JN042271

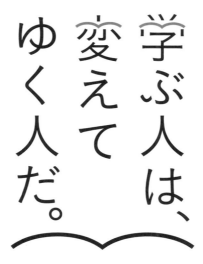

学ぶ人は、
変えて
ゆく人だ。

目の前にある問題はもちろん、

人生の問いや、

社会の課題を自ら見つけ、

挑み続けるために、人は学ぶ。

「学び」で、

少しずつ世界は変えてゆける。

いつでも、どこでも、誰でも、

学ぶことができる世の中へ。

旺文社

7日間完成

文部科学省後援
英検®1級
予想問題ドリル
[6訂版]

英検®は，公益財団法人 日本英語検定協会の登録商標です。

はじめに

　もうすぐ試験本番―そんなときに一番大事な英検対策は，試験形式に慣れることです。
　『7日間完成 英検 予想問題ドリル』シリーズは，7日間で試験本番に向けて，直前の総仕上げができる問題集です。目安として1日1セットずつ学習することで，最新の試験形式に慣れることができ，合格への実力が養成されるように構成されています。
　本書には以下のような特長があります。

本番に限りなく近い予想問題！
過去問分析を基にした本番に近い予想問題を収録しています。
学習スタイルに合わせて音声が聞ける！
リスニングアプリ「英語の友」を使ってスマホでの音声再生が可能です。また，PCからの音声ファイルダウンロードにも対応しています。
面接（スピーキングテスト）にも対応！
本書1冊で面接対策までカバーしています。
採点・見直しが簡単にできる！
各Dayの筆記試験・リスニングテストは採点・見直し学習アプリ「学びの友」対応。
解答をオンラインマークシートに入力するだけで簡単に採点ができます。

　本書を活用し，合格に向かってラストスパートをかけてください！
　皆さんの英検1級合格を心より願っています。

Contents

編集協力：株式会社シー・レップス，鹿島由紀子，Ed Jacob，内藤香，株式会社友人社，Peter Vincent，
Nadia McKechnie，Jason A. Chau

デザイン：相馬敬徳（Rafters）　　**装丁イラスト**：根津あやぼ　　**録音**：ユニバ合同会社

ナレーション：Ann Slater，Chris Wells，Emma Howard，Michael Rhys，Jack Merluzzi，Julia Yermakov，大武芙由美

本書の使い方

本書を以下のような流れに沿って使うことで，7日間で対策をすることができます。

> ❶試験について知る
> 本冊p.5「英検1級の試験形式と攻略法」をよく読んで内容を把握しましょう。

── Day 1～7に7日間取り組む ──

> ❷問題を解く
> 模試 に挑戦しましょう。
> ●制限時間内に解きましょう。
> ●付属のマークシートもしくは自動採点サービス（詳しくはp.4）で解答しましょう。

> ❸答え合わせをする
> 別冊の「解答と解説」で答え合わせをしましょう。
> ●どの技能も7割以上正解していれば，合格の可能性は高いでしょう。

音声について

本書の音声は，以下の2通りでご利用いただけます。

音声ファイルで再生

詳しくはp.4をご覧ください。収録箇所は 🔊001 などで示しています。

アプリ「英語の友」（iOS/Android）で再生

❶「英語の友」公式サイトより，アプリをインストール

（右の二次元コードから読み込めます）

https://eigonotomo.com/   英語の友 検索

❷ライブラリより本書を選び，「追加」ボタンをタップ

※本アプリの機能の一部は有料ですが，本書の音声は無料でお聞きいただけます。アプリの詳しいご利用方法は「英語の友」公式サイト，あるいはアプリ内のヘルプをご参照ください。
※本サービスは予告なく終了することがあります。

Web特典について ※本サービスは予告なく終了することがあります。

アクセス方法

❶以下のURLにアクセス（右の二次元コードから読み込めます）

　https://eiken.obunsha.co.jp/yosoudrill/

❷「1級」を選択し，以下の利用コードを入力

　xkcarf ※すべて半角アルファベット小文字

特典内容

音声ファイルダウンロード

「音声データダウンロード」からファイルをダウンロードし，展開してからオーディオプレーヤーで再生してください。音声ファイルはzip形式にまとめられた形でダウンロードされます。展開後，デジタルオーディオプレーヤーなどで再生してください。

※音声の再生にはMP3を再生できる機器などが必要です。
※ご利用機器，音声再生ソフト等に関する技術的なご質問は，ハードメーカーまたはソフトメーカーにお願いいたします。

自動採点サービスについて

本書収録の筆記試験・リスニングテストを，採点・見直し学習アプリ「学びの友」で簡単に自動採点することができます。（ライティングは自己採点です）

□ 便利な自動採点機能で学習結果がすぐにわかる
□ 学習履歴から間違えた問題を抽出して解き直しができる
□ 学習記録カレンダーで自分のがんばりを可視化

❶「学びの友」公式サイトへアクセス（右の二次元コードから読み込めます）

　https://manatomo.obunsha.co.jp/ ［学びの友 ［検索］

❷アプリを起動後，「旺文社まなびID」に会員登録（無料）
❸アプリ内のライブラリより本書を選び，「追加」ボタンをタップ

※iOS／Android端末，Webブラウザよりご利用いただけます。アプリの動作環境については「学びの友」公式サイトをご参照ください。なお，本アプリは無料でご利用いただけます。
※詳しいご利用方法は「学びの友」公式サイト，あるいはアプリ内ヘルプをご参照ください。
※本サービスは予告なく終了することがあります。

英検1級の試験形式と攻略法

筆記試験（100分）

1 短文の語句空所補充	目標時間12分	22問

短文または会話文中の空所に適する語句を，4つの選択肢から1つ選ぶ問題です。出題される品詞はさまざまですが，同じ設問の選択肢においてはすべて同じ品詞・形となっています。22問のうち，単語が18問程度，2〜3語からなる句動詞が4問程度出題されます。

攻略法 短文の意味を瞬間的に捉え，空所に入る語句を素早く選ぶ必要があります。空所にどのような意味の言葉が入るかを考える際は，文の前半と後半（もしくは1文目と2文目）の結びつきを捉え，それがイコールの内容になるのか，反対の内容になるのかを突き止めましょう。また，接頭辞，接尾辞，語根，派生語についての知識をつけておき，未知の単語の意味を推測する手がかりにしましょう。1級の語句はほかの級と比べてレベルが圧倒的に高いので，事前に語彙力強化をしておくことをお勧めします。語彙力強化のためには，インターネット上の記事，雑誌，英字新聞などを読んだときに，ノート形式で語彙表現のまとめをしておくことが効果的です。その際，例文あるいはある程度の意味のまとまりごとに書き留めておくと記憶に残りやすくなります。

2 長文の語句空所補充	目標時間15分	6問

長文中の空所に適する語句を，4つの選択肢から1つ選ぶ問題です。長文は3段落程度からなる350語前後のものが2つあり，それぞれ空所が3箇所あります。選択肢の語句は5語程度からなる文の一部です。

攻略法 筆記1で求められる語彙力に加え，文章の論旨の展開を正確に把握し，文の整合性を判断する力が求められます。一文一文の意味をじっくり捉えていくのではなく，速読を行って，論旨の展開を追いかけましょう。そのために，however（逆接），consequently / as a result（結果）などの「つなぎ言葉」に注目するくせをつけておきましょう。選択肢の内容はそれぞれ大きく異なり，ひっかけのような出題はありません。模試を解く際は，選択肢を見る前に空所の内容を予想してみるのも良いトレーニングとなるでしょう。この後には筆記3の長文をさらに2つ読まなければならないので，余力を残しておくつもりで効率的に解答していきましょう。

3 長文の内容一致選択 | 目標時間**28分** | **7**問

長文に関する質問に対して, 4つの選択肢から1つ選ぶ問題です。長文は全部で2つです。1つ目の長文は3段落程度からなる500語前後のもので, 設問が3題。2つ目の長文は7〜8段落程度からなる800語前後のもので, 設問が4題。設問の形式には, 完全な疑問文に対する答えを選ぶものと, 未完成の英文を完成させる答えを選ぶものの2通りがあります。

攻略法 まずタイトルと設問にざっと目を通して, あらかじめどんなことが問題として問われているのかを理解した上で本文を読み進めます。筆記2と同様に, 全文にわたって精読していく必要はありませんが, 重要と思われる箇所はしっかりと理解できるまで目を通しましょう。そのためには, 本筋と関係のないディテールを読み飛ばすなど, めりはりをつけて読み進めるスキルが必要となります。それぞれの段落が何を述べるために構成されているかを見極め, 以後の展開を予測しながら読むと, 理解しやすくなります。正解のほとんどは本文の内容を言い換えた文となっているので, 設問文からキーワードを特定し, 該当する箇所を本文から素早く探し出せるようにしておきましょう。

4 英作文（要約問題） | 目標時間**20分** | **1**問

アカデミックな, または社会性の高い幅広い分野のテーマに関する長文が1つ提示され, その内容を自分の言葉で90〜110語の英文に要約する問題です。長文は3段落程度からなる300語前後の長さです。

攻略法 要約問題は「内容・構成・語彙・文法」の4つの観点で採点されます。具体的には英文の要点を適切に捉えた要約になっているか, 要約が論理的な文章になっているかという点や, 1級にふさわしい語彙や文法を正しく, 工夫しながら使えているか, という点が重要だと考えられます。初めに長文に目を通し, 全体の要旨を正しくつかみましょう。全文を精読する必要はありませんが, 長文の趣旨から外れた要約を作成してしまうと大幅に減点されるおそれがあるので, しっかりとポイントを把握することが重要です。それと同時に, 要約に際して省くべき具体例や補足の部分を見極める必要があります。なお, 長文の表現をそのまま使うのではなく, できるだけパラフレーズして要約を作成できるように意識しましょう。最後には, 基本的なスペルや文法のミスがないか必ず確認を。

5 英作文（意見論述問題）　｜　目標時間25分　｜　1問

社会的問題に関するTOPICが出され，それに対する自分の考えとその理由3つを200〜240語の英文にまとめる問題です。「序論」「本文」「結論」で構成することが求められます。TOPICはYes/No形式で答えるものと，Agree/Disagree形式で答えるものの2通りがあります。

攻略法　意見論述問題は要約問題と同様に「内容・構成・語彙・文法」の4つの観点で採点されます。具体的には求められた内容が解答に含まれているか，解答の構成や展開がわかりやすく論理的な文章になっているかという点や，1級にふさわしい語彙や文法を正しく，工夫しながら使えているか，という点が重要だと考えられます。まずはしっかりとTOPICを把握しましょう。TOPICはメディアでよく取り上げられるものが多いので，普段から社会情勢に対して問題意識を持ち，背景知識などを集めておくようにしましょう。次に，自分の意見・主張を決めますが，筋の通る理由や具体例とセットで考えをめぐらせ，一番解答を書きやすい主張に決定するとスムーズです。Yes/No（あるいはAgree/Disagree）双方の立場で考え得る主張を書き出すと，作文をするための素材が整いやすいでしょう。なお，このプロセスは手早く済ませ，執筆と見直しにしっかりと時間を充てましょう。効果的なパラフレーズを取り入れつつも，主張の伝わりやすさを意識しましょう。見直しの際は，初歩的な文法ミスや時制の不一致などのチェックも忘れずに。

リスニングテスト（約35分）

Part 1 会話の内容一致選択　｜　放送回数1回　｜　10問

会話とその内容に関する質問を聞いて，質問の答えとして適切なものを4つの選択肢から1つ選ぶ問題です。No. 1〜No. 8は男女2名による短めの会話，No. 9は同じく男女2名による長めの会話，No. 10は3名による長めの会話で，解答時間は10秒です。

攻略法　放送される会話文は，家庭，学校，職場でのやりとりが主です。口語表現が多く使われる中で，話者の心理や，その場の状況を読み取ることが必要になります。暗示的であったり皮肉的であったりする発言も多くあるので注意しましょう。ビジネスに関する話題も多く，やや専門的な語句・表現が使われることがあるので，ビジネス関連の背景知識や語句も確認しておきましょう。

Part 2 文の内容一致選択　｜　放送回数1回　｜　10問

説明文とそれに関する質問を聞いて，質問の答えとして適切なものを4つの選択肢から1つ選ぶ問題です。5つの説明文に対して質問は2つずつあります。解答時間はそれぞれ10秒です。

攻略法　説明文のテーマは多岐にわたります。タイトルを注意深く聞き，少しでもヒントを得ましょう。説明文の冒頭も，まずはテーマについての概要を説明する内容となっていることがほとんどです。ただし質問とは直接関係のない内容も多いので，聞き逃しても慌てず，続きのリスニングに集中しましょう。年号などの詳細については，リーディングに取り組むときよりも入念に把握し，メモをしながら聞き取りましょう。

Part 3 **Real-Life**形式の内容一致選択　｜　放送回数1回　｜　5問

実生活における指示文・メッセージ・アナウンス・説明を聞く問題です。英文放送前に10秒与えられ，問題冊子に印刷されている Situation と Question を読みます。それから放送を聞き，Questionの答えとして適切なものを4つの選択肢から1つ選びます。解答時間は10秒です。

攻略法　英文が流れる前の10秒間に，Situation（あなたの状況）と Question（あなたが何をするべきか）を必ず把握しましょう。その後は英文に集中し，とりわけ冒頭を聞き逃さないよう注意しましょう。問われる内容があらかじめわかるので，自分が知りたい情報が聞こえるのを待ち，解答が済んだら次の設問に目を通してもよいでしょう。

Part 4 インタビューの内容一致選択　｜　放送回数1回　｜　2問

3分～3分半程度のインタビュー形式の英文を聞き，質問の答えとして適切なものを4つの選択肢から1つ選ぶ問題です。質問は2つあり，解答時間はそれぞれ10秒です。

攻略法　インタビューでは，さまざまな分野で活躍する人たちが，その職業についた理由，その仕事の良い点と悪い点，職業柄注意していることなど，その職業に関連する事柄を述べます。まずは，どんな職業に就いている人物かを冒頭でしっかりと聞き取りましょう。またインタビュアーによる手短な質問も正確に把握しましょう。全体的には長いリスニングとなりますが，話題が切り替わる度に整理してメモを取っていきましょう。

リスニングテストの指示文

1級のリスニングテストで放送される英語の指示文は以下の通りです。

The listening test for the Grade 1 examination is about to begin. Listen carefully to the directions. You will not be permitted to ask questions during the test. This test has four parts. All of the questions in these four parts are multiple-choice questions. For each question, choose the best answer from among the four choices written in your test booklet. On your answer sheet, find the number of the question and mark your answer. You are permitted to take notes for every part of this listening test.

Part 1 Now, here are the directions for Part 1. In this part, you will hear 10 dialogues, No. 1 through No. 10. Each dialogue will be followed by one question. For each question, you will have 10 seconds to choose the best answer and mark your answer on your answer sheet. The dialogue and the question will be given only once. Now, we will begin the Grade 1 listening test.

Part 2 Here are the directions for Part 2. In this part, you will hear five passages, (A) through (E). Each passage will be followed by two questions, No. 11 through No. 20. For each question, you will have 10 seconds to choose the best answer and mark your answer on your answer sheet. The passage and the questions will be given only once. Now, let's begin.

Part 3 Here are the directions for Part 3. In this part, you will hear five passages, (F) through (J). The passages represent real-life situations and may contain sound effects. Each passage will have one question, No. 21 through No. 25. Before each passage, you will have 10 seconds to read the situation and question written in your test booklet. After you hear the passage, you will have 10 seconds to choose the best answer and mark your answer on your answer sheet. The passage will be given only once. Now, let's begin.

Part 4 Finally, here are the directions for Part 4. In this part, you will hear an interview. The interview will be followed by two questions, No. 26 and No. 27. For each question, you will have 10 seconds to choose the best answer and mark your answer on your answer sheet. The interview and the questions will be given only once. This is an interview with ...

Your time is up. Stop writing and wait quietly until the answer sheets have been collected.

面接（スピーキングテスト）（約**10**分）

5つのトピックが書かれたカードが渡され，1分間で1つのトピックに関するスピーチの準備をし，2分間のスピーチをします。スピーチの後にはいくつかの質問に答えます。

問題	形式・課題詳細
自由会話	面接委員と簡単な日常会話を行う。
スピーチ	与えられた5つのトピックの中から1つを選び，スピーチを行う。
Q & A	スピーチの内容やトピックに関連した質問に答える。

面接（スピーキングテスト）については，本冊p.120「1級の面接（スピーキングテスト）はどんなテスト？」でより詳しく説明しています。

筆記試験

試験時間 筆記100分

1　To complete each item, choose the best word or phrase from among the four choices. Then, on your answer sheet, find the number of the question and mark your answer.

(1) Due to the outbreak of civil war, neighboring countries got ready for a major (　　　) of refugees. They prepared housing, food, drinking water, and other basic supplies.

1 overthrow　　**2** influx　　**3** uptake　　**4** onset

(2) This university is a coeducational institution (　　　) with the Baptist Church.

1 allocated　　**2** pampered　　**3** affiliated　　**4** implicated

(3) Professor John Markle had planned to write an entire novel over the summer, but he found the (　　　) impossible. In the end, it took him two years to complete.

1 prelude　　**2** ploy　　**3** feat　　**4** feint

(4) *A:* Excuse me, but would you mind signing this petition to limit private gun ownership?

B: Sorry, but I like hunting, so I'm not a (　　　) of strict restrictions on gun ownership.

1 proponent　　**2** curfew　　**3** connoisseur　　**4** pickpocket

(5) The president determined that opening a new office in Singapore posed (　　　) risks, so he decided to postpone the decision for one or two years.

1 insatiable　　**2** uninhibited　　**3** inherent　　**4** unrepentant

(6) *A:* I don't feel like I'm a very effective teacher.

B: I couldn't disagree with you more. You've had a (　　　) effect on many of your students.

1 frenetic　　**2** punitive　　**3** voracious　　**4** profound

(7) **A:** Oh, no! I spilled juice all over your blouse. I'm so (   ).
B: Please don't worry about it. I can wash it off easily.
1 frumpy   **2** clumsy   **3** nifty   **4** feisty

(8) Judy wanted to start dating when she was 14 years old, but her parents told her that she could only go out if she and her date were (   ) by an adult.
1 remitted   **2** succumbed   **3** chaperoned   **4** hinged

(9) Even though there was a general consensus to go ahead with the project, the manager remained (   ) that it was a bad idea and would result in substantial loss.
1 inevitable   **2** adamant   **3** arbitrary   **4** obligatory

(10) The woman was caught stealing from the store, and a week later she was (   ) by the authorities.
1 prolonged   **2** prosecuted   **3** perturbed   **4** demolished

(11) With all the support and additional training offered to the employee, it became clear that he would continue to fail at even the simplest tasks. He was completely (   ).
1 scarce   **2** docile   **3** inept   **4** ornate

(12) The young man inherited millions of dollars from his grandfather, but he soon (   ) his fortune by gambling and partying.
1 impaired   **2** recuperated   **3** enhanced   **4** squandered

(13) The jury found the defendant guilty of first degree murder, disregarding his claim that he had (   ) pulled the trigger of the gun.
1 intermittently   **2** conventionally
3 cordially   **4** inadvertently

(14) The computer expert installed a sophisticated new software program to (   ) the billing operations of his company.
1 galvanize   **2** nullify   **3** expedite   **4** rummage

(15) The furniture company went bankrupt. The profits from the (   ) of its inventory helped pay off the investors.
1 consignment   **2** liquidation   **3** custody   **4** diminution

Day 1
Day 2
Day 3
Day 4
Day 5
Day 6
Day 7

(16) The Prosecutor's Office decided to (   ) two foreign diplomats on espionage charges, which caused an international dispute.

1 repeal   **2** harass   **3** indict   **4** stimulate

(17) The couple divorced after three years of marriage. They discovered that they were simply not (   ) with each other.

1 sustainable   **2** compatible   **3** opportune   **4** indigenous

(18) The politician was (   ) for his insensitive and offensive remarks regarding victims of the tragedy.

1 lambasted   **2** commended   **3** extolled   **4** revised

(19) Children who (   ) in class are often just trying to attract attention.

1 act up   **2** play down   **3** pan out   **4** give out

(20) The company's annual report was discredited by stockholders, for it (   ) several major losses the company had suffered during the year.

1 held down   **2** holed up   **3** glossed over   **4** ground out

(21) The vice-president shouted at the sales manager during the meeting. No one had ever seen the vice-president (   ) at anyone like that, for he was generally a calm person.

1 plug away   **2** wind up   **3** bang out   **4** lash out

(22) Minami never gives up. When she fails at something or gets a bad score on a test, she just (   ) the failure and makes an even greater effort the next time around.

1 shrugs off   **2** bows out   **3** waves off   **4** turns out

Day 1
Day 2
Day 3
Day 4
Day 5
Day 6
Day 7

2 *Read each passage and choose the best word or phrase from among the four choices for each blank. Then, on your answer sheet, find the number of the question and mark your answer.*

The Predicted EV Revolution

Practical electric cars have been around since the late 19th century, yet the internal combustion engine has dominated automobile production since its inception. With growing concern over climate change and localized pollution, local authorities and national governments are increasingly looking toward electric vehicles, or EVs, to offset the damage caused by our reliance on fossil fuels. Important—perhaps largely symbolic—proclamations have already been made by some European governments and local governments in the USA and other regions. Although not yet formal laws, officials expressed the intention to ban (*23*) by the middle of the century, while many cities already run Car-Free days.

Such proposals have not been met with universal approval. Some people feel that the focus on emissions is myopic and ignores, for example, other particulate matter created by brake wear, tire wear, and road surface abrasion, which can be breathed in and is linked to cardiopulmonary toxicity and other illnesses. Critics also argue that EVs are only as clean as the source of their energy which, in many places, still means heavily polluting fossil fuels. For a real EV revolution to take place, it needs to be accompanied by (*24*).

Still others argue that the answer does not lie in replacing conventional automobiles with ostensibly emission-free EVs, but rather with reducing (*25*). This would require enormous investment in clean forms of urban transport as well as convincing urban dwellers to forgo their cars. As more and more people choose to live in cities, solutions need to be found quickly to meet the increased demand for reliable transportation. This means not only ensuring that urban transport is clean, safe and economically viable, but also trying to convince an increasingly exercise-averse population to walk and ride bicycles rather than hop into a car.

(23) **1** symbols of automobile domination
      2 over-reliance on electricity
      3 the use of the term "climate change"
      4 the sale of diesel and petrol vehicles

(24) **1** particular matters related to toxicity
     2 new means of producing pollutants
     3 a revolution in renewable energy production
     4 switching the focus to road surface abrasion

(25) **1** the number of non-renewable energy plants
     2 the amount of personally owned vehicles as a whole
     3 the population increase in heavily polluted areas
     4 the economic woes of urban migrants

Drunk to the Gills

As anybody who has imbibed a little too much alcohol can attest to, it can certainly (**26**). Images of St. Bernards trekking across the Alps to warm up freezing mountaineers with a snifter of brandy have added to the image of alcohol's ability to keep the cold out. The truth is not quite so positive, as alcohol causes blood vessels in the skin to dilate, thereby shunting blood from the core to the periphery, which in turn inundates the brain with messages saying the body is hot. This confusion in sensory perception can be fatal in humans, but in a couple of fish, drinking in the cold is key to survival.

Scientists have discovered that goldfish and their wild relatives, crucian carp, effectively create their own alcohol in the form of ethanol in order to live. The discovery explains their extraordinary ability to survive winters in lakes covered by ice, where oxygen is at a premium and temperatures plummet. The lack of oxygen means the fish are unable to breathe, and therefore must rely on anaerobic generation of energy, which does not require access to fresh air but has the potentially fatal side-effect of producing lactic acid. Goldfish and crucian carp possess a second set of proteins controlling energy production which allows them to convert (**27**).

The discovery not only explains the hardiness of these fish but could also have important implications for future research. This survival trait may be due to whole genome duplication, which has led to the evolution of biological novelty and allowed some species (**28**). Whole genome duplication means that two sets of genes are created in some animals, allowing the original genome to help the animal grow and develop as normal, while the other genome is effectively free to mutate and adapt with less risk to the animal carrying them becoming injured or deformed. While certainly interesting, practical applications look to be a long way off.

(26) **1** feel like it is warming you up
        2 affect peripheral vision acuity
        3 aid in the rescue of stranded climbers
        4 cause positive changes in sensory perception

(27) **1** oxygen into fresh air
        2 ice into much warmer water
        3 the lactic acid into alcoholic waste
        4 air into fatal levels of alcohol

(28) **1** to mutate beyond all recognition
        2 to create biologically exact clones of themselves
        3 to consume alcohol more than humans do
        4 to thrive in previously inhospitable environments

Day 1
Day 2
Day 3
Day 4
Day 5
Day 6
Day 7

The Development of Modern Education

The word "education" itself can be traced to the Latin words *educatio*, meaning to rear or bring up, and *educo*, meaning to lead or train, although the roots of education date back to preliterate times. In prehistory, when the majority of humans belonged to hunter-gatherer societies, education was primarily concerned with adults passing to children the skills and knowledge required to feed and protect the society. Such education was more sophisticated than one may imagine, involving the identification and memorization of edible foods, sources of water, awareness of dangers, hunting and trapping skills, and the creation and use of weapons. Such skills and knowledge were passed from generation to generation orally, often by storytelling, and also through imitation and the practical use of the knowledge being imparted.

As societies became more advanced, they began to expand their knowledge and abilities beyond the limits of what could be properly learned through imitation and the oral tradition, and thus formal education began to develop. Schools that could be recognizable as such, with seats for students and a teacher, existed in ancient Egypt and mainly focused on training the children of well-to-do parents to become scribes, as reading and writing were greatly sought-after skills. As societies settled, the education of both children and adults reflected the cultures and needs of each society, varying from combat skills to natural history, the arts, mathematics, philosophy, and religion.

Over time, religion became particularly important in the development of formal education, especially in Europe, and dominated much of how students would be taught for many years. Many schools were founded on religious principles during the High Middle Ages, around the 11th, 12th, and 13th centuries, and primarily served to train members of the clergy. At the time, the clergy were among the most educated members of society, so it is perhaps not surprising that cathedral schools paved the way for the first European universities, including the University of Oxford, the University of Naples, and the University of Bologna.

Although very important in the development of higher education, such universities were actually not the first institutions to offer such advanced scholarly opportunities. The Academy, founded by the philosopher Plato around 387 BC, can lay claim to being the first school for higher education, and it is also the source for the English words "academic" and "academia." Situated outside the city walls of ancient Athens, schooling at the Academy started out as informal gatherings of prominent philosophers, mathematicians, and other scholars, gradually becoming an established seat of learning for students like Aristotle. The Academy arguably influenced universities throughout history not only for its standards of scholarship, but also for its exclusivity. Although it was not believed to have charged fees, at least during Plato's time, membership was open only to the privileged, which many people feel continues to be a feature of modern elite universities around the world.

---

(29) What was the primary driving force behind early forms of education?
  1 The transmission of stories between communities was the only way to preserve local cultures.
  2 Adults learned to read and write by copying signs and symbols in nature, which were then used to develop community relationships.
  3 Survival of primitive communities depended on successful inter-generational understanding of important knowledge.
  4 As early societies were mostly nomadic, there was no need for any form of education.

(30) How did the evolution of increasingly settled and advanced cultures affect the development of education?
  1 The needs of societies were reflected in the development of the education systems that each one introduced and nurtured.
  2 As societal structures evolved, the desire for educational institutions became less pronounced.
  3 The development of advanced societies was stunted by adherence to traditional oral transmission of knowledge and skills.
  4 Settled communities remained the preserve of the affluent, and education was not considered to be a key requirement.

(31) In what ways could modern universities be said to be similar to the first of such institutions?
  1 Theological thought and study remain the priority for the majority of schools of higher learning throughout the world.
  2 The architecture and structure of schools and universities have remained largely unchanged for thousands of years.
  3 The way in which students are selected is still based on informal selection criteria developed by early philosophers.
  4 From the earliest iterations of institutions of higher education, there has been a tendency to cater to a select portion of society.

筆記試験

Day
1
Day
2
Day
3
Day
4
Day
5
Day
6
Day
7

Patient-Focused Drug Development

For all the talk about the latest discoveries in drugs, genetics, and molecular biology, significant obstacles to converting them into medical therapies remain. Some of these obstacles have to do with the science: Finding a practical application for even the most thrilling discovery may take large investments of time and money. However, others are legal and philosophical issues external to the research itself. Since the 1960s, the highest priority in the development and testing of new drugs and other therapies has been safety. Standards established by regulatory bodies and pharmaceutical industry associations lay out in great detail the mechanisms by which potentially harmful side effects are to be identified, reported, and studied. There is a simple process for halting a clinical trial because of evidence that the drug being investigated is dangerous. Additionally, requirements that long-term use be studied have become very stringent, under the assumption that it may take years of continual use for adverse effects to present themselves.

This thinking has its origin in the events following the release of the sedative thalidomide in 1957. Developed and first marketed in what was then West Germany, thalidomide not only had a tranquilizing or calming effect but also relieved nausea. It was thus considered an ideal medication for pregnant women suffering from morning sickness, and because it was available over the counter without a prescription, it was an instant success. What no one knew until the women's pregnancies began coming to term was that thalidomide caused birth defects, most frequently malformation of the arms and legs but also disruption of nerve, heart, and lung development. About 10,000 babies were affected, mostly across Europe. Up to half of them did not survive infancy. How could such a tragedy have happened in developed countries in which biochemical and pharmaceutical research were so highly advanced? At the time, scientists believed the placental barrier prevented drugs from crossing from a mother's bloodstream to her fetus. Therefore, there was little perceived risk that a drug taken by the mother could cause damage to the baby, and it was not routine to test new substances for effects during and after pregnancy. Thalidomide had been tested on rodents and pronounced ready for the market.

By the time its United States manufacturer and distributor applied for approval with the Food and Drug Administration (FDA) in 1960, safety concerns had so intensified that thalidomide was no longer available over the counter in West Germany, and biologist and reviewer Frances Oldham Kelsey declined to approve its distribution without further testing. Subsequent research that definitively established the link between thalidomide and birth defects vindicated her caution, and the publicity accelerated the push for more exacting safety requirements in clinical trials. When the U.S. Congress unanimously passed the Kefauver Harris Amendment to the Federal Food, Drug and Cosmetic Act in 1962, these concerns became law. Kefauver Harris required pharmaceutical companies to submit proof of not only efficacy but also safety. There were also new requirements that potential side effects be disclosed and that patients participating in clinical trials give formal consent after being apprised of the accompanying risks.

Given the state of medical research of the era, it is difficult to regard these regulations as anything but positive developments. Fewer than twenty babies were born in the United States with thalidomide-related birth defects. Though it was never released for sale commercially, it was tested extensively in pursuit of FDA approval. The concern decades later is that science has advanced in ways that the practices governing clinical trials have not. Researchers have developed possible methods of attacking terminal diseases, especially cancers and autoimmune disorders, from multiple specific pathways. But as Peter Huber wrote in *The Cure in the Code*, "The studies that Washington had traditionally required to prove that drugs work can't be completed any faster than diseases typically progress." Even serious side effects are of low importance to patients facing certain death without a new treatment, but current regulations and clinical practices make their compromises for them. And it is increasingly common to treat an extremely ill patient with a "cocktail" of several drugs at once. This makes determining the effectiveness of any one drug in the mixture very difficult. Finally, the highly controlled safety testing required in clinical trials is expensive, which means that innovators with ideas for treating rare diseases have exceptional difficulty finding the funding to get their new therapies through the approval process.

What would a truly advanced system for getting effective new treatments to the market look like? Some have supported "right-to-try" laws at the state level, which would make it legal for patients to take drugs under study before the FDA has given them federal approval, as long as strict informed consent rules were enforced. Others favor relaxing regulations applied to clinical trials of patients with terminal or severely debilitating diseases. Marc Joffe notes that, paradoxically, the example of thalidomide supports their case: "In 1964, an Israeli doctor gave thalidomide tablets to a leprosy patient suffering extreme pain. The medication not only allowed the patient to sleep but reversed his symptoms. Eventually, thalidomide became a common treatment for leprosy and was later found to be effective against AIDS and cancer."

Day 1
Day 2
Day 3
Day 4
Day 5
Day 6
Day 7

(32) What does the author of the passage say is true of the standards of regulatory bodies and pharmaceutical industry associations?
  1 They are designed to be neutral on the legal and philosophical debates that now surround research into new medical treatments.
  2 They remove some of the obstacles to making new and complicated treatments available to patients.
  3 They are intended to discover both side effects that occur immediately and those that only occur over time.
  4 They did not prevent serious side effects from causing widespread problems in the United States, despite their emphasis on safety.

(33) Frances Oldham Kelsey is an example of a scientist who
  1 ran tests that confirmed that thalidomide caused birth defects and other side effects that had been linked to it.
  2 worked with the United States Congress to write new legislation governing the conducting of clinical trials.
  3 developed a method of testing new pharmaceutical products that did not involve rodents.
  4 believed new treatments should be rigorously tested before they were approved for sale to the public.

(34) Peter Huber believes that traditional requirements for clinical trials
  1 ensure that doctors have the best available information about the combination of drugs that will help their patients.
  2 have motivated scientists to develop innovative treatments that require less safety testing before approval.
  3 prevent patients with serious diseases from making their own decisions about whether a treatment is worthwhile.
  4 have not kept the public safe from more recent drugs that are as potentially dangerous as thalidomide.

(35) What does Marc Joffe demonstrate by citing the leprosy patient?

1 More bad side effects of thalidomide continued to be discovered after its use had been restricted for years.

2 A drug can be beneficial to some patients even if it is too dangerous for the majority of patients to use.

3 Seriously ill patients are not always qualified to judge which therapies will best relieve their symptoms.

4 Attacking a serious disease through multiple pathways is usually the most effective way to treat patients.

Day 1
Day 2
Day 3
Day 4
Day 5
Day 6
Day 7

4 English Summary

- Instructions: Read the article below and summarize it in your own words as far as possible in English.
- Suggested length: 90-110 words
- Write your summary in the space provided on your answer sheet. <u>Any writing outside the space will not be graded.</u>

During the 20th century, various Native American tribes came into tremendous wealth when they began operating casinos or when large deposits of gold or other resources were discovered on their reservations. Over the years, there were assertions being made that greed was causing certain tribes to use a process called "disenrollment" to expel large numbers of their members. Critics have claimed that those tribes were disenrolling people because revenues from things like gambling and mineral wealth are shared out equally among members, so reducing populations meant the remaining individuals each received a greater share of the wealth.

Disenrollment is frequently carried out based on what is known as "blood quantum." According to many tribes' regulations, if Native Americans marry non-Natives, their children are at risk of losing their status as a member of the tribe. For example, the Navaho tribe does not permit individuals who have less than 25 percent "Navaho blood" to be members. However, it can sometimes be difficult for members to prove that they have enough Native ancestry to remain in the tribe when supporting documents have been damaged or lost.

Members who are disenrolled lose access to a wide range of benefits, including housing subsidies, health care, and scholarships provided by the tribe. In addition, even though members who have been disenrolled still consider themselves to be part of the tribe, they are at risk of losing their cultural identity and also frequently come to feel socially isolated after being cut off from friends and neighbors whom they may have known for their entire lives. Non-Natives may see them as Native Americans, and they sometimes face racial discrimination because of it. At the same time, they lack the support mechanisms and the sense of community that other Native Americans who still belong to the tribe have.

5 English Composition

- Write an essay on the given **TOPIC**.
- Give THREE reasons to support your answer.
- Structure: introduction, main body, and conclusion
- Suggested length: 200-240 words
- Write your essay in the space provided on your answer sheet. <u>Any writing outside the space will not be graded.</u>

TOPIC

Should life-prolonging treatment be encouraged?

Day 1
Day 2
Day 3
Day 4
Day 5
Day 6
Day 7

リスニングテスト

試験時間 リスニング約**35**分

There are four parts to this listening test.

Part 1	Dialogues: 1 question each	Multiple-choice
Part 2	Passages: 2 questions each	Multiple-choice
Part 3	Real-Life: 1 question each	Multiple-choice
Part 4	Interview: 2 questions	Multiple-choice

※Listen carefully to the instructions.

Part 1　◀))001～011

No. 1
1 Open a simple checking account for now.
2 Put some money into a higher-yield account.
3 Consider a high-yield checking account.
4 Let his current account mature before making changes.

No. 2
1 Better training for her staff.
2 The same salary as everyone else.
3 A 10 percent raise.
4 A substantial promotion.

No. 3
1 She often comes to work late.
2 She is not to blame for the problem.
3 She has a bad temper.
4 She is not getting her work done.

No. 4
1 Ted will make a purchase.
2 Ted will withdraw money from an ATM.
3 Janice will pay Ted's debt for him.
4 Janice will pay Ted back the remaining debt.

No. 5
1. He is worried that it lacks balance.
2. He believes it is working very well.
3. He likes it but he is often hungry.
4. He thinks it is not very effective.

No. 6
1. Take some time off to recuperate.
2. Prepare for his presentation this weekend.
3. Get a part-time job to make money.
4. Talk to her sister about his experience.

No. 7
1. He wishes it were cooler.
2. He thinks it will rain later.
3. He likes hot weather.
4. He does not want it to rain.

No. 8
1. To urge her to turn in her thesis right away.
2. To tell her that he will be her thesis advisor.
3. To inform her that her thesis needs rewriting.
4. To check whether she has gone to work.

No. 9
1. Resolving conflicts between captains and crew.
2. Getting crew members to extend their contracts.
3. Avoiding vandalism by crew members.
4. Training captains to be more responsible.

No. 10
1. He likes having time to study new things.
2. He wishes he had more free time to enjoy life.
3. His financial circumstances worry him.
4. He wants to return to meaningful work.

Day 1
Day 2
Day 3
Day 4
Day 5
Day 6
Day 7

(A) *No. 11*

1 To create a mutual base for European countries.
2 To gain access to strategic territories.
3 To derive benefits from natural resources.
4 To avoid claims of sovereignty.

No. 12

1 They all agreed to military cooperation.
2 They are allowed to reject claims of sovereignty.
3 They all signed the treaty in 1959.
4 None of them are allowed to claim sovereignty.

(B) *No. 13*

1 It was used as a means to inspire creativity in manufacturing.
2 It was largely overlooked until Mies van der Rohe took over.
3 All of the directors, except the founder, were architects.
4 The students studied in five different cities.

No. 14

1 Its liberal approach helped to remodel German politics in the 1930s.
2 The Nazi Party pressured the school to design university campuses.
3 Many students from the United States attended the Bauhaus.
4 Numerous staff members went on to work in schools overseas after the war.

(C) *No. 15*

1 The Egyptians devised a unique construction process.
2 They were worshipped for symbolic and sacrificial reasons.
3 They were constructed by diverse civilizations.
4 The shape and design helped to increase their durability.

No. 16

1 It represented the creation of the earth.
2 It influenced both the shape and placement of the pyramids.
3 The sun is one of the original Seven Wonders of the World.
4 The sun was known to rise in the west in ancient Egypt.

(D)	*No. 17*	**1** Over 5,000 comets.
		2 Comets could be seen without a telescope.
		3 The comet he spotted orbits the sun.
		4 A comet that bears his name.
	No. 18	**1** Following the invention of the telescope.
		2 Over 2,000 years ago.
		3 Just before the invasion of England.
		4 As the Bayeux Tapestry was being created.
(E)	*No. 19*	**1** People can have physical symptoms.
		2 University students are less likely to be affected.
		3 Symptoms of the addiction are exaggerated.
		4 The price of smartphones can cause stress and worry.
	No. 20	**1** Children get closer to their friends while ignoring their parents.
		2 The health warnings on products scare children.
		3 It is shown to negatively influence their behavior.
		4 It causes them to always interrupt their parents.

リスニングテスト

Day 1
Day 2
Day 3
Day 4
Day 5
Day 6
Day 7

(F)　*No. 21*　***Situation:*** You're a marketing manager for a company. The vice-president of sales makes the following announcement to all employees of the company.

　　　　Question: What does the new policy require your department to do?

　　　　1 Involve the vice-president of sales in brochure development.

　　　　2 Consult department heads before distributing brochures.

　　　　3 Sign off on any product specifications and claims.

　　　　4 Send brochure proofs to relevant engineers.

(G)　*No. 22*　***Situation:*** You plan to buy a house in the U.S., and a realtor has shown you four houses for consideration. You're mainly concerned about making money, low maintenance, and low risk. The realtor tells you the following.

　　　　Question: Which house best suits your needs?

　　　　1 The home on Oakwood Way.

　　　　2 The home on El Portal.

　　　　3 The place on Lockwood Circle.

　　　　4 The house on Fairmont Drive.

(H)　*No. 23*　***Situation:*** You have just moved into a dormitory at the university. You listen to a phone message explaining how to use voicemail.

　　　　Question: What is one step you need to take to create your main mailbox?

　　　　1 Press 9.

　　　　2 Enter a passcode.

　　　　3 Enter your dormitory number.

　　　　4 Press 0.

(I)   **No. 24**   ***Situation:*** You want to join a gym to use exercise equipment about three times a week. You will go before work for 30 minutes on weekdays starting at 6:30 a.m. You hear the following sales pitch from a gym trainer.

            Question: What is your best deal?

            1 The Right On plan.

            2 The Muscle Tone plan.

            3 The Fitness Plus plan.

            4 The Top Shape plan.

(J)   **No. 25**   ***Situation:*** You hear an announcement over your dormitory public address system.

            Question: What is one of the things you are asked to do after leaving the building?

            1 Stand about 30 meters away from the building.

            2 Find the fire inspector at the exit of the building.

            3 Wait two minutes before returning to your dorm.

            4 Wait for authorization to return to your dorm.

No. 26　**1** He started modeling part-time in New York to make money for school.
　　　　2 He was recruited to model by a scouting agent who visited his university.
　　　　3 While traveling in Europe, he modeled to make money to continue his travels.
　　　　4 While attending modeling school, he was introduced to an agency.

No. 27　**1** He had to go on a strenuous diet for an extended period.
　　　　2 He could never get enough work due to fierce competition.
　　　　3 He was hospitalized for several serious diseases he came down with.
　　　　4 He could not adjust to the culture there, which affected his health.

Day
1

Day
2

Day
3

Day
4

Day
5

Day
6

Day
7

筆記試験

試験時間 筆記100分

1 To complete each item, choose the best word or phrase from among the four choices. Then, on your answer sheet, find the number of the question and mark your answer.

(1) The tourism industry is suffering from the effects of a prolonged recession, and fears of terrorism will only ( ) the situation.
1 exacerbate   **2** placate   **3** insinuate   **4** inaugurate

(2) After her breast cancer surgery, Jill was warned by her doctor that it was of ( ) importance to take the prescribed medication daily and to come in for regular checkups.
1 paramount   **2** innocuous   **3** exclusive   **4** inopportune

(3) Carrie was shocked to hear her best friend ( ) lie to the teacher about her frequent absences from class, telling him the falsehood that her father was seriously ill.
1 pensively   **2** meekly   **3** empirically   **4** blatantly

(4) The founder of the company is ill and can no longer do his work effectively, but he will not ( ) any of his authority to his assistants.
1 dissolve   **2** assimilate   **3** relinquish   **4** reprieve

(5) The river is characterized by rapids and waterfalls in the mountains, but once it reaches the plains, it slowly ( ) its way to the sea.
1 revolves   **2** loiters   **3** meanders   **4** tarnishes

(6) My Jeep has good ( ) with its four-wheel drive, and I really need it on the icy mountain road leading to the ski lodge.
1 dissonance   **2** traction   **3** fluctuation   **4** deviation

(7) Bob kept his body lean by exercising daily and ( ) all sweets and fatty foods.
1 procuring   **2** deciphering   **3** forestalling   **4** forgoing

(8) During the negotiations, the ambassador argued that the neighboring state's ( ) over the island was not recognized by international law and that it should be returned to his own country.

    1 sovereignty   **2** credibility   **3** coincidence   **4** solidarity

(9) The ( ) heat of the afternoon was in stark contrast to the frigid temperatures of the night before.

    1 discerning   **2** intriguing   **3** stifling   **4** numbing

(10) *A:* Let me treat you to lunch today.
    B: No, you paid last time. Let me ( ) and treat you this time.

    1 enjoin   **2** vanquish   **3** grind   **4** reciprocate

(11) The woman ( ) the advances of her male colleague, telling him that she preferred not to date anyone from the office.

    1 justified   **2** spurned   **3** spawned   **4** heeded

(12) There are many ( ) within Christianity, Roman Catholicism being the largest and the oldest.

    1 denominations   **2** prophecies
    3 pundits   **4** recapitulations

(13) Due to the lack of water and high temperatures, deserts are considered among the most ( ) places on Earth.

    1 inhospitable   **2** unbridled   **3** impartial   **4** lucrative

(14) *A:* Hey, Ted. I heard you just won over $100,000 in the lottery. How does it feel?
    B: I'm ( ). It's like a gift from heaven.

    1 euphoric   **2** jaded   **3** ubiquitous   **4** brusque

(15) Antoni enjoys creating new dishes. His ( ) in the kitchen will surely make him a famous chef one day.

    1 paternity   **2** intransigence   **3** ingenuity   **4** haughtiness

(16) This budget increase will enable the ( ) of the projects scheduled for the current fiscal year.

    1 containment   **2** destitution
    3 implementation   **4** incrimination

Day 1
Day 2
Day 3
Day 4
Day 5
Day 6
Day 7

(17) Doctors were warned to thoroughly wash their hands after treating patients in the ward, for each had a disease that was highly (   ).
1 contagious   **2** outrageous   **3** gallant   **4** vicarious

(18) At first, the young man was reserved, for most of the people at the party were strangers. However, he soon lost his initial (   ) and began socializing with others.
1 inhibitions   **2** artifacts   **3** tumors   **4** diversities

(19) Suzanne was a capable negotiator, so the union had confidence she would (   ) a satisfactory settlement with company representatives.
1 make over   **2** skim off   **3** pull off   **4** tack on

(20) Unfortunately, Tom never saved any money, so he had nothing to (   ) on after losing his job.
1 opt out   **2** hand down   **3** fall back   **4** run up

(21) *A:* I'm sorry, officer. I didn't know I was speeding.
B: You're expected to (   ) the law at all times. And since you were going 20 miles per hour over the speed limit, I have no choice but to write you a ticket.
1 object to   **2** abide by   **3** stand by   **4** descend on

(22) Crime in the neighborhood skyrocketed over the last several years, so the mayor vowed to (   ) on drug dealers and other criminals.
1 crack down   **2** carry out   **3** break down   **4** belt out

Read each passage and choose the best word or phrase from among the four choices for each blank. Then, on your answer sheet, find the number of the question and mark your answer.

Canine Separation Anxiety

Dogs of all breeds may feel separation anxiety when left alone in the house. They might bark or whine incessantly or, in extreme cases, destroy furniture, rugs, or doors. However, dogs can usually be cured of this problem. When dogs do not identify their human family as their masters, (23   ). The dog's misconception that it is the leader is often the source of separation anxiety. Dogs are pack animals that operate within a simple social hierarchy of "those who lead" and "those who follow."

Dogs take their roles in the pack very seriously. When followers, they obey with their famous canine loyalty. When leaders, they protect their followers. When a dog believes it is the pack's leader, it feels powerless to defend its followers—the human family—when they leave the house. Emotional discomfort sets in.

Proper training is the solution. For example, it is important to ignore your pet when it barks or whimpers to get your attention. You, as the leader, decide when to feed, pet, punish, and reward. You are master of your own time; your dog has no claim on it, and should never be led to believe that it does. (24   ), and the sooner it understands this, the better. As soon as people get back home, they often want to hug their pets. However, it is important to delay the exchange of affection for a couple of minutes to reinforce that your dog follows your schedule, instead of the other way around.

It can (25   ) to ignore your pet's whimpering and put on a stern face when you really feel like smothering it in hugs. But in the long run, a human who acts as the leader will make the dog happier. You can hug your dog and frolic together as much as you want, as long as you don't let it decide when.

---

(23) **1** they can act aggressively toward them
     2 they stop eating and lose weight
     3 they always feel lonely and sad
     4 the result can be unwanted behavior

(24) **1** The dog is the leader of the pack
     2 The dog doesn't make the rules
     3 You must always make the dog happy
     4 The dog can't tell what time it is

1 be a simple affair
    2 often require outside assistance
    3 take a lot of willpower
    4 seem to make no sense

Sputnik 1

The world's first artificial satellite, Sputnik 1, was launched into elliptical low-Earth orbit by the Soviet Union in 1957. The launch and successful deployment of Sputnik not only represented what is generally considered to be the first major development of the Space Age, but also (　**26**　). The ensuing "Sputnik crisis" led to the start of the Space Race, triggering political upheaval, a clamor to develop new technology, and massive scientific, military and educational investments, including the creation of NASA.

The launch took place during the decades-long Cold War, when sensationalist propaganda was rife on all sides. However, the Soviets had been deliberately cagey about publicizing their advancements in rocketry as the government feared that secrets could be leaked and any failures would be exploited by Western propaganda to ridicule the Soviet Union and further (　**27**　). For this reason, despite its unprecedented success and the fact that the Soviet Union had beaten the United States to this major scientific landmark, the launch was not immediately publicized in Soviet propaganda. When the news was formally announced it shocked many people in the U.S. who, until then, believed that the U.S. was the world's unrivaled technological superpower. Elsewhere, the news was greeted with a mix of trepidation for the future and astonishment at the accomplishment of such a feat.

The spherical design and antenna placements of Sputnik 1 allowed it to transmit on 20.005 and 40.002 MHz equally in all directions, regardless of the satellite's rotation, which meant that both scientists and amateur radio operators throughout the world were able to track its progress as it completed its 21-day mission. Compared to modern satellites, it was decidedly low-tech, equipped with no sensors for speed, altitude or atmospheric readings, and only four external antennas to broadcast radio pulses, although this (　**28**　). By monitoring the craft, considerable deductions about the upper atmosphere could be made, and important data regarding drag and propagation of radio signals could be gathered.

(26)   **1** urged politicians to temporarily shut down NASA
     2 stunned people and governments around the world
     3 transmitted the news seamlessly across the globe
     4 convinced onlookers an invasion was imminent

(27)   **1** enhance its status as the leader in space technology
     2 demonize it as restrictively formal and oversensitive
     3 characterize it as backward and technologically inferior
     4 acknowledge its ideological prowess and standing

(28)   **1** far from rendered the mission technologically insignificant
     2 had no considerable impact on satellite development
     3 prevented the accumulation of qualitative data
     4 allowed the experiment to drag on indefinitely

Day 1
Day 2
Day 3
Day 4
Day 5
Day 6
Day 7

Read each passage and choose the best answer from among the four choices for each question. Then, on your answer sheet, find the number of the question and mark your answer.

Conspiracy Theories

Throughout history, events, occurrences, sightings, disappearances, and other newsworthy events from the moon landings to political assassinations have left many wondering about the exact circumstances surrounding them. For some, the official record of questionable, sensational or seemingly unexplainable events is unsatisfactory. This has led to unfounded speculation and theories that governments and other powerful actors are withholding the truth for nefarious reasons. Such theories are known as "conspiracy theories," and they often give rise to hypotheses that not only contradict the prevailing understanding of history or provable facts, but also include some outlandish claims. The pejorative term has been used for over a century, with some claiming conspiracy theorists have been identified further back, although the growth of media such as TV and especially the Internet has seen a recent explosion in the use of the term and an associated rise in conspiracy theories themselves.

Conspiracy theories are not the sole preserve of tabloid publications and fantastical websites, however, as they have been studied professionally. Political scientist Michael Barkun identified three principles of conspiracy theories, which are: "nothing happens by accident," "nothing is as it seems," and "everything is connected." He goes on to identify three major classifications of conspiracy theories: event conspiracy theories, relating to major events like the 9/11 terrorist attacks in the U.S.; systemic conspiracy theories relating to single groups seeking global domination, such as the rumored Illuminati; and super-conspiracy theories, under which interlinked conspiracies are controlled by an omnipotent evil force, including the bizarre claim that the planet is controlled by a race of shape-shifting lizards. Studies have also found that many conspiracy theories incorporate evidence used to discredit them as "proof" that they are true, claiming that such efforts confirm that powerful figures are nervous and trying to cover up the truth.

Regarding conspiracy theorists, three studies conducted at the Université Grenoble Alpes in France found that those prone to believe in conspiracy theories considered themselves to be "exceptionally perceptive and unique." This belief, and the need to feel unique or special, can manifest itself in people believing that they alone possess rare information about the events in question, concluding that hidden, malevolent forces are at work to obscure the truth from an oblivious, gullible public. But it is not only those with an inflated sense of self-worth who believe in conspiracy theories: Research by the University of Kent in the UK suggested that people could become favorable towards conspiracy theories while greatly underestimating the change in their attitude.

This does not explain the prevalence of conspiracy theories, however, or completely explain why they appeal to so many. People may be drawn to conspiracy theories because they offer a form of relief for those who feel they have no power over their own lives. They can ascribe difficulties and setbacks to the sinister forces in control. For some, however, the obsessive tendency to believe in and spread conspiracy theories could be the manifestations of more serious underlying psychological conditions such as schizophrenia or paranoia.

---

(29) What is true about the general perception of conspiracy theories and conspiracy theorists?

1 Most conspiracy theories are based on factual accounts of events that would otherwise remain unexplained.

2 The term "conspiracy theory" has generally been used to respectfully denote a way of thinking that challenges the status quo.

3 Conspiracy theorists tend to disregard mainstream accounts in favor of more offbeat suggestions.

4 Government attempts to cover up sensitive stories of paranormal activities are being uncovered by dedicated actors.

(30) How has academic study improved our understanding of conspiracy theories?

1 Academics have identified interlinked forms of evidence which support the legitimacy of conspiracy theories.

2 Conspiracy theories may seem bizarre, but academic research has established that they are governed by provable principles.

3 Academics have found that conspiracy theories have exposed a system of global domination established by certain powerful groups.

4 Although conspiracy theories appear random and disparate, research has shown they can be classified and have some similarities.

Day 1
Day 2
Day 3
Day 4
Day 5
Day 6
Day 7

(31) How could the propagation of conspiracy theories suggest an underlying psychological basis?

1 Conspiracy theorists could exhibit narcissistic tendencies as well as a belief that society is being misled as to the true nature of the world.

2 Psychologists dismiss credible theories by categorizing conspiracy theorists as suffering from mental illnesses.

3 Excessive control by political groups has resulted in psychological trauma which often manifests itself in belief in conspiracy theories.

4 By switching blame to conspiracy theorists, politicians can effectively mislead the public on many issues.

The Real Cost of the Louisiana Purchase

In 1803, the United States government made what is popularly referred to as the best real estate deal in the history of the country: the Louisiana Purchase. In exchange for 68 million francs, which at the time equated to around $15 million U.S. dollars, the U.S. received 827,000 square miles of land from France, effectively doubling the size of the young nation. Today, that would be tantamount to purchasing fifteen U.S. states and two Canadian provinces for the paltry sum of $310 million. Looking at these figures, it comes as no surprise that the Louisiana Purchase has been lauded as such a spectacular bargain. From a technical viewpoint, however, determining the actual price paid to acquire these lands is a more complicated matter, as calculating this figure requires one to look at the costs incurred in displacing the Native Americans that inhabited the Louisiana Territory.

In actual fact, the U.S. was not purchasing all of the Louisiana Territory from France. Instead, they were purchasing the sole right to colonize the land, which was primarily inhabited by indigenous tribes—it is estimated that a mere 60,000 non-natives inhabited these lands in 1803. Claiming the territory from its native inhabitants would prove to be a challenging undertaking, and over the course of the last two centuries, the U.S. government has made treaties, agreements, and statutes with well over 200 Native American tribes in this region. Between 1804 and 2012, it is estimated that the U.S. government paid various tribes a total sum of $2.6 billion for this land, which would be about $8.6 billion when adjusted for inflation.

The methods in which the U.S. government went about obtaining these lands from native tribes are a delicate topic. The first Indian cession of land within the Louisiana Territory is a prime example as to why. In 1804, William Henry Harrison, the governor of the Indiana Territory at that time, manipulated a handful of Sauk and Fox Indian tribe representatives into signing away 3.6 million acres of land, 1.6 million of which were part of the Louisiana Territory. The land was bought for about half a cent an acre, when the value at the time is reported to have been around 60 cents an acre. In the words of historian Herbert S. Channick, Harrison managed to secure such a lucrative deal because he "maneuvered a handful of drunken Indians into agreeing to a cession which they had no authority to make." Once the papers were signed, though, the U.S. government treated them as law, and the Sauk and Fox tribes were driven out of their land just a few decades later. Those that refused to leave were killed.

The U.S. government's efforts to procure these lands throughout the twentieth century, though considerably more civilized than their approach in the 1800s, have nevertheless failed to satisfy native tribes. A notable ongoing dispute centering around the U.S. seizure of Indian land within the Louisiana Territory is the Sioux Black Hills Land Claim. A portion of the Black Hills, a mountain range stretching across Wyoming and South Dakota, was annexed from the Sioux people by the U.S. government in 1877, shortly after the discovery of gold in the region. In 1980, the U.S. Supreme Court, finding this to be an unjust seizure of territory in direct violation of a treaty made with the Sioux in 1868, ordered $100 million to be paid to compensate the tribe. The Sioux refused this payment, reiterating their initial displeasure with this turn of events. They did not want financial compensation; they wanted their lands returned to them. In explaining the motivation for their refusal, Mario Gonzalez, general counsel for the Oglala Sioux Tribe, reported that "The Sioux Indians are very attached to their lands and particularly the Black Hills because that's the spiritual center of the Sioux nation." Interest has continued to accumulate on the unclaimed funds, which currently amount to well over $1 billion.

Even taking all of these tribal compensations and unpaid debts into account, the Louisiana Purchase is certainly deserving of its reputation as a phenomenal deal. Even a conservative estimate places the true value of these lands at an amount that is staggering in comparison to the $2.6 billion—or $8.6 billion when adjusted for inflation—that has been paid thus far. Take, for instance, the value of the land in North Dakota, one of the states carved out of the Louisiana Territory. Between 2010 and 2015 alone, over $100 billion of oil was extracted there. As historian Robert Lee puts it, "The Louisiana Purchase remains an unbelievable steal. But not of the type we've been taught. The land came cheap because of how little the United States paid the people who lived here long before the French laid claim to it."

Day 1
Day 2
Day 3
Day 4
Day 5
Day 6
Day 7

(32) What does the author of the passage imply about the Louisiana Purchase?

1 The French, though perhaps pressed at the time for funds, committed an irreparable logistical error in forfeiting ownership of the Louisiana territory.

2 The praise generally given in regard to the Louisiana Purchase is misguided, as the U.S. government concealed key aspects of the deal.

3 Even if the U.S. government had not paid France for the Louisiana Territory, the region still would have been seized by the growing population of settlers.

4 An accurate estimate of the cost incurred in the acquisition of the Louisiana Territory requires the tallying of numerous financial transactions.

(33) The example of William Henry Harrison's deal with tribal representatives serves to illustrate that

1 U.S. government representatives were on the whole unfair in their dealings with Indian tribes, but they only turned to violence as a last resort.

2 the tactics by which Indian lands were absorbed into U.S. territory, while perhaps effective, were nevertheless morally questionable.

3 Indian tribes were forced to negotiate deals according to the customs of a society drastically different than their own.

4 Indian tribes often ceded their lands for considerably less than they were worth due to their misunderstanding of land ownership in general.

(34) What is true of the Sioux people?

1 Although the Sioux would have likely accepted a reasonable financial payment for the Black Hills in the 1800s, that is no longer the case.

2 The tribe's leading figures are in support of allowing interest to further accumulate on the compensation for the Black Hills before accepting it.

3 The tribe is unwilling to negotiate any deal with the U.S. government that does not include the return of all or a portion of sacred lands.

4 The tribe remains protected by the terms of a treaty that was found to still be intact following a U.S. Supreme Court judgment.

(35) Which of the following statements would Robert Lee most likely agree with?

1 The state of North Dakota is arguably the most valuable piece of land that was acquired in the Louisiana Purchase.

2 Historians should refrain from describing the Louisiana Purchase as a lucrative deal until estimates of land acquisition prices have been finalized.

3 The U.S. government should compensate Indian tribes for the inhumane treatment they received during the acquisition of their lands.

4 Popular education regarding the Louisiana Purchase is misleading, as the amount paid to the French represents but a portion of the land's total price.

Day 1

Day 2

Day 3

Day 4

Day 5

Day 6

Day 7

English Summary

● Instructions: Read the article below and summarize it in your own words as far as possible in English.
● Suggested length: 90-110 words
● Write your summary in the space provided on your answer sheet. <u>Any writing outside the space will not be graded.</u>

Artificial intelligence is quickly becoming an important part of the American justice system, as police departments use facial recognition technology to identify suspects or employ software to analyze crime patterns. Perhaps its most controversial use, however, is in the sentencing of people convicted of crimes. Such sentencing software searches for and analyzes factors such as prior criminal records, types of crimes committed, etc., to determine the likelihood of the individual breaking the law again in the future. Although the software does not determine the sentence, many judges employ it when determining sentences.

In one experiment, however, the software was tested against ordinary people with no particular knowledge of law enforcement. Unlike the software, these people only read short descriptions of the defendants. Both the software and the people were asked to predict whether the defendant would reoffend within the next two years. The humans' overall accuracy was 67 percent, whereas the software was correct 65 percent of the time. Due to this disappointing performance, experts worry about the risk of judges being influenced by software that has been promoted as a highly sophisticated and accurate predictor of whether a defendant will reoffend.

One of the main selling points of AI is that computers should be able to make decisions based on data alone, without the biases that humans are likely to have. However, since AI is trained on huge volumes of data created by humans who may have racist attitudes toward Black people and other minorities, there are fears that it will inherit the biases present in the data. Indeed, this appears to be exactly what happened when one well-known program was nearly twice as likely to mistakenly label Black individuals as being at high risk of committing another crime. Until software becomes more accurate and can eliminate biases, law enforcement officials should be extremely cautious about its use.

5 English Composition

- Write an essay on the given **TOPIC**.
- Give THREE reasons to support your answer.
- Structure: introduction, main body, and conclusion
- Suggested length: 200-240 words
- Write your essay in the space provided on your answer sheet. <u>Any writing outside the space will not be graded.</u>

TOPIC
Should voting be compulsory?

Day 1
Day 2
Day 3
Day 4
Day 5
Day 6
Day 7

リスニングテスト

試験時間 **リスニング約35分**

There are four parts to this listening test.

Part 1	**Dialogues:** 1 question each	Multiple-choice
Part 2	**Passages:** 2 questions each	Multiple-choice
Part 3	**Real-Life:** 1 question each	Multiple-choice
Part 4	**Interview:** 2 questions	Multiple-choice

※Listen carefully to the instructions.

Part 1　◀))026～036

No. 1
  1 She has not thought about next week yet.
  2 She wants to go on a trip around the country.
  3 She basically plans to take it easy.
  4 She wants to catch up on her work.

No. 2
  1 To find a resort near a big city.
  2 To work a little while on vacation.
  3 To find an easily reachable resort.
  4 To choose a culture they both like.

No. 3
  1 He is relieved after hearing it.
  2 He will wait and see if it comes true.
  3 He is highly skeptical of it.
  4 He is surprised to hear it.

No. 4
  1 Most riders don't use drugs.
  2 More riders will be caught.
  3 The image of the race has not been damaged.
  4 A lot of people should share the blame.

No. 5   **1** Ask Ron to do all the work.
        2 Request a team-member change.
        3 Improve the current curriculum.
        4 Ask Ron to join their team.

No. 6   **1** Lack of communication about a project delay.
        2 A shortage of necessary staff for the project.
        3 Insufficient budgeting for project completion.
        4 Being overloaded with too many projects.

No. 7   **1** He most likely lied on his résumé.
        2 He does not suit the company's culture.
        3 He shows a clear lack of management skills.
        4 He deserves a chance to succeed.

No. 8   **1** She does not want to be a freelancer.
        2 Current part-time workers are irresponsible.
        3 Staff in Human Resources are unmotivated.
        4 The turnover of freelancers is high.

No. 9   **1** He wanted to know about special promotions.
        2 He wanted to talk to a salesperson.
        3 He wanted to know where he could see ITO notebooks.
        4 He wanted to get literature on ITO notebooks.

No. 10   **1** Establish a friendly rapport first.
        2 Come up with an acceptable offer.
        3 Introduce himself courteously at the start.
        4 Ask Lucas about culturally acceptable behavior.

Day 1
Day 2
Day 3
Day 4
Day 5
Day 6
Day 7

(A) **No. 11** **1** There are virtually no limits to what teachers can teach.
  2 The right kind of teaching can actually produce genius.
  3 Students think more creatively when given stimulating books and lectures.
  4 Students should be expected to solve problems independently.

No. 12 **1** Envision multiple solutions to problems or questions.
  2 Consider various creative concepts provided by teachers.
  3 Question teachers in order to gain greater self-confidence.
  4 Stimulate their curiosity by watching fun, creative programs.

(B) **No. 13** **1** The levels of CFCs in the atmosphere fluctuated.
  2 Atmospheric ozone decreased.
  3 The ozone hole markedly shrank.
  4 Dangerous ultraviolet rays suddenly increased.

No. 14 **1** Carbon dioxide is clearly causing global warming.
  2 Basing economic policy on scientific theory is risky.
  3 Reducing CFCs is costlier than reducing carbon dioxide emissions.
  4 Science cannot fully explain the role of the ozone layer.

(C) **No. 15** **1** It is a translation of the word "philosophy."
  2 Descartes used it to further the modern study of philosophy.
  3 Descartes was the first person to suggest it.
  4 Similar ideas had been expressed by other philosophers.

No. 16 **1** He was influenced by the work of Sir Isaac Newton.
  2 He had a vision while serving as a soldier.
  3 He was experimenting with merging calculus and philosophy.
  4 He remembered it while publishing his scientific studies.

(D) *No. 17*
1 Their cylindrical shape influenced early cameras.
2 They made still images appear animated.
3 They effectively blurred animation.
4 The first zoetropes were made by Greeks.

No. 18
1 They often included pottery and ceramics.
2 They were associated with mathematical concepts.
3 Inventors painted lamps and other cylindrical objects.
4 Early examples often featured animals.

(E) *No. 19*
1 It is a recent phenomenon brought about by advanced societies.
2 Equality became less prominent as humans became more sophisticated.
3 It has historically increased the power of the strongest communities.
4 Equality has been considered important since early civilizations began.

No. 20
1 Colonies that promoted the common good were healthier.
2 It is difficult to determine which civilization was the greatest.
3 Where equality flourished, so did the society.
4 Superior societies should value innovation over equality.

Day
1
Day
2
Day
3
Day
4
Day
5
Day
6
Day
7

(F)   *No. 21*   ***Situation:*** Upon returning home after work late Friday evening, you hear the following message on your answering machine. You absolutely need the package by the 12th.

Question: What should you do tomorrow?

1 Go to the Main Dispatch Office on 42nd Street.

2 Wait at home for the delivery.

3 Pick up your package from the sender.

4 Call the local FastEx office in Highland Park.

(G)   *No. 22*   ***Situation:*** You hear an announcement in a store while shopping. You are a senior citizen as well as a store member.

Question: How can you use the biggest total discount?

1 Apply for a rebate on any purchase you make.

2 Get the member's discount and apply for a rebate.

3 Combine the senior citizen discount and the rebate.

4 Shop after 8 p.m. for maximum discounts.

(H)   *No. 23*   ***Situation:*** You listen to a dentist giving you an explanation about your treatment options. You don't have dental insurance.

Question: If you follow his advice, what should you do?

1 Extract the decayed tooth.

2 Get a root canal.

3 Fill the cavity.

4 Get a gold crown.

(I) *No. 24* ***Situation:*** You are approaching your home by car and you see a policeman in the road ahead. He stops you and explains what is happening.

Question: What does he advise that you do?

1 Take only valuable possessions from your home.

2 Listen to the news while waiting at your home.

3 Stay away from your home for the time being.

4 Assist firefighters with their efforts to save structures.

(J) *No. 25* ***Situation:*** You attend an investment seminar in the U.S. You are 29 years old and hope to invest for your retirement or any possible future emergency. You have little time to manage your investments. You have $40,000 to begin with. You hear the following from a financial planner.

Question: According to the financial planner, what should you do?

1 Purchase an individual home.

2 Purchase undervalued stocks.

3 Invest in an index fund.

4 Invest in bonds giving dividends.

Day 1
Day 2
Day 3
Day 4
Day 5
Day 6
Day 7

No. 26   **1** She has staff try the food before it goes out to patients.
　　　　　2 She checks with doctors right before serving meals.
　　　　　3 She makes sure the food is cooked at the right temperature.
　　　　　4 She watches patients eat the food they have prepared.

No. 27   **1** The doctors give her information about patients' medical conditions.
　　　　　2 She personally visits each patient to check on their medical conditions.
　　　　　3 The doctors tell her what kinds of meals to prepare based on patients' conditions.
　　　　　4 She gets the information she needs from online reports about the patients.

Day
1

Day
2

Day
3

Day
4

Day
5

Day
6

Day
7

筆記試験＆リスニングテスト

1 To complete each item, choose the best word or phrase from among the four choices. Then, on your answer sheet, find the number of the question and mark your answer.

---

(1) Thanks to effective vaccination campaigns, polio is one disease that has been nearly (　　) in many countries.

1 condensed **2** eradicated **3** withheld **4** bolstered

(2) The tobacco industry has given up trying to (　　) the commonly accepted understanding that smoking causes lung cancer.

1 repudiate **2** compel **3** relegate **4** contemplate

(3) **A:** Jack just heard that Altrua Limited is going bankrupt, and he wants to write a front-page story about it.

B: It's certainly newsworthy, if true. But he only got that information from one source. Before the story goes to print, we've got to get it (　　).

1 coveted **2** corroborated **3** rejuvenated **4** suffocated

(4) Tetsuo has a good memory. He can (　　) many facts, names, and dates in his mind.

1 retain **2** heave **3** decimate **4** project

(5) One of the major car companies (　　) its production due to poor sales performance last year.

1 mitigated **2** recouped **3** mollified **4** curtailed

(6) The oil spill was considered the greatest environmental (　　) that the coastal region has ever experienced.

1 impediment **2** catastrophe **3** iniquity **4** consequence

(7) Social scientists are still able to reveal a pattern of (　　) even in societies embracing "equal rights."

1 verdict **2** stratification **3** tenacity **4** platitude

(8) The contract (　　　) that all shipments must be delivered on time, or there would be a penalty of $100 per day of delay.

1 derived　　　　**2** stipulated　　　　**3** reprimanded　　　**4** consecrated

(9) Narcotic drugs can have a (　　　) effect on the body if they are abused, sometimes leading to death.

1 regimental　　**2** cogent　　　　**3** detrimental　　　**4** strident

(10) Ken was surprised to see a birthday present and card on his desk after returning from the restroom. Someone had (　　　) put it there while he was away.

1 surreptitiously　**2** negligently　　**3** judiciously　　**4** retroactively

(11) Fifty-two (　　　) have been made to the country's constitution, but the constitution's relevance has not been weakened.

1 amendments　**2** recipients　　**3** enigmas　　　**4** epitaphs

(12) An agreement between the two leading parties appears (　　　). The negotiators are working late into the night to bridge the few remaining differences.

1 contingent　　**2** medieval　　　**3** imminent　　　**4** derisive

(13) **A:** Jim never fails to clarify the main point of whatever is discussed at meetings.
B: You're right. He's always sharp and (　　　).

1 incipient　　　**2** incisive　　　**3** vindictive　　　**4** voluptuous

(14) Before leaving for work, James had a (　　　) that something bad would happen that day. It turned out to be true, for he had a minor car accident just a few hours later.

1 consultation　**2** mutation　　　**3** retribution　　**4** premonition

(15) It is commonly known that a (　　　) lifestyle is not good for health. It is important to get away from TVs and computers and get some exercise during the day.

1 sedentary　　**2** vigorous　　　**3** fervent　　　**4** frugal

(16) The senator decided to drop out of politics after the election (　　　), in which he was soundly defeated.

1 harangue　　**2** breakthrough　**3** remnant　　　**4** debacle

Day 1
Day 2
Day 3
Day 4
Day 5
Day 6
Day 7

(17) The citizens of the city were shocked to hear that their police chief had been a juvenile (   ) in his youth and had committed several crimes.

1 deliberator   **2** quotient   **3** collaborator   **4** delinquent

(18) *A:* I hope I'm not being too (   ). I should have called you before dropping in.

    B: Don't worry about it. I wasn't doing anything anyway.

1 dismissive   **2** intrusive   **3** conducive   **4** dissuasive

(19) The two tennis champions (   ) in the final match of the International Cup to determine who would be the world's top player.

1 stirred up   **2** squared off   **3** fanned out   **4** boiled over

(20) After years of work, researchers believe they are finally (   ) on an effective cure for the common cold.

1 marking up   **2** brushing up   **3** zeroing in   **4** raking off

(21) In a strange twist of events, Bruce (   ) divorcing his wife and marrying his marriage counselor.

1 jacked up   **2** found out   **3** dished out   **4** wound up

(22) Helen had a great time at her farewell party, but she seemed fairly (   ) during her speech. I thought she was going to cry.

1 ripped off   **2** buckled down   **3** watered down   **4** choked up

2

Read each passage and choose the best word or phrase from among the four choices for each blank. Then, on your answer sheet, find the number of the question and mark your answer.

筆記試験＆リスニングテスト

Day 1
Day 2
Day 3
Day 4
Day 5
Day 6
Day 7

Busyness and Creativity

We live in a state of increasing busyness, bombarded by news, messages, social media updates and more from our omnipresent digital companions, meaning our minds are becoming more occupied than ever before. It is estimated that we digest up to five times as much information or more on a daily basis than we did only twenty-five years ago, and (**23**) has been shown to adversely affect our creative abilities. Creativity is often awakened by "switching off" and allowing our minds to wander, which is hard when a stream of information demands our brains remain in linear thinking mode. So is the answer sustained idleness rather than constant, if superficial, engagement? As with many things in life, the solution lies in moderation rather than extremes.

While exposing ourselves to excessive stimulation reduces our capacity to be creative, (**24**). In experiments led by the psychology department of Rider University in New Jersey, subjects given certain constraints for a task were found to be more creative, and even continued to be once those rules were lifted. These somewhat contrary findings might not be as conflicting as they first appear. Constantly checking the Internet has become second nature to many of us, and therefore habitual and addictive. Tapping into our creative well could be as simple as introducing some smartphone restrictions.

Striking a balance between keeping busy and allowing the mind to run free is an approach that has helped some of the world's most creative minds envisage and develop groundbreaking inventions and theories. Albert Einstein, for example, took regular breaks from his experiments and thinking sessions to relax and listen to music, while Nikola Tesla had an insight about rotating magnetic fields while out for a stroll. Many others, including Apple co-founders Steve Jobs and Steve Wozniak, have extolled the benefits of tuning out for a while (**25**). While extended periods of idleness can be counterproductive, so too can prolonged, uninterrupted periods of busyness, so stepping away from the screen may do much more than give your eyes a rest.

---

(23) **1** our inability to remain focused
   2 this interruption to the neurotransmitters
   3 this constant drain on our attention
   4 our need to continually update social media

1 it does not lead to addictive behavior
   2 conflicts with rule imposition also follow
   3 we can no longer set appropriate boundaries
   4 imposing some limits can enhance it

1 to recharge their creative batteries
   2 to reconnect with people on social media
   3 and embracing prolonged periods of laziness
   4 to focus on the most important tasks

Hashtag Democracy

The breakneck speed at which social media continues to expand has repercussions beyond friends oversharing salacious private details, and (**26**). Nowadays everyone from teenagers to world leaders can and do share predominantly unfiltered views to those willing to listen and engage in discussion and debate. Whereas one could argue that social media has done much to democratize access to media by giving an outlet to those who wish to express themselves, it is becoming increasingly clear that it has a role in disrupting, and thereby affecting, the political process.

The influence of social media cannot be ignored, as over 60 percent of U.S. adults now turn to platforms like Twitter and Facebook for their news, and politicians and others have seized the opportunity to reach them. However, despite the array of news organizations available today, many people rely on stories shared within their own self-selected, often circumscribed, digital bubbles. This has led to a strange paradox in which the exponential growth rate of news outlets at our disposal has resulted in many of us restricting ourselves to overtly ideological ones, contributing to (**27**). This paradox is seen by some as leading to the undermining of democracy itself.

Misinformation campaigns can spread like wildfire on social media, which, unlike most traditional media outlets, are not held to the same moral and legal standards. Due to their size and reach, many argue that it is time for the likes of Twitter and Facebook to adhere to the same regulations and punishments as other broadcasters, as they have effectively become media companies. Serious issues are routinely discussed on these channels, which can negatively affect public debate, yet social media could be used to help save democracy. Social media platforms use algorithms which analyze our viewing habits to force-feed us similar items we may be interested in, and this could be the key to bursting our digital bubbles. These same algorithms, many argue, should be used in more positive ways to enhance debate and democracy by (*28*   ).

---

(26)   **1** family members are rightly concerned
      2 democracy is struggling to keep pace
      3 politicians are turning a blind eye
      4 the effect remains relatively negligible

(27)   **1** greater insights into political thought
      2 society broadening its horizons on social issues
      3 increased partisanship and polarized political opinion
      4 growing support for liberal-leaning agendas

(28)   **1** encouraging us to interact more belligerently
      2 upgrading our social media connections
      3 punishing and condemning those who oppose democracy
      4 exposing us to alternative perspectives

Day 1
Day 2
Day 3
Day 4
Day 5
Day 6
Day 7

The History of Globalization

Most of us assume that globalization is a relatively new concept in the history of mankind, a concept marked by such business trends as worldwide express delivery services, multinational coffee chains, the Internet, and the offshoring of production facilities and call centers. In fact, globalization has been with us since the first people exited Africa, the birthplace of humankind, tens of thousands of years ago. Since that time, migrants, merchants, religious missionaries, warriors, and others have brought their values, ideas, customs, and products to new regions of the world, stimulating significant changes. To fully understand globalization, it should be viewed in its broadest context, not merely within the narrow contexts of economics, trade, politics, or religion, for it has been interwoven in the vast tapestry of human history in so many ways.

Nayan Chanda, author of *Bound Together: How Traders, Preachers, Adventurers, and Warriors Shaped Globalization* and member of the Yale Center for the Study of Globalization, argues that globalization "has worked silently for millennia without being given a name, and it moves through a multitude of threads connecting us to faraway places from an ancient time." As long as people travel and migrate, as long as people trade, globalization will always be with us. To stress this point, Chanda had his DNA tested and discovered, unsurprisingly, that his ancient lineage stretched back to India and, before that, Africa. Chanda reminds us that migrations continue to move around the globe, for "migrants constitute 20 percent of the population in some 41 of the world's largest countries."

Many scholars may criticize Chanda's primary concepts in his book, which hold that globalization has unfolded gradually throughout much of human history and that our current global undertakings have their roots in the past, as too simple. However, his astute knowledge of the historical evolutionary events of globalization and his weaving together of individuals, societies, and cultures is as convincing as it is impressive. In drawing parallels with today, Chanda postulates that modern multicultural corporations are modeled after the crown-sponsored trading houses of England, Portugal, and Holland, whose far-reaching global influences could be traced back to far earlier roots in the ancient empires of Mesopotamia. Furthermore, Chanda believes that development of convertible currencies and credit cards, the lifeblood of modern trade, can be traced back to gold and silver mining in Mexico and Peru by early Spanish invaders, who shipped back their treasures to their motherland.

The U.S. is often seen as the progenitor of modern globalization, but in their times, Roman, Mongol, and British empires were likewise seen as the initiators and instigators of globalization. The global power shifts are unlikely to halt in the future. Western powers today are fearful of the flood of Chinese products bombarding the world, for some view the Chinese success as a portent for a new age of Chinese-dominated globalization. Yet efforts to halt change are futile. This is because, though people today have difficulty keeping up with the rapid changes brought by globalization, change cannot be contained. However, petty tribalism, another inheritance from our past, blocks us from making the necessary holistic global changes needed to combat global climate change, powerful pandemics, international economic crises, and humanitarian disasters. It seems that we all need to view globalization differently if we, as fellow humans, are to survive and thrive.

---

(29) What do we learn about the development of globalization?

1 Globalization has been with us in some form since the earliest migrations of humans to distant lands.

2 Though globalization has long played a role in human life, it has developed into something dramatically different today.

3 Attempts to comprehend the development of globalization in its entirety are futile, so it is best to analyze it through particular fields of study.

4 Experts have reached a consensus that globalization is a contemporary concept which opens a whole different way of conducting business.

(30) What does the author imply about the work, *Bound Together: How Traders, Preachers, Adventurers, and Warriors Shaped Globalization*?

1 The concepts presented in the book about how globalization unfolded and its parallels to modern times are overly simple.

2 The book is the best ever about the history of globalization and how it affects our daily lives.

3 Chanda's explanations about the evolution of globalization are more convincing than his parallels to modern times.

4 Chanda's grasp of globalization's past events and his explication of complex interlocking relationships are brilliant.

筆記試験＆リスニングテスト

Day 1
Day 2
Day 3
Day 4
Day 5
Day 6
Day 7

(31) What does the author imply about the evolutionary flow of globalization?

1 A nation that is best able to overcome its tendency toward petty tribalism is likely to be the leader of globalization.

2 Those nations that have historically been at the forefront of globalization are eventually destined to lose their dominant role.

3 The evolution of globalization is unpredictable, so it is natural that nations struggle to maintain their own interests.

4 Because of its success in importing goods worldwide, China is destined to stop being the new center of globalization.

Acoustic Ecology

Are we losing our ability to listen? We are surrounded by sound—perhaps "bombarded" would be a more fitting word in reference to our urban environments—but the vast majority of people live a daily existence with very little awareness of the sounds around them. Just in case you don't consider yourself to belong to this group of non-listeners, here's a simple test to assess your personal listening skills: Name five sounds that you heard today. If you fail to complete the list within a few minutes, rest assured that you are by no means alone.

The deterioration of the human ability to consciously listen, or at least the perception of this phenomenon, was one concern that led R. Murray Schafer, a Canadian musician, composer, and former communications professor, to propose and begin to develop the interdisciplinary field of acoustic ecology in the 1960s. Schafer believed that the visual modality was overly and increasingly dominant in society, often to the detriment of sound awareness. He advocated that the acoustic environment be listened to as a musical composition and that the members of a society be responsible for the content of this composition. This is certainly a profound concept and, although it is unlikely that such a frame of mind could be attained on a widespread level, Schafer has nevertheless made a laudable contribution to improving sound awareness around the world.

Schafer's seminal work was based on an ambitious effort entitled the World Soundscape Project, which he spearheaded in the 1970s. The project aimed at investigating and documenting the relationship between people and the acoustic environment in which they live. The project's first endeavor was a field study of the soundscape of Vancouver, Canada, that employed sound-level measurements, sound recordings, and descriptions of a range of sound features. The project was then followed by similar studies in several small towns across Europe. In analyzing the various soundscapes, Schafer and his colleagues classified sound sources into three broad categories: "keynotes" or background sounds that represent an underlying tonality; "sound signals" or foreground sounds that attract attention; and "soundmarks," particular prominent identifying features, such as coastal surf, waterfalls, wildlife, bells, and sounds created through various traditional activities. This work highlighted the fact that the sounds of a particular community, both natural and artificial, can characterize and express the community's identity, just as local architecture, customs, and culture do.

Unfortunately, however, with the ongoing advance of urbanization, many unique soundscapes have disappeared or become submerged under the homogenous onslaught of indistinguishable noise that marks the contemporary city. Moreover, as the sounds of the natural world are increasingly replaced by traffic, construction, and other unpleasant sonic features that define our urban environments, sound is increasingly becoming something that we try to block out rather than listen to. One could argue that the lack of sound awareness in society today is due to the scarcity of appealing sounds and the consequential effect that we must indeed ignore sound for our mental well-being. But this argument has several flaws, one being that closing ourselves off from "bad" sounds simultaneously restricts our potential to appreciate "good" sounds. More importantly, perhaps, is that choosing to simply shut out ambient noise on a conscious level overlooks the subconscious adverse effects of noise, such as stress and other negative impacts on mental health. Furthermore, we should keep in mind Schafer's appeal that all members of a society bear responsibility for the composition of the soundscape and, as such, we should pay attention to the sounds of our living environments, be aware of what we like and do not like, and take appropriate action to help preserve pleasing sounds and decrease or prevent offensive ones.

One technique for gaining awareness of environmental sound is the so-called "soundwalk" that was pioneered by Schafer and his peers. Although a variety of approaches can be applied, the method basically involves strolling in a particular location and listening discriminatively to the soundscape while simultaneously making critical assessments of each audible sound and judging its contribution to the overall sonic environment. For most people, a concentrated effort to carefully listen to each and every sound that enters the ears would undoubtedly reveal a myriad of sounds that would normally escape notice.

Acoustic ecology today is somewhat of an umbrella term that encompasses work being done by academics, city planners, sociologists, engineers, architects, and sound artists, among others. The implications of this relatively new area of study are far-reaching: noise pollution has been and remains to be a particular concern within the field, and appropriately so. Noise levels continue to rise due to increasing transportation volumes and the expanding use of audible machinery and technology. Meanwhile, sounds of the natural world continue to disappear. However, during this period of transition, the effect of sound on our behavior and

Day
1
Day
2
Day
3
Day
4
Day
5
Day
6
Day
7

health remains a largely neglected topic. Now more than ever, a deeper appreciation for sound and its role in our lives is needed.

---

(32) According to the passage, Schafer was motivated to develop the field of acoustic ecology because he
 1 was concerned about the changing sound environment and how it negatively affects people.
 2 wanted to document unique soundscapes that were disappearing in the modern world.
 3 believed people were paying insufficient attention to the sounds around them.
 4 argued that the visual and acoustic modalities we encounter are actually inseparable.

(33) Schafer states that all the sounds of a community
 1 shape the character of its citizens as much as the visual modality does, though people are unconscious of this.
 2 make up the community soundscape, which can be measured in units of "keynotes."
 3 are natural in the sense that they evolved over time to fit the character of that particular community.
 4 reflect that community's identity as much as other significant cultural characteristics do.

(34) The author suggests that
 1 noise pollution is causing people to become permanently hard of hearing.
 2 people are correct in assuming there is little they can do about halting noise pollution.
 3 ignoring noise pollution reduces our stress level and is arguably best for our well-being.
 4 urban noise pollution causes people to want to ignore most sounds in the environment.

(35) A soundwalk is an example of a technique to
1 increase our ability to both hear and evaluate various sounds in the environment.
2 improve our understanding of the physical nature of sound and its role in our lives.
3 foster our appreciation of environmental sounds and how each of them enlivens us.
4 stimulate our unconscious so that we can awaken sounds we have heard in the past.

Day 1
Day 2
Day 3
Day 4
Day 5
Day 6
Day 7

● Instructions: Read the article below and summarize it in your own words as far as possible in English.
● Suggested length: 90-110 words
● Write your summary in the space provided on your answer sheet. <u>Any writing outside the space will not be graded.</u>

Every 10 years, after a census is conducted in the United States to count the nation's current population, the shapes and sizes of the nation's election districts are thoroughly reviewed and compared with the freshly acquired data. Then, if necessary, the election districts are changed to reflect shifts in population and ensure equal representation for each citizen. However, there are some politicians who do not approach this process honestly by utilizing a technique called "gerrymandering," which alters the shapes and sizes of voting districts in order to gain an unfair advantage in elections. Both the Republican and Democratic parties have frequently been guilty of this practice.

Gerrymandering is deeply undemocratic and is a practice that has existed for more than 200 years. In particular, gerrymandering has made it difficult for minorities, such as Black people, to be fairly represented in American politics. For example, racist politicians may use a technique called "cracking," in which minorities are split up into multiple districts, making it nearly impossible for them to elect someone from the party they favor. On the other hand, another method known as "packing" concentrates minority voters into one district. Although it is easy for them to elect a representative in that one area, it is unlikely that they will be able to elect candidates in other districts.

While gerrymandering based on race is illegal in the United States, the United States Supreme Court has effectively upheld the use of gerrymandering in many cases, allowing political parties to gain advantage in elections. This means that minorities are still affected by it because there is a strong correlation between a person's race and the party the person votes for. This decision has enabled parties to defend discriminatory maps under the pretense that the redrawn maps are more representative of the people and not discriminatory towards any particular group.

5　English Composition

- Write an essay on the given **TOPIC**.
- Give THREE reasons to support your answer.
- Structure: introduction, main body, and conclusion
- Suggested length: 200-240 words
- Write your essay in the space provided on your answer sheet. <u>Any writing outside the space will not be graded.</u>

TOPIC

Should elderly parents be cared for at home?

Day 1
Day 2
Day 3
Day 4
Day 5
Day 6
Day 7

Listening Test

There are four parts to this listening test.

Part 1	Dialogues: 1 question each	Multiple-choice
Part 2	Passages: 2 questions each	Multiple-choice
Part 3	Real-Life: 1 question each	Multiple-choice
Part 4	Interview: 2 questions	Multiple-choice

※Listen carefully to the instructions.

Part 1 ◀))051~061

No. 1
1 John is not familiar with the office party.
2 John does not like to attend office parties.
3 John has few friends at the office.
4 John hopes to get closer to his colleagues.

No. 2
1 Give Tim a call.
2 Meet Rachel.
3 Buy some food.
4 Leave work early.

No. 3
1 A textbook written for American MBA students.
2 A business-English textbook for English learners.
3 Case studies that students developed by themselves.
4 Case-study materials for business graduate students.

No. 4
1 Inform her supervisor about Derrick's false claim.
2 Present her idea to improve assembly line efficiency.
3 Help correct problems with the automation equipment.
4 Confront Derrick about his false assertion.

No. 5
1 His responsibilities are not as promised.
2 He spends almost all day on administrative tasks.
3 He wants the management title he deserves.
4 His clients are extremely difficult to work with.

No. 6
1. The vice-president of sales is being unfair.
2. The woman's account is not deemed important.
3. There is an unofficial freeze on hiring.
4. All staff in the company are overworked.

No. 7
1. Wait before making a final decision.
2. Send Phillip to a smaller school.
3. Get some family counseling.
4. Seek advice from Phillip's teacher.

No. 8
1. Find a university closer to home.
2. Move to a more convenient location.
3. Concentrate more on her reading.
4. Continue to live with her parents.

No. 9
1. Convey the woman's request.
2. Consider the woman's application.
3. Call back with important information.
4. Set up an interview for next week.

No. 10
1. They will likely get a seat on the 11:00 a.m. flight.
2. They will probably have to take the 1:00 p.m. flight.
3. They will be well compensated for the delay.
4. They will get seats on a flight with another airline.

Day 1
Day 2
Day 3
Day 4
Day 5
Day 6
Day 7

(A)   *No. 11*   **1** They located language families that shared similar words and phrases.
2 They distinguished language families primarily by grammatical differences.
3 They delineated language families primarily by geographical proximity.
4 They grouped languages into families that shared an evolutionary history.

No. 12   **1** A massive amount of data would have to be analyzed.
2 Different systems of classification yield different results.
3 There is little interest in classifying world languages.
4 There are too many languages in the world.

(B)   *No. 13*   **1** They need to be more ruthless to beat competitors.
2 They should learn from the airline industry's mistakes.
3 They are in no position to give advice about virtue.
4 They can boost profits by behaving morally.

No. 14   **1** It is essential in the cutthroat world of business.
2 The needs of their shareholders are a bigger priority.
3 It needs to be studied again before being applied.
4 They can use it to get rid of unwanted employees.

(C)   *No. 15*   **1** It is the oldest mausoleum in the world.
2 The emperor built it to commemorate the birth of his child.
3 Each side is a mirror image of the other.
4 The materials took over sixteen years to transport by elephant.

No. 16   **1** There is not enough water for visitors to drink.
2 Millions of visitors help to conserve it.
3 The government set up a foundation to restore it.
4 It is suffering from adverse environmental conditions.

(D) *No. 17* **1** The 1930s saw more and more people visiting the seaside.
2 British weather is not particularly suited for open-air swimming.
3 Places with Italian names are very popular.
4 British people like to sunbathe in cafés.

No. 18 **1** They have closed recently as foreign travel is cheaper than ever.
2 They have closed because rich people don't like chemicals.
3 They are beginning to open in foreign countries as temperatures rise.
4 They are becoming popular once again for various reasons.

(E) *No. 19* **1** Frustration with his fountain pen becoming blocked with ink.
2 The articles he wrote while working for a newspaper.
3 The properties of the ink used to print newspapers.
4 His previous experiments with quick-drying ink.

No. 20 **1** Some people still use the inventor's name for them.
2 They are exclusively of the disposable variety.
3 They are unrecognizable from the initial versions.
4 They no longer use metal.

Day 1 Day 2 Day 3 Day 4 Day 5 Day 6 Day 7

(F)   *No. 21*   ***Situation:*** Your young child will be going on a field trip, and you have already submitted the permission slip. She is allergic to eggs and peanuts. You call the school after hours and hear the following recording.

Question: What does the school ask you to do?

1 Call the school office about your daughter's allergies.
2 Fill out an online meal request form.
3 Prepare a lunch for your daughter.
4 Purchase a special meal.

(G)   *No. 22*   ***Situation:*** You will go to the U.S. in September this year to study in a university in California but have not yet applied for a visa. You attend a presentation with all students planning to study abroad and hear the following from the Director of Student Affairs.

Question: What should you do?

1 Go to the tables in Room 1601.
2 Gain advice in Room 1404.
3 Get assistance in Room 1604.
4 Attend the session in Room 1412.

(H)   *No. 23*   ***Situation:*** You are enrolled in a doctoral program at a university in the U.S. You meet with your department academic advisor, who tells you the following. You hope to have Dr. Sheila Carlson on your dissertation committee.

Question: What should you do first?

1 Schedule your comprehensive examination.
2 Request a list of approved faculty members.
3 Fill out the Doctoral Committee Form.
4 Make an appointment with Robin Wright.

(I)   *No. 24*   ***Situation:*** You are a volunteer for a program called Forward in Cambodia and are at a pre-departure orientation meeting. You will work with the program's conservation group in Cambodia. You hear the following from the program's executive director.

Question: Where will you go first after you arrive in Phnom Penh?

1 To a hospital for a medical check-up.
2 To an apartment to deposit your belongings.
3 To a guesthouse for a one-night stay.
4 To a bus station to catch a minivan.

(J)   *No. 25*   ***Situation:*** You hear a flight attendant make an announcement. You are transferring to another flight.

Question: What should you do?

1 Follow the blue signs.
2 Follow the red lines.
3 See a representative.
4 Go through immigration.

Day
1
Day
2
Day
3
Day
4
Day
5
Day
6
Day
7

No. 26 **1** He read about Central Asia in *National Geographic* when he was a boy.

2 He had read some interesting books on Mongolia before planning the trip.

3 He had heard that the people of Central Asia were friendly and generous.

4 He wanted to film a documentary of the trip for several television networks.

No. 27 **1** He had read the book *The Royal Road to Romance* about adventures on the Mississippi.

2 He is exhausted from his world travels and wants to stay closer to home for a while.

3 Since he was a boy, he wanted to be a writer like Mark Twain and write about people living on the Mississippi.

4 He is fascinated by why people choose to live on a river that will invariably flood.

筆記試験＆リスニングテスト

Day
1

Day
2

Day
3

Day
4

Day
5

Day
6

Day
7

筆記試験&リスニングテスト

試験時間 **筆記100分** リスニング約35分

1 *To complete each item, choose the best word or phrase from among the four choices. Then, on your answer sheet, find the number of the question and mark your answer.*

---

(1) The substance in red wine known as tannin is believed to (　　) the negative effects of fatty foods, so some nutritionists believe that a little red wine is good for you.

1 inhibit　　　　**2** revoke　　　　**3** instigate　　　　**4** retract

(2) The professor was so angry with his class that he scolded and yelled at them. His (　　) lasted for over 10 minutes.

1 specimen　　　　**2** riptide　　　　**3** patronage　　　　**4** tirade

(3) The man's nerves were (　　) by the constant noise of traffic from the freeway near his apartment, so he decided to move.

1 botched　　　　**2** crusted　　　　**3** frayed　　　　**4** thwarted

(4) When the multimillionaire died, he (　　) his collection of modern art to the national museum. "We are delighted to receive such a gift," said a museum spokesperson.

1 bequeathed　　**2** detested　　　　**3** extradited　　　　**4** impeached

(5) The house was spacious and beautiful, but the garden had been poorly maintained and therefore (　　) from the property's overall appearance.

1 aggravated　　**2** detracted　　　**3** plundered　　　**4** illuminated

(6) The (　　) coffee shops throughout the city are a sign of the rising popularity of the beverage.

1 precocious　　**2** forthright　　　**3** dilapidated　　　**4** ubiquitous

(7) After negotiations reached a stalemate, the two sides agreed to bring in a third party to (　　) a solution.

1 mediate　　　　**2** subjugate　　　**3** substantiate　　　**4** liberate

Day 1
Day 2
Day 3
Day 4
Day 5
Day 6
Day 7

(8)   Although doctors believed that Jack was cured of his disease, a sudden (   ) occurred within the year.

1 rebuttal   **2** debris   **3** relapse   **4** eclipse

(9)   After his shoulder operation, the footballer was given time to (   ) at a center for injured athletes before returning to training.

1 impinge   **2** plagiarize   **3** stray   **4** convalesce

(10)   Because of the heavy rains, no one could reach the mountain village for over a week. The villagers were in great need due to the (   ) of supplies.

1 glut   **2** lure   **3** dearth   **4** deluge

(11)   The salaries of waiters in many countries (   ) less than half of their total income. They usually earn more from tips.

1 feign   **2** constitute   **3** fabricate   **4** provoke

(12)   *A:* What did Alice mean in her (   ) comment about disappearing?
       B: I'm not sure, but I think she was hinting that she intends to resign.

1 latent   **2** homogeneous   **3** cryptic   **4** lethargic

(13)   The landscape surrounding the castle was (   ), with only a few leafless trees and dark, craggy rocks. Local townspeople did not like to go there.

1 solvent   **2** bleak   **3** suave   **4** opulent

(14)   The police chief stressed that the views expressed in the media were mere (   ), for the investigation was still in its early stages and no one had been charged.

1 indentation   **2** speculation   **3** arbitration   **4** consummation

(15)   The patient was given a (   ) to replace the blood he had lost during surgery.

1 transmission   **2** maceration   **3** transfusion   **4** migration

(16)   Considering the author is known to be a very (   ) person who usually prefers to be alone, fans were surprised and pleased at his eagerness to give a speech.

1 optimistic   **2** austere   **3** feasible   **4** introverted

(17) Kelly was unpleasantly shocked when she saw what the designer had done to her office, for she could not find anything new that was (   ) pleasing.

1 precariously   **2** aesthetically   **3** haphazardly   **4** audaciously

(18) Scientists had no logical explanation for the result of their latest experiment, so it was considered an (   ).

1 anomaly   **2** arousal   **3** endowment   **4** edifice

(19) *A:* Why isn't Lloyd hanging out with Jarod these days? They used to be best friends.

B: Lloyd (   ) with him. They both dated the same girl, and it didn't end well.

1 stood down   **2** struck down   **3** backed out   **4** fell out

(20) The offer Steve received for his used car was not as high as he wanted, so he decided to (   ) for a better offer.

1 fall flat   **2** carry over   **3** take down   **4** hold out

(21) The report was over 40 pages long, and there was no time to study it before the meeting. I only managed to (   ) it briefly.

1 leaf through   **2** squeeze by   **3** branch out   **4** root for

(22) In addition to recording the interviews she did, the reporter liked to (   ) a few notes as she listened.

1 jot down   **2** rail against   **3** fret over   **4** sink into

Day 1
Day 2
Day 3
Day 4
Day 5
Day 6
Day 7

2 Read each passage and choose the best word or phrase from among the four choices for each blank. Then, on your answer sheet, find the number of the question and mark your answer.

When Languages Die

There are around 6,500 languages remaining in the world, which sounds like an extraordinary number until you consider that around 400 languages have become extinct over the past century alone. Around half of the world's population now speak one of the top ten languages, leaving less-widespread tongues in peril, with experts estimating that 50 percent of the languages existing today could disappear by the end of this century. UNESCO tracks endangered languages in the Atlas of the World's Languages in Danger, which currently lists 576 as critically endangered, (*23*).

The loss of these languages means a lot more than simply a local dialect no longer being used. At stake is not just the loss of what many consider obscure languages, but also their associated cultures, emotions and behaviors, which often follow the oral tradition and cannot always be translated. An example of one of the more unusual and intriguing languages under imminent threat is sfyria, which uses no words at all; instead, those who "speak" the language do so by whistling. Restricted to a mountainous area of Greece, sfyria has been spoken for over two millennia and allows speakers to communicate over staggering distances of up to four or more kilometers. Passed down from generation to generation, mostly as a closely-guarded secret, it is now spoken by only a handful of people and looks set to become another economic victim as the younger generation leave the countryside (*24*).

Surprisingly, sfyria is not the only example of a whistled language, as others exist within Europe and also throughout Africa, with some attracting officially protected status. Silbo Gomero, a whistled form of Spanish spoken in the Canary Islands, was named a Masterpiece of the Oral and Intangible Heritage of Humanity by UNESCO in 2009 and has (*25*). The government has also sought to protect the language by making it part of the national curriculum, using it in tourism campaigns, and making it a feature of festivals and rituals.

---

(23) **1** although new languages are secretly born every day
  2 with thousands more deemed endangered or threatened
  3 and many others rebounding exponentially
  4 considered to be a beneficial linguistic development

(24)   **1** only to be thwarted by language deficiencies
        2 and spread cultural secrets far and wide
        3 due to educational and linguistic difficulties
        4 to seek greater financial opportunities in Athens

(25)   **1** since witnessed something of a revival
        2 inspired new tonal languages to develop
        3 been allowed to fade from memory
        4 now taken on startling new forms

Barefoot and Minimalist Running

In 2009, the book *Born to Run* by Christopher McDougall caused a couple of profound and largely unexpected changes to the sport of running. Unlike many books about running which cover training tips, famous runners, or high-profile races, *Born to Run* had almost none of those things. The book chronicled the author's encounters with the Tarahumara people of northern Mexico, who run great distances in flimsy sandals made from old tires and other scrap, and also documented his research into the (**26**). This more nuanced look at why and how we run subsequently turned conventional wisdom about modern running shoes on its head, creating an industry-shaking upheaval and surge of interest in barefoot and minimalist running.

Accompanying what many considered to be not only a return to a more natural way of running, but perhaps even the reclamation of our birthright as distance runners, was a (**27**) aiming for increasingly long distances. Participation in ultramarathons, ranging from 50km to 200km and more, grew exponentially, bringing what were once fringe events competed in by the brave and perhaps foolhardy into the mainstream. As more and more runners sought to emulate the feats of the Tarahumara, footwear manufacturers struggled to catch up with the new demand for minimalist footwear. While certainly noticeable, the minimalist explosion was to be rather short-lived.

(**28**) back sometime around 2015, when some of those originally enamored with barefoot and minimalist running seemed to pine for the cushioning and protection of conventional modern running shoes. Manufacturers shifted their emphasis from minimalist to maximalist, replacing wafer-thin soles aimed at increasing proprioception with soft, pillowy soles designed to make you feel as if you're floating on clouds. However, for many of those who embraced minimalist running, barefoot running, and ultra running as their style of choice, the shifting of the spotlight has had little impact, irrespective of whether or not it may one day return.

---

(26) **1** wisdom of less-civilized communities and groups
     2 socio-anthropological aspects of running throughout human history
     3 conventions and regulations regarding Olympic sports
     4 growing trend toward running in groups

(27) **1** marked decrease in those
     2 resurgence of atavistic communities
     3 proliferation in the number of runners
     4 mimicry of the brave characters of yesteryear

(28) **1** The trend of anthropology soon came
     2 The author left Mexico and traveled
     3 All of those endeared to maximalism shifted
     4 The pendulum of popularity began to swing

筆記試験＆リスニングテスト

Day
1

Day
2

Day
3

Day
4

Day
5

Day
6

Day
7

Read each passage and choose the best answer from among the four choices for each question. Then, on your answer sheet, find the number of the question and mark your answer.

Cultural Climate Change

The scientific evidence for climate change is now all but indisputable, regardless of those who still wish to deny its veracity. We are growing sadly accustomed to hearing we will be facing a future of extreme weather, droughts, rising sea levels, mass extinctions and much more. Despite the very real issues these scenarios present, those presenting them to the public often overlook how climate change could fundamentally affect us on a cultural level, and by doing so, they are possibly missing a major psychological tool in persuading the naysayers. Like other bad news, we may shake our heads in frustration or fret for an uncertain future, but we can go about our day to day lives because for many, the effects are not immediate and not close enough to home to cause pressing concern. They are not on our doorstep, so to speak, so we can shut them out for now. Elsewhere, however, people cannot afford to be so complacent.

In some parts of the world, activities that revolve around the ocean, like surfing, swimming, sailing or simply sunbathing on the beach, are not only central to the economic sustainability of the region, but also to the culture that binds the community together. In mountainous areas, climbing, hiking, and winter sports like skiing or snowboarding perform the same functions and are touchstones of the community's culture and lifestyle. When oceans, beaches, mountains and other geographical features come under threat from climate change, so do the cultures and communities that depend on them. This could mean the loss of traditional construction methods or local craftsmanship, a source of food becoming extinct, or mass migration leading to communities becoming scattered and cultural ties being broken. While these serious and very real impacts of climate change matter greatly to those being affected, they are rarely taken into account in governmental studies and programs.

These emotional effects have been used by the arts to successfully convey the dangers of climate change in a way that people can relate to their daily lives. Countless books, movies, plays and poems paint a dystopian view of the future and many allude, either explicitly or otherwise, to man-made climate change. As the arts are much more accessible to the general public than scientific publications, they have the power to resonate with more people. Works like *The Windup Girl* by Paolo Bacigalupi, *Finitude* by Hamish MacDonald, and *From Here* by Daniel Kramb have all taken climate change as their central theme: They do not portray the future, if things do not change drastically, in a promising way.

What they all touch upon is the very real effects that everyday people will face, like destroyed communities, collapse of infrastructure, lack of food and potable water, extreme weather destroying entire communities, and loss of amenities we take for granted like electricity and gas. This more immediate, tangible vision could be the key to both tackling climate change in the future and preserving our environment and the cultures it supports.

---

(29) What consequence of the increased coverage devoted to climate change is referred to in the article?

1 The evidence for man-made climate change is not overwhelming, so people around the world should not worry.

2 Although climate change seems to be affecting our planet, scientists remain frustrated that they cannot show clear patterns of causation.

3 We are increasingly informed of the physical impacts of climate change on the planet, yet we may be oblivious to the effects on civilization as a whole.

4 As sea levels rise and migration increases, we will need to fortify our homes to shut out water and protect against poor construction.

(30) How might local communities be under threat from climate change?

1 As the impact of climate change increases, governments are forced to divert funding from smaller communities to sustain entire regions.

2 Local communities are increasingly being asked to sacrifice established ways of life in order to combat climate change.

3 The tourist industry in local communities could be adversely affected as more people choose to go surfing than skiing.

4 Communities built around geographical factors could see their entire way of life disappear due to climate change.

(31) How can the arts be more successful than scientists in alerting a skeptical public to the dangers of climate change?

1 Dystopian literature generally helps people feel better about destruction of community and lack of resources.

2 Scientists can write poems and songs about climate change and distribute them effectively on the Internet.

3 The arts personalize climate change, meaning that the public can more accurately perceive how it will affect their lives on a practical level.

4 Scientific literature is too emotional for many readers; therefore, the arts offer momentary escape from destruction and loss of amenities.

Day 1
Day 2
Day 3
Day 4
Day 5
Day 6
Day 7

The Impact of Invasive Species

Scientists have long been concerned about the changes taking place today in ecosystems due to invasive species. Famed Harvard biologist Edward O. Wilson argued that invasions of alien species are second only to habitat destruction in their impact on species extinction. English ecologist Charles Elton, who initiated the scientific study of invasive alien species in his seminal work *The Ecology of Invasions by Animals and Plants* in 1958, wrote, "We must make no mistake. We are seeing one of the greatest historical convolutions in the world's fauna and flora." Elton and his team of researchers hoped to better understand the impact of alien species by uncovering underlying patterns and answering such questions as follows: Are certain species better adapted to invasions? Why are certain environments, like the Hawaiian Islands, more prone to invasions? And why have the American gray squirrels been so successful in overrunning the British Isles? The researchers collected volumes of case studies in an effort to answer these and other questions.

Elton argued that there was a link between biological diversity—the variety and populations of an ecosystem's species—and that ecosystem's overall health. Ecosystems with greater diversity had greater "biotic resistance" that helped maintain their integrity. In his medical model, a non-invaded ecosystem with sufficient diversity was considered healthy, while an ecosystem invaded by alien-species was considered diseased. Elton introduced other models to help explain the transitions he saw taking place. He argued that ecosystems were similar to a marketplace, with a limited number of job openings, or niches. All species, whether native or alien, had to compete for a niche space, similar to multitudes of candidates applying for a job opening.

This idea of niches helped Elton and following ecologists explain why certain smaller, more isolated ecosystems, like those in Hawaii, were more likely to be invaded. The biodiversity was less complex, supporting fewer species, than in larger ecosystems, especially continental ecosystems. Therefore, they had more niches available for invaders. Native species in smaller ecosystems also had less competition than larger systems. Therefore, they were less tough and less resistant. Elton wrote, "The balance of relatively simple communities of plants and animals is more easily upset than that of richer ones, and thus, more vulnerable to invasion."

Half a century of research since Elton's early work has confirmed that invasive species can and do change ecosystems in a variety of ways, by spreading disease among natural species, by altering the environment in a way that favors their survival, and by eating other species. However, the compilation of cases show a pattern that Elton would not have expected—alien species rarely drive out native species. Looking at the case of the gray squirrels that Elton was particularly intrigued with, the rise in the number of gray squirrels coincided with the decrease in the populations of Eurasian red squirrels so loved by British people. There are less than 30,000 of these red squirrels in Britain today. It seemed obvious to most observers that this invading species had overrun the native species and directly caused its decline.

But this case, which became a popular model for illustrating how an alien species drives out a native species, is actually more complex than initially believed. In fact, there is evidence that the red squirrel's decline was not entirely caused by gray squirrels, for the red squirrel's decline had started long before the arrival of their supposed nemesis. Populations of red squirrels had already died out in certain areas of the British Isles in the 19th century, and they had to be reintroduced. However, two-thirds of all gray squirrels were carriers of a viral skin disease that the red squirrels were susceptible to, and this certainly sped up the red squirrel's decline.

Rather than outcompete, the majority of invasive alien species simply fit in to their adopted ecosystem without damaging effects, for almost any given ecosystem is able to harbor even greater diversity—far from the tightly structured systems envisioned by Elton and Wilson. "What invasions have shown is that there are plenty of unused resources," says Ted Grosholtz, marine biologist at the University of California at Davis. "Ecosystems can absorb a lot of new species." South Florida, a crossroads for trade in exotic flora and fauna, has hosted 300 new invasive plant species, while researchers have counted at least 250 non-native species in San Francisco Bay. Marine ecosystems have shown themselves to be particularly open to invasive species over the past several centuries, as ships and other transport vehicles have unintentionally introduced life forms from distant lands. And yet despite the introduction of exotic crabs, sponges, worms, clams, and marine diseases to San Francisco Bay, not a single native marine species has been shown to have been made extinct by the invaders.

All this leads to the conclusion that invasions of terrestrial and marine ecosystems are not a simple win-or-lose, zero-sum game, where one new species drives out another. Researchers have found that, despite the earlier fears of ecosystem damage or collapse, invaded ecosystems offer an even richer diversity.

Day 1
Day 2
Day 3
Day 4
Day 5
Day 6
Day 7

(32) How does Edward O. Wilson's theory about invasive species compare with that of Charles Elton's?

1 After years of research, they both came to the conclusion that invasive species were more benign than they first assumed.

2 Wilson believed that species invasion was a minor problem, while Elton greatly feared the destructive power of invasive species.

3 They were similar in that they both believed ecosystems were under attack by invasive species, and that the consequences could be severe.

4 They both set out to ask numerous questions about the effects of invasive species, but were never able to get satisfactory answers.

(33) What did Elton imply about niches?

1 Niches basically stood for the number of native species in a particular ecosystem, which decreased when non-native species invaded.

2 Various species are in constant competition for niches, so the introduction of invasive species has a negative overall effect on the end result.

3 Ecosystems with few available niches had greater diversity and were therefore less vulnerable than those that had many open niches.

4 Smaller ecosystems have fewer niches than larger ecosystems, making the larger ecosystems more vulnerable to alien species.

(34) The case of the decreasing population of red squirrels in Britain supports the idea that

1 the disappearance of native species is not necessarily a direct result of invasive species.

2 diseases introduced by invasive species cause more extinctions than any other cause.

3 the introduction of native species has more drastic consequences than most researchers can predict.

4 two species that are similar to each other cannot coexist in the same ecosystem in the long run.

(35) What is the author's conclusion about invasive species?

  1 Species have been invading ecosystems since the beginning of time, and such invasions are a natural part of the evolutionary process.

  2 In most cases, invasive species cannot adapt sufficiently to their adopted homes to survive in the long term.

  3 Ecosystems are more adaptable than once assumed, and they often benefit from the introduction of alien species.

  4 Due to the complexity of ecosystems, researchers will never fully understand the impact of invasive species on native species.

Day 1
Day 2
Day 3
Day 4
Day 5
Day 6
Day 7

- Instructions: Read the article below and summarize it in your own words as far as possible in English.
- Suggested length: 90-110 words
- Write your summary in the space provided on your answer sheet. <u>Any writing outside the space will not be graded.</u>

As tourists have become increasingly conscious of the effects travel can have on the environment, many are turning to ecotourism, which is often said to be a more sustainable way to explore the world. This industry has become so popular that it is now estimated to be valued at over 170 billion dollars worldwide. In theory, ecotourism places a strong emphasis on preserving natural landscapes, wildlife, and local cultures, while minimizing travelers' negative impacts on the environment. Despite this, critics frequently express concerns about ecotourism, particularly the negative effects that it has had on indigenous peoples, such as the Maasai of Kenya and Tanzania.

Numerous tourist parks showcasing Africa's incredible wildlife, culture, and scenic landscapes have been established on lands traditionally belonging to the Maasai people, helping to make ecotourism a substantial revenue source for these countries. However, the Maasai themselves have rarely shared in the profits, as the parks were mainly operated by Western businesses. Furthermore, ecotourism has also resulted in the loss of land and resources for the Maasai people, who have been displaced by the establishment of protected areas on their ancestral territories. These areas have restricted their access to grazing lands and sacred sites, which are essential for both their livelihood and cultural identity.

While ecotourism has been less than ideal for the Maasai historically, there have been many sustainable ecotourism initiatives aimed at involving and empowering the Maasai community. For example, Campi ya Kanzi and the Mara Naboisho Conservancy have successfully adopted a participatory and inclusive approach, where the Maasai have been involved in decision-making and management processes. They have also ensured that the Maasai receive fair and equitable benefits from ecotourism activities, such as employment opportunities, income generation, and infrastructure development.

5 English Composition

- Write an essay on the given **TOPIC**.
- Give THREE reasons to support your answer.
- Structure: introduction, main body, and conclusion
- Suggested length: 200-240 words
- Write your essay in the space provided on your answer sheet. <u>Any writing outside the space will not be graded.</u>

TOPIC

Agree or disagree: Free trade is desirable

Day 1
Day 2
Day 3
Day 4
Day 5
Day 6
Day 7

Listening Test

Part 1	Dialogues: 1 question each	Multiple-choice
Part 2	Passages: 2 questions each	Multiple-choice
Part 3	Real-Life: 1 question each	Multiple-choice
Part 4	Interview: 2 questions	Multiple-choice

※Listen carefully to the instructions.

Part 1   ◀))076~086

No. 1
1 He is a regular customer of the airline.
2 He is planning a business trip.
3 He already owns his Mexican address.
4 He wants to pay at the airport.

No. 2
1 To reschedule his appointment.
2 To cancel his appointment.
3 To make a new appointment.
4 To check his appointment time.

No. 3
1 Unused items should be given away.
2 The man needs to purchase newer styles.
3 The closet needs to be organized according to season.
4 Most remaining clothes are very shabby.

No. 4
1 Review her smartphone calendar first thing every morning.
2 Call her dentist to apologize for forgetting her appointment.
3 Get a new app for her smartphone.
4 Write all her appointments down on a calendar.

No. 5
1 The cleaners did not perform as promised.
2 The cleaning staff suggested throwing his pants away.
3 A new stain appeared on his pants.
4 The cleaners are unreasonably expensive.

No. 6
1 He hopes to have a tennis injury healed.
2 He is interested in holistic healing issues.
3 He hopes to listen to a famous speaker.
4 He can meet someone he knows there.

No. 7
1 He was feeling sick at the conference.
2 He could not get the ticket he wanted.
3 He wanted to avoid a delayed return.
4 He found the conference boring.

No. 8
1 Inform some people that she will be late.
2 Mail some letters for her.
3 Pick up a package for her.
4 Show her where the post office is.

No. 9
1 Train agents to handle more complex questions.
2 Conduct regular customer satisfaction surveys.
3 Refer certain calls to specialized agents.
4 Communicate more regularly with Operations.

No. 10
1 Apologize to the clients in person.
2 Make sure to keep her informed.
3 Try to multitask effectively.
4 Update the progress reports.

Day 1
Day 2
Day 3
Day 4
Day 5
Day 6
Day 7

(A) **No. 11**
1 Its famous chalk cliffs.
2 The nearby Chalk Sea.
3 Its factories, where chalk is made.
4 Chalks of various colors.

No. 12
1 Remains of microorganisms settled on sea bottoms.
2 Fossils decomposed in the powerful sea currents.
3 Small living creatures left deposits on cliff walls.
4 Shells of marine mollusks floated to the surface and hardened into rock.

(B) **No. 13**
1 It was primarily for military defense.
2 It served as a precise solar calendar.
3 It was used for important religious rituals.
4 It was a gathering place for the Chavin elite.

No. 14
1 It was employed as a political tool by leaders.
2 It served to strengthen the civilization's military.
3 It solidified the importance of farmers.
4 It was used to educate the common people.

(C) **No. 15**
1 Activists were plotting a coup.
2 There were negative reviews about some books.
3 Activists used books to challenge the government.
4 A book celebration got out of hand.

No. 16
1 The number of rebels in the country.
2 The rare success of the local economy.
3 The dangers of reading banned books.
4 The wealth disparity among its population.

(D)	*No. 17*	**1**	The plot of a famous movie.
		2	Unsuccessful attempts to drive somebody insane.
		3	A difficult and time-consuming diagnosis.
		4	The use of various techniques to cover deception.

No. 18

1 Leaders use it when they build relationships with foreign governments.
2 It could affect people's trust in government.
3 It helps leaders adopt riskier policies.
4 It allows dictators to isolate themselves from society.

(E)   *No. 19*

1 They were able to compete at a high level.
2 They developed the ability to overpower larger prey.
3 They were able to hunt more successfully.
4 They were able to walk upright.

No. 20

1 It has remained largely unchanged.
2 Modern athletes can continue their careers longer than before.
3 Competitive running has become religious.
4 It has become varied and lucrative.

Day 1
Day 2
Day 3
Day 4
Day 5
Day 6
Day 7

(F) *No. 21* ***Situation:*** You represent a Japanese investment group and confer with an investment banker in the U.S. about real estate. You have money you must invest within six months. The investment banker gives you the following advice.

Question: According to the advice, what is your best investment option?

1 A restaurant chain.

2 A lifestyle center.

3 A traditional shopping mall.

4 A new type of entertainment center.

(G) *No. 22* ***Situation:*** You want to reserve a tennis court for this weekend for you and your friends. You can play for two hours anytime between 10 a.m. and 4 p.m. You want to spend as little money as possible. A reservation clerk tells you the following.

Question: According to the clerk, what should you reserve?

1 Two courts for 2 p.m. on Sunday.

2 One outdoor court on Saturday for 2 p.m.

3 One court for Saturday and another for Sunday.

4 Make no reservations until Saturday.

(H) *No. 23* ***Situation:*** You receive a message on your cellphone from your company's testing team assigned to a software development project. You have a contract with a coding company that offers a money-back guarantee.

Question: According to the message, what should you do first?

1 Find a new coding company.

2 Consult with legal experts.

3 Call InTech to get more information.

4 Negotiate a reduced payment to InTech.

(I) **No. 24** ***Situation:*** You are in charge of purchases at a research company. A technical specialist gives you some advice.

Question: According to the technical specialist, what should you do in the short run?

1 Purchase a more powerful mainframe.
2 Switch to powerful workstations.
3 Buy the hardware she needs.
4 Search for the best deals.

(J) **No. 25** ***Situation:*** You will give a poster presentation at a conference and attend a meeting with other presenters before the conference's plenary session. You hear the following from one of the conference organizers.

Question: What are you asked to do now?

1 Go to the room next door.
2 Go to your assigned room in Building Three.
3 Check any audio-visual equipment you will use.
4 Check-in at the lobby of Crystal Hall.

Day 1
Day 2
Day 3
Day 4
Day 5
Day 6
Day 7

No. 26 **1** They accelerate corporate technology development for Jump Start's corporate investors.
2 They educate corporations and startups about new technology that can help them expand their businesses.
3 They introduce corporations to entrepreneurs and gain access to new startup technologies.
4 They offer training and support to startup entrepreneurs to help their business grow.

No. 27 **1** There are simply too few entrepreneurs and startups in Japan.
2 Japanese corporations are less interested in startups than foreign corporations.
3 Large Japanese corporations compete directly with startups and stifle them.
4 Foreign startups are more aggressive and overwhelm Japanese startups.

Day
1

Day
2

Day
3

Day
4

Day
5

Day
6

Day
7

筆記試験&リスニングテスト

試験時間 筆記**100**分 リスニング約**35**分

1

To complete each item, choose the best word or phrase from among the four choices. Then, on your answer sheet, find the number of the question and mark your answer.

(1) "Organic gardening" usually makes use of (   ) comprised of biodegradable waste and leaves to help boost the fertility of the soil.

1 antibiotics   **2** compost   **3** trivia   **4** dregs

(2) The government reduced rice production levels by setting (   ) for farmers.

1 annotations   **2** spheres   **3** quotas   **4** stems

(3) Any student who has been expelled from this university may apply for (   ) as a student. The academic dean will make the final decision.

1 recompense   **2** reinstatement   **3** integrity   **4** felicity

(4) The doctor prescribed medication to help lessen the effects from the (   ) damage caused by the severe stroke.

1 communal   **2** congenial   **3** cerebral   **4** authentic

(5) The presidents of the two nations rejected a peace proposal that included the (   ) of peacekeeping forces along their mutual borders.

1 disavowal   **2** deportment   **3** denigration   **4** deployment

(6) These bicycle gears should be regularly (   ) with oil or grease to prevent their wear over time.

1 fomented   **2** lubricated   **3** reinforced   **4** rescinded

(7) The political cartoonist is famous for his (   ) of influential people, which exaggerate their features and make them appear humorous.

1 adages   **2** caricatures   **3** patriots   **4** outskirts

(8) To test the effectiveness and safety of the new drug, one-third of the study group was given the drug, another third was given a (   ), and the last third was given nothing.

1 placebo   **2** tweak   **3** manifest   **4** gust

筆記試験&リスニングテスト

Day
1

Day
2

Day
3

Day
4

Day
5

Day
6

Day
7

(9) The firm was (   ) with phone calls following a TV report that questioned the safety of its latest product.

1 inundated **2** commiserated **3** enveloped **4** adorned

(10) **A:** This storm has caused a lot of damage. Did you see pictures of the flooding downtown?

B: I sure did. Some cars were almost completely (   ). You could barely see their tops.

1 appalled **2** elongated **3** submerged **4** enervated

(11) **A:** Jack heard that you don't want him on the new project team. He's a little upset.

B: What he heard was (   ). I'd love to have him on the project team, but he already has more than enough work to do.

1 misconstrued **2** skeptical **3** indeterminable **4** insubstantial

(12) The students were easily (   ) on the day before their winter vacation, so the teacher decided to let them do some fun activities.

1 mocked **2** distracted **3** disfigured **4** elaborated

(13) Mary was (   ) to hear that her first novel won a top literary prize. She decided to hold a party to celebrate the event.

1 ecstatic **2** despondent **3** enraged **4** spontaneous

(14) The detectives tried to (   ) the truth about the robbery by questioning the suspects one by one, but their stories were contradictory, leaving the investigators even more confused.

1 improvise **2** raid **3** elicit **4** levitate

(15) Ken's mother likes to wear (   ) clothes with bright colors and unique designs.

1 distinctive **2** alleged **3** callous **4** formidable

(16) Bill had looked forward to working on an automobile assembly line, but after several months, he found the work (   ) and wanted to find a new job.

1 mundane **2** devious **3** luminous **4** celestial

(17) If you remain silent and avoid talking to others, you'll be seen as being indifferent and (   ).

1 turbulent **2** lascivious **3** wanton **4** aloof

(18) The employee carried out her duties (   ). In fact, her work was so careless and her service so poor that customers often complained.

1 expediently   **2** eruditely   **3** genetically   **4** perfunctorily

(19) Charles couldn't help (   ) during class, as he had been up most of the night writing his essay.

1 passing away   **2** bubbling over   **3** nodding off   **4** boxing up

(20) Faulty wiring was the likely cause of the fire, but the fire inspector said they would not (   ) the possibility of arson until a thorough investigation had been completed.

1 strike up   **2** bail out   **3** think through   **4** rule out

(21) Many volunteers were eager to (   ) after the hurricane and help clean up, so the town recovered much more quickly than officials had first predicted.

1 own up   **2** nose around   **3** strike off   **4** pitch in

(22) The party starts at 8:00, and there will be a lot of people. You'd better (   ) at Jill's house by 8:30 if you want to get anything good to eat.

1 hit out   **2** turn up   **3** throw over   **4** spin off

Day 1
Day 2
Day 3
Day 4
Day 5
Day 6
Day 7

2 *Read each passage and choose the best word or phrase from among the four choices for each blank. Then, on your answer sheet, find the number of the question and mark your answer.*

The Impact of Nicolaus Copernicus

In the late 15th century, planetary theory was a contentious issue, and the terms "astronomy" and "astrology" were largely synonymous, themselves subdivisions of the larger "science of the stars." In contemporary terms, some may consider astrology (**23**), concerned mostly with horoscopes and annual prognostications, but at the time clear distinctions were not made. However basic and erroneous they may look in hindsight, mathematical techniques were widely used at the time to form a more nuanced understanding of the heavens, producing theoretical tools and tables of motions to explain the situation and movement of the planets.

This historical backdrop provides part of the reason that the discoveries and theories of Nicolaus Copernicus were so revolutionary. At the time, the accepted understanding of celestial bodies put the stationary Earth at the center of the universe, with other planets and stars revolving around it in an order that was hotly contested. Copernicus developed the heliocentric model of the universe, placing the static sun at its center with other planets, including ours, (**24**). He published his findings in his groundbreaking book, *On the Revolutions of the Heavenly Spheres*, in 1543, which paved the way for other great discoveries from the likes of Galileo, Newton and Kepler.

Copernicus lived in an era when religion was very important and the Catholic Church wielded considerable power, so when word of his work attracted interest in the Vatican, it was a cause for both encouragement and alarm. Although the church was a major sponsor of science, including astronomy, it had also sometimes persecuted those who presented new scientific theories. This background could explain why Copernicus initially resisted publication of *On the Revolutions*, fearing scorn and criticism, particularly from religious circles, and led him to (**25**). Although his book did not attract a great deal of controversy during his lifetime, defense of the theory it presented would lead to the infamous trial of Galileo in the 16th century.

---

(23) **1** to be largely the preserve of academia
  2 thoroughly lacking in rigorous thought and process
  3 to be something of a pseudoscience
  4 a mere trifle and affectation

(24)   1 effectively irrelevant in cosmic terms
       2 revolving around indeterminate stars and bodies
       3 competing for relevance in celestial order
       4 falling into a determined order and orbit

(25)   1 request posthumous publication of his theory
       2 dedicate the book to Pope Paul III
       3 demand astronomical fees for publication rights
       4 focus on the fields of economics and diplomacy

Palm Oil Plantations

Palm oil makes up 33 percent of the world's vegetable oil market and is used for everything from cooking to the creation of biofuels. However, a recent study by the International Union for the Conservation of Nature (IUCN) shows that palm oil farming has been disastrous for the environment. It has devastated fragile ecosystems in countries such as Indonesia and Malaysia, where new palm oil plantations (26). The expansion of palm oil plantations threatens over 190 endangered species, including orangutans, gibbons, and tigers. Even worse, as demand for palm oil increases, further development would threaten the environments of more than half of all endangered mammals and nearly two-thirds of all threatened birds.

Palm oil certified as "sustainable" is only minimally better at preventing the destruction of virgin tropical forests. Certification for sustainability was set up to assure consumers that palm oil plantations were not causing deforestation. A spokesperson for the Roundtable on Sustainable Palm Oil (RSPO), which certifies about 20 percent of all palm oil, argues that the certification system (27). Though the system has been imperfect, it has played a significant role in the fight against deforestation. Richard George of Greenpeace UK claims, however, that it is simply not true. His watchdog organization has "time and again caught RSPO members destroying forests for palm oil, including trashing orangutan habitat."

Unfortunately, there is no easy solution to the problem. One major issue is the (28). It is often simpler to cut down virgin forests than deal with complex ownership issues of formerly farmed plantations. In addition, plantations are often relegated to degraded land where crop yields are low. In an attempt to halt further environmental damage, the EU has passed legislation to ban palm-oil use in biofuels by 2030. However, an outright ban of the oil would likely result in an increase in production of other types of oil, such as soy, corn, and rapeseed. These oil crops use up to as much as nine times the land occupied by palm oil plantations, which would result in massive destruction of wildlife ecosystems in other regions of the world, such as Argentina and Brazil. In other words, a ban would likely shift the problem to other ecosystems and result in even wider devastation and biodiversity loss.

---

(26) **1** encroach into virgin forests
      2 are replacing older plantations
      3 host a variety of threatened species
      4 introduce the latest farming techniques

(27) **1** has had a largely positive effect
      2 is not very promising
      3 must expand to other countries
      4 needs to be revamped

(28) **1** setting of new palm oil plantations
      2 fragility of tropical ecosystems
      3 complexity of palm oil harvesting
      4 competitive advantages of palm oil

Day 1
Day 2
Day 3
Day 4
Day 5
Day 6
Day 7

Read each passage and choose the best answer from among the four choices for each question. Then, on your answer sheet, find the number of the question and mark your answer.

The Hunters Aiding Science

Whaling has been part of the indigenous Alaskan culture for centuries, but back in 1977, the International Whaling Commission (IWC) threw it into jeopardy by setting a quota of zero for bowhead whale hunting. The IWC concluded that there were perilously low numbers of whales because, believing that whales were scared of ice, they only counted those they could see swimming in open water. In protest, the Alaska Native whaling captains formed their own group and sought to prove that whales were not afraid of ice and the numbers were much higher than previously estimated. A second group of scientists backed their claim and the ban was lifted, which not only came as a relief to the communities hunting whales for subsistence, but also saw the beginning of new alliances between hunters and scientists.

Such relationships have allowed scientists like Hans Thewissen to get close to whales in ways he could not have done before, and conduct experiments that were once impossible. As whales are a protected species, Thewissen and other scientists generally have to observe them from afar, and he had very few opportunities to conduct experiments on fresh carcasses. Although it may seem a little macabre, by following the whaling captains on their seasonal hunts, he has been able to make several breakthroughs in understanding whale behavior and biology, including the discovery that bowhead whales have a sense of smell. Once again, the suggestion that whales had a sense of smell came from the hunters who reported that the whales tended to swim far from shore when campfires were built, leading them to believe they could smell them. Although the suggestion that whales could smell was initially dismissed, as being able to smell things in the air seems useless to animals that live in water, Thewissen proved that it was surprisingly true after he gained access to a fresh bowhead whale skull and examined its brain.

The willingness of the hunters to share not only their knowledge, including information about whale anatomy previously unknown to science, but also the spoils of their catch has greatly aided the scientists in their research. Such cooperation was not always forthcoming, however, and the relationships needed to be nurtured over a long period before trust was developed. At first, still reeling from the 1977 IWC quota, many hunters were concerned that any knowledge they shared would be used against them by government agencies to shut down the hunts. In return, the scientists had to work to show that their desire to accompany the hunters was purely scientific and not motivated by politics or the desire to expose what many believe to be a barbaric practice. Public opinion against whaling continues to grow around the world, and when coupled with environmental problems threatening the habitat of the region, it could spell the end of the whale hunting tradition in Alaska. In this regard, the records of the scientists could help preserve the local knowledge of whales for future generations.

(29) How did estimates regarding whale numbers from the IWC compare to data from Alaska Native hunters?

1 The findings of the IWC confirmed that Alaska Natives were right in suggesting that whales do not like the cold.

2 The knowledge of the hunters in this case turned out to be superior to the initial findings reached by the IWC.

3 Scientists offered to interpret the data to solve any problems between the hunters and the IWC.

4 The IWC found that whale numbers had remained steady despite many centuries of hunting.

(30) What effect has the work between scientists and hunters had on the understanding of whales?

1 The work has allowed scientists to get fresh meat for their campfires and learn about macabre hunting practices.

2 Scientists have been able to dismiss some widely held beliefs about whales by observing them from a distance.

3 Scientists have not only benefited from a previously unavailable proximity to whales, but also from local expertise.

4 Although valuable from a sociological standpoint, the work has not resulted in any new scientific knowledge.

(31) How has the relationship between the Alaska Native hunters and scientists evolved over time?

1 While friendly at first, there is growing distrust on both sides which threatens to derail the entire program.

2 Both the hunters and the scientists have worked to politicize widespread concerns about the whaling industry.

3 Despite initial misgivings, the relationship has been effective and may help Alaska Native hunters preserve their heritage.

4 Although it was beneficial at first, the hunts and invasive scientific experiments now threaten the environment.

筆記試験＆リスニングテスト

Day 1
Day 2
Day 3
Day 4
Day 5
Day 6
Day 7

The Rise of AI Armies

The idea of killer robots usually conjures images from science fiction films like *Terminator* and *Robocop*, but lethal autonomous weapons have not only been developed but are currently in use. A fixed-position sentry gun, developed by Samsung for the South Korean government, can perform surveillance and is reportedly capable of firing autonomously, and it is not alone. The UK is developing a drone destined to replace human-piloted warplanes, which will not only carry air-to-air and air-to-ground weaponry and operate intercontinentally but will also incorporate full autonomy. Other countries, including Russia and the U.S., are developing autonomous weapons including tanks, warships, submarines and humanoid robots.

Two systems in particular, under development by the U.S. government, have led academics to warn that they could leave humans completely defenseless. The U.S. Defense Advanced Research Projects Agency (DARPA) is aiming to create drones able to track and kill targets independent of contact with their handlers. Academics like Stuart Russell, Professor of Computer Science at the University of California, Berkley, argue that such research could breach the Geneva Conventions and could lead to an apocalyptic scenario where humanity is in the hands of amoral machines. The pace in which the technology is advancing means that ostensibly self-aware, highly-armed machines could be deployed in battle within years rather than decades, which has greatly increased the level of concern.

Even those at the forefront of robotics technology and artificial intelligence (AI), including founders of AI and robotics companies and Silicon Valley executives, have been pushing the United Nations to ban the further development and use of autonomous weapons. The reason behind the call to prohibit such weapons is to stop the current arms race for killer robots and prevent it from going any further. In a letter to the United Nations, signed by over a hundred specialists from twenty-six countries, it is argued that such an arms race could bring about the "third revolution in warfare," following the development and use of gunpowder and nuclear arms. This arms race could be unlike anything we have seen in the past, as lethal autonomous weapons could allow for armed conflicts on scales scarcely imaginable.

Another major concern is the removal of the human factor and, by extension, the moral factor. A machine that is simply programmed to locate and destroy a target is able to do so regardless of what that target is. This raises the terrifying possibility of innocent populations being targeted by terrorists and despots. It is the moral element which has prompted the call for lethal autonomous weapons systems to be added to the list of weapons banned under the United Nations Convention on Certain Conventional Weapons (CCW) along with chemical and other weapons.

On top of this, there is, as with all computer-controlled machines, the added risk of malfunction and hacking. It is for these and other reasons that the call to pursue AI for peace, rather than further industrializing war, is growing increasingly louder.

Even the man dubbed the "Godfather of Artificial Intelligence," Professor Geoffrey Hinton, is against the deployment of autonomous weapons, although he believes that this should not turn people against AI as a whole. Not only is he against weaponized AI systems, he also fears the use of AI by the government to increase surveillance of the civilian population, and how his research could be abused by the security services. Despite these concerns, he remains optimistic about the beneficial uses of AI. Having lost his first wife to cancer and seeing his second wife also succumb to the disease, he believes medicine will become far more efficient as a result of AI, as costs could be greatly reduced, and human error brought down to almost zero.

Morality is not the only human element related to the use of AI in warfare, and it could explain why armed forces are keen to use such systems on the battlefield. Intelligent robots do not tire, are able to learn while working, can be much more cost-efficient, and are perhaps less likely to make mistakes. Given how draining warfare can be on personnel and the societies affected, it seems understandable that armed forces are keen to exploit AI for military purposes, although the potential consequences could be catastrophic. Whereas a machine performing repetitive tasks in a factory can be strictly monitored and unplugged if necessary, an intelligent war machine operating covertly and autonomously thousands of miles away is much more difficult to control. The risk of innocent lives being lost and atrocities being committed by autonomous machines means further development must be closely monitored. The future of warfare may be headed into the realms of science fiction. It remains to be seen whether scientists, military strategists, politicians and other leaders are ready for the revolution.

---

(32) What is true about the current state of autonomous weapons systems around the world?

1 The development of autonomous weapons systems is advancing at such a pace that they are already opposing their handlers.

2 Amoral machines are demanding to be allowed to operate internationally and not be limited to fixed positions.

3 Military forces are developing weapons systems that can not only operate independent of humans, but actually replace them.

4 Autonomous weapons systems are destined to be deployed in battle alongside tanks and submarines only under strict legal constraints.

Day 1
Day 2
Day 3
Day 4
Day 5
Day 6
Day 7

(33) How do a growing number of technology specialists and leaders feel about the use of autonomous weapons?

1 Specialists in AI technology believe the prohibition of autonomous weapons will lead to a new arms race.

2 Even those who have led the development of AI systems are concerned about their use in armed conflicts.

3 Many people involved in the development of AI weapons feel that the United Nations should not stand in the way of their deployment.

4 Such leaders have helped to revolutionize warfare and hope to see barriers to deployment lifted.

(34) Why do some people consider the moral argument for the banning of AI systems to be as important as the safety argument?

1 Making such weapons autonomous could lead them to destroying targets using unconventional methods and tactics.

2 The technology involved should be better put to use by combating hacking and fighting terrorism.

3 Autonomous weapons are currently too simple and could cause governments to be less efficient in surveilling civilians in peacetime.

4 The technology could target innocent civilians in numerous harmful ways.

(35) What elements that differentiate AI systems from humans need to be strongly considered before using autonomous weapons in battle?

1 The cost of AI weapons systems greatly outweighs the benefits of having them replace soldiers and other military personnel.

2 Autonomous weapons may not be prone to physical limitations but they lack the principles that could prevent war crimes.

3 AI systems have no concept of the potential outcomes of warfare and are unable to correct any mistakes they make.

4 Robotic weapons systems are much more prepared for the future of armed conflict than military leaders and politicians.

筆記試験&リスニングテスト

Day
1

Day
2

Day
3

Day
4

Day
5

Day
6

Day
7

（筆記試験の問題は次のページに続きます。）

4 English Summary

●Instructions: Read the article below and summarize it in your own words as far as possible in English.
●Suggested length: 90-110 words
●Write your summary in the space provided on your answer sheet. <u>Any writing outside the space will not be graded.</u>

As the recent increase in heatwaves and natural disasters around the world suggests, global warming is becoming extremely serious, and current efforts to reduce it may not be effective. As a result, a growing number of researchers are suggesting that humanity's best hope may be to explore a concept known as "geoengineering." This refers to utilizing advanced technology in order to counteract the impacts of global warming on a global scale. Many scientists believe it could buy us valuable time to transition to a more sustainable and low-carbon future.

One possible geoengineering approach is solar radiation management, which involves reflecting a small portion of the sun's energy back into space. This could be achieved by injecting tiny particles called aerosols into the upper atmosphere to create artificial clouds, or by utilizing giant space-based mirrors. These clouds or mirrors would prevent sunlight from warming the planet, just as ash from volcanic eruptions has cooled the Earth in the past. Another method is carbon dioxide removal, in which devices, such as artificial trees with plastic leaves that are more efficient at absorbing carbon than real leaves are, would be used. The carbon would then be kept underground or in other long-term storage facilities.

While geoengineering holds promise, it also raises serious concerns. For instance, it may have unintended consequences for ecosystems and weather. One possibility is that altering the reflectivity of the Earth's surface could affect rainfall patterns and disrupt regional climates. In addition, relying on geoengineering as a "quick fix" could potentially affect the urgency of reducing greenhouse gas emissions. This could hinder attempts to bring about a more environmentally friendly energy system. Therefore, it is crucial to approach geoengineering with caution and a deep understanding of its potential impacts while continuing to prioritize efforts to decrease greenhouse gasses through sustainable practices and renewable energy sources.

5 English Composition

- Write an essay on the given **TOPIC**.
- Give THREE reasons to support your answer.
- Structure: introduction, main body, and conclusion
- Suggested length: 200-240 words
- Write your essay in the space provided on your answer sheet. <u>Any writing outside the space will not be graded.</u>

TOPIC

Agree or disagree: Animal testing should be banned immediately

Day 1 Day 2 Day 3 Day 4 Day 5 Day 6 Day 7

Listening Test

There are four parts to this listening test.

Part 1	Dialogues: 1 question each	Multiple-choice
Part 2	Passages: 2 questions each	Multiple-choice
Part 3	Real-Life: 1 question each	Multiple-choice
Part 4	Interview: 2 questions	Multiple-choice

※Listen carefully to the instructions.

Part 1   ◀)) 101~111

No. 1
1 She thought she would get a price discount.
2 She forgot that the sales tax had increased.
3 She did not accurately remember the product's price.
4 She did not take into account state tax differences.

No. 2
1 A long-distance telephone operator.
2 The person whom the woman is calling.
3 The woman's customer in Indianapolis.
4 The person placing the call.

No. 3
1 Carrie is overly critical of her colleagues.
2 The manager purposefully creates mistrust.
3 Several team members are untrustworthy.
4 William favors certain team members over others.

No. 4
1 He cannot stand watching the program.
2 He will only watch a few episodes at a time.
3 He likes the stories but not the acting.
4 He enjoys it more than true-life violence.

No. 5
1 She would prefer living in an urban area.
2 She does not want to retire overseas.
3 She would rather live near a beach.
4 She wants to live closer to the U.S.

No. 6
1 Getting visas took longer than expected.
2 The embassy information online was inaccurate.
3 They had to leave their passports at the embassy.
4 The visa application was unnecessarily complex.

No. 7
1 Her final report.
2 Her midterm test.
3 Her final test.
4 Her lack of class participation.

No. 8
1 Open her own restaurant.
2 Get funding from other sources.
3 Work to gain expertise.
4 Keep her current job.

No. 9
1 Get in touch with Maximum regarding a new arrangement.
2 Demand more from an underperforming property manager.
3 Contact Standard Management and inform them of their decision.
4 Demand a better performance from both management companies.

No. 10
1 Sharing confidential information with the press.
2 Providing inaccurate information to her boss.
3 Meeting the press without Marketing personnel present.
4 Ignoring a warning she had been given.

Day 1
Day 2
Day 3
Day 4
Day 5
Day 6
Day 7

(A) **No. 11** **1** As an interior designer of sounds.

2 As a lover and creator of music.

3 As a business person who understands other business people.

4 As an inventor of business identities.

No. 12 **1** By getting them to focus on their true customers.

2 By convincing them to play attractive children's songs.

3 By choosing sounds that fit their brand image.

4 By having toys play gentle music to slow shoppers down.

(B) **No. 13** **1** He took part in expeditions paid for by the Spanish monarchy.

2 He wasn't allowed to land in Greenland.

3 He spent many years competing with Christopher Columbus in Canada.

4 He went on to inherit land settled by his father.

No. 14 **1** They can only be verified by linguists.

2 They are generally accepted to be factual.

3 They are considered too extraordinary to be true.

4 They are thought to be way off the mark in Iceland.

(C) **No. 15** **1** Some runners don't think they are challenging enough.

2 They are considered to be simpler than organized races.

3 Some runners prioritize them over other events.

4 They demand sports equipment manufacturers to invest more in FKT.

No. 16 **1** They have led to the development of new technology.

2 They have changed the way sporting events are viewed.

3 They have made people more skeptical of record attempts.

4 Fewer sporting events are resonating with sponsors.

(D)   *No. 17*   **1** They avoid negative feedback and depressing news.

                             2 Most writers choose to end their careers.

                             3 Different writers adopt different approaches.

                             4 Writers try to block out inspiration.

          No. 18   **1** It can cause financial difficulties.

                             2 Many creatives complain about their industry.

                             3 Self-help groups have failed to address the problem.

                             4 It is now recognized as an incurable disease.

(E)   *No. 19*   **1** It can help with balance and bone strength.

                             2 Balanced vegetarian diets can improve health.

                             3 Vegetarian diets are considered to increase the risk of cancer.

                             4 Vegan diets should not be followed.

          No. 20   **1** In the latter part of the 19th century.

                             2 Indians introduced it to Greece in ancient times.

                             3 The first vegetarians lived in Manchester.

                             4 Vegetarianism may date back to the 7th century BC.

Day 1
Day 2
Day 3
Day 4
Day 5
Day 6
Day 7

(F)　**No. 21**　***Situation:*** You are running a marathon overseas, and the chartered bus you are on arrives at the stadium where the marathon will begin. You hear the following announcement on the bus.

Question: What does the speaker recommend you do in the last 20 minutes before the marathon begins?

1 Do your final stretch or warm-up routine.

2 Take your final sips of water.

3 Go to the restroom one last time.

4 Stay within your starting zone.

(G)　**No. 22**　***Situation:*** Your child is in the second grade of an elementary school in the U.S. You attend a PTA meeting at the school. You have volunteered to help with the school's annual Auction and Book Fair. You hear the following from the president of the PTA.

Question: What are you asked to do?

1 Visit local stores to ask for donations.

2 Organize sale items before the Fair.

3 Prepare baked goods for the auction.

4 Sell donated products on October 16th.

(H)　**No. 23**　***Situation:*** You are a 58-year-old business executive on vacation. You are staying at a four-star hotel and decide to stay an additional night. You want to get the best price possible.

Question: What does the front-desk clerk recommend that you do?

1 Get the senior's rate.

2 Ask for a corporate discount.

3 Book a room online.

4 Book a room directly with the hotel.

(I)   *No. 24*   ***Situation:*** You work in the human resources department of a university and receive a message on your cellphone from the head instructor for math and science at an affiliated high school. You oversee instructors at the high school. You will be on a business trip this coming Monday.

Question: What should you do first?

1 Gather teachers together to resolve issues.
2 Send an e-mail to teachers.
3 Go to the school to support Tim.
4 Begin looking for new teachers.

(J)   *No. 25*   ***Situation:*** You plan to renew your driver's license so you call the Department of Motor Vehicles. You want the simplest, fastest way of renewal. Your license expires in 45 days. You changed residences last year. You get the following advice.

Question: What should you do?

1 Download an application form online.
2 Make a DMV appointment online.
3 Renew your license online.
4 Renew your license by mail.

Day 1
Day 2
Day 3
Day 4
Day 5
Day 6
Day 7

No. 26

1 He was interested in economics and helping people make investments.

2 He was interested in how architecture can help make people's lives better.

3 His friend, who was a real estate agent, told him about the business.

4 His parents ran a real estate business and hoped he would eventually take over.

No. 27

1 He maintains a wide network of real estate agents and obtains leads from them.

2 He turns to people he knows to introduce sales leads only at times of recession.

3 He maintains another type of real estate business besides house sales.

4 He saves up money during the good years to support his business in difficult times.

Day
1

Day
2

Day
3

Day
4

Day
5

Day
6

Day
7

1級の面接（スピーキングテスト）はどんなテスト？

面接（スピーキングテスト）では，与えられたトピックについてのスピーチをしたり，それに関する質問に答えたりします。
まず面接の流れをつかみ，その後に予想問題を確認しましょう。

1 入室

係員の指示に従い，面接室に入ります。あいさつをしてから，係員に面接カードを手渡し，指示に従って，着席しましょう。

2 氏名・受験級の確認と日常会話

面接委員が自己紹介をした後，受験者の氏名と受験級を確認します。その後，簡単な日常会話をします。

3 トピックカードの受け取りとスピーチの考慮 （1分間）

5つのトピックが書かれたトピックカードが面接委員から渡されます。トピックを1つ選び，スピーチの内容を考えましょう。考える時間は1分間です。メモを取ることはできません。

指示例 **Let's begin the test. Here is the topic card.** You have one minute to choose one topic from the five choices and prepare your speech.

┌─ トピック選びのポイント ─────────────────────────────┐
☐ 5つのトピックには素早く目を通し，自分の得意そうな分野のものを選ぶ。
☐ 最近ニュースで見たトピックなど，話題を展開しやすそうなものを選ぶ。
☐ 知らない単語が混ざっているトピックは避けるか，内容を推測する。
└──┘

4 スピーチ（2分間）

選んだトピックを面接委員に伝え，スピーチを行います。スピーチの時間は2分間で，2分を超えてしまった場合は，途中でも中止しなければなりません。

指示例 **Your time is up. Please tell us which topic you chose.**

→ I have chosen the fourth topic: Does using social network services affect people's everyday behavior?

OK. You have two minutes to give your speech. **Please begin.**

┌─ スピーチのポイント ─────────────────────────
- □ まずトピックに対する自分の意見を明確に伝える。
- □ 自分の意見を裏づける理由を論理的に述べる。
- □ 具体的な例を挙げる。
- □ 発話ははっきりと，ごまかしたり必要以上に早口になったりしないよう注意する。
- □ 関係のない話題など，余計な内容を盛り込まない。
- □ 結論をしっかりと述べる。

5 Q&A（4分間）

面接委員から，受験者が行ったスピーチやトピックに関連する質問がいくつかなされます。考慮時間はありませんので，その場で自分の意見を考えて述べましょう。

指示例 **We are going to ask you some questions about your speech.** Do you want to explain a bit more about ...?

指示例 **I'd like to move slightly away from the topic.** Do you think it is important to ...?

┌─ Q&Aのポイント ─────────────────────────
- □ 面接委員からの質問をよく聞き，理解してから答える。（考慮時間はないが，一呼吸おいても構わない。）
- □ スピーチと同様，自分の意見や立場をまず明確にする。
- □ Yes. や No. だけではなく，そう考えた理由も必ず述べる。
- □ 自身のスピーチで述べた意見と矛盾しないよう注意する。（新しい理由や情報を足すことは構わない。）

6 トピックカードの返却と退室

試験が終了したら，トピックカードを面接委員に返却し，あいさつをして退室しましょう。

Grade 1 TOPIC CARD

1. Is the labor reform law effective enough to make Japanese workers take more holidays?

2. Should home schooling be more accepted in Japan?

3. Will globalization reduce national awareness?

4. Does using social network services affect people's everyday behavior?

5. Agree or disagree: Surrogate delivery is not ethical

解答解説

ここでは，4つ目のトピックをスピーチ解答例とし，解説しています。

トピックの訳

1. 労働改革法は，日本の労働者により多くの休暇を取らせるための十分な効果がありますか。
2. ホームスクーリングは日本でもっと受け入れられるべきですか。
3. グローバル化は国民意識を薄めるでしょうか。
4. SNSの使用は，人々の日々の行動に影響を与えますか。
5. 賛成か反対か：代理出産は倫理的ではない。

🔊 126

スピーチ解答例

Considering the large amount of time most people spend using social networks these days, it seems only natural that it will affect how we live our daily lives. Some of these effects can be positive. For example, many people now exercise more and follow healthier lifestyles. This is due to the many apps on their smartphones, as well as the lifestyle advisers and other activists who have become "influencers" through Facebook, Twitter and other social network sites. Others are involved in political and social activities due to the rich and up-to-date information available on social networking sites. However, there also are negative effects. Social media allows people to be more outspoken and post their opinions instantly, without time for reflection. This can lead to conflicts and personal attacks. In the worst cases, this may develop into "cyber bullying." Another problem is that by using social media, people often portray idealized versions of themselves, a sort of fake identity and fake pride. In other cases, people are made to buy things they don't need or can't afford. Some pay huge amounts, trying to look like the attractive and idealized personalities they follow online. Social media can be very useful. However, it is also very important to be aware of how it can control our behavior.

解説 4つ目のトピック「SNSの使用は，人々の日々の行動に影響を与えますか」を選んだ場合のスピーチ。解答例ではまず，「今日人々がSNSを使用する時間を考慮すると，それが日常生活に影響を与えるのは自然なことのように思える」として，自身がYesの立場であることを説明している。その次に，そうした影響の良い点と悪い点を挙げることで，議論を展開している。良い点としては，SNSで情報を発信する「インフルエンサー」たちの影響で人々がより健康な生活をするようになっていることや，SNSの情報発信によって政治活動などに人々が積極的に関われるようになっていることなどを例に挙げている。悪い点については，SNSは人々の率直な意見を素早く拡散するため「ネットいじめ」につながる恐れがあること，またSNSで見栄を張るために散財する人もいることを説明している。SNSによって影響を受ける人々の行動について以上の例を挙げたうえ，結論では，「SNSはとても便利である。しかし，それがどれほどわれわれの行動を左右するか認識することもとても重要である」とスピーチを締めくくっている。

MEMO

MEMO

MEMO

MEMO

4 English Summary

Write your English Summary in the space below. (Suggested length: 90-110 words)

（解答欄：5 / 10 / 15 / 20）

Day 1 解答用紙（1級）

筆記解答欄

問題番号	1	2	3	4
(1)	①	②	③	④
(2)	①	②	③	④
(3)	①	②	③	④
(4)	①	②	③	④
(5)	①	②	③	④
(6)	①	②	③	④
(7)	①	②	③	④
(8)	①	②	③	④
(9)	①	②	③	④
(10)	①	②	③	④
(11)	①	②	③	④
(12)	①	②	③	④
(13)	①	②	③	④
(14)	①	②	③	④
(15)	①	②	③	④
(16)	①	②	③	④
(17)	①	②	③	④
(18)	①	②	③	④
(19)	①	②	③	④
(20)	①	②	③	④
(21)	①	②	③	④
(22)	①	②	③	④

（1）

問題番号	1	2	3	4
(23)	①	②	③	④
(24)	①	②	③	④
(25)	①	②	③	④
(26)	①	②	③	④
(27)	①	②	③	④
(28)	①	②	③	④
(29)	①	②	③	④
(30)	①	②	③	④
(31)	①	②	③	④
(32)	①	②	③	④
(33)	①	②	③	④
(34)	①	②	③	④
(35)	①	②	③	④

（2 / 3）

リスニング解答欄

	問題番号	1	2	3	4
Part 1	No.1	①	②	③	④
	No.2	①	②	③	④
	No.3	①	②	③	④
	No.4	①	②	③	④
	No.5	①	②	③	④
	No.6	①	②	③	④
	No.7	①	②	③	④
	No.8	①	②	③	④
	No.9	①	②	③	④
	No.10	①	②	③	④
Part 2	A No.11	①	②	③	④
	No.12	①	②	③	④
	B No.13	①	②	③	④
	No.14	①	②	③	④
	C No.15	①	②	③	④
	No.16	①	②	③	④
	D No.17	①	②	③	④
	No.18	①	②	③	④
	E No.19	①	②	③	④
	No.20	①	②	③	④
Part 3	F No.21	①	②	③	④
	G No.22	①	②	③	④
	H No.23	①	②	③	④
	I No.24	①	②	③	④
	J No.25	①	②	③	④
Part 4	No.26	①	②	③	④
	No.27	①	②	③	④

注意事項

（HBの）黒鉛筆またはシャープペンシル以外の筆記具を使用してマーク・記入した場合、解答が無効となるので、注意してください。

※ 5 の解答欄は裏面にあります。

5　English Composition

Write your English Composition in the space below. (Suggested length: 200-240 words)

5

10

15

20

25

4　English Summary

Write your English Summary in the space below. (Suggested length: 90-110 words)

5

10

15

20

Day 2　解答用紙（1級）

リスニング解答欄

問題番号		1	2	3	4
Part 1	No.1	①	②	③	④
	No.2	①	②	③	④
	No.3	①	②	③	④
	No.4	①	②	③	④
	No.5	①	②	③	④
	No.6	①	②	③	④
	No.7	①	②	③	④
	No.8	①	②	③	④
	No.9	①	②	③	④
	No.10	①	②	③	④
Part 2	A No.11	①	②	③	④
	No.12	①	②	③	④
	B No.13	①	②	③	④
	No.14	①	②	③	④
	C No.15	①	②	③	④
	No.16	①	②	③	④
	D No.17	①	②	③	④
	No.18	①	②	③	④
	E No.19	①	②	③	④
	No.20	①	②	③	④
Part 3	F No.21	①	②	③	④
	G No.22	①	②	③	④
	H No.23	①	②	③	④
	I No.24	①	②	③	④
	J No.25	①	②	③	④
Part 4	No.26	①	②	③	④
	No.27	①	②	③	④

筆記解答欄

問題番号		1	2	3	4
1	(1)	①	②	③	④
	(2)	①	②	③	④
	(3)	①	②	③	④
	(4)	①	②	③	④
	(5)	①	②	③	④
	(6)	①	②	③	④
	(7)	①	②	③	④
	(8)	①	②	③	④
	(9)	①	②	③	④
	(10)	①	②	③	④
	(11)	①	②	③	④
	(12)	①	②	③	④
	(13)	①	②	③	④
	(14)	①	②	③	④
	(15)	①	②	③	④
	(16)	①	②	③	④
	(17)	①	②	③	④
	(18)	①	②	③	④
	(19)	①	②	③	④
	(20)	①	②	③	④
	(21)	①	②	③	④
	(22)	①	②	③	④
2	(23)	①	②	③	④
	(24)	①	②	③	④
	(25)	①	②	③	④
	(26)	①	②	③	④
	(27)	①	②	③	④
	(28)	①	②	③	④
3	(29)	①	②	③	④
	(30)	①	②	③	④
	(31)	①	②	③	④
	(32)	①	②	③	④
	(33)	①	②	③	④
	(34)	①	②	③	④
	(35)	①	②	③	④

注意事項

（HBの）黒鉛筆またはシャープペンシル以外の筆記
具を使用してマーク・記入した場合、解答が無効と
なるので、注意してください。

4 English Summary

Write your English Summary in the space below. (Suggested length: 90–110 words)

5
10
15
20

Day 3 解答用紙（1級）

筆記解答欄

問題番号	1	2	3	4
(1)	①	②	③	④
(2)	①	②	③	④
(3)	①	②	③	④
(4)	①	②	③	④
(5)	①	②	③	④
(6)	①	②	③	④
(7)	①	②	③	④
(8)	①	②	③	④
(9)	①	②	③	④
(10)	①	②	③	④
(11)	①	②	③	④
(12)	①	②	③	④
(13)	①	②	③	④
(14)	①	②	③	④
(15)	①	②	③	④
(16)	①	②	③	④
(17)	①	②	③	④
(18)	①	②	③	④
(19)	①	②	③	④
(20)	①	②	③	④
(21)	①	②	③	④
(22)	①	②	③	④

1

問題番号	1	2	3	4
(23)	①	②	③	④
(24)	①	②	③	④
(25)	①	②	③	④
(26)	①	②	③	④
(27)	①	②	③	④
(28)	①	②	③	④
(29)	①	②	③	④
(30)	①	②	③	④
(31)	①	②	③	④
(32)	①	②	③	④
(33)	①	②	③	④
(34)	①	②	③	④
(35)	①	②	③	④

2
3

リスニング解答欄

	問題番号	1	2	3	4
Part 1	No.1	①	②	③	④
	No.2	①	②	③	④
	No.3	①	②	③	④
	No.4	①	②	③	④
	No.5	①	②	③	④
	No.6	①	②	③	④
	No.7	①	②	③	④
	No.8	①	②	③	④
	No.9	①	②	③	④
	No.10	①	②	③	④
A	No.11	①	②	③	④
	No.12	①	②	③	④
B	No.13	①	②	③	④
	No.14	①	②	③	④
C	No.15	①	②	③	④
	No.16	①	②	③	④
D	No.17	①	②	③	④
	No.18	①	②	③	④
E	No.19	①	②	③	④
	No.20	①	②	③	④
F	No.21	①	②	③	④
G	No.22	①	②	③	④
H	No.23	①	②	③	④
I	No.24	①	②	③	④
J	No.25	①	②	③	④
Part 4	No.26	①	②	③	④
	No.27	①	②	③	④

Part 2
Part 3

注意事項

（HBの）黒鉛筆またはシャープペンシル以外の筆記
具を使用してマーク・記入した場合、解答が無効と
なるので、注意してください。

※ **5** の解答欄は裏面にあります。

5   English Composition

Write your English Composition in the space below. (Suggested length: 200-240 words)

<table>
<tr><td></td></tr>
</table>

4 English Summary

Write your English Summary in the space below. (Suggested length: 90-110 words)

(Answer grid with line markers: 5, 10, 15, 20)

リスニング解答欄

	問題番号	1 2 3 4
Part 1	No.1	① ② ③ ④
	No.2	① ② ③ ④
	No.3	① ② ③ ④
	No.4	① ② ③ ④
	No.5	① ② ③ ④
	No.6	① ② ③ ④
	No.7	① ② ③ ④
	No.8	① ② ③ ④
	No.9	① ② ③ ④
	No.10	① ② ③ ④
Part 2	A No.11	① ② ③ ④
	No.12	① ② ③ ④
	No.13	① ② ③ ④
	B No.14	① ② ③ ④
	No.15	① ② ③ ④
	No.16	① ② ③ ④
	C No.17	① ② ③ ④
	No.18	① ② ③ ④
	D No.19	① ② ③ ④
	No.20	① ② ③ ④
	E No.21	① ② ③ ④
Part 3	F No.22	① ② ③ ④
	G No.23	① ② ③ ④
	H No.24	① ② ③ ④
	I No.25	① ② ③ ④
	J No.26	① ② ③ ④
Part 4	No.27	① ② ③ ④

Day 4 解答用紙（1級）

筆記解答欄

問題番号	1 2 3 4		問題番号	1 2 3 4
1 (1)	① ② ③ ④		2 (23)	① ② ③ ④
(2)	① ② ③ ④		(24)	① ② ③ ④
(3)	① ② ③ ④		(25)	① ② ③ ④
(4)	① ② ③ ④		(26)	① ② ③ ④
(5)	① ② ③ ④		(27)	① ② ③ ④
(6)	① ② ③ ④		(28)	① ② ③ ④
(7)	① ② ③ ④		3 (29)	① ② ③ ④
(8)	① ② ③ ④		(30)	① ② ③ ④
(9)	① ② ③ ④		(31)	① ② ③ ④
(10)	① ② ③ ④		(32)	① ② ③ ④
(11)	① ② ③ ④		(33)	① ② ③ ④
(12)	① ② ③ ④		(34)	① ② ③ ④
(13)	① ② ③ ④		(35)	① ② ③ ④
(14)	① ② ③ ④			
(15)	① ② ③ ④			
(16)	① ② ③ ④			
(17)	① ② ③ ④			
(18)	① ② ③ ④			
(19)	① ② ③ ④			
(20)	① ② ③ ④			
(21)	① ② ③ ④			
(22)	① ② ③ ④			

注意事項

（HBの）黒鉛筆またはシャープペンシル以外の筆記
具を使用してマーク・記入した場合、解答が無効と
なるので、注意してください。

切り取り線

4　English Summary

Write your English Summary in the space below. (Suggested length: 90-110 words)

5　10　15　20

Day 5　解答用紙（1級）

筆記解答欄

問題番号	1	2	3	4
(1)	①	②	③	④
(2)	①	②	③	④
(3)	①	②	③	④
(4)	①	②	③	④
(5)	①	②	③	④
(6)	①	②	③	④
(7)	①	②	③	④
(8)	①	②	③	④
(9)	①	②	③	④
(10)	①	②	③	④
(11)	①	②	③	④
(12)	①	②	③	④
(13)	①	②	③	④
(14)	①	②	③	④
(15)	①	②	③	④
(16)	①	②	③	④
(17)	①	②	③	④
(18)	①	②	③	④
(19)	①	②	③	④
(20)	①	②	③	④
(21)	①	②	③	④
(22)	①	②	③	④

1

問題番号	1	2	3	4
(23)	①	②	③	④
(24)	①	②	③	④
(25)	①	②	③	④
(26)	①	②	③	④
(27)	①	②	③	④
(28)	①	②	③	④

2

問題番号	1	2	3	4
(29)	①	②	③	④
(30)	①	②	③	④
(31)	①	②	③	④
(32)	①	②	③	④
(33)	①	②	③	④
(34)	①	②	③	④
(35)	①	②	③	④

3

リスニング解答欄

	問題番号	1	2	3	4
Part 1	No.1	①	②	③	④
	No.2	①	②	③	④
	No.3	①	②	③	④
	No.4	①	②	③	④
	No.5	①	②	③	④
	No.6	①	②	③	④
	No.7	①	②	③	④
	No.8	①	②	③	④
	No.9	①	②	③	④
	No.10	①	②	③	④
Part 2 A	No.11	①	②	③	④
	No.12	①	②	③	④
B	No.13	①	②	③	④
	No.14	①	②	③	④
C	No.15	①	②	③	④
	No.16	①	②	③	④
D	No.17	①	②	③	④
	No.18	①	②	③	④
E	No.19	①	②	③	④
	No.20	①	②	③	④
Part 3 F	No.21	①	②	③	④
G	No.22	①	②	③	④
H	No.23	①	②	③	④
I	No.24	①	②	③	④
J	No.25	①	②	③	④
Part 4	No.26	①	②	③	④
	No.27	①	②	③	④

注意事項

（HBの）黒鉛筆またはシャープペンシル以外の筆記
具を使用してマーク・記入した場合、解答が無効と
なるので、注意してください。

※ 5 の解答欄は裏面にあります。

5 English Composition

Write your English Composition in the space below. (Suggested length: 200-240 words)

5

10

15

20

25

4　English Summary

Write your English Summary in the space below. (Suggested length: 90-110 words)

5
10
15
20

Day 6　解答用紙（1級）

筆記解答欄

問題番号	1	2	3	4
(1)	①	②	③	④
(2)	①	②	③	④
(3)	①	②	③	④
(4)	①	②	③	④
(5)	①	②	③	④
(6)	①	②	③	④
(7)	①	②	③	④
(8)	①	②	③	④
(9)	①	②	③	④
(10)	①	②	③	④
(11)	①	②	③	④
(12)	①	②	③	④
(13)	①	②	③	④
(14)	①	②	③	④
(15)	①	②	③	④
(16)	①	②	③	④
(17)	①	②	③	④
(18)	①	②	③	④
(19)	①	②	③	④
(20)	①	②	③	④
(21)	①	②	③	④
(22)	①	②	③	④

（問題番号 1）

問題番号	1	2	3	4
(23)	①	②	③	④
(24)	①	②	③	④
(25)	①	②	③	④
(26)	①	②	③	④
(27)	①	②	③	④
(28)	①	②	③	④
(29)	①	②	③	④
(30)	①	②	③	④
(31)	①	②	③	④
(32)	①	②	③	④
(33)	①	②	③	④
(34)	①	②	③	④
(35)	①	②	③	④

（問題番号 2 / 3）

リスニング解答欄

	問題番号	1	2	3	4
Part 1	No.1	①	②	③	④
	No.2	①	②	③	④
	No.3	①	②	③	④
	No.4	①	②	③	④
	No.5	①	②	③	④
	No.6	①	②	③	④
	No.7	①	②	③	④
	No.8	①	②	③	④
	No.9	①	②	③	④
	No.10	①	②	③	④
Part 2　A	No.11	①	②	③	④
	No.12	①	②	③	④
B	No.13	①	②	③	④
	No.14	①	②	③	④
C	No.15	①	②	③	④
	No.16	①	②	③	④
D	No.17	①	②	③	④
	No.18	①	②	③	④
E	No.19	①	②	③	④
	No.20	①	②	③	④
Part 3　F	No.21	①	②	③	④
G	No.22	①	②	③	④
H	No.23	①	②	③	④
I	No.24	①	②	③	④
J	No.25	①	②	③	④
Part 4	No.26	①	②	③	④
	No.27	①	②	③	④

注意事項

（HBの）黒鉛筆またはシャープペンシル以外の筆記
具を使用してマーク・記入した場合、解答が無効と
なるので、注意してください。

※ 5 の解答欄は裏面にあります。

記入上の注意（記述形式）

・太枠に囲まれた部分のみが採点の対象です。指示事項を守り、文字は、はっきりと分かりやすく、濃く、書いてください。

・数字の１と小文字のl（エル）、数字の２とＺ（ゼット）など似ている文字は、判別できるよう書いてください。

・消しゴムで消す場合は、消しくず、消し残しがないようしっかりと消してください。

・解答が英語以外の言語を用いている、質問と関係がない、テストの趣旨に反すると判断された場合、０点と採点される可能性があります。

5 | English Composition

Write your English Composition in the space below. (Suggested length: 200-240 words)

5

10

15

20

25

4 English Summary

Write your English Summary in the space below. (Suggested length: 90-110 words)

5
10
15
20

Day 7 解答用紙（1級）

筆記解答欄

問題番号	1	2	3	4
(1)	①	②	③	④
(2)	①	②	③	④
(3)	①	②	③	④
(4)	①	②	③	④
(5)	①	②	③	④
(6)	①	②	③	④
(7)	①	②	③	④
(8)	①	②	③	④
(9)	①	②	③	④
(10)	①	②	③	④
(11)	①	②	③	④
(12)	①	②	③	④
(13)	①	②	③	④
(14)	①	②	③	④
(15)	①	②	③	④
(16)	①	②	③	④
(17)	①	②	③	④
(18)	①	②	③	④
(19)	①	②	③	④
(20)	①	②	③	④
(21)	①	②	③	④
(22)	①	②	③	④

1

問題番号	1	2	3	4
(23)	①	②	③	④
(24)	①	②	③	④
(25)	①	②	③	④
(26)	①	②	③	④
(27)	①	②	③	④
(28)	①	②	③	④
(29)	①	②	③	④
(30)	①	②	③	④
(31)	①	②	③	④
(32)	①	②	③	④
(33)	①	②	③	④
(34)	①	②	③	④
(35)	①	②	③	④

2
3

リスニング解答欄

	問題番号	1	2	3	4
Part 1	No.1	①	②	③	④
	No.2	①	②	③	④
	No.3	①	②	③	④
	No.4	①	②	③	④
	No.5	①	②	③	④
	No.6	①	②	③	④
	No.7	①	②	③	④
	No.8	①	②	③	④
	No.9	①	②	③	④
	No.10	①	②	③	④
Part 2 A	No.11	①	②	③	④
	No.12	①	②	③	④
B	No.13	①	②	③	④
	No.14	①	②	③	④
C	No.15	①	②	③	④
	No.16	①	②	③	④
D	No.17	①	②	③	④
	No.18	①	②	③	④
E	No.19	①	②	③	④
	No.20	①	②	③	④
Part 3 F	No.21	①	②	③	④
G	No.22	①	②	③	④
H	No.23	①	②	③	④
I	No.24	①	②	③	④
J	No.25	①	②	③	④
Part 4	No.26	①	②	③	④
	No.27	①	②	③	④

注意事項

黒鉛筆またはシャープペンシル以外の筆記
具を使用してマーク・記入した場合、解答が無効と
なるので、注意してください。

※ 5 の解答欄は裏面にあります。

5　English Composition

Write your English Composition in the space below. (Suggested length: 200-240 words)

5

10

15

20

25

7日間完成

文部科学省後援

英検®1級
予想問題ドリル

[6訂版]

解答と解説

Contents 解答と解説

旺文社

筆記試験
解答と解説

問題編 p.10〜23

筆記

1

問題	1	2	3	4	5	6	7	8	9	10	11	12	13	14	15	16	17	18	19	20
解答	2	3	3	1	3	4	2	4	2	2	2	3	4	4	3	2	3	1	1	3

問題	21	22
解答	4	1

2

問題	23	24	25	26	27	28
解答	4	3	2	1	3	4

3

問題	29	30	31	32	33	34	35
解答	3	1	4	3	4	3	2

4 **5** 解説内にある解答例を参照してください。

1

(1) 解答 **2**

「内紛の勃発により, 近隣諸国は難民の大規模流入に対する備えをした。住宅や食料, 飲料水, そのほかの基本的な生活必需品を用意した」

解説 内紛勃発で近隣諸国がいろいろと用意をしたのは, 難民が大量に流入することが予想されたためだと考えられる。**1**「転覆」, **3**「摂取」, **4**「襲撃」。

(2) 解答 **3**

「この大学は, バプテスト教会系列の男女共学校だ」

解説 人や団体同士が提携・所属・付属している状態を, affiliate の過去分詞 affiliated「提携した」を用いて表す。**1**「割り当てられた」, **2**「甘やかされた」, **4**「関与した」。

(3) 解答 **3**

「ジョン・マークル教授は夏の間に小説を1冊書き終えるつもりだったが, そのような芸当は不可能であることに気づいた。結局, 書き終えるのに2年かかった」

解説 「小説を書き終えるつもりだったが, ( ) は不可能だとわかった」という流れなので, 空所には小説を書き上げることを表す語が入るはず。**3**「芸当, 偉業」が正解。**1**「前兆」, **2**「策略」, **4**「見せかけ」。

(4) 解答 **1**

A「すみませんが, 個人による銃の所持の制限を求めるこの嘆願書にご署名いただけませんか」

B「申し訳ないのですが, 私は狩猟が好きで, 厳重な銃規制の支持者ではありません」

解説 Bは狩猟が好きなのだから, 銃規制には反対の旨を述べるはず。not の後なので「支持者」という意味の proponent を選ぶ。**2**「門限」, **3**「目利き」, **4**「すり」。

(5) 解答 **3**

「社長はシンガポールでの新オフィス開設には内在するリスクがあることを見極め, 決断を1, 2年先送りすることにした」

解説 risk を修飾する語として適切なのは, **3**「内在する, 固有の」。**1**「飽くことのない」, **2**「遠慮のな

い」，4「後悔していない」。

(6) 解答 4

A「私は自分のことを教師としてあまり有能だとは感じておりません」

B「私の意見は正反対ですね。あなたは多くの生徒に多大な影響を与えてきたのです」

解説 I couldn't disagree with you more. は「これ以上の反対はできないだろう」，つまり「全く逆の立場だ」という意味なので，これに続く B の発言は A の発言と対照的な内容になる。4が正解。1「熱狂した」，2「厳しい」，3「貪欲な」。

(7) 解答 2

A「まあ，大変！　あなたのブラウスにジュースをぶちまけてしまったわ。私ってとてもどんくさいわね」

B「心配しないで。簡単に洗い落とせるわ」

解説 誤ってジュースをこぼしてしまったのだから，自分自身のことを「どんくさい，不器用」と言ったと考えるのが自然。1「あか抜けない」，3「気のきいた」，4「元気がいい」。

(8) 解答 3

「ジュディは14歳のときに男女交際を始めたいと思ったが，デートに行けるのは彼女と相手が大人に付き添われる場合だけだと両親に言われた」

解説 14歳の女の子が両親からデートを許してもらう条件を考えると，大人に「付き添われる」必要があると考えられる。1「送金されて」，2 succumb「屈する」の過去分詞，4「ちょうつがいをつけられて」。

(9) 解答 2

「そのプロジェクトを進めることに大多数の合意があったのだが，マネージャーは，それは悪いアイデアであり，かなりの損失を出す結果になるだろうと断固主張していた」

解説 Even though から，前半の内容と後半の内容が対照的になることを考えると，that 節の内容は the manager の考えを表しているはず。be adamant that ... で「…ということを断固主張している」という意味になる2が正解。1「必然的な」，3「恣意的な」，4「義務的な」。

(10) 解答 2

「その女性は店で盗みを働くのを見つかり，1週間後に当局によって起訴された」

解説 女性は盗みを働いたのだから，「起訴された」と考えるのが自然。the authorities「当局」とは，ここでは起訴する機関のことなので，「検察」などと考えればよい。1「引き延ばされた」，3「動揺させられた」，4「破壊された」。

(11) 解答 3

「その従業員に提供されたすべてのサポートと追加研修をもって，彼はどんなに簡単な仕事でも失敗し続けるであろうことが明らかになった。彼は全くの無能であった」

解説 どんな簡単な仕事もこなせないということは，「技量に欠ける，無能」ということ。1「不足して」，2「従順な」，4「飾り立てた」。

(12) 解答 4

「その若者は祖父から数百万ドルの遺産を相続したが，すぐにギャンブルやどんちゃん騒ぎでその財産を浪費した」

解説 後半の節は前半の節と逆接でつながっている。ギャンブルやどんちゃん騒ぎをしたというのだから，大金はすぐに「浪費された」はず。1「健康を害した」，2「回復した」，3「高めた」。

(13) 解答 4

「陪審員団は，被告は第一級殺人で有罪であるとの評決を下し，不注意で銃の引き金を引いてしまったという被告の主張は受け入れなかった」

解説 殺人罪で有罪が言い渡された被告が，自分を弁護するためにどんな主張をしていたのか考える。「引き金を引いた」，つまり「撃った」のは「不注意」だったと訴えるのが自然。1「断続的に」，2「慣例的に」，3「心から」。

(14) 解答 3

「そのコンピュータ専門家は，自社の請求書作成業務を手早く片づけるため，新しい精巧なソフトウェアをインストールした」

解説 新しいソフトを導入した理由として適切なのは，請求書作成業務を「手早く片づける」ため。1「～に刺激を与える」，2「～を無効にする」，4「～をくまなく捜す」。

(15) 解答 2

「その家具会社は倒産した。会社の在庫品整理から得た利益は出資者への返済に役立った」

解説 この会社は倒産したのだが，2文目に利益を得て出資者に金を返したとある。金をどう工面したのかを考えると，在庫の「整理，清算」が適切。1「託送品」，3「保護」，4「減少，減損」。

(16)　**解答** 3

「検察庁が2人の外国人外交官をスパイ容疑で起訴する決定を下したところ，国際的な論争が巻き起こった」

解説 検察庁がすることは，「〜（人）を起訴する」こと。1「〜（法律など）を廃止する」，2「〜（人）を困らせる」，4「〜を刺激する」。

(17)　**解答** 2

「その夫婦は結婚して3年後に離婚した。彼らはお互いにどうしても気が合わないとわかったのだ」

解説 compatible with 〜はコンピュータについて使うと「〜と互換性がある」，人について使うと「〜と気が合う」という意味。1「（環境を）維持できる，耐え得る」，3「（時間や行為などが）好都合の」，4「土着の，生まれつきの」。

(18)　**解答** 1

「その惨事の被害者に関して無神経で侮辱的なコメントを述べたことで，その政治家は厳しくとがめられた」

解説 被害者に対して無神経なコメントをしたら，「とがめられる」はず。2「褒められて」，3「激賞されて」，4「修正されて」。

(19)　**解答** 1

「授業中に悪さをする子供たちは，たいてい気を引こうとしているだけである」

解説 子供が注意を引くためにする行動として考えられるのは，1「悪さをする，行儀悪くする」。2「〜を軽く扱う」，3「成功する」，4「力が尽きる」。

(20)　**解答** 3

「その会社の年次報告書は，株主に信用してもらえなかった。その年に社がこうむったいくつかの巨額の損失をごまかしたからである」

解説 年次報告書が信頼できないのは，損失を「ごまかした」から。1「〜を抑制した」，2「身を隠した」，4「〜（たばこなど）をもみ消した」。

(21)　**解答** 4

「副社長は，会議で営業部長に対して大声を張り上げた。副社長がそのように誰かを痛烈に批判するのを誰も見たことがなかった。彼は通常はおだやかな人だったからだ」

解説 at anyone like that「そのように誰かに向かって」とあるのだから，空所に入るのは1文目の shouted に近い意味の単語のはず。4が正解。1「〜に根気よく励む」，2「〜を（…で）終わりにする」，3「〜を大きな音で演奏する」。

(22)　**解答** 1

「ミナミは決してあきらめない。何かで失敗したり，テストの点数が悪かったりしても，彼女はただ失敗など気にも留めず，それどころか次の機会のためにさらなる努力をするのだ」

解説 1文目にミナミはあきらめない人だとあるので，失敗したときの態度としては「気にしない」が最も適切。2「お辞儀をして退出する」，3「〜をはねつける，拒絶する」，4「〜を追い出す」。

2

全訳
予測されたEV車革命
　実用的な電気自動車は19世紀後期より普及しているが，内燃エンジンが誕生してからは，それが自動車生産を支配してきた。気候変動や局地汚染に関する関心が高まるにつれ，地方自治体や政府は電気自動車，つまりEV車が，人間の化石燃料への依存によって引き起こされた被害を相殺してくれることに，次第に期待を寄せるようになった。重要な，そしておそらく大い

に象徴的な宣言が，ヨーロッパ数カ国の政府，米国の地方自治体，その他の地域によってすでになされている。いまだ正式な法律ではないにしても，当局は今世紀半ばまでにディーゼル車とガソリン車の販売を禁止する意向を表明しており，一方ですでに多くの都市はカーフリーデーを実施している。
　こうした提案は世界的な承認を得てはいない。排出に焦点を当てることは近視眼的で，例えばブレーキやタイヤの摩耗，そして路面の磨り減りによってできる

粒子状物質を無視していると感じる人々もいる。そして物質が呼吸で吸いこまれて心肺毒性やそのほかの病気にもつながることがある。批評家たちはまた, EV車はそのエネルギー源と同じくらいクリーンなだけだと主張する。そのエネルギー源とは, 今でも多くの場所で多量の汚染をする化石燃料を指す。本当のEV車革命が実現するためには, **再生可能エネルギー生産における革命も伴う必要があるのだ。**

さらに, 従来型の自動車を表面上は排ガスを出さないEV車で置き換えることに答えがあるのではなく, むしろ個人所有の自動車の全体数を減らすことにあると主張する人々もいる。これには, クリーンな形式の都市交通への莫大な投資および, 車を我慢するよう都市の住民を説得することを要する。都市で生活することを選ぶ人が増えているので, 信頼のおける交通機関への高まる需要に見合う解決法をすぐに見つけなければならない。これは, 都市交通がクリーンかつ安全で経済的実現性があるということを保証するばかりでなく, 増加する運動嫌いの人々を説得して, 自動車に飛び乗るよりも歩いたり自転車に乗ったりさせようとすることを意味するのだ。

(23) 解答 **4**

解説 世界の電気自動車に対する期待について述べている段落なので, それ以外の車を禁止するという流れが自然。1「自動車支配の象徴」, 2「電気への過度の依存」, 3「『気候変動』という用語の使用」。

(24) 解答 **3**

解説 EV車のエネルギー源（つまり電気）もクリーンに生産しなくてはならない, というのがこの段落の論旨なので3が正解。1「毒性に関連する特定の問題」, 2「汚染物質を生産する新たな手段」, 4「路面の磨り減りへと焦点を変えること」。

(25) 解答 **2**

解説 空所後の「クリーンな都市交通への投資」や「車を我慢するよう都市住民を説得」から2が正解。1「非再生可能エネルギー工場の数」, 3「汚染の激しい地域における人口増加」, 4「都市移住者の経済的悩み」。

全訳
すっかり酔っぱらう

酒をちょっと飲みすぎたことのある人なら誰でも証言できるとおり, 酒は確かに体が温かくなるような感

じがすることがある。セントバーナード犬が凍える登山者を温めるため少量のブランデーを携えてアルプスを旅する情景が, 酒には寒さを防ぐ力があるという印象を強めた。真実はそんなに有益なものではない。アルコールは皮膚の中にある血管を拡張し, それによって血液を中心部から末端へと流し, その結果として, 体が温かいというメッセージが脳に押し寄せるのだ。知覚におけるこの混乱が, 人間においては致命的にもなり得るが, 2種類の魚の場合は寒いときの飲酒が生存への鍵となる。

科学者たちは, 金魚とその近縁野生種であるヨーロッパブナが, 生きるためにエタノールという形で体内に効率的にアルコールを作り出すことを発見した。その発見で, 氷に覆われた湖の中で, 冬を生き抜く魚たちの類いまれな能力の説明がつく。そこでは酸素が非常に貴重で水温が急に下がる。酸素不足だと魚は呼吸できず, 酸素を必要としないエネルギー生成に頼らなくてはならない。これだと新鮮な空気は必要ないものの乳酸を作り出すという命にかかわる可能性さえある副作用を伴う。金魚とヨーロッパブナはエネルギー生成をコントロールする予備のタンパク質複合体を持っており, それが乳酸をアルコール性の老廃物に変えることを可能にするのだ。

発見はこれらの魚たちの耐寒性を説明するだけでなく, 将来の研究に向けての重要な暗示となり得る。この生存特性は全ゲノム重複に起因するのかもしれない。それが生物の新規性の進化へとつながり, いくつかの種がかつて生存に適さなかった環境で育つことを可能にしたのだ。全ゲノム重複は, 数種の動物の中で遺伝子が2セット創造されることを意味する。すると元のゲノムは動物がいつものように成長し発達するのを助け, もう一方のゲノムはそのゲノムを持つ動物が傷ついたり変形したりするリスクが少ないままで効果的に自由に変化し順応していく。確かに興味深いが, 実用化はまだまだ先の話のようだ。

(26) 解答 **1**

解説 次の文の「凍える登山者を温める」「酒には寒さを防ぐ力がある」という記述から, 1が正解。2「周辺視野の鋭敏さに影響する」, 3「動けなくなった登山者の救助に役立つ」, 4「知覚に好ましい変化を引き起こす」。

(27) 解答 **3**

解説 第2段落の冒頭に「エタノールという形で体内に効率的にアルコールを作り出す」とあるので, 3が

正解。**1**「酸素を新鮮な空気に」，**2**「氷をもっとずっと温かい水に」，**4**「空気を致死量のアルコールに」。

(28) 解答 **4**

解説 空所前に「生存特性」とあることから，**4**が正

解。**1**「それと認識できないほどに変形すること」，**2**「生物学的に精密な自分たちのクローンを作ること」，**3**「人間よりも多量のアルコールを摂取すること」。

3

全訳

近代教育の発達

education（教育）という言葉自体は，「養育する，育てる」という意味のラテン語 educatio と，「導く，訓練する」という意味の educo にさかのぼることができるが，教育のルーツは文字文化が誕生する前までさかのぼる。先史時代，大多数の人間が狩猟採集社会に属していたころ，主として教育とは，大人が子供に社会を養ったり守ったりするのに必要な技術と知識を伝えることであった。こうした教育は想像以上に洗練されたもので，食用になる食べ物，水源，危険の認知，狩りとわなの技術，そして武器の製造・使用などについて教えられていた。そのような技術と知識は，ある世代から次の世代へと口頭で受け継がれ，多くの場合，物語として話したり，あるいは模倣をしたり，与えられた知識を実際に使ったりすることで伝えられた。

社会が発展するにつれ，人々の知識と能力はさらに拡大し始め，模倣や従来の口頭伝承を通じて適切に身につけられる限界を超えてしまった。これが公教育の始まりであった。学校だと認識できる，つまり生徒用の席があり先生がいる学校は，古代エジプトで存在しており，裕福な親を持つ子供を教育して書記官にすることに主眼が置かれていた。読み書きは非常に需要の高いスキルだったのである。社会が落ち着くと親の教育も子供の教育も各社会の文化とニーズを映し出すようになり，それは戦闘技術から博物学，芸術，数学，哲学，そして宗教に至るまで，さまざまであった。

時がたつにつれ，公教育の発展という点において，宗教が特に重要になった。とりわけヨーロッパがそうで，生徒への教え方の大部分を長年宗教が支配していた。中世盛期の11〜13世紀には，多くの学校が宗教的な教えに基づいて設立され，主に聖職者たちの教育に役立てられていた。当時，聖職者は最高の教育を受けた社会構成員であったので，聖堂学校がオックスフォード大学，ナポリ大学，ボローニャ大学といったヨーロッ

パ初の大学へとつながったのは，おそらく驚くべきことではない。

このような大学は，より高度な教育の開発において非常に重要だったが，実際には先進的な学問的機会を提供する最初の機関というわけではなかった。アカデメイアは，紀元前387年ごろにプラトンが設立した学園だが，より高度な教育を授けるための初めての学校であると主張できるのはこの学校であり，その名は academic（学究的な）と academia（学究的な生活）という英単語の語源にもなっている。古代アテネの城壁の外にあったことから，アカデメイアでの教育は，卓越した哲学者や数学者らによる非公式の集まりとして始まり，アリストテレスのような生徒たちの学びの場として徐々に定着していった。アカデメイアはおそらく，その学問的な水準だけでなく，その排他性においても，歴史を通して大学に影響を与えた。授業料は，少なくともプラトンの時代は徴収していなかったと思われていたが，メンバーになれたのは特権階級だけで，多くの人が感じていることだが，それは現代の世界中のエリート大学の特徴として続いているのである。

(29) 解答 **3**

「昔の形態の教育の裏に存在した主な原動力は何か」
1 コミュニティー間で話を伝承していくことが地域文化を守る唯一の方法だった。
2 成人は自然の中で標識やシンボルを書き写すことで読み書きができるようになり，それがコミュニティーの結びつきを生み出すために使われた。
3 原始的なコミュニティーが生き抜けるかどうかは，重要な知識を世代をまたいで理解することに成功するかどうかにかかっていた。
4 昔の社会はほとんど遊牧社会だったので，どんな形態の教育であろうとニーズは一切なかった。

解説 初期の教育については，第1段落に有史以前の教育について説明がある。第2文には「主として教

とは，大人が子供に社会を養ったり守ったりするのに必要な技術と知識を伝えることであった」とあり，同段落最終文には「そのような技術と知識は，ある世代から次の世代へと口頭で受け継がれた」とある。この内容に一致する**3**が正解。

(30) 解答 **1**

「文化がますます安定し，進化していくことにより，教育の発展にはどのような影響があったか」

1 社会のニーズが，それぞれの社会が導入し，育んだ教育制度の発展に反映されていた。

2 社会構造が進化するにつれ，教育機関を求める声は弱まっていった。

3 先進社会の発展は，知識と技術を従来どおり口頭伝承していくことに執着したため，阻害された。

4 安定したコミュニティーは裕福な人々の領分のままであり，教育を重要で欠かせないものと見る向きはなかった。

解説 進んだ文化と教育の関係については，第2段落に説明がある。同段落最終文の「社会が落ち着くと親の教育も子供の教育も各社会の文化とニーズを映し出すようになった」という内容に合う**1**が正解。

(31) 解答 **4**

「現代の大学はどのような点で最初の教育機関と似ていると言われているか」

1 神学的な考えと研究は，世界中の至る所にある，高等教育を施す大多数の大学で優先されたままである。

2 学校や大学の構造や体制は，何千年もおおむね変わらずにきた。

3 学生の選考方法は，昔の哲学者が作り出した非公式の選考基準にいまだに基づいている。

4 高等教育機関が古くから繰り返してきたように社会の上流階級を相手にする傾向がある。

解説 初めての大学と現代の大学の共通点については，最終段落で述べられている。最後の2文では，大学は昔から排他的で，プラトンの時代でも特権階級にしか門戸が開かれていなかったと説明した後，「それは現代の世界中のエリート大学の特徴として続いているのだ」と述べている。この内容に合う**4**が正解。

全訳
患者中心の医薬品開発

　医薬品，遺伝学，分子生物学の最新の発見については議論されているにもかかわらず，それらを内科的治療に転換するための重大な障害はいまだに存在している。そうした障害のいくつかは技術的な問題である。最も心弾むような発見にとってさえ，実践上の用途を見つけるためには時間と金の莫大な投資が必要となる。しかし，そのほかの障害は，研究そのものを取り巻く法的，哲学的問題である。1960年代以来，新しい薬剤と治療法の開発・検査における最重要事項は，安全性だ。取締機関と製薬工業協会が定めた基準は，有害が疑われる副作用を特定し，記録し，研究する方法を極めて詳細に説明している。調査中の薬物が危険だという証拠により臨床試験を中止する簡単な方法がある。それに加えて，連続使用の副作用が現れるには何年もかかるだろうという前提のもと，長期間の使用を検査する必要条件は非常に厳しくなった。

　この考え方は1957年の鎮痛剤サリドマイドの発売に続く出来事に端を発する。当時の西ドイツで開発され，発売されたサリドマイドは，鎮静・沈静効果があるだけではなく，吐き気を軽減した。そのため，つわりで苦しむ妊婦のための理想的な薬剤と考えられ，処方箋がなくても店頭で入手できたこともあり，たちまち大当たりした。妊娠が臨月に差しかかるまで誰にもわからなかったのは，サリドマイドが先天性異常を引き起こすことだった。最も多いのは腕や脚の奇形だったが，神経，心臓，肺の発達途絶なども引き起こした。主にヨーロッパ全土でおよそ1万人の赤ちゃんが影響を受けた。その半数が幼少期に亡くなった。生化学および薬学研究が高度に進んだ先進国で，なぜこのような悲劇が起こり得たのだろう。当時，科学者たちは，胎盤関門が母親の血流から胎児へと薬剤が流れるのを防ぐと考えていた。それゆえ，母親が飲んだ薬が赤ちゃんに害を与えるリスクはほとんど知られておらず，新物質が妊娠中や妊娠後に与える影響を検査することは慣例となっていなかった。サリドマイドはげっ歯動物でテストされ，市販できると断言されたのだ。

　1960年に米国の製造販売業者が食品医薬品局（FDA）に申請するころには，安全に対する懸念が非常に高まっていたためサリドマイドは西ドイツではもはや市販されておらず，生物学者で審査官のフランシス・オールドハム・ケルシーはさらなる検査をせずに販売を認めることを拒否した。それに続く調査がサリドマイドと出生異常の関連性を決定的に証明し，彼女の懸念の正当性が立証され，報道は臨床試験におけるより厳しい安全要件を求める動きを加速させた。1962年，米国議会が満場一致で連邦食品・医薬品・化粧品法にキーフォーバー・ハリス医薬品改正法を通し，これらの懸念が法律になった。キーフォーバー・ハリス（医薬品改正）法は医薬品製造会社に，効能だけでなく，

安全性についても証明を提出することを要求した。そこにはさらに，潜在的副作用を開示すること，臨床試験に参加する患者はそれに伴うリスクを知らされた後に正式に承諾すること，という新たな要件もあった。

　当時の医学研究の状況を考えると，これらの規則を前向きな動きと見なさないわけにはいかない。米国で20人未満の赤ちゃんがサリドマイド関連の出生異常を伴って生まれた。商業的に売り出されることはなかったが，FDAの認可を求めて大規模に試験されていたのだ。数十年たっての懸念は，科学が進歩しているのに，臨床試験を管理する実務が伴っていないということだ。研究者たちは，特にがんや自己免疫疾患などの終末期疾患に取り組む可能な限りの方法を多様で特異的な経路から開発している。しかし，ピーター・ヒューバーが『The Cure in the Code』の中で書いたように，「従来，薬の効き目を証明するのにワシントンが要求した研究は，疾病の一般的な進行より先に完了することはできない」。新しい治療がなく生命の危機に直面している患者にとっては，重大な副作用さえ重要度が低いが，現在の規則や臨床試験は勝手に彼らを譲歩させている。さらに，症状が極めて重い患者に，一度に数種類の薬剤の「カクテル」を投与することがますます一般的になってきている。このため，混ぜ合わせた中の1つの薬の効果を決めることは非常に難しい。最後に，臨床試験に要する高度に管理された安全性試験は高価で，希少疾患の治療アイデアを持つ革新者が新しい治療法を認可してもらおうとしても，そのプロセスを通すための資金援助先を見つけるのは極めて困難だということになる。

　効果的な新しい治療法を市場に出す真に進んだシステムとはどのようなものだろう。州レベルでの「試す権利」法を支持する意見もある。それなら，厳しいインフォームド・コンセント規則が実施される限り，FDAが連邦政府の認可を出す前に患者が研究中の薬剤を服用することが合法になる。末期あるいは極めて重い病気の患者の臨床治療への申請基準緩和を支持する意見もある。マーク・ジョフは逆説的にではあるが，サリドマイドの例が彼らの主張の根拠となると述べる。「1964年に，イスラエルの医師が極度の痛みに苦しむハンセン病患者にサリドマイドの錠剤を投与した。その投薬治療のおかげで患者は眠ることができたばかりか症状も改善した。やがてサリドマイドはハンセン病の一般的治療になり，後にはエイズやがんにも有効であることがわかった」。

(32) 解答 **3**

「文章の著者は取締機関と製薬工業協会が定めた基準について正しいのはどれだと述べているか」

1 新しい医学療法への研究をとりまく法的，哲学的議論に基づいて，中立であるよう計画されている。

2 新しい複雑な治療を患者が利用できるよう障害のいくつかを取り除く。

3 すぐに起こる副作用と，時を経て起こるものの両方を見つけることを意図している。

4 安全性を強調しているにもかかわらず，米国内に深刻な問題を引き起こす深刻な副作用を防ぐことができなかった。

解説 取締機関と製薬工業協会が定めた基準については，第1段落で述べられている。調査中の薬物が危険な場合，臨床試験を中止することができることに加え，長期間の使用を検査する必要条件が厳しくなったという説明から，この内容に一致する**3**が正解。

(33) 解答 **4**

「フランシス・オールドハム・ケルシーは…科学者の例である」

1 サリドマイドが出生異常を引き起こしたことや，そのほかの副作用もそれに関連していることを確かめる検査を行った

2 臨床試験実施を管理する新しい法律を作るために米国議会で働いた

3 げっ歯類動物を使わずに新しい薬剤製品を検査する方法を開発した

4 新しい治療は一般に売ることが認められる前に厳しく検査されるべきだと信じる

解説 フランシス・オールドハム・ケルシーについては，第3段落に説明がある。サリドマイドの安全に対する懸念が高まっていた1960年当時，さらなる検査をせずに販売を認めることを拒否した，と述べている。この内容に合う**4**が正解。

(34) 解答 **3**

「ピーター・ヒューバーは，臨床試験のための従来の必要条件は…と考えている」

1 患者を助ける薬剤の組み合わせについて，利用できる最良の情報を医師が有することを保証する

2 認可前に安全性試験をあまり要求されない革新的治療を開発するよう科学者を刺激した

3 重病を抱える患者が，治療が価値あるものかどうかを自分で決定することを阻む

4 サリドマイドと同じくらい危険な可能性のある最近

の薬剤から国民を安全に守っていない

解説 ピーター・ヒューバーについての記述は，第4段落にある。著書の中で，「従来，薬の効き目を証明するのにワシントンが要求した研究は，疾病の一般的な進行より先に完了することはできない」と述べているところから，この内容に合う**3**が正解。

(35) 解答 2

「マーク・ジョフがハンセン病患者を引用して明らかにしたことは何か」

1 サリドマイドのさらに悪い副作用が，何年も使用が禁止された以後も見つかり続けた。

2 薬剤は，大多数の患者にとって使用が危険すぎるとしても，ある患者にとっては有益になり得る。

3 重病の患者は，どの治療法が自分たちの症状を最も緩和するかを判断するのに適格とは言えない。

4 さまざまな経路で重病に取り組むことは，通常，患者を治療する最も有効な方法である。

解説 ハンセン病患者の例については，最終段落に述べられている。痛みに苦しむハンセン病患者にサリドマイド錠剤を投与したところ，眠れたばかりか症状も改善した。また後にはエイズやがんにも有効であるとわかった，とある。この内容に合う**2**が正解。

4

問題文の訳

　20世紀にさまざまなアメリカ先住民族は，カジノの経営を始めたり，彼らの居留地で金やその他の大量の資源の埋蔵物が発見されたりしたことで，非常に裕福になった。長年の間，ある一定の部族は強欲さが原因で「除籍」と呼ばれるプロセスを利用し，多数の部族民を追放していたという主張がなされていた。批判的な人たちの主張によれば，そのような部族が部族民を除籍していた理由は，ギャンブルや鉱物資源といったものから得られる収入が部族民に平等に分配されているためで，部族民の数を減らすことは，残った部族民ひとりひとりの富の取り分が大きくなることを意味していた。

　除籍は，いわゆる「ブラッド・クオンタム」（血の量）に基づいて実行されることが多い。多くの部族の規則によれば，もしアメリカ先住民が非先住民と結婚した場合，その子どもたちは部族民としての地位を失うリスクがある。例えばナバホ族は「ナバホ族の血」が25％未満の者が部族民になることを認めていない。しかしながら時には，裏付けとなる書類が損傷していたりなくなっていたりすると，部族にとどまるのに十分な先住民の祖先がいることを部族民が証明するのが困難なこともありうる。

　除籍された部族民は，部族によって提供される住宅補助や医療，奨学金を含む多様なメリットを享受できなくなる。加えて，除籍された部族民がそれでもなお自分自身を部族の一員だと考えているとしても，文化的アイデンティティを失うリスクがあるし，さらにずっと知り合いだったかもしれない友人や近隣の人々と切り離されたあとに社会的に孤立していると感じるようになることも多い。非先住民は彼らのことをアメリカ先住民と見なすかもしれず，そのせいで彼らは人種差別に直面することもある。同時に，今も部族に属している他のアメリカ先住民にはある支援の仕組みや共同体意識を彼らは欠いてしまうのだ。

解答例

　There has been criticism that some Native American tribes are exploiting a process called disenrollment to reduce the number of tribal memberships so that the remaining members can have a greater proportion of wealth from revenue sources. The targets of this process are often Native Americans of mixed race, who often lack documentation to support their Native American status. Disenrolled people not only

解答例の訳

　一部のアメリカ先住民族が部族民の数を減らし，残った者たちが収入源からより多くの取り分を得られるようにするため，除籍と呼ばれるプロセスを不当に利用しているという批判がある。このプロセスのターゲットは，2つ以上の人種の血を受け継いでいるアメリカ先住民であることが多く，彼らはアメリカ先住民の地位を裏付ける書類を持っていないことがしばしばある。除籍された人々は経済的なメリットを失うだけではなく，自分がいまだに一員であると感じている部

lose economic benefits but can also lose cultural and social connections to the tribe that they still feel they are a part of. On top of that, they also have a difficult time becoming accepted into non-Native society. (101語)

族との文化的・社会的つながりも失いかねない。それに加えて，彼らは非先住民の社会に受け入れてもらうことにも苦労するのだ。

解説 トピックは第1段落第2文 Over the years, there were assertions being made that greed was causing certain tribes to use a process called "disenrollment" to expel large numbers of their members. より「部族による除籍の利用」だとわかる。各段落の要旨は，第1段落：先住民族の間で，分配される富の取り分を増やすために，除籍を利用した部族民の追放が行われてきた。第2段落：除籍は「血の量」に基づいて行われ，一定量に満たないと除籍されるのだが，書類の紛失などにより部族にとどまる資格があることを示すことができないこともある。第3段落：除籍されると部族にいることで得られたメリットや，文化的アイデンティティを失い，社会的に孤立し，非先住民からは差別されることもある。解答の際はこれらを問題文とは異なる表現に言い換えてまとめる。なお，第1段落のカジノや埋蔵物といった具体的な収入源の話，第2段落の「ナバホ族の血」の話，第3段落の住宅補助や医療，奨学金の話はいずれも具体例なので解答に含める必要はない。ただし，具体例は一律に排除するのではなく，それ自体が重要な情報を内包していることもあるし，語数調整に使える場合もあるので，その内容をきちんと把握しておくことが大切である。解答例では，第1段落の，先住民族が部族民を減らすために除籍を利用していることについて some Native American tribes are exploiting a process called disenrollment to reduce the number of tribal memberships と表現している。exploit「～を不当に利用する」を使うことで，批判的な内容を上手に伝えている。また，第3段落の，除籍された人たちが部族にいたメリットや文化的アイデンティティを失って社会的に孤立してしまうことについては，not only ～ but also ... を用いて Disenrolled people not only lose economic benefits but can also lose cultural and social connections to the tribe とわかりやすくまとめている。

5

問題の訳
TOPIC：延命医療は奨励されるべきか。

解答例①

Life-prolonging treatment, which is basically aimed at helping patients with a small chance of full recovery live longer, should not be encouraged. The three factors related to my position are the patients' true wishes, the strain on the family, and the patients' control over their lives.

Patients in this situation are required to undergo long-term, stressful treatment. Some of them who cannot breathe for themselves are put on artificial respirators and administered intravenous drips while lying in bed, which restricts them from moving freely. This situation is too painful for them to endure.

解答例①の訳

延命医療とは，完全な回復があまり見込めない患者が長生きする一助となることを基本的な目的としていますが，奨励されるべきではありません。私の立場に関連する3つの要因があります。患者が本当に望むこと，家族への負担，そして自分の命について患者が判断して決めることです。

このような境遇にいる患者は，長期に及ぶストレスの多い治療を受ける必要があります。自分では呼吸できない患者の中には，人工呼吸器を装着され，ベッドに横になりながら点滴を投与されている人もいます。そのせいで自由に動くことが制限されます。この状況は，患者にとってあまりにも過酷で耐え難いものです。

その一方で，患者の家族もまた2つの苦しみに耐えないといけません。精神的な苦痛と経済的な負担です。

On the other hand, the patients' families also must bear two kinds of pain: mental and financial. Mentally, they have the burden of having to watch their family members' condition slowly deteriorate with time. Financially, long-term treatment forces the families to pay for expensive medical care.

Finally, patients must face a reality in which they start to lose control over their lives. In many cases, they become too ill to make decisions about their own treatment, which means their families may have to make choices that may not accurately reflect the true wishes of the patients.

Therefore, it is essential for patients and their families to understand how life-prolonging treatment can impact their lives. Unless these things are considered carefully, it is inappropriate to encourage this kind of treatment. （222語）

精神的には，家族の状態が時間とともにゆっくり悪化していくのを見守っていなければならないという負担がのしかかります。経済的には，長期の治療によって家族は高額の医療費を支払わなければなりません。

最後に，患者は，自分の命が自分の思い通りにならなくなっているのだ，という現実を直視しなければなりません。多くの場合，患者の病状がひどいため，治療について自分で決定することができません。つまり，患者が本当に望むことを正確には反映していないかもしれなくても，家族が選択を迫られることがあり得るということです。

以上の理由から，患者とその家族にとって，延命治療が患者の生涯にどう影響するのかを理解することが不可欠です。こうしたことを慎重に考えないのならば，延命治療のような治療を奨励することは適当ではありません。

解説 序論では，トピックに対して反対の立場を表明し，それには「患者が本当に望むこと」，「家族への負担」，「患者自身による命のコントロール」という3つの要因がかかわると述べている。本論にあたる第2〜4段落では，3つの要因について詳しく述べ，反対理由を説明している。患者と家族のそれぞれの立場から延命治療について説明することで情報が整理され，問題点が明確に伝わる内容になっている。最終段落では全体のまとめとして結論を述べている。単に第1段落の内容を言い換えるのではなく，it is essential for patients and their families to understand how life-prolonging treatment can impact their lives と延命治療問題の要点に言及することで，主張に一層の厚みを持たせている。

解答例②

Life-prolonging treatment is not always given to patients in serious condition, but it must be encouraged. Society as a whole needs to deeply consider increasing hospital resources, prioritizing patients' needs, and improving the quality of healthcare.

First of all, from a moral standpoint, if the means of preserving the lives of patients is at all possible, doctors must treat them. Such an effort would require a lot of resources. Increased funding frees hospitals from having to prioritize certain medical cases over others, allowing them to value the lives of all patients.

Since lifesaving medical procedures are amongst the riskiest, it is understandable that doctors may gradually become pragmatic about the advice they give to terminally ill patients. For example, if they believe patients

解答例②の訳

延命治療は必ずしも重病の患者に施されてはいませんが，促されるべきです。社会全体で，病院の資金を増やすこと，患者のニーズを優先すること，そして医療の質を向上させることについて深く考える必要があります。

まず，倫理的な観点から見て，患者の命を守る手段が多少でもあるのならば，医師は患者を治療しなければなりません。そのような努力のためには，たくさんの資金が必要となるでしょう。資金を増やせば，病院はある患者を別の患者より優先させる必要がなくなり，すべての患者の命を大切にできるのです。

命を救うために行う医療処置は，最もリスクのある行為に数えられます。よって，医師が末期患者に与えるアドバイスにおいて徐々に実利的になるかもしれないことは，理解できます。例えば，もし患者が医療ミスや誤った管理のことで後に病院を訴えるかもしれないと思えば，医師は病院の法的責任を減らすため，治療の早期終了を勧めることで先手を打つかもしれませ

might later sue hospitals for any perceived malpractice or mismanagement, they may act first by recommending ending treatment early to lessen hospital liability. However, doing so would instead compromise their real obligation to respect patients' wishes.

Finally, a greater attempt is needed in improving research and care to reduce any debilitating side effects that may impact a patient's quality of life after complex treatments. Extending life in a way that is beneficial to the patient is the ethically correct approach.

In sum, patients' lives are needlessly ended early. Only by having the highest of standards when it comes to healthcare for the terminally ill can society prove itself to be truly humane.

(235語)

ん。しかしむしろ，そのような行為は患者の意思を尊重するという医師本来の義務を踏みにじることになるでしょう。

最後に，もっと努力して研究と医療ケアを進歩させ，患者を衰弱させるような副作用を減らしていく必要があります。これらの副作用は複雑な治療を受けた患者の暮らしに影響を与えかねません。患者にとってメリットのある方法で延命することが，倫理的に正しい方法です。

まとめると，患者の命は不必要に早期に終わらせられています。終末患者の医療について最高の水準を設ける場合にのみ，社会が真に人道的であると証明されるのです。

Day
1

解説 序論では，トピックに対して賛成の立場を表明し，検討すべき事項として，「病院の資金増」，「患者のニーズを優先すること」，「医療の質の向上」の3点を挙げている。本論ではこの検討事項に沿って自分の考えを詳しく説明している。3つの理由については，倫理的な観点から，「医師の責任」（第2段落），「患者の意思の尊重」（第3段落），「終末患者治療のあるべき姿」（第4段落）を挙げている。最後の段落は結論部だが，いったん patients' lives are needlessly ended early と言ってから自分の考えを述べることで，自分の立場の正当性を読み手に強く訴える内容になっている。

リスニングテスト
解答と解説

問題編 p.24〜30

リスニング

Part 1	問題	*1*	*2*	*3*	*4*	*5*	*6*	*7*	*8*	*9*	*10*
	解答	2	3	3	4	2	1	1	1	1	4

Part 2	問題	*11*	*12*	*13*	*14*	*15*	*16*	*17*	*18*	*19*	*20*
	解答	3	2	2	4	4	2	3	2	1	3

Part 3	問題	*21*	*22*	*23*	*24*	*25*
	解答	4	4	2	2	4

Part 4	問題	*26*	*27*
	解答	1	1

Part 1 🔊 001〜011

No. 1 解答 **2**

★：Excuse me, ma'am. I'd like to open a checking account here and make a $30,000 deposit. Please tell me what to do.

☆：Just fill out this form. With that amount, you may want to put part of it into a certificate of deposit. It'll give you a much higher interest rate.

★：I see. That's a kind of savings account, right?

☆：That's correct, but you leave the money in the account for a set period of time, from three months up to several years. You shouldn't take it out until it matures, or there will be a penalty.

★：OK, then I'll put $20,000 into one of those and the remaining $10,000 into a checking account.

Question：What does the woman recommend the man do?

★：すみません。こちらに当座預金口座を開設して3万ドル預金したいのです。どうしたらいいか教えてください。

☆：この用紙に必要事項を記入してください。それだけお預けになるのでしたら，一部は譲渡性預金にされてはどうですか。金利がずっと高くなります。

★：そうですか。それは普通預金口座の一種ですよね？

☆：そうですが，一定期間，3カ月から数年間ですが，お金を口座に入れたままになります。満期になるまでは引き出さない方がいいです。違約金が発生しますから。

★：わかりました，では2万ドルを譲渡性預金にして，残りの1万ドルを当座預金にします。

質問：女性は，男性にどうすることを勧めているか。

1 今は単なる当座預金口座を開設する。

2 利回りがよりよい口座にお金の一部を預ける。

3 利回りのよい当座預金口座を検討する。

4 現在持っている口座が満期になってから変更する。

解説　女性はその発言の中で，「譲渡性預金に一部を入れること」，「譲渡性預金を開設したら引き出さないこと」を助言している。a much higher interest rate を a higher-yield account と言い換えている **2** が正解。checking account「当座預金口座」，certificate of deposit「譲渡性預金」，savings account「普通預金口座」。

No. 2　解答　3

●：Why do you need a raise, Alice? Can't you get by on your current salary?

☆：It's not that. Everyone except me got a 10 percent increase, which seems unfair, especially since I have more experience than anyone else.

●：And because of your experience, you've always received the highest remuneration among all the staff. Moreover, everyone's wage is based on what they bring into the company, and you're not invoicing enough to justify an increase at this time.

☆：That's because I spend half my time training everyone else. Just ask them. My true contribution is double what I invoice clients.

Question：What would it take to satisfy Alice?

●：なぜ昇給が必要なんだい，アリス。今の給料ではやっていけないの？

☆：そうではないんです。私以外の全員は10％の昇給があって，それは不公平だと思います。特に私はほかの誰より経験があるんですから。

●：そしてその経験があるから，君はいつも全スタッフの中で一番高い報酬を得てきたんじゃないか。それに，全員の賃金は会社にどれだけ利益をもたらしているかに基づくわけで，今の時点で君は昇給を正当化するほど請求書を送っていないよ。

☆：それは，私がほかのみんなの指導に時間の半分を使っているからです。みんなに聞いてください。私の本当の貢献度は，クライアントに送る請求額の倍はあります。

質問：アリスを満足させるには何が必要か。

1 彼女のスタッフの研修の向上。　　　　**2** ほかのみんなと同じ給料。
3 10％の昇給。　　　　　　　　　　　**4** かなりの昇進。

解説　女性は不満を訴えている。その内容は Everyone except me got a 10 percent increase, which seems unfair から，自分だけ10％の昇給がないことが不満の原因だとわかる。**3**が正解。invoice は「〜に請求書を起こす，送る」という意味で，ここでは「売上を出す，成績を上げる」ことを示唆している。

No. 3　解答　3

★：I spoke to Michael yesterday, and he tells me that Stella blew up at him again because he arrived at work a few minutes late. His train was delayed, so it really wasn't his fault.

☆：I'm not surprised. Everybody's been walking on eggshells around her. Even a minor issue can set her off.

★：Well, Michael says he can't work with her anymore, so he's avoiding her.

☆：We need to tell the manager about this. It's getting to the point that her disposition is affecting our work.

★：I agree. We all have our disagreements sometimes, but the way she handles them is just not professional.

Question：What do the speakers say about Stella?

★：マイケルと昨日話したら，彼が仕事に数分遅刻したら，ステラがまた彼に怒ったと言っていたよ。電車が遅れたから，実際は彼のせいではなかったんだ。

☆：驚かないわね。みんな彼女には細心の注意を払っているわ。どんな些細なことでも彼女を怒らせかねないから。

★：それが，マイケルがもう彼女とは仕事をできないと言っていて，彼女のことを避けているんだ。

☆：この件はマネージャーに伝えた方がいいわね。彼女の気質が私たちの仕事に悪い影響を与え始めているわ。

★：同感だよ。みんな時には意見が合わないこともあるけれど，そうなったときの彼女の対応はプロらしくないね。

質問：話者はステラについて何と言っているか。

1 彼女はよく仕事に遅刻する。　　　　**2** その問題で彼女は悪くない。
3 彼女は短気だ。　　　　　　　　　　**4** 彼女は仕事を終わらせていない。

解説　男性も女性もステラのことをよく思っていない。その理由は男性の最初の発言の Stella blew up at him again や女性の最初の発言の Even a minor issue can set her off. から，彼女の怒りっぽい性格にあるとわかる。**3**が正解。

No. 4　解答　4

●：Say, Janice, I've been looking for you. Remember that $100 I lent you the other day? I need it back to pay a few bills, like garbage and a few utilities.

☆：That's right, Ted. But remember, I already paid you back 40 last week.

●：Oh, you're right. So you just owe me 60, then.

☆：If you have a few minutes now, we can stop at the ATM down the street and I'll get it for you.

●：That would be great, Janice. I hate to bother you about it now but I'm completely broke myself this week.

Question：What will most likely happen next?

●：ジャニス，ちょっと。君を探していたんだ。先日貸した100ドルのこと覚えている？　いくつか請求書の支払いをするのに，それを返してもらわないといけないんだ。ごみの収集や公共料金とかね。

☆：そうだったわね，テッド。でも思い出して，先週すでに40ドル返したわよ。

●：ああ，そうだね。ということは，君に貸しているのは60ドルだ。

☆：今ちょっと時間があるなら，この先のATMに一緒に寄ってもらえれば，お金をおろすわ。

●：それは助かるよ，ジャニス。こんなことで今君に迷惑をかけたくはないんだけど，僕も今週は一文無しなんだよ。

質問：次に一番起こりそうなことはどれか。

1 テッドは物を購入する。　　　　　　　　**2** テッドはATMからお金をおろす。
3 ジャニスはテッドの借金を肩代わりする。　**4** ジャニスは借金の残りをテッドに返済する。

解説　これからの具体的な行動について，女性は最後の発言で，If you have a few minutes now, we can stop at the ATM down the street and I'll get it for you. と述べている。I'll get it for you とはここでは「あなたのために60ドルを手にする」，つまり借金を返すということ。**4**が正解。

No. 5　解答　2

☆：Paul, are you going to eat all that?

★：Believe it or not, Nancy, I'm on a diet. Except for carbohydrates and sugars, I can eat anything. There is no limit on fats or proteins.

☆：Really? I'd go crazy without bread, pasta, or fruit.

★：Well, I love this diet. I can eat this whole steak, and still lose weight. I've already lost 20 pounds.

☆：It doesn't sound very healthy. Why not eat a more balanced diet and get some exercise?

★：I've tried the balanced diet thing, and it doesn't work for me. And as for exercise, I started riding my bicycle to work every day.

Question：How does the man feel about his current diet?

☆：ポール，それを全部食べるつもりなの？

★：ナンシー，信じられないだろうけど，僕はダイエット中なんだ。炭水化物と糖類以外なら，何を食べても構わないんだ。脂肪もタンパク質も制限はないんだよ。

☆：本当？　パンやパスタや果物がなかったら，私なら気が変になるわ。

★：まあ，僕はこのダイエットをとても気に入っているんだ。このステーキを丸々食べられて，それでも体重が減るんだからね。もう20ポンド痩せたよ。

☆：それってあまり健康によさそうではないわね。もっとバランスの取れた食事をして，少し運動したらどうなの？

★：バランスのいい食事とやらは試してみたけど，僕には向かないんだよ。運動はというと，毎日自転車で通勤し始めたよ。

質問：男性は現在の自分のダイエットについてどう思っているか。

1 バランスが取れていないことを心配している。　**2** 大変うまくいっていると思っている。
3 気に入ってはいるが，空腹なことが多い。　　　　**4** あまり効果的ではないと思っている。

解説 男性はダイエットについて「とても気に入っている」と言っており，ステーキを食べても構わないのに，すでに20ポンド（10キロ弱）体重が減ったことを満足げに話している。**2**が正解。

No. 6　解答　**1**

☆：Have a good weekend, Ryan. You have plans?

●：Yeah, I have two tests and a presentation next week, so I'll spend the weekend preparing. I also have my part-time job on Saturday. I need to work to pay for expenses.

☆：Well, I hope you can at least rest up a little on Sunday to be in shape for the hectic week ahead.

●：I wish I could. No rest for the weary.

☆：If you don't unwind, you'll end up collapsing like my sister. She had to drop out of college.

●：I know, but I really don't see any chance for slowing down in the near future.

Question：What does the woman say the man should do?

☆：良い週末を，ライアン。何か予定はあるの？

●：うん，来週テストが2つとプレゼンが1つあるから，週末はその準備をするつもりなんだ。土曜日にはアルバイトもある。いろんな費用の支払いのために働かないといけないんだ。

☆：そう，日曜日に少しは休息をとって，これから先のとても忙しい週を体調を崩さずにすごせるといいわね。

●：そうできればいいんだけどなあ。疲れていても休んでいる暇はないんだ。

☆：リラックスしないと，私の姉みたいに倒れてしまうわ。彼女は大学をやめないといけなかったんだから。

●：わかっているけど，当面は落ち着く見込みが本当にないんだ。

質問：女性は男性にどうするべきだと言っているか。

1 元気になるために少し休む時間をとる。　　**2** 今週末にプレゼンの準備をする。
3 お金を稼ぐためにアルバイトをする。　　**4** 女性の姉に男性の経験について話す。

解説 女性の I hope you can at least rest up a little on Sunday to be in shape for the hectic week ahead という発言と，If you don't unwind, you'll end up collapsing like my sister. という発言は内容的に同じことで，しっかり休みなさいということ。**1**が正解。recuperate「回復する」。

No. 7　解答　**1**

●：Boy, Sarah! Today is sure to be a scorcher.

☆：You're telling me! It's only 9:00 in the morning, and it's already almost 30 degrees.

●：Personally, I don't see it happening, but the weather forecast said it might rain this afternoon. That might help.

☆：Let's hope so, Jim.

Question：What does Jim imply about the weather?

●：うわ，サラ！　今日は間違いなく猛暑になるよ。

☆：全くそのとおりね！　まだ朝の9時だというのに，もう30度近くあるんだから。

●：個人的にはそんな感じはしないんだけれど，天気予報によると，今日の午後は雨が降るかもしれないんだって。それだと助かるな。

☆：降るように願いましょう，ジム。

質問：ジムは天気について何を示唆しているか。

1 涼しくなればいいのにと願っている。　　**2** 後で雨が降るだろうと思っている。
3 暑い天気が好きだ。　　**4** 雨は降ってほしくない。

解説 男性の発言にある scorcher は「猛暑日」という意味。男性は雨が降るという天気予報について触れ，That might help. と言っているのだから，**1**が正解。雨が降るというのは男性自身の予測ではなく，むしろ「そんな感じはしない」と言っているので，**2**は不適。You're telling me.「全くそのとおりだ」。

No. 8 解答 1

☆：Hello. Leigh Stein's phone.

●：Hello. This is Richard Butler from the university. May I speak to Leigh? It's rather urgent.

☆：I'm sorry, Mr. Butler. She's working at the library right now, and she's left her phone. I'll make sure she calls you back when she comes back.

●：Please tell her to call me this afternoon before 4:00 p.m. I'm her graduation thesis advisor. She hasn't submitted her thesis to me yet, and it's due no later than 5:00.

☆：All right, I'll tell her.

Question：What does Richard Butler call Leigh Stein for?

☆：もしもし。これはリー・スタインの電話です。

●：もしもし。大学のリチャード・バトラーです。リーと話せますか。緊急の用件なんです。

☆：すみません，バトラーさん。彼女はちょうど図書館で働いているところで，電話を置いて行ってしまったんです。彼女が帰ったら折り返し電話させるようにします。

●：今日の午後4時までに私に電話するよう伝えてください。私は彼女の卒業論文の指導教官です。彼女はまだ私に論文を提出していなくて，それを5時に間に合うように提出しないといけないのです。

☆：わかりました，伝えます。

質問：リチャード・バトラーは何のためにリー・スタインに電話したのか。

1 彼女に直ちに卒業論文を提出するよう命じるため。
2 自分が卒業論文の指導教官になることを彼女に伝えるため。
3 彼女の卒業論文は書き直す必要があると伝えるため。
4 彼女が仕事に行ったかどうか確かめるため。

解説　男性が電話をかけた理由は最後の発言で述べられている。She hasn't submitted her thesis to me yet, and it's due no later than 5:00. から **1** が正解。graduation thesis「卒業論文」。

No. 9 解答 1

☆：We have a request to train Japanese ship captains on how to improve their management of Philippine crew members. It will be a two-day program.

★：What kind of budget are we talking about?

☆：It's pretty decent, enough to bring in an expert or two, perhaps someone from the Philippine Embassy.

★：Did you do a needs analysis?

☆：Not a complete one. They have good English skills according to the test results. The company has two main concerns. One is getting Philippine crew members to look at their work more comprehensively.

★：What do you mean by that?

☆：Well, for example, if a Japanese crew member comes across a rope lying on the deck that shouldn't be there, he'll put it where it belongs. Philippine crew members often think that is not their job. They stick to what's spelled out in their

☆：日本人船長たちへの研修の申し込みがありました。どうすればフィリピン人船員をもっと上手に管理できるのか，についてです。2日間の研修になる予定です。

★：予算についてはどのような話をしているのですか。

☆：なかなかの額で，専門家をおそらくフィリピン大使館から1，2名連れてくるのに十分です。

★：ニーズの分析はしましたか。

☆：完全ではありませんが。テスト結果を見ると，彼らの英語の能力は十分です。クライアント企業には主に2つの懸念があります。1つはフィリピン人船員がもっと包括的に仕事に向き合うようにすることです。

★：それはつまりどういうことですか。

☆：そうですね，例えば日本人船員なら，甲板上でそこにあってはならないロープを見つけた場合，しかるべき場所に戻すでしょう。フィリピン人船員の場合は，それは自分の仕事ではないと考えることが多いのです。契約書に書かれている

contracts.

★：I see. Anything else?

☆：Yes, sometimes Japanese captains have scolded a crew member in front of others, which caused a loss of face. The crew member often holds a grudge after something like that, even when the captain tries to patch things up.

★：So how do they settle a problem like that if someone refuses to talk things out?

☆：I'm not sure. The company hopes that someone in the Philippine Embassy can help answer that. One captain I spoke to said that going through a third party, someone the Philippine crew members like and trust, is the best way.

★：This sounds like an interesting project. Let me know when you'd like me to get started on it.

Question：What is one issue that needs to be addressed in the training?

ことに固執するんです。

★：なるほど。ほかにもありますか。

☆：はい，時々日本人船長はある船員をみんなの前で叱ったのですが，そのせいで面目を失うことになりました。その船員はそのような出来事の後にしばしば恨みを抱くようになっています。船長が関係修復を試みていてもです。

★：でも，物事の解決を拒んでいる人がいる場合，彼らはそのような問題をどのように解決するのですか。

☆：わかりません。クライアント企業は，フィリピン大使館の人がその答えを出す助けになることを願っているのです。私が話をした船長の1人は，フィリピン人船員たちが好意を持っていて信頼している第三者を通じて進めるのが最善の方法ではないかと言っていました。

★：面白そうなプロジェクトですね。取りかかる時期が来たら教えてください。

質問：研修で取り組むべき問題の1つは何か。

1 船長と船員の間のいさかいを解決すること。　　**2** 船員に契約を延長してもらうこと。
3 船員による蛮行を回避すること。　　**4** 船長を研修してもっと責任感を持たせること。

解説 研修の目的については，前半で「フィリピン人船員の管理」と言っており，後半で具体的な内容が述べられる。The crew member often holds a grudge after something like that, even when the captain tries to patch things up. から，船長と船員の関係は穏やかではないことがわかる。さらに 男性の how do they settle a problem like that if someone refuses to talk things out? という質問に，女性が The company hopes that someone in the Philippine Embassy can help answer that. と答えていることから，その問題を解決したいと思っていることもわかる。**1** が正解。

No. 10 　解答　4

★：Hey, look who's here!

☆：Hi, Jack. We've missed you! How's retired life treating you?

●：It's not all it's cracked up to be. I have a lot of free time on my hands, too much in fact. I miss coming in to the office.

★：Have you thought about getting a part-time job?

●：Well, I don't really need the money, but yeah, I sure have.

☆：And what have you found?

●：Not much. The only jobs available are things like bagging groceries or working as a sales clerk. That's not exactly how I want to spend my time.

☆：I would've thought that with your experience, you could do some consulting.

★：ねえ，誰かと思ったら！

☆：こんにちは，ジャック。あなたがいなくて寂しかったわ！　引退後の生活はどう？

●：期待していたほどよくはないね。自由な時間はたくさんあるのだけれど，実際のところ持て余している。通勤が恋しいよ。

★：アルバイトをすることは考えたことある？

●：まあ，お金はそこまで必要ないんだけれど，そうだね，考えたことは確かにあるね。

☆：それで何か見つけたの？

●：あんまり。やらせてもらえる仕事と言えば，食料品の袋詰めか，販売員の仕事しかないんだ。そのようなことに自分の時間を使いたいとは思わないね。

☆：あなたの経験があれば，コンサルティング業務

●：Believe me, I've looked. Most jobs require technology experience, something I'm not strong in.

★：I know. Even I feel too old to keep up with all the recent developments, especially all the apps.

●：You don't suppose there's any chance of me getting some part-time work here, do you?

☆：I certainly wouldn't count on it. In fact, there's talk that we may lay off staff this year or next.

★：I may be out there looking for work with you sooner than I'd like.

☆：Have you thought about doing some volunteer work? There must be a lot of NGOs and such that could use your help.

●：Yeah, I've been leaning that way, unless a paying job turns up soon. Anyway, don't let me keep you from your work. I'll stop by and say hello to Denise before I take off.

★：Good seeing you, Jack. Take care.

Question：What does Jack say about his new life?

ができるのではないかと思っただろうけど。

●：調べたさ，本当に。ほとんどの仕事はテクノロジー分野の経験が必須なんだ。僕があまり強くない分野だよ。

★：そうだね。僕だって最近の発展すべてについていくには年を取りすぎたと感じるよ。中でもあれこれあるアプリにね。

●：僕がここで何かアルバイトの職を得られるチャンスはないかな？

☆：私なら間違いなくそれはあてにしないわ。実際，今年か来年に従業員を解雇するかもしれないという話があるの。

★：僕も，やりたいとも思わないうちからあなたと一緒に仕事探しをすることになるかもしれないよ。

☆：ボランティアの仕事について考えたことはある？　あなたの力を活用できるNGOなどの組織がたくさんあるはずよ。

●：そうだね，そんなふうに気持ちが傾いてきていたんだ。有給の仕事がすぐに見つからないならね。さて，仕事の邪魔をしてはいけないね。帰る前にデニースのところに寄ってあいさつしてくるよ。

★：会えてよかったわ，ジャック。気をつけて。

質問：ジャックは新しい人生について何と言っているか。

1 新しいことを勉強する時間を持てることが気に入っている。
2 人生を楽しむための自由な時間がもっとあればよいのにと思っている。
3 経済的な状況が彼を悩ませている。
4 有意義な仕事に戻りたいと思っている。

解説　会話の中心的な話題はこれからのジャックの仕事について。ジャックは The only jobs available are things like bagging groceries or working as a sales clerk. と現状を説明した後，That's not exactly how I want to spend my time. と述べているので，どんな仕事でもいいわけではないことがわかる。それを meaningful を使って表している **4** が正解。I don't really need the money と言っているので **3** は誤り。

(A)

The Antarctic Treaty

Despite being one of the most inhospitable places on the planet, the Antarctic was the subject of claims of sovereignty from numerous countries throughout the twentieth century. Governments from countries like the United Kingdom, Norway, France and Argentina created bases and claimed territorial space around them, although many of these claims overlapped, which raised the unpleasant prospect of conflict. While the majority of the bases were created ostensibly in the name of scientific research, the continent is recognized as a strategic military location and could be home to vast natural resources which could be exploited for commercial gain.

In order to protect the region and prevent claims of sovereignty leading to military conflict, the Antarctic Treaty was signed in 1959, and entered into force in 1961. Signed by the original twelve countries that were active in the region during the International Geophysical Year of 1957 to 1958, the treaty now has 53 signatories. As a major instrument of international law, it provides, amongst other things, that Antarctica "shall be used for peaceful purposes only." Rare in its scope and objectives, the treaty allows signatories to both claim territory for themselves and to deny claims by other signatories at the same time, thereby maintaining the status quo and protecting this important natural environment.

Questions

No.11 What is one reason countries might be interested in claiming territory in Antarctica?

No.12 What is true about the signatories to the Antarctic Treaty?

南極条約

南極は地球上で最も不毛な土地の1つであるにもかかわらず，20世紀を通してこの土地に対して数々の国が主権を主張した。英国やノルウェー，フランス，アルゼンチンといった国々の政府が基地を設け，その周囲の領有権を主張したが，多くの主張内容が重複しており，衝突という好ましくない面を引き起こした。多数の基地は表向きには科学調査という名目で設けられたが，この大陸は戦略的な軍事拠点と考えられており，営利目的で開発可能な天然資源が膨大に存在する可能性があった。

この地域を保護し，主権の主張が軍事衝突に発展するのを防ぐため，南極条約が1959年に採択され，1961年に発効した。採択したのは，国際地球観測年（1957～1958年）に最初から参加していた12カ国で，現在の条約加盟国数は53に上る。国際法の主要な協定の1つとして，南極条約はさまざまなことを規定しているが，そのうちの1つは，南極は「その利用は平和目的に限定される」というものである。この条約の範囲と目的はほかにあまり例がないのだが，加盟国は自国のために領有権を主張できると同時に，ほかの加盟国の領有権を否定できる。そのおかげで現状が維持され，この重要な自然環境が保護されるのだ。

No. 11 解答 3

「国家が南極の領有権を主張することに興味を示しかねない理由の1つは何か」

1 欧州諸国のための共通拠点を設けるため。　　**2** 戦略上重要な領土に行けるようにするため。

3 天然資源から恩恵を得るため。　　**4** 主権の主張を避けるため。

解説　多くの国が南極の主権を主張する理由については，the continent is recognized as a strategic military location and could be home to vast natural resources which could be exploited for commercial gain と，2つ挙げられている。2つ目の理由に一致する**3**が正解。

No. 12 解答 2

「南極条約の加盟国について正しいことは何か」

1 全加盟国が軍事協力することで合意した。　　**2** 加盟国は主権の主張を却下することができる。

3 全加盟国が条約を1959年に採択した。　　**4** どの加盟国も主権を主張することは認められていない。

解説　南極条約について後半で詳しく説明されている。その特徴として the treaty allows signatories to both claim territory for themselves and to deny claims by other signatories at the same time という説明があるので，**2** が正解。

(B)

The Bauhaus

The Bauhaus, established in Germany in 1919, was the most influential modernist art school of the 20th century. Founded by Walter Gropius, a pioneer of modernist architecture, the school existed in three cities: Weimar, Dessau and Berlin. Inspired by what they saw as a loss of creativity in manufacturing, the founders sought to redefine art's purpose in society. Although the founder was an architect, as were the two subsequent directors, the Bauhaus had no architecture department in its first years. In fact, architecture wasn't strongly emphasized until Mies van der Rohe became the final director in 1930.

The Bauhaus has influenced the fields of architecture, art, graphic design, industrial design, typography and more. It's hard to believe, therefore, that it was open for only fourteen years. Having been under pressure from the Nazi government who accused it of being "un-German" and a front for communists and social liberals, the Bauhaus closed its doors in 1933. Its legacy and impact are largely due to many of the key figures of the Bauhaus emigrating to the United States following World War II. Walter Gropius taught at Harvard, Mies van der Rohe designed the campus and taught at the Illinois Institute of Technology, and Josef Albers taught at Yale.

Questions

No.13　What is true about the study of architecture at the Bauhaus?

No.14　What reason is suggested for the enduring influence of the Bauhaus?

バウハウス

バウハウスは1919年にドイツで設立され，20世紀で最も影響力のあるモダニズム芸術の学校だった。設立したヴァルター・グロピウスはモダニズム建築のパイオニアで，この学校は3都市に存在した。ヴァイマル，デッサウ，ベルリンである。各学校の創立者たちにインスピレーションを与えたのは，もの作りにおいて彼らが創造力の欠如であると見なしたものであり，社会における芸術の目的を再定義しようとした。設立者は建築家であり，彼に続いた2人の校長もそうであったが，バウハウスは初めの数年は建築学部がなかった。むしろ，建築を強く重視するようになったのは，1930年にミース・ファン・デル・ローエが最後の校長に就任してからであった。

バウハウスは，建築，芸術，グラフィックデザイン，工業デザイン，タイポグラフィをはじめとする多くの分野で影響を与えてきた。従って，開校していたのがわずか14年だったというのは信じがたい。この学校を「非ドイツ的」で共産主義および社会自由主義の代表組織だと糾弾するナチスの圧力にさらされたことで，バウハウスは1933年に閉校した。この学校の遺産と影響力は，バウハウスの多くの重要人物が第二次世界大戦後にアメリカ合衆国に移住したことに帰している。ヴァルター・グロピウスはハーバード大学で教鞭をとり，ミース・ファン・デル・ローエはそのキャンパスを設計し，イリノイ工科大学で教えた。ヨセフ・アルバースはイエール大学で教壇に立った。

No. 13　解答　2

「バウハウスにおける建築学について正しいことは何か」

1 もの作りにおいて創造力を刺激する手段として用いられた。

2 ミース・ファン・デル・ローエが引き継ぐまでほとんど気にされていなかった。

3 設立者を除く全校長が建築家だった。

4 学生たちは5つの異なる都市で学んだ。

解説 前半で述べている architecture wasn't strongly emphasized until Mies van der Rohe became the final director in 1930 に一致する **2** が正解。

No. 14 **解答** **4**

「バウハウスの影響力がいつまでも衰えない理由として何が示唆されているか」

1 そのリベラルな手法が1930年代にドイツの政治を再構築するのに役立った。

2 ナチ党が学校に圧力をかけて大学のキャンパスを設計させた。

3 米国出身の多くの学生がバウハウスに通っていた。

4 多くの職員が戦争後に海外の学校で仕事を続けた。

解説 バウハウスがいつまでも影響力を持っている理由については，後半で Its legacy and impact are largely due to many of the key figures of the Bauhaus emigrating to the United States following World War II. という説明がある。key figures は「重要人物」のこと。これを staff members で言い換えている **4** が正解。

(C)

Pyramids

Pyramids are most commonly associated with Egypt, but they are not unique to that country. In fact, various styles of pyramids were built in areas as diverse as Sudan, Mexico, China, India, and Greece. Pyramids were constructed for various reasons, including for use as tombs and places of worship, and even for human sacrifice. The design itself was chosen for both practical and symbolic reasons. For practicality, the weight distribution in a pyramid, with most of the weight at the bottom, allowed early civilizations to create stable monumental structures using drystone building techniques. This stability has enabled the greatest pyramids to stand for millennia.

For an appreciation and understanding of their symbolism, the Egyptian pyramids are arguably the best place to turn. Pyramids are thought to represent the primordial mound that created the earth according to ancient Egyptian beliefs. Their shape is also reminiscent of the sun's rays. The latter reason is given more credence as the setting sun was considered to be the realm of the dead, and all Egyptian pyramids were built on the west bank of the Nile, where the sun sets. The Great Pyramid in Giza, built over 4,000 years ago, is the only one of the original Seven Wonders of the World still in existence.

Questions

No.15 Why have some pyramids been able to last for thousands of years?

No.16 How is the sun associated with the Egyptian pyramids?

ピラミッド

ピラミッドから最もよく連想されるのはエジプトだが，ピラミッドはエジプト固有のものではない。実際，さまざまな形のピラミッドがスーダン，メキシコ，中国，インド，ギリシャなど広い地域で建設されている。ピラミッドが建設された理由はさまざまであり，墓や礼拝場として使用するため，あるいは人間をいけにえとして差し出すために建てられたものもある。そのデザイン自体は，実用性と象徴性の両面から選ばれた。実用性については，ピラミッドにおける重量の配分は，底部が最も重くなっており，そのおかげで，昔の文明でも安定した巨大構造物を石積みの技術を使って作ることができたのだ。このように安定していることで巨大ピラミッドは何千年もの間，建っていられるのである。

ピラミッドの象徴性を正しく評価・理解する上で，エジプトのそれはおそらく目を向けるのに最適のものである。ピラミッドは，古代エジプトの信仰によると，地球を作り出した原始時代の山を表していると考えられている。また，その形は太陽光を思い出させる。より信頼できるのは，この2つ目の理由の方だ。というのも，沈む太陽は死者の世界であると考えられており，すべてのエジプトのピラミッドは，日が沈むナイル川西岸に建てられているからである。ギザの大ピラミッドは，4,000年以上前に建てられたピラミッドで，世界七不思議のうち唯一現存するものである。

No. 15　解答　4

「なぜ一部のピラミッドは何千年も建っていられるのか」

1 エジプト人が独特の建築方法を考え出したから。

2 それらは，象徴であるという理由，そしていけにえを差し出すという理由で崇拝されたから。

3 それらは多様な文明社会によって建設されたから。

4 その形やデザインのおかげで耐久性が向上したから。

解説　ピラミッドが何千年も建っていられる理由は，the weight distribution in a pyramid, with most of the weight at the bottom, allowed early civilizations to create stable monumental structures ... という説明の後で This stability has enabled the greatest pyramids to stand for millennia. と言っており，その構造が鍵であることがわかる。ピラミッドの構造を The shape and design と言い表している **4** が正解。

No. 16　解答　2

「太陽はどのようにエジプトのピラミッドと結びつけて考えられているか」

1 それは，地球の創造を表していた。　　　　　　**2** それは，ピラミッドの形と設置の両方に影響した。

3 太陽は世界七不思議の1つである。　　　　　　**4** 太陽は古代エジプトでは西から昇るとされていた。

解説　ピラミッドと太陽の関係については，後半に Their shape is also reminiscent of the sun's rays. とあるので，まずピラミッドの形が太陽に関係していることがわかる。続けて，日没が死者と関連づけられていたという説明の後，all Egyptian pyramids were built on the west bank of the Nile, where the sun sets とあることから，ピラミッドは方角も考慮されて建てられたことがわかる。よって **2** が正解。

(D)

Halley's Comet

　　　Although over 5,000 comets have been identified and billions more are thought to exist, arguably the most famous comet is Halley's Comet. Halley's Comet is named after the English astronomer Edmond Halley. In 1705, he was the first person to determine that the comet orbits the sun and calculated how long it would take to complete its orbit. The comet is visible from Earth every 75 or 76 years and recorded sightings date back into antiquity. The comet can be seen without a telescope and was last seen in 1986, meaning it is set to return in 2061.

　　　Halley may have been the first to recognize that the comet that bears his name revolves around the sun, but he was not the first to see it. Indeed, his studies of historical comet sightings led him to conclude that similar accounts of the same comet existed. The first sighting of Halley's is believed to have taken place in China in 239 BC. Perhaps its most famous appearance, however, was shortly before the invasion of England by William the Conqueror in the year 1066. William took this as a sign that he would be successful, and the comet is featured on the Bayeux Tapestry which chronicles the invasion.

Questions

No.17　What did Edmond Halley discover?

No.18　When was Halley's Comet first spotted?

ハレー彗星

　5,000を超える彗星が見つかっており，存在する彗星の数は数十億に上ると考えられているが，おそらく最も有名な彗星はハレー彗星だろう。ハレー彗星は，イギリス人天文学者であるエドモンド・ハレーにちなんで名づけられた。1705年，彼は初めてこの彗星が太陽を周回していることを突き止め，1周するのにどれくらいの時間がかかるのか計算した。ハレー彗星を地球から見ることができるのは75〜76年に1度で，古代の昔にすでに目撃されている記録がある。ハレー彗星は望遠鏡を使わなくても見ることができ，最後に見られたのは1986年のことである。つまり，次に戻ってくるのは2061年ということだ。

　ハレーは，自分の名前を持つ彗星が太陽の周りを回っていることを知った最初の人物だったかもしれない。し

かし，初めて目撃した人物は彼ではない。実際，彼は歴史に残っていた彗星の目撃情報を研究し，同一の彗星について似た報告が存在するとの結論に達した。ハレー彗星が初めて目撃されたのは，紀元前239年の中国においてだと考えられている。しかし，おそらくその出現で最もよく知られているのは，征服王ウィリアムによるイングランド侵攻直前の1066年のことだ。ウィリアムはこれを成功の予兆だと考えた。このときのハレー彗星の姿は，イギリス侵攻を年代順に記録しているバイユーのタペストリーに描かれている。

No. 17 　解答 　3

「エドモンド・ハレーは何を発見したか」

1　5,000個を超える彗星。

2　彗星は望遠鏡なしでも見られること。

3　見つけた彗星が太陽を周回していること。

4　彼の名前を持つ彗星。

解説 　天文学者のハレーについては，he was the first person to determine that the comet orbits the sun という説明があるので3が正解。後半に he was not the first to see it（＝ Halley's Comet）とあることからもわかるとおり，4ではないので注意。

No. 18 　解答 　2

「ハレー彗星が初めて見つけられたのはいつのことか」

1　望遠鏡の発明に続いて。

2　2,000年以上前。

3　イングランド侵攻直前。

4　バイユーのタペストリーが作られたとき。

解説 　初めての目撃情報については，The first sighting of Halley's is believed to have taken place in China in 239 BC. とある。in 239 BC. は現在から見て2,000年以上前なので，2が正解。

(E)

Smartphone Addiction

The invention and development of smartphones has arguably made our lives easier. However, researchers are increasingly beginning to recognize that convenience and connectivity come at a price. It is estimated that around 11 percent of all people in Western countries suffer from technology addiction. The psychological effects of smartphone use can include anxiety and stress. In one study, researchers found that over 80 percent of university students have imagined their phones ringing when they were not. Even more worrying, many people actually experience physical withdrawal symptoms when not using the devices, including increased blood pressure and heart rate.

Sadly, it is not only adults that are at risk. A study by Mott Children's Hospital and Illinois State University in the U.S. looked at how the use of smartphones by parents could affect their children's behavior. They asked parents about technology-related interruptions, which are called "technoference," when communicating with their children. Around half of the parents interviewed said that smartphone use affected possible interaction with their children at least once a day. The study appears to show that technoference may lead to symptoms like hyperactivity and irritability in children. Perhaps it is not surprising, then, that some academics suggest that smartphones should carry health warnings.

Questions

No.19 What have researchers discovered about smartphone addiction?

No.20 How might "technoference" be affecting children?

スマホ中毒

　スマートフォンの発明と発達により，おそらく私たちは生活しやすくなった。しかしながら，研究者たちにとって一層明らかになりつつあるのだが，便利さとつながりやすさは代償を伴う。概算では欧米の全人口の約11％がテクノロジー中毒を患っている。スマートフォンの使用による精神的な影響には，不安やストレスが含まれる。ある研究で研究者たちが発見したことによると，大学生の80％以上は，スマートフォンが実際には鳴っていないの

に鳴っているように感じたことがあった。さらに心配なことに，スマートフォンを使っていないときに実際に体に禁断症状が現れる人も多くいる。その症状には血圧ならびに脈拍数の上昇がある。

　悲しいことに，危険にさらされているのは成人だけではない。アメリカのモット小児病院とイリノイ州立大学は，その共同研究において，親がスマートフォンを使用することで子供の行動にどのような影響が出るかを調べた。研究チームは親にテクノロジーが関係する中断について尋ねた。つまり，子供たちとコミュニケーションをとっている際に起こる，いわゆる「テクノフェアレンス」について質問したのである。面談した親の約半数は，少なくとも1日に1回，子供との触れ合いがスマートフォンの利用に影響されたと答えた。この研究は，テクノフェアレンスは子供の多動やいらいらといった症状につながりかねないことを表しているようだ。となると，一部の研究者らはスマートフォンに健康に関する警告を付けておくべきだと提案しているが，それも驚くようなことではないかもしれない。

No. 19 　解答 1
「スマートフォン中毒について研究者は何を発見したか」
1 身体的症状が現れる人もいる。
2 大学生は影響を受けにくい。
3 中毒症状は誇張されている。
4 スマートフォンの値段がストレスと心配を引き起こし得る。
解説 研究者が発見したスマートフォン中毒の症状については，大学生を対象とした実験の説明の後で，many people actually experience physical withdrawal symptoms when not using the devices, including increased blood pressure and heart rate と述べている。これを言い換えた1が正解。

No. 20 　解答 3
「『テクノフェアレンス』が子供にどのように影響している可能性があるか」
1 子供たちは親を無視する一方で友達との距離を縮めている。
2 製品に書いてある健康に関する警告が子供たちを怖がらせる。
3 子供たちの行動によくない影響を与えることが示されている。
4 そのせいで子供は常に大人の邪魔をしてしまう。
解説 technoference の影響については technoference may lead to symptoms like hyperactivity and irritability in children と説明されている。hyperactivity and irritability を negatively influence their behavior で言い換えている3が正解。

Part 3 　◀))018〜023

(F) No. 21 　解答 4

As you know, we screwed up with our new printer brochures. They contained several inaccuracies, including specifications. We ended up discarding tens of thousands of them, which cost us a small fortune. We need to put some extra preventive measures in place to avoid recurrences. Anyone sending specifications for any product to the marketing department should second check them with the head of their departments, who should then sign off on them. This means department heads take responsibility for their accuracy. After galley proofs are returned to the marketing department from printers, the proofs need to be checked by the engineers in charge of product development. Marketing will assure that the pertinent engineers obtain galleys in a timely manner. These engineers must then assure claims and specifications are accurate and then return the galleys to the marketing department. I know this adds a layer of work, but it needs to be done and done efficiently and quickly.

状況：あなたは企業でマーケティング部長をしている。営業本部長が全社員に次の発表をする。

質問：新方針はあなたの部署に何をするよう求めているか。

ご存じの通り，当社の新型プリンターのパンフレットは使い物になりませんでした。仕様を含め，誤りがいくつもありました。結局，何万枚というパンフレットを処分し，その費用はかなりの金額に上りました。われわれは，再発を防ぐためにさらなる防止策を講じる必要があります。すべての製品について仕様書をマーケティング部に送る際は，各部門長とともに内容をもう一度チェックしてください。部門長はそれから承認の署名をするようにしてください。これはつまり，部門長が正確性について責任を負うということです。校正紙が印刷所からマーケティング部に戻ってきたら，製品開発担当エンジニアが校正紙をチェックしてください。マーケティング部が，該当のエンジニアが適切なタイミングで校正紙を受け取れるようにします。次に，校正をしたエンジニアは，宣伝文句と仕様が正確であることを確認した後，確実に校正紙をマーケティング部に戻してください。これによって作業が増えることはわかっていますが，する必要があることですし，しかも効果的かつ迅速に行わなければなりません。

1 パンフレットの作成に営業本部長に加わってもらう。

2 パンフレットを配布する前に部門長に相談する。

3 すべての製品仕様書と宣伝文句を承認する。

4 パンフレットの校正紙を適切なエンジニアに送る。

解説 マーケティング部がすべきことはまず，Anyone sending specifications for any product to the marketing department から，仕様書を各部から受け取ること。そして，After galley proofs are returned to the marketing department from printers や Marketing will assure that the pertinent engineers obtain galleys in a timely manner. から，印刷所と担当エンジニアの間に立って，校正紙が確実に届くようにすることもその役割だと判断できる。正解は**4**。

(G) No. 22 解答 **4**

I think we've narrowed your purchase choice to four properties, each with their good points. The house on El Portal is a beauty and will appreciate significantly, but it's in a forested fire zone. There have been two major fires that have burned homes there in the last thirty years. The mansion on Lockwood Circle has an amazing view, but it's also got a lot of property and massive decking, so upkeep will cost a bundle over the long run. The place on Fairmont Drive is a newer home in a gated community for additional safety from theft. Newer homes require less maintenance and you'll see a lot of appreciation on that house. And finally, the house on Oakwood Way is a splendid older Victorian. Be aware, though, that it requires substantial renovation and then occasional repairs after that. Moreover, finding fixtures and parts for older homes can be a challenge.

状況：あなたは米国で家を購入する計画をしており，不動産業者から検討のために4件の家を見せてもらった。あなたが主に懸念していることは，お金を稼げるか，維持がしやすいか，そしてリスクを低く抑えられるかである。不動産業者は次のように言う。

質問：どの家があなたのニーズに最も合致するか。

さて，購入物件の選択肢は4件まで減りましたが，どの物件にも良い点があります。エル・ポータルの家は美しく，今後大きく価値を上げるでしょう。ただし，森林に覆われた火災危険地域内にあります。過去30年の間に，域内の家屋を燃やした大きな火事が2回ありました。ロックウッド・サークルにある邸宅は，眺望がすばらしいのですが，土地が広くデッキも広大なため，長期的には維持費がかさむでしょう。フェアモント・ドライブの物件はほかよりも新しく，住民以外の立ち入りが制限されている敷地内にありますので，その分，窃盗に対する安全性は高くなっています。家は新しいほど維持に手間がかかりませんし，今後，家の評価も大いに上がるでしょう。そして最後に，オークウッド・ウェイの物件ですが，こちらは壮麗なビクトリア様式の旧館です。ただし，認識いただきたいのですが，かなりの修繕が必要で，その後も時々修理が必要になります。さらに，歴史のある家で使われている備えつけの調度品や部品を探すことは，容易ではありません。

解説　Situation で making money, low maintenance, low risk という３つの条件が与えられている。これをすべて満たすのは，additional safety from theft と less maintenance という特徴を備え，将来的に a lot of appreciation on that house が期待できる**4**のフェアモント・ドライブの家である。

(H) No. 23　解答　2

Welcome to University Voicemail! To create your main mailbox, press the pound key, enter your student identification number, press the pound key again, enter a secret six-digit passcode, and press the pound key a third time. Your information will be repeated back. Confirm by pressing 1 or revise by pressing 2. After creating your main mailbox, you can add up to four sub-mailboxes at any time so callers can leave messages for separate individuals. Mailbox owners can create sub-mailboxes now by pressing 0. To repeat these instructions, press 9.

状況：あなたは大学の寮に入ったばかりである。あなたはボイスメールの使い方を説明した電話メッセージを聞く。

質問：メイン・メールボックスを作る際に行う手順の１つはどれか。

大学ボイスメールへようこそ！　メイン・メールボックスを作るには，シャープボタンを押してから学生番号を入力し，再度シャープボタンを押してから６けたの暗証番号を入力し，３度目のシャープボタンを押します。あなたが入力した内容が繰り返して読まれます。1を押して確定するか，2を押して訂正してください。メイン・メールボックスを作ると，その後はいつでも，最大4つまでサブ・メールボックスを追加できますので，電話をかけてきた人が個別にメッセージを残すことができます。メールボックスをすでに持っている方は，今0を押せばサブ・メールボックスを作ることができます。以上の説明を繰り返す場合は，9を押してください。

1 9を押す。　　　　　　　　　　　　　2 暗証番号を入れる。
3 自分の寮の番号を入れる。　　　　　　4 0を押す。

解説　メイン・メールボックスは，press the pound key → enter your student identification number → press the pound key again → enter a secret six-digit passcode → press the pound key a third time という手順で作成する。enter a secret six-digit passcode に当てはまる**2**が正解。

(I) No. 24　解答　2

We offer various plans to suit every need and schedule. First is our Muscle Tone plan at \$40 a month that gives you access to all the equipment in our gym mornings from 6:00 to 8:00 and then evenings after 7:00, but not weekends. Our Right On plan at \$50 a month lets you take advantage of our gym and join any class at any time you choose for a total of up to four hours a week. Our Top Shape plan at \$40 lets you choose from up to three classes a week, but without access to the gym for individual workouts. Finally, our Fitness Plus plan at \$80 a month gives you unlimited access to all equipment and any class at any time, from 6 a.m. to 11 p.m.

状況：あなたはジムに加入し，週3回ほど運動器具を使いたいと思っている。あなたは平日の仕事に行く前の30分間，午前6時半から利用するつもりである。あなたはジムのトレーナーによる次のような勧誘を聞く。

質問：あなたにとって最も良い契約はどれか。

あらゆるニーズとご都合に応えるため，当ジムではさまざまなプランをご用意しております。まず，マッスル・トーン・プランは月額40ドルで，ジム内のすべての器具を，朝は6時から8時まで，夜は7時以降ご利用いただけます。週末はご利用いただけません。ライト・オン・プランは月額50ドルで当ジムをご利用いただくプランです。最大で週4時間，お好きな時間にお好きなクラスを受講していただけます。トップ・シェイプ・プランは40ドルで，毎週3クラスまでお選びいただけます。ただし，お1人でのトレーニングではジムを利用することはで

きません。最後に，フィットネス・プラス・プランは月額80ドルで，制限は一切なく，午前6時から午後11時までのすべての器具をご利用いただけ，どのクラスでもご参加いただけます。

1 ライト・オン・プラン。 **2** マッスル・トーン・プラン。

3 フィットネス・プラス・プラン。 **4** トップ・シェイプ・プラン。

[解説] Situation から，利用するのは平日の朝の30分だけ。月額40ドルで access to all the equipment in our gym mornings from 6:00 to 8:00 という**2**のマッスル・トーン・プランが一番の好条件となる。トップ・シェイプ・プランも40ドルだが，個人で器具を使ってトレーニングすることができないので不適。

(J) No. 25 [解答] 4

We will begin a fire drill in two minutes. When the alarm sounds, make sure the windows are closed in your room, take a towel, leave your room, and close but do not lock the door behind you. Proceed to one of the four exits and move at least 50 meters away from the building. The six fire escapes should be used only when an exit is blocked. They should not be used during this fire drill. Do not re-enter the building until the fire inspector gives permission, which could take 20 minutes. Failing to comply with these instructions could result in a $75 fine and a 25-day suspension.

状況：あなたは寮の拡声装置でアナウンスを聞く。

質問：建物から出た後でするように指示されていることの1つは何か。

2分後に消防訓練を始めます。警報が鳴ったら，部屋の窓が閉まっていることを確認し，タオルを持って部屋を出てください。ドアは閉めますが，鍵はかけないでください。4カ所ある出口のどれか1つまで進んだら，建物から少なくとも50メートル離れてください。6カ所ある非常口を使うのは，出口が封鎖されているときだけです。今回の消防訓練の間は，非常口は使わないようにしてください。防火検査員から許可が出るまでは，建物に戻ってはいけません。許可が出るまで20分かかるかもしれません。以上の指示に従わない場合は，75ドルの罰金と25日間の停学処分になることがあります。

1 建物から30メートルほど離れたところに立つ。 **2** 建物の出口にいる防火検査員を見つける。

3 自分の寮に戻るまで2分待つ。 **4** 自分の寮に戻る許可を待つ。

[解説] 指示されている内容は，出口から出ること，建物から50メートル以上離れること，非常口は使わないこと，許可が出るまでは建物に戻らないこと。permission を authorization で言い換えている**4**が正解。

Part 4 ◀)) 024～025

★：Welcome to KPIX radio's Jeremy Steven show. Today, our guest is Jon Melcher, who was an international fashion model for four years. Thanks for joining us today, Jon.

●：Thanks for having me, Jeremy.

★：Tell me, was the modeling life as glamorous as it looks?

●：I wish I could say yes, but I can't. It's been a lot of blood, sweat, and tears, and the pay I made in the U.S. and in Europe would surprise you. Male models generally make a lot less than their female counterparts.

★：How did you get started?

●：I went to university in New York and needed money for school, so I thought I'd try out modeling. I worked for an agency, and after a few months, I was asked to do some jobs in Europe. I then dropped out of university to do modeling full-time. I did some runway work in Paris and Milan, but the competition was just too intense and I couldn't save anything. In fact, I barely earned enough to live on. I returned to New York, but competition there was just as tough, real dog eat dog. Then I was offered a contract to work in Tokyo. The pay is much better in Asia, where name brand fashions have really caught on, and there's a big demand for Western models.

★：And how was your experience in Tokyo?

●：Overall, it was a blast. It's a great city. But there were some downers, too. I mean, during the first few jobs I did, I was told I was too fat. I couldn't believe it. There were two types of models, the muscular, macho types and the super thin types. I fell into the thin type, but I wasn't thin enough. The sizes of the clothes I modeled were made for ultra-skinny people. I was told to lose about 10 to 15 pounds, so I starved myself for several months. I became anemic looking. I mean, you could count my ribs when I took my shirt off. That wasn't good for my health, so I often came down with colds, but I did get a lot of jobs.

★：And most of it was runway work?

●：Yes, but I did a variety of work, such as magazine and catalog photo shoots, TV commercials, and even the occasional acting job on Japanese TV programs to fill up my schedule. The big fashion shows and the TV ads paid the best. Many of the other projects were just filler work, and I made very little from those. I got a lot of jobs my first two years in Japan, but then the competition became more intense, with a lot of young Western models flooding into Japan.

★：When did you decide to leave modeling?

●：After four years of modeling, I'd finally saved up a fair amount of money. I continued to work as a model in Tokyo part-time and enrolled in a university there, graduating in Marketing. After graduating, I became a copywriter and gave up modeling completely to avoid any conflict of interest with clients I was writing for. It was great to be out of modeling and eat anything I wanted to without worrying about being told off for being too fat.

★：Thanks, Jon, for your fascinating stories about the modeling world.

●：Thanks for having me, Jeremy.

Questions

No.26　What is one thing Jon says about his career?

No.27　What is one thing Jon says about modeling in Tokyo?

★：KPIX ラジオ，ジェレミー・スティーブン・ショーへようこそ。本日のゲストは，ジョン・メルヒャーさんです。国際的なファッションモデルとして4年間活動されました。ジョン，今日は来てくれてありがとう。

●：呼んでくれてありがとう，ジェレミー。

★：モデル業の生活は魅力的に見えるけど，実際そうだったのか話を聞かせてくれる？

●：そのとおりさ，と言えればいいんだけどね，言えないね。たくさんの血と汗と涙を流してきたし，アメリカやヨーロッパで僕がもらっていた報酬を聞いたら驚くよ。一般的に，男性モデルは女性モデルよりもずっと稼ぎが悪いんだ。

★：モデル業を始めたきっかけは？

●：ニューヨークの大学に通っていて，学費が必要だったんだ。だからモデルをやってみようと思って。ある事務所で仕事をして数ヵ月したころ，ヨーロッパでの仕事の依頼があったんだ。それから大学をやめて，モデル業1本に絞った。パリやミラノでファッション・ショーに出たんだけど，競争がとにかく激しくて，何の蓄えもできなかったよ。実際のところ，生活していくだけのお金を稼ぐのがやっとだったんだ。ニューヨークに戻っても競争は変わらぬ厳しさで，本当に食うか食われるかなんだ。それから東京での仕事の契約をオファーされたんだ。有名ブランド・ファッションがとても流行しているアジアの方が支払いがずっと高くて，欧米人モデルの需要も多いんだ。

★：東京での体験はどうだった？

●：全体的に見れば楽しかった。すばらしい街だよ。でも気が滅入るようなこともあったよ。というのも，最初

の数回の仕事で太りすぎだと言われたんだ。信じられなかったよ。モデルには2つのタイプがあったんだけど，それは筋骨隆々のマッチョ・タイプと，超細身タイプだったんだ。僕は細身タイプの方に入ったけど，それには細さが足りなかった。僕がモデルをした服のサイズは，とんでもなく痩せている人のために作られていたんだ。だいたい10〜15ポンド体重を落とすように言われたよ。だから数カ月間，自分を飢餓状態にしたね。弱々しい見た目になったよ。というか，シャツを脱ぐと肋骨を数えることができたんだ。それは自分の健康にはよくないことだから，よく風邪をひいたけど，仕事をたくさんもらったことは確かだね。

★：ほとんどはファッション・ショーの仕事だったの？

●：そうだよ，でも，いろんな仕事をしたよ。雑誌やカタログの写真撮影，テレビCM，そして俳優として日本のテレビ番組に出たことも時々あった。スケジュールを埋めるためにね。大きなファッション・ショーやテレビCMの仕事は支払いが一番よかった。そのほかの仕事の多くは，ただ空いた時間を埋めるだけの仕事だったし，大した稼ぎもなかった。日本に来て2年はたくさん仕事をしたけれど，それから競争がもっと激しくなったんだ。若い欧米人モデルがどっと日本に押し寄せて来たからね。

★：モデル業から身を引く決意をしたのはいつごろだったの？

●：4年間モデルの仕事をしていたら，ようやくかなりの額のお金を貯めることができた。アルバイトとして東京でモデルの仕事を続けながら，都内の大学に入って，マーケティング学科を卒業したんだ。卒業後はコピーライターになって，モデルの仕事は完全にやめたよ。コピーを書いているクライアントと利害関係が対立しないようにするためにね。モデル業を離れ，太りすぎだと叱られる心配をすることなく何でも食べられるのは，すばらしいことだった。

★：ジョン，モデル業界について非常に興味深い話を聞かせてくれて，ありがとう。

●：お招きいただきありがとう，ジェレミー。

No. 26 解答 1

「自身のキャリアについてジョンが述べていることの1つは何か」

1 学費を稼ぐためにニューヨークでモデルのバイトを始めた。

2 大学を訪れていたスカウトにモデルをしないかと誘われた。

3 ヨーロッパ旅行をしていたときに，旅行を続けるお金を稼ぐためにモデルをした。

4 モデル学校在学中に，事務所へ紹介された。

解説 キャリアのきっかけについて，I went to university in New York and needed money for school, so I thought I'd try out modeling. と説明している。**1**が正解。フルタイムで働くようになったのは後のことなので，まずはアルバイトだったと考えられる。

No. 27 解答 1

「東京でのモデルの仕事についてジョンが述べていることの1つは何か」

1 長期間ダイエットに奮闘しなければならなかった。

2 競争が激しいために十分な仕事を得られたことがなかった。

3 いくつか重病を患い，入院した。

4 そこの文化になじめず，その影響が健康にも出た。

解説 ジョンは東京でのつらい経験について，太りすぎだと言われ，必死に痩せた話をしている。**1**が正解。

筆記試験
解答と解説

問題編 p.32〜45

筆記

1

問題	1	2	3	4	5	6	7	8	9	10	11	12	13	14	15	16	17	18	19	20
解答	1	1	4	3	3	2	4	1	3	4	2	1	1	1	3	3	1	1	3	3

問題	21	22
解答	2	1

2

問題	23	24	25	26	27	28
解答	4	2	3	2	3	1

3

問題	29	30	31	32	33	34	35
解答	3	4	1	4	2	3	4

4　　**5**　　解説内にある解答例を参照してください。

1

(1)　解答 1
「観光業界は長引く不況の影響に苦しんでおり，テロへの恐怖はその状況を悪化させるだけだろう」
解説　低調な観光業界において，テロの恐怖は状況を「さらに悪くする」ものだと考えられる。**2**「〜をなだめる，〜の怒りを静める」，**3**「〜をほのめかす」，**4**「〜を始める，就任させる」。

(2)　解答 1
「乳がんの手術後，ジルは医師から，処方薬を毎日飲んで定期的に健康診断に来ることが最も重要だと忠告された」
解説　of importance は important と同じ意味。どんなに重要かを表す語として適切なのは**1**の paramount「最高の」。of paramount importance で「最高に重要な」という意味になる。**2**「無害の」，**3**「排他的な」，**4**「折の悪い」。

(3)　解答 4
「キャリーは，一番の親友が授業を頻繁に欠席すること

について，彼女の父親は重病だと先生に公然と嘘をついていると聞いてショックを受けた」
解説　先生に嘘をつく様子を表す副詞として最も適切なのは，**4**「露骨に，公然と」。**1**「物思いに沈んで」，**2**「従順に」，**3**「経験に基づいて」。

(4)　解答 3
「その会社の創立者は病気で，もはや効果的に仕事をすることはできないが，補佐役たちには自分の権限を少しも譲らないだろう」
解説　「効果的に仕事ができない」という前半と逆接でつながって「誰にも権限を〜しないだろう」という文脈。**3**「(権利など)を譲渡する」ことはないと考えられる。**1**「〜を解散する，溶かす」，**2**「〜を吸収する，同化させる」，**4**「〜の刑の執行を延期する」。

(5)　解答 3
「その川は山中の急流と滝が特徴だが，ひとたび平野部に至ると，海へとゆっくり曲がりくねっていく」
解説　川の流れについて述べているので，**3**「曲がり

くねる」が適切。急流や滝との対比からも正解が導けるだろう。**1**「旋回する」，**2**「ぶらぶら歩く」，**4**「曇る，脱色する」。

(6) 解答 2
「私のジープは四輪駆動で牽引力（けんいん）が強く，スキー小屋に続く凍った山道を通るときに本当に必要となる」

解説 四輪駆動で凍った道で必要になるのだから，**2**「牽引力，トラクション」に優れているはず。traction「トラクション」とは道路を滑らずに引っ張っていく力のこと。**1**「不一致，不協和（音）」，**3**「変動，揺れ」，**4**「逸脱」。

(7) 解答 4
「ボブは毎日運動し，甘いものと脂肪の多い食品をすべて控えることで体をスリムに保っていた」

解説 形容詞の lean は「細い」（≒thin）という意味。細い体型を維持するために必要なことを考えると，甘いものや脂肪の多いものは**4**「差し控える」べき。**1**「〜を獲得する，手に入れる」，**2**「〜を解読する」，**3**「〜を未然に防ぐ」。

(8) 解答 1
「その交渉の中で大使は，その島に対する隣国の統治権は国際法で認められておらず，自分の国に返還されるべきだと主張した」

解説 大使は「島は返還されるべきだ」と言っているので，島に対する隣国の「統治権」は国際法で認められていないと考えられる。**2**「信用性，威信」，**3**「偶然の一致」，**4**「団結，連帯意識」。

(9) 解答 3
「息が詰まるような午後の暑さは，前夜の凍るような気温とは全く対照的だった」

解説 「前夜の凍るような気温とは全く対照的」なのだから，**3**「息が詰まるほど暑い」と考えられる。in stark contrast to 〜 は「〜と全く対照的に」という意味。**1**「洞察力のある」，**2**「好奇心をそそる」，**4**「しびれさせるような」。

(10) 解答 4
A「今日ランチをおごらせてよ」
B「いや，君はこの前払っただろ。今度は僕がお返しをして君におごる番だよ」

解説 前回はAがおごってくれたのだから，今回はBがおごることで「返礼する」のだと考えられる。**1**「〜

を課す，命じる」，**2**「〜を打ち破る」，**3**「〜をすりつぶす」。

(11) 解答 2
「社内の人と付き合うのは好きではないと言って，その女性は同僚男性が言い寄ってきたのをはねつけた」

解説 advance は通例複数形で「〜（人）に言い寄ること」という意味。社内の人と付き合うのは嫌なのだから，言い寄られても「はねつけた」はず。**1**「〜を正当化した」，**3**「〜を引き起こした，多量に産んだ」，**4**「〜に気をつけた」。

(12) 解答 1
「キリスト教の中には多くの教派があり，ローマカトリック教が最大にして最古である」

解説 後半が独立分詞構文なっている。ローマカトリック教はキリスト教の「教派」の1つなので，**1**が正解。**2**「予言」，**3**「専門家」，**4**「要約」。

(13) 解答 1
「水がなく気温が高いため，砂漠は地球上で最も生きにくい場所の1つだと見なされている」

解説 水がなくて気温が高い場所は，「生存に適さない」場所だと言える。**2**「抑制のない，激しい」，**3**「偏りのない，公平な」，**4**「もうかる」。

(14) 解答 1
A「やあ，テッド。君がたった今宝くじで10万ドル以上当てたって聞いたよ。どんな気持ちだい？」
B「ものすごく幸せさ。まるで天国からの贈り物のようだよ」

解説 宝くじを当てた気持ちを尋ねられている。感情を表す形容詞は**1**か**2**だが，「天国からの贈り物のようだ」と言っているので，**1**「幸福感にあふれた」が正解。**2**「飽き飽きした」，**3**「至る所にある」，**4**「ぶっきらぼうな，無愛想な」。

(15) 解答 3
「アントニは新しい料理を創り出すことが好きだ。厨房における彼の創意工夫は，いつか必ず彼を有名なシェフにするだろう」

解説 料理を創作することが好きなのだから，**3**「創意工夫」が彼を有名にするであろうシェフとしての特性である。**1**「父であること」，**2**「妥協しないこと，頑迷」，**4**「高慢さ」。

(16) 解答 3

「この予算増加により, 今会計年度に予定されているプロジェクトの実施が可能になる」

解説　予算増により, プロジェクトをどうすることができるか考える。3「実施, 実行」が正解。1「抑制」, 2「極貧」, 4「有罪にすること」。

(17) 解答 1

「医師たちは, その病棟の患者を治療した後は徹底的な手洗いをするよう警告された。患者一人一人が非常に伝染性の高い病気を持っていたからである」

解説　徹底した手洗いが奨励されていたのだから, 患者は伝染病にかかっていたと考えられる。1「伝染する, うつりやすい」が正解。2「非道な」, 3「勇敢な, 堂々とした」, 4「身代わりの」。

(18) 解答 1

「その若者は最初, 遠慮がちだった。パーティーの出席者のほとんどが知らない人だったからだ。しかし, すぐに初めのためらいがなくなり, ほかの人たちと交流し始めた」

解説　lost his initial ... から, 最初はあった何を失ったのかを考える。1文目に「最初は遠慮がちだった」とあるので, なくなったのは「遠慮する気持ち」だと推測できる。1「(心理的な) 抑制, ためらい」が正解。2「工芸品」, 3「腫瘍」, 4「相違点」。

(19) 解答 3

「スザンヌは有能な交渉人なので, 会社側の代表者と満足のいく合意を成し遂げるだろうと組合は確信していた」

解説　交渉での話なので, 満足のいく合意を「成し遂げる」と考えるのが自然。1「～を作り直す」, 2「～を着服する」, 4「～を添える」。

(20) 解答 3

「不運にも, トムは全く貯金をしなかったので, 失業してから当てにするものが何もなかった」

解説　貯金がないということは, 失業後に「頼る」ものがないということ。fall back on ～ で「～を当てにする, (最後の) 頼みとする」という意味。1「～から手を引く」, 2「～を後世に残す, (判決) を言い渡す」, 4「～ (出費・借金など) を増やす」。

(21) 解答 2

A「すみませんでした。スピードが出すぎているなんてわからなかったのです」

B「あなたは常に法律に従うことが求められています。時速20マイルの速度超過でしたから, 違反切符を切らざるを得ません」

解説　Bは警察官の発言。常に法律を「守る」ように言っていると考えるのが自然。1「～に反対する」, 3「～を支持する」, 4「～に押しかける」。

(22) 解答 1

「過去数年で近郊の犯罪が急激に増えたので, 市長は麻薬ディーラーやそのほかの犯罪者を取り締まることを誓った」

解説　犯罪の増加に対してすべきことは, 取り締まり。crack down on ～ で「～を厳しく取り締まる」という意味になるので, 1が正解。2「～を実行する」, 3「～を壊す」, 4「～を大声で歌う」。

2

全訳

犬の分離不安

　どんな種類の犬でも, 家にぽつんと置き去りにされると分離不安を感じる。犬は絶え間なくほえたり, 悲しそうに鳴いたり, 極端な場合は家具や敷物やドアを壊したりする。しかし, 犬のこの問題はたいていの場合治すことができる。犬が人間の家族を主人だと見なしていないと, 結果が好ましくない行動につながることがある。自分がリーダーだという犬の思い違いが, しばしば分離不安の原因となっているのだ。犬は群れ意識を持つ動物であり, 「率いる者」と「従う者」という極めて単純な社会的序列の枠内で行動する。

　犬は, 群れにおける自らの役割を極めて真剣にとらえる。従う者であるときは名高い犬特有の忠実さをもって従う。リーダーであるときは従う者を守る。自分が群れのリーダーだと確信しているときに, 従う者たち, つまり人間の家族が外出すると, 犬は彼らを守る力がないと感じる。犬は不安になり始める。

　これを解決するのは適切な訓練だ。例えば, ペットがあなたの気を引こうとほえたり弱々しく鳴いたりし

ても，無視することが大切だ。あなたが，リーダーとして，いつ食事を与え，かわいがり，罰を与え，褒美を与えるかを決めるのである。あなたは自分の時間を思うままに使うことができる，犬にはあなたの時間について何ら要求する権利はないし，決してその権利があると思わせてはいけない。犬がルールを決めるのではなく，そして犬がそのことを理解するのは早ければ早いほど良い。人々はしばしば，帰宅するとすぐにペットを抱きしめたがる。しかし，愛情の交換は数分間先延ばしにして，犬があなたの予定に合わせるのであって，その逆ではないという原則を強調することが重要である。

ペットがクンクン鳴くのを無視したり，本当は力いっぱい抱きしめてやりたいのにいかめしい顔を装ったりするには，意志の力を大いに必要とするかもしれない。しかし，長い目で見れば，主人らしく振舞う人間の方が，犬をより幸せにするのだ。好きなだけ犬を抱きしめたり，一緒に遊び回ったりするのは構わない。ただし，それがいつなのかを犬に決めさせることがなければの話である。

(23) 解答 **4**

解説 犬の問題行動を一言でunwanted behaviorとまとめた**4**が正解。**1**「犬は飼い主の家族に対し攻撃的になることがある」，**2**「犬は食べるのをやめ，体重を減らす」，**3**「犬はいつも寂しく，悲しく感じる」。

(24) 解答 **2**

解説 前の文で，飼い主がリーダーなので，いつ何をするかを決める，と述べている。この内容を受けている**2**が正解。**1**「犬は群れのリーダーである」，**3**「あなたはいつも犬を幸せにしておかなければいけない」，**4**「犬には今何時かがわからない」。

(25) 解答 **3**

解説 犬と遊んであげたいのに我慢するには意志の力がいる。**3**が正解。**1**「単純なことである」，**2**「しばしば外部の助けを要する」，**4**「全く意味を成さないように思える」。

全訳

スプートニク1号

世界初の人工衛星スプートニク1号は，1957年ソビエト連邦によって楕円形の低地球軌道に打ち上げられた。スプートニクの打ち上げとうまくいった配置は，一般的に考えられていた宇宙時代の初めての重要な進展を象徴するだけでなく，世界中の人々と政府を驚かせた。その後の「スプートニク危機」は宇宙競争の始まりにつながり，政治激変，新しい技術を開発するべきだと言う民衆の声，NASAの創設を含む科学・軍事・教育への巨額の投資を引き起こした。

打ち上げが実行されたのは何十年と続いた冷戦のさなかで，センセーショナルな宣伝戦略が両陣営を飛び交っていたときだった。しかし，ソビエト連邦はロケット学における自国の進歩を宣伝することには意図的に慎重だった。というのも政府は，秘密が漏れることや，失敗しようものならば欧米がそれを宣伝戦略に利用し，ソ連を笑いものにした上に，ソ連は発展が遅く技術的に劣っているととらえることを恐れたのだ。この理由から，前代未聞の成功と，ソ連が米国より先にこの大きな科学的出来事に到達したという事実があったにもかかわらず，ソビエトの宣伝戦略において打ち上げが直ちに公表されることはなかった。それが正式に発表されると，そのニュースは，それまで米国こそ世界に無類の技術超大国だと信じていた米国の多くの人々を驚かせた。そのほかの国では，そのニュースは未来への不安とこのような業績を成し遂げたことへの驚きで迎えられた。

スプートニク1号の球状のデザインとアンテナ設置のおかげで，人工衛星の回転に関係なく全方向に20.005メガヘルツと40.002メガヘルツで電波信号を送れるようになった。それはつまり，全世界の科学者とアマチュア通信士の両方が，スプートニクが21日間のミッションを完了するまで，その過程を確認できることを意味した。現代の人工衛星に比べて，明らかに低い技術レベルで，速度や高度や大気数値の感知装置も備えておらず，ラジオ波を送信するためにはたった4本の外部アンテナしかなかったが，それでもこれはミッションを決して技術的に取るに足らないものにしなかった。宇宙船をモニターすることによって，上層大気についての相当な推論を立てることができたし，無線信号の障害と伝達に関する重要なデータも集めることができたのだ。

(26) 解答 **2**

解説 スプートニクの打ち上げ成功は，「宇宙時代の初めての重要な進展を象徴するだけでなく…」という文脈より，世界の受け止め方として，**2**が入るのが適切。**1**「一時的にNASAを閉鎖させるよう政治家たちを駆りたてた」，**3**「世界中に切れ目なくニュースを伝えた」，**4**「侵略が目前に迫っていると傍観者たちを説得した」。

(27) 解答 3

解説 ソ連はその成功にもかかわらず，マイナス面が強調されるのを懸念していたという文脈なので，**3**が適切。**1**「ソ連の宇宙技術におけるリーダーとしての地位を向上させる」，**2**「ソ連を限定的に堅苦しく神経過敏だと悪者扱いする」，**4**「ソ連の観念的な武勇と名声を認める」。

(28) 解答 1

解説 空所の直前にalthoughがあるので，「あらゆる点で現代の技術には劣る」という前半とは対象的な内容が入る。**1**が正解。**2**「人工衛星の発展に大きな影響はなかった」，**3**「質的データの集積を妨げた」，**4**「実験をいつまでもだらだらと長引かせることを許した」。

3

全訳

陰謀説

歴史を通じて，事件，出来事，目撃，失踪，そのほか月面着陸から政治的暗殺まで報道価値のある出来事は，それらを取り巻く正確な状況について多くの人々に不思議な思いを残してきた。疑わしく，世間を騒がせるような，一見説明のつかない出来事の公的な記録には満足しない人がいるのだ。これが政府やそのほかの権力をもつ当事者が，不正な理由で真実を伏せているという事実無根の憶測や説につながった。そうした説は「陰謀説」として知られ，しばしば歴史や立証可能な事実の一般的な理解に矛盾するだけでなく，突飛な主張を含む仮説を生みだした。その軽蔑的な用語は1世紀以上にわたって使われ，陰謀論者と称する人々も以前から確認されていたが，テレビや特にインターネットなどメディアの普及で，その言葉の使用が急増し，陰謀説そのものも関連してよく見られるようになっている。

しかしながら，陰謀説はタブロイド出版物や空想的なウェブサイトだけの領分ではなく，専門的に研究されている。政治科学者マイケル・バークンは陰謀説の3つの原則を明らかにした。それは「何事も偶然には起こらない」，「見た目通りのことはない」，「すべては関連している」ということだ。さらにバークンは陰謀説を大きく3つの分類に特定した。米国の9.11テロ攻撃のような大きな事件に関連した事件陰謀説，噂のイルミナティのような世界支配を求める単独グループに関連した組織陰謀説，そして超陰謀説の下では，連結された陰謀が全能の邪悪な勢力によって支配されているというのだ。そこには姿を変えることのできるトカゲ種に地球が支配されているというばかげた主張も含まれている。さらに多くの陰謀説では，その説の信頼性を傷つけるために使われた証拠こそ説が真実であることの「証」であるとしており，権力者たちが不安に

なり，真実を隠そうとしているのをそうした努力が裏づけていると主張していることが研究でわかった。

陰謀論者に関しては，フランスのグルノーブルアルプス大学で行われた3つの研究で，陰謀説を信じがちな人は自分たちを「並はずれて鋭敏でユニークだ」と見なしていることが明らかになった。この信念と，自分をユニークで特別だと感じる必要性が，問題の事件について自分だけが貴重な情報をもっていると信じ，秘密の邪悪な勢力が無関心でだまされやすい大衆から真実を覆い隠そうと働いていると結論づける人々の中に現れる可能性があるのだ。しかし，陰謀説を信じるのは自意識過剰な人々だけではない。英国のケント大学による調査は，人々は陰謀説に賛同するようになることがあり，その際自分たちの態度の変化を極めて少なく見積もると示唆している。

しかしこれは，陰謀説の流行を説明するものではなく，陰謀説がこれほど多くの人を引きつける理由の完全な説明にもならない。自分自身の生活も支配できないと感じる人々に一種の安心を与えてくれるため，人は陰謀説に引きつけられるのかもしれない。困難や挫折を，支配する邪悪な力のせいにできるからだ。しかし，ある人々にとっては，陰謀説を信じ広める強迫観念的傾向は，統合失調症や被害妄想といった，より深刻な潜在的精神疾患の現れである可能性もある。

(29) 解答 3

「陰謀説と陰謀論者への一般的な認識について何が正しいか」

1 大部分の陰謀説はそうでなければ説明がつかない，出来事の事実に基づいている。

2「陰謀説」という言葉は一般的に，現状に意義を唱える考え方への敬意を示して使われている。

3 陰謀論者は一風変わった思いつきの方を好み，主流の説を無視しがちである。

4 超常現象の機密事件を隠ぺいしようとする政府の試みは熱心な活動参加者によって暴露されている。

解説 陰謀説と陰謀論者の概要は第1段落で述べられている。しばしば歴史や立証可能な事実の一般的な理解に矛盾するだけでなく突飛な主張を含む仮説を生みだしたという説明に一致する**3**が正解。

(30) 解答 **4**

「学術研究は，陰謀説についての私たちの理解をどのように改善したか」

1 学者たちは陰謀説の正当性を支える連結された形の証拠を特定した。

2 陰謀説は奇妙に見えるが，学術調査はそれらが証明可能な原則で管理されていることを立証した。

3 陰謀説が特定の権力団体によって確立された地球支配のシステムを暴露したことを，学者たちは発見した。

4 陰謀説はでたらめで全く異なるように見えるが，それらは分類でき，いくつかの類似点があることが研究でわかった。

解説 陰謀説の研究については，第2段落で説明されている。陰謀説の3つの原則で類似点を挙げ，3つの分類も示していることから，この内容を別の言葉で言い換えた**4**が正解。

(31) 解答 **1**

「陰謀説の伝播は潜在する心理学的基盤をどのように示し得るか」

1 陰謀論者は，世界の本質について社会は間違った方向に導かれているという信念と共に，自己陶酔的な傾向を示すことがある。

2 心理学者たちは，陰謀論者を精神疾患にかかっていると分類することで，信頼できる説を退ける。

3 政治団体による過度の管理が，心理的トラウマとなり，しばしば陰謀説への信用として現れる。

4 陰謀論者への非難に切り替えることで，政治家たちは多くの問題に関して大衆を効果的に間違った方向に導くことができる。

解説 第3段落以降，どのような人が陰謀説を信じがちなのか，陰謀論者の心理的側面が説明されている。自分を特別だと見なし，自分だけが貴重な情報を持っていると信じ，秘密の邪悪な勢力がだまされやすい大衆から真実を覆い隠そうとしていると結論づける人々，と定義していることから，**1**が正解。

全訳
ルイジアナ買収の真のコスト

　1803年，米国政府は一般にアメリカの歴史上最高と言われる不動産取引を行った。ルイジアナ買収である。当時の約1,500万ドルに等しい6,800万フランと引き換えに，米国はフランスから82万7,000平方マイルの土地を受け取り，若い国家は事実上2倍の大きさになった。今日だと米国の15州とカナダ2州をわずか3万1,000万ドルで購入するのに等しいだろう。こうした数字を見るに，ルイジアナ買収が目覚ましい好条件取引だったと褒めたたえられているのも驚きではない。しかし，専門的な観点から見ると，これらの土地を手に入れるために支払われた実際の金額を決めるのは，もっと複雑な問題だ。なぜなら，この数字を計算するには，ルイジアナ準州に住んでいたアメリカ先住民を強制退去させることで背負い込んだコストを見る必要があるからだ。

　実際，米国はフランスからすべてのルイジアナ準州を購入したわけではない。そうではなく，もともと土着の民族が住んでいた土地に植民地を作る独占権を購入したのだ。1803年にはこれらの土地の先住民以外の住民はたったの6万人だったと見積もられる。結局先住民から領土を奪うのは困難な仕事であり，過去2世紀にわたり，米国はこの地域の200以上のアメリカ先住民部族と条約，協定，法規などを取り交わしてきた。1804年から2012年の間に，米国政府は様々な部族に総額26億ドル，インフレ調整をすると約86億ドルの土地代を払ったと推測される。

　米国政府が先住民族からこれらの土地を獲得した手段は，取り扱いの難しい問題だ。ルイジアナ準州内の土地の最初の先住民譲渡は，その理由の申し分ない例である。1804年，当時のインディアナ準州の知事だったウィリアム・ヘンリー・ハリソンは，ソーク族とフォックス族の数人の代表を巧みに操って360万エーカーの土地を放棄させた。そのうち160万エーカーがルイジアナ準州だった。土地は1エーカー当たり半セントで買い上げられたが，当時の価値は1エーカー当たり約60セントだったと報告されている。歴史家ハーバート・S・チャニックの言葉によれば，ハリソンがこれほど有利な取引を確保できたのは，彼が「少数の酔っぱらったインディアンを巧みに操って，彼らには何の権限もない譲渡契約に合意させた」からである。それでも，書類が署名されると，米国政府はそれを法律として扱い，ソーク族とフォックス族はたった数十年後には自分たちの土地から追い出された。出て行かない者は殺害された。

これらの土地を手に入れるための20世紀における米国政府の努力は，1800年代のやり方よりはかなり礼儀正しくはあったが，やはり先住民族を満足させることはできなかった。ルイジアナ準州内の先住民の土地の米国による押収をめぐる現在進行中の有名な争議は，スー族ブラック・ヒルズ土地所有権要求である。ワイオミングとサウス・ダコタにまたがる山岳地帯，ブラック・ヒルズの一部は1877年，その地で金が発見された直後，米国政府によってスー族から横取りされた。1980年，米国最高裁は，これは1868年にスー族との間で交わされた条約に明らかに違反した領土の不正押収であるとして，スー族への賠償金として1億ドルの支払いを命じた。スー族はこの事件の成り行きへの当初からの不満を再度主張し，支払いを拒絶した。彼らは金銭の賠償ではなく，自分たちの土地を返還して欲しいと思っていたのである。彼らの拒絶の動機を説明するにあたり，オグララ・スー族評議会のマリオ・ゴンザレスは，「スー・インディアンは自分たちの土地，特にブラック・ヒルズに非常に愛着を持っている。なぜならそこはスー民族の魂の中心だからだ」と発表している。未請求の資金への利子は増え続け，現在では優に10億ドルを超えている。

こうした部族補償と未払いの負債を考慮に入れても，ルイジアナ買収は驚異的な取引という評判に間違いなく値する。控え目な見積もりでさえ，これらの土地の本当の価値はこれまで支払われた26億ドル（インフレ調整して86億ドル）に比べると驚異的である。例えば，ルイジアナ準州から切り分けられた州の1つノース・ダコタの土地の価値を見てみよう。2010年から2015年の間だけでも，そこで1,000億ドル以上の石油が抽出された。歴史家ロバート・リーが言うには，「ルイジアナ買収は今でも信じられないもうけ物だ。しかし，私たちが教えられた類のものではない。土地が安かったのは，フランスが権利を主張するずっと前からここに住んでいた人々に，米国がほんの少ししか払わなかったせいだ」。

(32) 解答 4

「文章の著者はルイジアナ買収について何を示唆しているか」

1 フランスは，おそらく当時資金がなくて困っていたにもかかわらず，ルイジアナ準州の所有権を失って，取り返しのつかない事業上の過ちを犯した。
2 ルイジアナ買収に関して一般に与えられている称賛は，米国政府が取引の鍵となる側面を隠しているので，誤った方へ導かれている。

3 たとえ米国政府がルイジアナ準州の代金をフランスに払わなかったとしても，その地域は今でも定住者の増大する人口で占拠されていただろう。
4 ルイジアナ準州の獲得にかかった費用を正確に見積もるには，数々の金融取引を合算する必要がある。

解説 第1段落の終盤で，これらの土地を手に入れるために支払われた実際の金額は，アメリカ先住民を強制退去させることで背負い込んだコストを見る必要があると述べている。したがって，この内容に合う4が正解。

(33) 解答 2

「部族代表とのウィリアム・ヘンリー・ハリソンの取引の例は，…ことを説明している」

1 米国政府代表は概してインディアンとの取引において不当だったが，暴力に頼ったのは最終手段としてだけだった
2 インディアンの土地を米国の領土に吸収した戦略は，効果的だっただろうが，やはり道義的に疑わしかった
3 インディアンの部族は，自分たちとは極端に異なる社会の慣習に従って取引の交渉をすることを余儀なくされた
4 インディアンの部族は，概して土地の所有権に関する誤解のせいで，しばしば本来の価値よりかなり安く土地を譲渡した

解説 ウィリアム・ヘンリー・ハリソンの取引の例は第3段落に述べられている。ハリソンがインディアンの代表を巧みに操って格安な取引に合意させ署名させたと述べている。この内容から，2が正解。

(34) 解答 3

「スー族について正しいのは何か」

1 スー族は1800年代にはブラック・ヒルズの妥当な支払いを受け入れただろうが，もはやそんなことはない。
2 部族の主だった人々は，受け取る前にブラック・ヒルズの補償金への利息をさらに増やすのに賛成している。
3 部族は，聖なる土地全体あるいは一部の返還を含まない取引を，米国政府と交渉する気はない。
4 部族は，米国最高裁の判決に従い，いまだに変わっていない条約で守られている。

解説 スー族に関しては第4段落に記述がある。ブラック・ヒルズの土地所有権要求について説明されており，スー族が補償金の受け取りを拒否しているとあ

る。この内容に合う**3**が正解。スー族は当初から不満だったともあるので，**1**は不適。

(35) 解答 **4**

「次の文のうちロバート・リーがおそらく同意するのはどれか」

1 ノース・ダコタ州は，ルイジアナ買収で獲得された中でほぼ間違いなく最も貴重な土地である。

2 歴史学者たちは，土地取得の見積価格が最終的に判明するまで，ルイジアナ買収をもうかった取引だと説明するのを控えるべきだ。

3 米国政府は，彼らの土地を取得する際にインディアンの部族が受けた非人道的な扱いに対して，補償すべきだ。

4 フランスに支払った金額は土地の総額の一部なので，ルイジアナ買収に関する一般向けの教育は誤解を招く恐れがある。

解説 ロバート・リーの言葉は最終文にある。ルイジアナ買収は教えられたような取引ではなく，土地が安かったのは米国の支払いが少なかったせいだ，と述べている。この内容に一致する**4**が正解。

4

問題文の訳

　警察が容疑者を特定するのに顔認識テクノロジーを利用したり，犯罪のパターンを分析するためのソフトウエアを使用したりする中，人工知能（AI）は急速に米国司法制度の重要な一部になりつつある。しかしながら，おそらく最も議論をかもしている利用法は，犯罪で有罪とされた人物に判決を下す際の利用である。そのような判決用のソフトウエアは，その人物が将来再び法を破る見込みについて判断を下すために，前科や，犯した罪の種類といった要素を調べて分析する。ソフトウエアが判決を決めることはないのだが，判決を決める際にそれを利用する裁判官は多い。

　しかしながら，ある実験において，そのソフトウエアを法の執行に関する特別な知識を一切持たない普通の人々と比較したテストが行われた。ソフトウエアとは異なり，これらの人々は被告人に関する短い説明を読んだだけだった。ソフトウエアも普通の人々も，被告人が今後2年以内に再び罪を犯すかどうか予想するように求められた。人間の全体的な正確さは67パーセントだったが，ソフトウエアが正しかった確率は65パーセントだった。このがっかりするような成績が原因で，専門家たちは，被告人が再犯するかどうかについての非常に洗練されていて正確な予言者として売り込まれてきたソフトウエアの影響を裁判官が受けることのリスクを懸念している。

　AIの主要なセールスポイントの1つは，コンピュータは人間ならおそらく持っているであろう偏見もなく，データだけに基づいて決定を下すことができるはずである，というものだ。しかしながらAIは，黒人やその他の少数派の人々に対して人種差別的な態度をとっている可能性がある人間によって作られた大量のデータを使って学習しているので，データに存在する偏見を受け継いでしまう恐れがある。実際，まさにこのようなことが起きたと思われることとして，ある有名なプログラムが，黒人を別の罪を犯すリスクが高いと誤って分類する可能性が2倍近く高かったことがあった。ソフトウエアがより正確になって偏見を排除することができるようになるまで，法執行当局の人々は，その利用に関して極めて慎重であるべきである。

解答例

　These days, in the U.S., AI software is increasingly being used to help judges sentence criminals who have been convicted of crimes. It makes predictions about whether a criminal is likely to offend again by checking and analyzing data related to the criminal. However, there are grave concerns that this will have an adverse influence on judges'

解答例の訳

　最近アメリカでは，裁判官が有罪とされた犯罪者に判決を下すのに役立てるため，AIを使ったソフトウエアがますます利用されている。それは，犯人が再び罪を犯す可能性があるかどうかについて，その犯人に関するデータを調べて分析することで予測する。しかしながら，とりわけそれはあまり信用できないかもしれないことを示した実験があったため，これ（＝AIソフトウエアの利用）が裁判官の判断に有害な影響を及ぼ

Day
3

37

decisions, especially because there was an experiment which showed it may not be very reliable. Furthermore, since the AI has been trained on data that could contain human biases, there are fears that the software might also be biased. Therefore, the software should be used cautiously until it is improved. (107語)

すだろうという深刻な懸念がある。さらに，AIは人間の偏見が含まれている可能性があるデータを使って学習してきたので，ソフトウエアも偏見を持っているかもしれないという不安がある。それゆえに，ソフトウエアは改善されるまで慎重に利用されるべきである。

解説 トピックは第1段落第2文 Perhaps its most controversial use, however, is in the sentencing of people convicted of crimes. から，「判決を下す際のAIの利用」だとわかる。各段落の要旨は，第1段落：最も物議をかもしていることとして，判決を下す際にAIを使ったソフトウエアを利用する裁判官が多い。第2段落：AIを使ったソフトウエアはあまり正確でないことが実験で明らかになり，それを利用するリスクを懸念する声がある。第3段落：AIを使ったソフトウエアの問題点は，元データに人間の偏見が含まれている可能性があるため，AIの判断も偏見を持ったものになりかねないことであり，その慎重な利用が求められている。解答の際はこれらを問題文とは異なる表現に言い換えてまとめる。なお，第1段落の顔認識テクノロジーや，犯罪パターンを分析するソフトウエアの話は，本題への導入の中で具体例として挙げられているだけなので，解答には含めない。第2段落に出てくる具体的なパーセンテージも不要である。解答例では，まず全体の構成として，However, Furthermore, Therefore という接続表現を適切に用いることで，各段落の要旨をわかりやすく伝えている。第2段落のAIを使ったソフトウエアを利用することへの懸念については，there are grave concerns that this will have an adverse influence on judges' decisions とまとめている。grave は serious，adverse は negative の類義語で，このような語句を使うことで表現力の高さを示すことができる。第3段落の，AIが学習するデータに人間の偏見が含まれている可能性があるため AIの判断にも偏見が存在しかねないことについては，since the AI has been trained on data that could contain human biases, there are fears that the software might also be biased と，関係代名詞を用いてわかりやすく表現している。

5

問題の訳
TOPIC：投票は義務であるべきか。

解答例①

　It is my opinion that forcing people to vote in elections is not only undemocratic and difficult to enforce, but may also lead to people voting randomly for people they do not support.

　First of all, the right to vote is a right, not a duty. Although some people choose not to vote because they are apathetic, many others do so because they do not like any of the candidates, or because they are not interested in the issue being voted on. In a democracy, people should have the right to vote or not vote as they choose.

　Secondly, it is very difficult to enforce

解答例①の訳

　私の意見では，選挙での投票を強制することは，非民主的であり，実際に行うことは難しいばかりか，人々が支持していない人にでたらめに投票することにつながりかねません。

　まず，投票権は権利であって，義務ではありません。関心がないという理由で投票の棄権を選ぶ人もいますが，多くの人が棄権を選ぶ理由は，気に入った候補者がいない，あるいは投票によって決まる事柄に興味がないからです。民主主義社会では，人々が好きなように投票する権利あるいはしない権利があるべきです。

　2つ目に，義務投票制の実施はとても難しいことです。投票しない人には罰金を課すという考えがあります。しかし，多数の人が投票しないことを選んだら，罰

compulsory voting. One idea is to fine people who do not vote. However, if a large number of people choose not to vote, the administrative costs of fining them would be enormous. It would be better for governments to spend the money on campaigns to encourage people to vote than on prosecuting people who do not.

And lastly, some people are just not interested in politics. If voting were to be compulsory, it might lead to people choosing parties without researching their policies carefully. This could lead to parties people do not really want being elected.

Although it is regrettable that so many people these days choose not to exercise their right to vote, compulsory voting is not desirable for both ethical and practical reasons. (230語)

金を課すのにかかる管理費用は膨大な額になるでしょう。政府はそのお金を使って投票促進キャンペーンをした方が，投票しない人を訴えるよりよいでしょう。

最後に，一部の人はただ政治に興味がありません。投票が義務化されたら，念入りに政策を調べずに政党を選ぶ人が出てくるかもしれません。これでは実際には望まれていない政党が選ばれることになりかねません。

最近ではたくさんの人が投票権を行使しないという選択をしており，残念なことではありますが，義務投票制は倫理的にも実用性の面でも望ましくないのです。

解説 序論では，トピックに対して反対の立場を表明し，「民主的でないこと」，「実施困難なこと」，「でたらめな投票」という3つの理由を簡単に挙げている。その具体的な説明が第2～4段落の本論部分で，「民主主義社会には投票しない権利もあるべき」（第2段落），「義務投票はコストがかかるので実用的でない」（第3段落），「有権者がでたらめに投票する」（第4段落）と，反対理由を順番に詳しく述べている。最後の段落は1文でまとめている。Although it is regrettable that so many people these days choose not to exercise their right to vote と譲歩することで，賛成派の共感も得る効果が期待できる。

解答例②

Voting is not only our right but also our duty. By making voting compulsory, we can encourage people to be more politically aware and force political parties to consider the needs of all voters.

First of all, it is our civic duty to vote. In the past, many men and women fought and died to secure the right to vote for us. It is a cornerstone of democracy. If we want to live in a democratic society, we should be prepared to take part in the democratic process by voting.

The next point to consider is that when people are required to vote, they tend to educate themselves about the policies of the parties they have to choose from. This is a good thing as it leads to a better-informed electorate, as well as an elected government that reflects the wishes of the people.

And finally, if everyone has to vote, political parties will have to work harder to appeal to all

解答例②の訳

投票とは，単なる権利ではなく，私たちの務めでもあります。投票の義務化によって，人々の政治への意識を高めることができますし，さらに政党にすべての有権者のニーズをよく考えさせることができます。

まず初めに，投票は市民の務めです。かつて，男女を問わず多くの人々が戦い，命を落とし，私たちに代わって投票権を守ってくれました。それが民主主義の礎です。民主主義社会で暮らしたいと思うのなら，投票によって民主主義のプロセスに参加する心構えができていないといけません。

次に考えるべき点は，投票が義務である場合，人々は自分たちが選ぶ政党の政策について，自ら学ぶ傾向があるということです。これは良いことです。そのおかげで有権者の知識が増えますし，さらに選挙で誕生した政府には市民の願いが反映されるからです。

そして最後になりますが，もし全員が投票しなければならなければ，政党は社会のあらゆる部門に訴えかけるために，さらに努力しなければならなくなるでしょう。現在は年齢が高いほど投票者の数も多い傾向があるので，政党はこの層をターゲットとしています。

sectors of society. At present, older people tend to vote in higher numbers, so political parties target them. However, if voting is compulsory, political parties have to appeal to younger people, too. This in turn leads to young people becoming more interested in politics.

Compulsory voting is good for society as it safeguards democracy, leads to a better-informed electorate, and encourages political parties to consider the needs of all members of society. (234 語)

しかし，投票が義務ならば，政党は若い層にも訴えかけなければなりません。その結果，若者が政治にもっと興味を持つことにつながるのです。

義務投票制が社会にとって良い理由は，それが民主主義を守り，有権者の知識を増やし，社会の全構成員のニーズを考慮するように政党の背中を後押しするからです。

解説　序論では，トピックに対して賛成の立場を表明し，「人々の政治に対する意識の高まり」と「政党による全有権者のニーズの考慮」を挙げている。ここでは理由が2つしかないが，本論を読むと，「人々の政治に対する意識の高まり」について，さらに理由を2つに分けて説明していることがわかる。具体的には，第2段落で「民主主義社会で生きる者の務めとしての投票」について，第3段落では「投票の義務化によって有権者が政治の勉強をすること」について述べている。第4段落は投票義務化が政党に与える良い効果について述べていて，すなわち義務化の結果誕生した政権は全有権者のニーズを無視できないと述べている。最後の段落では，本論で挙げた3つの理由を簡潔にまとめることで結論としている。

リスニングテスト
解答と解説

問題編 p.46〜52

リスニング

Part 1

問題	1	2	3	4	5	6	7	8	9	10
解答	3	3	3	1	2	1	2	4	4	1

Part 2

問題	11	12	13	14	15	16	17	18	19	20
解答	4	1	3	2	4	2	2	4	4	3

Part 3

問題	21	22	23	24	25
解答	1	2	3	3	3

Part 4

問題	26	27
解答	3	1

Part 1　◀》026〜036

No. 1　解答　3

★: Oh, hi, Mary. How are you doing?
☆: Not bad, but I'm really busy trying to get ahead in my work. I'm going on vacation next week, you know.
★: Oh, that's right. Where are you planning to go?
☆: I haven't decided for sure, but I'll take a short local trip to Carmel, perhaps for just a day or two. I'll mostly hang around in town, do a lot of reading, catch up on some TV programs, and make up for my lack of sleep this week.
★: Sounds good. I hope you have fun.
Question: How can Mary's plans for next week be best described?

★: やあ，メアリー。調子はどう？
☆: 悪くはないけど，仕事を先に進めようと頑張っているから，本当に忙しいのよ。私は来週休暇を取るでしょう。
★: ああ，そうだったね。どこへ行く予定なの？
☆: まだはっきり決めてはいないけど，近場のカーメルへ短い旅をするつもりよ。おそらく1日か2日ね。ほとんどは市内をぶらぶらしたり，たくさん本を読んだり，見逃したテレビ番組を見たり，今週の睡眠不足の埋め合わせをしたりするわ。
★: いいね。楽しんでね。
質問: 来週のメアリーの予定についてどのように説明するのが一番よいか。

1 まだ来週のことは考えていない。　**2** 国内を旅して回りたいと思っている。
3 基本的にゆっくりするつもりである。　**4** 仕事の遅れを取り戻したいと思っている。

解説 メアリーの最後の発言 I'll mostly hang around in town, do a lot of reading, catch up on some TV programs, and make up for my lack of sleep this week. から，のんびり過ごすつもりでいることがわかる。**3**が正解。take it easy「気楽にのんびり過ごす」，catch up on 〜「〜の遅れなどを取り戻す」。

No. 2　解答 3

★：Where shall we go on vacation this summer? We need to plan something.
☆：Well, I like the tropics, as you know. How about a nice resort in Thailand or Bali?
★：We only have five days, and I don't want to spend a large part of our vacation on a plane. How about some place closer, someplace like Vietnam?
☆：But I don't like big cities. I want to just relax on a beach.
★：We could stay in a quiet beach resort in some place like Da Nang. And there's a nonstop there from Tokyo.
☆：That would work. Let's search for a resort online, then.
Question：What was the man and woman's solution to their differences?

★：今度の夏の休暇はどこに行こうか。何か計画をしないと。
☆：そうね，知っての通り，私は熱帯地方が好きなのよね。タイやバリのすてきなリゾート地なんてどうかしら？
★：5日間しかないんだから，休暇の多くの時間を飛行機に費やすのはごめんだよ。もっと近い所はどう？　ベトナムとかは？
☆：でも大都市は嫌いなの。ただビーチでリラックスしたいの。
★：ダナンのような場所にある静かなビーチリゾートに滞在してもいいんじゃない。東京から直行便もあるしね。
☆：それならいいわね。じゃあネットでリゾート探しをしましょう。
質問：男性と女性は意見の相違をどのように解決したか。

1 大都市近くのリゾートを見つけることによって。　**2** 休暇中に少し仕事をすることによって。
3 簡単に着けるリゾートを見つけることによって。　**4** 2人とも好きな文化を選ぶことによって。

解説　女性はタイやバリのリゾートでゆっくりしたいと思っている。一方の男性は飛行機に長く乗るのは嫌で，How about some place closer, someplace like Vietnam? とより近い場所を提案している。これに女性はいったん反対するが，ベトナムのダナンにもリゾートがあると言われ，That would work. と答えている。**3** が正解。

No. 3　解答 3

★：Hasn't the weather been outrageous, Julie? It's already the middle of April, and it still feels like winter.
☆：Yeah, I know what you mean, Danny. We've only had a day or two of real spring days, and the rest of the time it's been dreary and downright freezing.
★：I'm thinking about escaping somewhere down south for a few days to thaw out.
☆：Well, you may want to wait and see. The forecast shows warming and blue skies by next week.
★：Yeah, right. Well, that's not going to stop me. I've heard that one too many times before.
Question：How does Danny feel about the weather forecast?

★：ジュリー，ここのところとんでもない天気だよね？　もう4月の半ばなのに，まだ冬みたいだ。
☆：うん，わかるわ，ダニー。本当に春めいた日は1日か2日しかなくて，後はずっと気のめいるような，本当に凍える日ばかりだもの。
★：どこか南の方へ2，3日，温まりに逃げ出そうと思っているんだ。
☆：でも，様子を見た方がいいと思うわ。予報では，来週までには暖かくなって晴れると言っているわ。
★：さあ，どうだか。まあ，そんなことでは僕を止められやしない。そんな予報は前にも嫌と言うほど聞いたことがあるからね。
質問：ダニーは天気予報のことをどう思っているか。

1 予報を聞いて安心している。　**2** それが本当になるか事態を見守るつもりだ。
3 予報をひどく疑っている。　**4** 予報を聞いて驚いている。

解説　ジュリーが天気予報について The forecast shows warming and blue skies by next week. と言うと，ダニーは Well, that's not going to stop me. I've heard that one too many times before. と頭から信用していない発言をしている。**3** が正解。

No. 4　解答　1

★：Hey, Angela. Did you see that program last night about the latest sports scandal?

☆：You mean the Tour of California doping scandal?

★：Yeah. Apparently the race is riddled with drug users. I love cycle racing, but this ruins the sport for everyone.

☆：I think it's way overblown. I mean, one or two riders get caught and suddenly everyone is blamed.

★：Yeah, but the only way to ensure confidence in the integrity of the sport is to test everyone, and then act firmly and swiftly when a racer has clearly cheated.

Question：What does Angela imply about the scandal?

★：やあ，アンジェラ。昨夜のあのテレビ番組を見た？　最新のスポーツ界のスキャンダルについて放送していた番組だよ。

☆：ツアー・オブ・カリフォルニアでの薬物使用スキャンダルのこと？

★：そう。どうやら，あのレースは薬物使用者だらけらしい。僕は自転車レースが大好きなのに，この事件のせいでみんながこのスポーツを嫌になってしまうよ。

☆：話がすごく誇張されていると思うわ。つまり，ライダーが1人か2人捕まったら，突然みんなが責められるのね。

★：うん，でも，このスポーツが清廉潔白に行われていることを確実に信じてもらう唯一の方法は，全員を検査して，そしてあるレーサーが明らかに不正を行っていたのであれば，速やかに断固たる行動を取ることだね。

質問：アンジェラがこのスキャンダルについて示唆していることは何か。

1 ほとんどのライダーは薬物を使っていない。　　**2** もっと多くのライダーが捕まるだろう。
3 レースのイメージは損なわれなかった。　　**4** 多くの人々に責任がある。

解説　会話の後半でアンジェラはone or two riders get caught and suddenly everyone is blamed. と述べている。つまり，不正を行っていたのは一部の選手で，ほとんどの選手は無実だと彼女は考えているので，**1**が正解。be riddled with「～だらけである」。

No. 5　解答　2

●：How's the team teaching working out for you?

☆：Not great, Michael. Ron's not pulling his weight, so I end up doing everything. And on top of that, he often criticizes the way I teach.

●：That's not right. You should put your foot down and insist he do his share. Is he at least helping with curriculum development?

☆：Not really. What little he's done doesn't fit with our lesson plans. I've confronted Ron before about this, but it has no effect. I'm ready to ask the vice principal if I can change partners.

●：Yes, you should definitely do that.

Question：What does the man suggest the woman do?

●：チーム授業の進捗はどう？

☆：順調じゃないわ，マイケル。ロンが十分に協力してくれないから，すべて自分でやるはめになっているの。それに加えて，彼は私の教え方をよく批判するのよ。

●：それはよくないね。断固として彼に自分のすべきことはするように主張するべきだ。少なくともカリキュラム作りは手伝ってくれているの？

☆：そうでもないわ。わずかながら彼がしたこともあるけど，私たちのレッスン計画にはそぐわないの。以前にこの件をロンに面と向かって伝えたのだけど，効果はないわ。副校長にパートナーを変えられるか聞くつもりよ。

●：そうだね，絶対そうすべきだよ。

質問：男性は女性にどうするように提案しているか。

1 ロンにすべての作業をするように頼む。　　**2** チームメンバーの変更を要求する。
3 現在のカリキュラムを改善する。　　**4** ロンにチームに加わるように頼む。

男性は you should definitely do that（= ask the vice principal if she can change partners）と最後に言っているので**2**が正解。

No. 6 　解答　**1**

☆：Can you believe it? No word yet about the upcoming software development project, and it's the end of March already.

★：That's absolutely crazy. Money was allocated months ago, and team members have already been chosen by Research and Development. So I mean, what's up? Is there a glitch?

☆：Rumor has it that Sales wants to change requirement specifications before we begin, probably tacking on some additional functions.

★：Well, I wish they'd at least let us know what's up so we could make better use of our time. I could've been working on something else these last few weeks.

☆：Exactly. It's not only wasteful, but downright rude.

Question：What is the problem they are discussing?

☆：信じられるかしら。今度のソフトウエア開発プロジェクトについてまだ何も連絡がないのよ。もう3カ月も終わりだというのに。

★：完全に正気の沙汰じゃないね。何カ月も前に予算はついているし，チームメンバーだって研究開発部がすでに選んでいる。つまり，どうしたって言うんだ？　何かうまくいっていないのかな。

☆：噂だと営業部は，私たちが始動する前に要求仕様を変えたいと思っているらしいわ。おそらく，いくつか機能を追加しようとしているのよ。

★：でも，少なくともどうなっているのか知らせてくれたらいいのに。そうすればもっと時間を有効に使えるんだから。この数週間で別のことを進められたのに。

☆：その通り。無駄なだけでなく，全くもって失礼だわ。

質問：彼らが話している問題は何か。

1 プロジェクトの遅れについてコミュニケーションが足りていないこと。
2 プロジェクトに必要なスタッフの不足。
3 プロジェクトをやり遂げるには不十分な予算。
4 プロジェクトが多すぎて負担が過剰にかかっていること。

話題の中心は何も進まないプロジェクトについてだが，特に会話の後半で男性が I wish they'd at least let us know what's up so we could make better use of our time と言い，何も情報が回ってこないことを問題視している。これに女性も同調しているので**1**が正解。

No. 7 　解答　**2**

●：What's your impression of the new director? He's been here for almost three months now.

☆：Honestly, I can't think of anything good to say. I'm taken aback by his lack of empathy and management skills.

●：I think you're being overly harsh. After all, he came to us with a stellar résumé showing a record of success. That said, his old school, top-down approach isn't a great fit here at Intech.

☆：You're being too kind. I can't believe the president would hire anyone like that. Look at his results the last three months. The whole department's in an uproar.

●：新ディレクターの印象はどう？　彼がここに来てもうじき3カ月になるよね。

☆：正直に言うと，何もほめるところがないわ。彼の思いやりとマネジメントスキルのなさにはびっくりよ。

●：君は厳しすぎると思うよ。結局彼は，成功実績が書かれた輝かしい経歴を持ってわれわれのところに来たんだよ。とは言え，彼の昔ながらのトップダウン方式は，わがインテック社にはあまり合っていないね。

☆：あなたは優しすぎるわ。社長があんな人を雇うなんて信じられない。ここ3カ月で彼が出した結果を見てよ。事業部全体が混乱しているわ。

Question：What does the man imply about the new director?

質問：男性は新ディレクターについて何を示唆しているか。

1 彼は履歴書で嘘の内容を記した可能性が高い。　　**2** 彼はこの会社の文化に合っていない。
3 彼は明らかにマネジメントスキルが欠落している。　**4** 彼は成功のチャンスを与えられるのに値する。

解説　男性は新ディレクターについて，he came to us with a stellar résumé showing a record of success と言い，続けて his old school, top-down approach isn't a great fit here at Intech. とも言っている。後半の内容に合う **2** が正解。be taken aback「驚く」，old school「旧来の」，in an uproar「(怒りなどで) 大騒ぎで」。

No. 8　解答　4

●：Hi, Melanie. How are things going at Human Resources?

☆：Not as well as I'd like. We've been losing a number of freelancers lately. They complain they're not being paid in a timely manner.

●：Are you serious? That's not just inefficient but totally inexcusable. It kills motivation and retention. Have you tried talking to anyone in Accounting?

☆：Of course, but I haven't gotten anywhere with them. They don't understand it's hard to find talented, reliable part-time staff and that it takes time to train new staff.

●：Yeah, what a waste! I hope you can eventually make a breakthrough and turn things around.

Question：What is the woman's problem?

●：こんにちは，メラニー。人事部の仕事は順調かい？

☆：なかなか思い通りにはいかないわ。最近フリーランスの人が何人もいなくなってしまったの。適切なタイミングで支払いがなされないと文句を言っているわ。

●：本当なの？　それは効率が悪いというだけでなく，全く言い訳できないことだよ。モチベーションはなくすし，会社に留めておくこともできないよ。経理部の人とは話してみたの？

☆：もちろんよ。でも彼らとはうまくいかなかったの。彼らは才能があって頼りになるパートタイムのスタッフを見つけることがどんなに大変か理解していないし，新しいスタッフの研修には時間がかかることも理解していないの。

●：そうだね，なんて無駄なことを！　最後には現状を打破できて，事態が好転するといいね。

質問：女性の問題は何か。

1 彼女はフリーランスになりたくない。　　　　**2** 現在のパートタイムの従業員は無責任である。
3 人事部のスタッフには意欲がない。　　　　　**4** フリーランスの人たちの離職率が高い。

解説　女性の問題は，給与支払いの問題で数々のフリーランスがいなくなったことと，経理部の理解がないこと。フリーランスがいなくなったことを turnover「離職率，転職率」を使って表している **4** が正解。

No. 9　解答　4

☆：Hello, ITO Computers. Can I help you?

★：Yes. I'd like some information about your new notebooks. Could you send me a brochure, including pricing, warranty information, and technical support services?

☆：Yes, of course. All the information can also be found on our website if you have Internet access.

★：Actually, I don't right now. That's one of the main reasons I'm planning to purchase a notebook.

☆：Well, in that case, we'll be happy to mail you the

☆：はい，ITOコンピュータです。どのようなご用件でしょうか。

★：はい。そちらの新型のノートパソコンについて知りたいのですが。価格と保証内容と技術サポート・サービスが書いてあるパンフレットを送っていただけないでしょうか。

☆：はい，もちろんです。インターネットに接続されているのでしたら，情報はすべて当社のウェブサイトにも載っております。

★：実は今は接続していません。ノートパソコンを

Day
4

information. Please give me your name and mailing address.

★：Sure. My name is David Wilson, and my address is 555 South Drive, Chicago, Illinois 60604.

☆：Over the next few weeks, we'll be setting up promotional booths in several shopping centers in the Chicago area to show our new line of notebooks.

★：That sounds good. So I'll be able to talk directly to your salesperson and try out the computers?

☆：That's right. And we're offering a free pair of speakers or a printer with every computer purchased during the promotional period.

★：Could you give me the dates and locations where you'll be setting up the booths?

☆：Yes, certainly. Just let me know what area of the city would be most convenient for you.

Question：Why did David call ITO Computers?

買おうと考えている大きな理由の1つがそれなんです。

☆：そうですか，それでしたら喜んでパンフレットをお送りいたします。お名前と郵送先のご住所をおっしゃってください。

★：はい。名前はデイビッド・ウィルソンで，住所はイリノイ州シカゴ60604のサウス・ドライブ555です。

☆：これから数週間の間，当社はシカゴ・エリア内にあるショッピングセンター数店舗で販売促進用のブースを設けて，ノートパソコンの新製品を展示することにしています。

★：それはいいですね。つまり，販売員の方と直接お話しして，パソコンを試すことができるわけですね。

☆：そうです。それから，販促期間中にパソコンをご購入いただくと，スピーカー1組かプリンターをもれなく無料でおつけいたします。

★：ブースを設置する日にちと場所を教えていただけますか。

☆：はい，かしこまりました。市内で一番行きやすい地区を教えてください。

質問：デイビッドはなぜITOコンピュータに電話したのか。

1 特別な販売促進について知りたかったから。
2 販売員と話したかったから。
3 ITOのノートパソコンをどこで見られるのか知りたかったから。
4 ITOのノートパソコンのチラシが欲しかったから。

解説　冒頭で男性が I'd like some information about your new notebooks. Could you send me a brochure ...? と言っており，ノートパソコンのパンフレットを欲しかったことがわかる。brochure を literature と言い換えている **4** が正解。

No. 10 解答 **1**

☆：OK, our business simulation is over. How do you think it went?

★：I can't understand why Lucas refused to accept my proposal for exclusive rights to our products in Brazil. I made him a good proposal, one that I was sure he couldn't refuse.

☆：What is your take on that, Lucas?

●：We never start negotiating like you did in Brazil without some kind of casual and friendly conversation first. You just started throwing numbers at me. Nobody trusts or likes that.

☆：はい，ビジネスシミュレーションは終わりました。どうでしたか。

★：ルーカスが私の提案を受け入れなかった理由がわかりません。ブラジルで当社の製品を独占して扱えるんですよ。彼には良い提案をしましたし，彼はそれを断われないだろうと私は確信していました。

☆：その点についてあなたの意見はどうですか，ルーカス？

●：あなたがブラジルでしたようなやり方では，交渉は決して始まりません。最初にカジュアルで

★ : Well, that's the way we do things in Switzerland. We don't like to waste people's time. Besides, I thought I gave you a polite greeting.

☆ : You need to consider, Bruce, that carrying out a negotiation in a foreign culture requires an understanding of that culture's social mannerisms.

★ : That's the first time I've ever been told I'm not courteous.

☆ : I don't think it's a matter of courtesy. It's more like establishing trust in a new social context, one that's quite different from the one in Switzerland.

● : Exactly. In many Latin cultures like ours, it's important to talk about family and personal things to first establish a relationship before getting down to business. You just can't rush things or you create hard feelings.

☆ : There's no doubt, Bruce, that you were prepared for the negotiation. You did an outstanding job with that. But there are other factors to consider when establishing a new business relationship.

★ : I see, I guess. I thought I would really win this negotiation with all the work that I put into it.

Question：What did Bruce fail to do, according to the other speakers?

気さくな会話もないなんて。あなたはただ私に数字を提示し始めただけです。そんなやり方は誰の信用も得られませんし，気に入る人はいません。

★：ですが，それがスイスでのわれわれのやり方です。私たちは人の時間を無駄にしたくはないのです。それに，私はあなたに礼儀正しくあいさつしたと思いますよ。

☆：ブルース，あなたはよく考える必要がありますよ。海外の文化圏で交渉を進めるには，その文化の社会的習慣を理解しなければなりません。

★：礼儀正しくないなんて言われたのは，今回が初めてです。

☆：礼儀正しいかどうかの問題ではないと思いますよ。それはもっと，スイスとは大きく異なる新しい社会的文脈の中で信頼を築けるかどうかの問題なのです。

●：その通りです。われわれのような多くのラテン文化では，家族や個人的なことについて話すことが重要で，それによってまず関係を築き，それから仕事の話をするのです。物事を急いではいけません。悪い感情を生んでしまいます。

☆：ブルース，あなたが交渉のための準備をしていたことは間違いありません。その点ではすばらしい仕事をしました。でも，新たなビジネス関係を構築する際にはほかにも検討すべき要因があるのです。

★：わかったように思います。やってきたことをすべてぶつけてこの交渉を本当に勝ち取ろうと思っていたのです。

質問：ブルースは，ほかの2人の話者によると，何ができていなかったのか。

Day **4**

1 まず友好的な関係を構築すること。
2 受け入れ可能な提案を考えること。
3 始めに丁寧に自己紹介すること。
4 ルーカスに文化的に受け入れてもらえる振る舞いについて尋ねること。

解説　会話では，ブルースとルーカスが女性とともにビジネスシミュレーションを振り返っている。ブルースの交渉の進め方について，ルーカスは We never start negotiating ... without some kind of casual and friendly conversation first. と問題点を指摘している。さらに it's important to talk about family and personal things to first establish a relationship before getting down to business と助言し，友好的な関係を築くことの重要さを伝えている。女性も同意見で，新しい社会や文化でどう信頼関係を築くかが大事だと述べているので，**1** が正解。

(A)

Teaching Creativity

There are many who believe we can't teach creativity because it is a gift that only comes naturally, like musical talent or even athletic ability. It is certainly difficult to teach genius, which is largely something with which a child must be born. However, we can teach creativity, or at least we can provide the environment and intellectual resources required for students to develop creative ways of looking at the world and solving problems. Teaching creativity means that students must be expected to do something other than listen to lectures, read textbooks, and memorize information. It requires students to solve problems and make use of the information and thinking methods available to them.

Teachers should encourage students to think "outside the box," and there are several things they can do to encourage this. They should help children see that there are often several solutions to a single problem or question. They can also create an atmosphere where there is often no single correct answer, and have children brainstorm or be imaginative through storytelling or games. It's important to give children more choices, and to back off from making too many decisions for them. Stimulate their senses by having them describe smells, colors, and flavors. Ask them to smell the flowers in a garden and then draw them. Teaching creativity requires teachers themselves to teach creatively.

Questions

No.11　What does the speaker imply about the teaching of creativity?

No.12　What should children be encouraged to do to think "outside the box"?

創造力教育

　創造力は，音楽の才能やさらに運動能力のように生まれながらにしか持ち得ない才能なので，教えることは不可能だと考える人は多い。確かに天賦の才を教えることは難しい。その大部分は，子供が生まれつき備えていなければならないものだからだ。しかし，創造力を教えることは可能である。あるいは，少なくとも，世の中を見つめ問題を解決する創造的な方法を生徒が身につけるのに必要な環境や知的資源を提供することはできる。創造力を教えるということは，生徒は講義を聞き，教科書を読み，情報を記憶するのとは違った何かをすることを当然期待されるということである。生徒には，問題を解決し，彼らが入手する情報と思考方法を活用することが求められる。

　教師は生徒に「箱の外で」考えるように促すべきであり，これを促進するために教師にできることはいくつかある。教師がすべきことは，1つの問題や疑問にはしばしばいくつかの解決法が存在することを子供が理解できるように助けることである。教師はまた，正解が1つに限定されないことが多い環境を作りだし，子供たちにブレーンストーミングをさせたり，物語やゲームを通じて彼らの想像力を豊かにしたりすることもできる。大切なのは，子供により多くの選択肢を与え，彼らに代わって多くの決定を下しすぎるのは控えることである。匂い，色，風味を描写させることで子供たちの五感を刺激しなさい。庭の花の匂いを嗅いでからその絵を描くように求めなさい。創造力を教えるとは，教師自身が創造的に教えることが求められるのである。

No. 11　解答　**4**

「話し手が創造力教育について示唆していることは何か」

1　教師が教えられることにはほぼ限度がない。

2　正しく教えることで実際に才能を生み出すことができる。

3　生徒は刺激を与えてくれる本や講義に触れることで，もっと創造的に考える。

4　生徒に期待すべきことは，自分自身で問題を解決することだ。

解説　英文全体が創造力教育に関する説明だが，It requires students to solve problems and make use of the information and thinking methods available to them. や It's important to give children more choices, and to back off from making too many decisions for them. などから，学生は受動的に知識を得るだけでなく，自ら能動的に動いて実際に問題解決に取り組んでいくことが大事だとわかる。**4** が正解。back off from ～「～を控える」。

No. 12　解答　1

「『箱の外で』考えるために，子供たちはどうすることが奨励されるべきか」
1 問題や疑問の解決法を複数思い描く。
2 教師によって提供されるさまざまな創造的な発想についてよく考える。
3 自信を高めるために教師に質問する。
4 好奇心を刺激するために面白くて創造的な番組を見る。

解説　think "outside the box" のために必要なことは，まず help children see that there are often several solutions to a single problem or question，次に have children brainstorm or be imaginative through storytelling or games，そして give children more choices, and to back off from making too many decisions for them と説明がある。言っていることはどれも実質的に同じで，解決法は1つでないことを知り，その上で自ら問題に対処できるようになること。**1** が正解。

(B)

The Ozone Hole

For decades, controversy has raged over chlorofluorocarbons, economically important gases also known as CFCs. In the 1970s, CFCs were blamed for depleting the ozone layer, which helps absorb the dangerous ultraviolet rays of the sun. The "ozone hole" over Antarctica was cited as evidence of a future global epidemic of skin cancer. It was claimed that even with a total ban on CFCs, it would take 50 years for the ozone layer to be restored. Thus, scientists were surprised by the amazing shrinkage of the ozone hole in 2002, and were further surprised to see a massive increase of ozone around the hole.

Although totally contrary to expectations, this dramatic fluctuation does not exonerate CFCs entirely, but it does show that scientists are still far from a complete understanding of atmospheric and climatic change. It also points to the dangers of basing economic policy on new scientific theories. The unexpected closing of the ozone hole should also make us skeptical of claims that carbon dioxide causes global warming. The cost of phasing out CFCs is estimated to be at least $40 billion, but costs of reducing carbon dioxide emissions to fight the alleged threat of global warming will be far higher.

Questions
No.13　What happened in Antarctica in 2002?
No.14　What does the speaker assert?

Day 4

オゾンホール

　何十年にもわたり，フロンガスを巡って激しい論争が行われてきた。フロンガスは経済的に重要な気体であり，CFC としても知られている。1970 年代に，太陽が発する危険な紫外線を吸収するのに役立つオゾン層を破壊するとして，CFC がやり玉に挙がった。南極大陸上空の「オゾンホール」は，将来世界的に皮膚がんが流行する証拠として引き合いに出された。CFC を全面的に禁止したとしても，オゾン層が修復されるには50年かかると言われた。したがって，オゾンホールが2002年に驚くほど縮小したことに科学者たちは驚き，ホールの周囲にオゾンが大量に増加したのを見てさらに驚いたのである。

　予想とは正反対だったものの，この劇的なオゾンの量の変動はCFCの容疑を完全に晴らすものではない。しかし，科学者が大気と気候の変化の完全な理解からはいまだ程遠いということを明らかにしているのは確かである。この変動はまた，新しい科学理論に基づいて経済政策を行うことの危険を示すものでもある。オゾンホールが予期せず閉じたことは，二酸化炭素が地球温暖化の原因であるという主張に対して私たちを懐疑的にするはずである。CFC の段階的廃止にかかるコストは少なくとも400億ドルと見積もられているが，地球温暖化なる脅威と闘

うために二酸化炭素排出量を削減するコストは，それをはるかに上回ることになる。

No. 13　解答　3

「2002年に南極大陸で何が起きたか」

1 大気中のCFCのレベルが変動した。　　**2** 大気中のオゾンが減少した。
3 オゾンホールが著しく縮まった。　　**4** 危険な紫外線が突然に増加した。

解説　2002年の出来事を説明しているところで，the amazing shrinkage of the ozone hole, a massive increase of ozone around the hole と述べられている。オゾンが増加し，ゆえにオゾンホールが縮まったのである。従って正解は**3**。

No. 14　解答　2

「話し手が主張しているのは何か」

1 二酸化炭素は明らかに地球温暖化の原因となっている。
2 科学理論に経済方針を基づかせることは危険である。
3 CFCを減らすことは二酸化炭素排出を減らすよりも費用がかかる。
4 科学はオゾン層の役割を完全には説明できない。

解説　後半の主張部分において，It also points to the dangers of basing economic policy on new scientific theories. と述べられているので，**2**が正解。**1**と**3**については，逆の意味の主張がなされており，**4**については述べられていない。

(C)

René Descartes

Born in France in 1596, René Descartes is often called the "Father of Modern Philosophy," such was his influence on the development of the modern study of the discipline. He is perhaps best known for his philosophical statement "cogito ergo sum," which translates as "I think, therefore I am." However, he wasn't the first person to suggest it. This philosophical line of thinking, that to be conscious that we are perceiving or thinking is to be conscious that we exist, can be traced back to classic philosophers such as Plato, Aristotle, and the 8th century Hindu philosopher, Adi Shankara.

Descartes' contributions to academia are not confined to philosophy, as he also contributed to scientific study and published a great number of mathematical works. While serving as a mercenary in the Protestant Dutch States Army, he formulated analytical geometry, which merged geometry and algebra. He claimed to have been informed of analytical geometry in a "vision." The use of algebra to explain geometry had an enormous impact on the subsequent study of mathematics. Descartes' work provided the basis for the calculus developed by Sir Isaac Newton. It also led to the philosophy that he is best remembered for.

Questions

No.15　What is true about the philosophical statement "I think, therefore I am"?
No.16　How did Descartes formulate the concept of analytical geometry?

ルネ・デカルト

1596年にフランスで生まれたルネ・デカルトは「近代哲学の父」と呼ばれることが多く，この学問の近代の研究の発展に与えた彼の影響とはそのようなものであった。彼はおそらく，「cogito ergo sum」という哲学的な発言で最も有名だ。これは「われ思う，ゆえにわれあり」と訳される。しかしながら，そのような意味のことを言ったのは，彼が最初ではない。この哲学的な理屈，つまり自分が知覚・思考していることを自覚することによって自分が存在していることを自覚するということは古典時代の哲学者であるプラトンやアリストテレス，そして8世紀のヒンズー教の哲学者であるアディ・シャンカラまでさかのぼることが可能である。

学問の世界でデカルトが貢献したのは哲学だけでなく，科学的な研究にも貢献したし，膨大な数の数学の研究についても発表した。プロテスタント派のオランダ軍に傭兵として従軍していたときは，解析幾何学を確立した。これは幾何学と代数学を1つにしたものである。デカルトは，ある「ビジョン」の中で解析幾何学について知らされたのだ，と主張した。代数を使って幾何学を説明することは，その後の数学の研究に多大な影響を与えた。デカルトの功績は，サー・アイザック・ニュートンが微分積分学を生む礎となった。それがまた，彼の名を最もよく知らしめる哲学にもつながったのである。

No. 15 　解答　**4**

「『われ思う，ゆえにわれあり』という哲学的な言葉について正しいことは何か」

1 「philosophy（哲学）」という単語の訳である。

2 デカルトは近代の哲学研究をより推し進めるためにそれを使った。

3 デカルトはそのように提示した最初の人である。

4 同様の考えはほかの哲学者によって表されていた。

解説　"I think, therefore I am." については，to be conscious that we are perceiving or thinking is to be conscious that we exist とその意味を説明した後に，can be traced back to classic philosophers such as Plato, Aristotle, and the 8th century Hindu philosopher, Adi Shankara と述べている。つまり，すでにあった考え方なので，**4**が正解。

No. 16 　解答　**2**

「デカルトはどのように解析幾何学の考えをまとめ上げたか」

1 彼はサー・アイザック・ニュートンの功績に影響を受けた。

2 彼は兵士として働いているときにビジョンを得た。

3 彼は微分積分学と哲学を1つにすることを試していた。

4 彼は科学的研究を発表している間にそれを思い出した。

解説　解析幾何学については，He claimed to have been informed of analytical geometry in a "vision." と説明している。細かなことは不明だが，解析幾何学ができあがるビジョンが彼の頭に湧いたのだと推測できる。解析幾何学ができたのは傭兵として従軍していたときのことなので，**2**が正解。

(D)

Zoetropes

A zoetrope is a form of pre-film animation device, which may be considered the forerunner to films. It is made using a cylinder with vertical slits and a series of still images which, when rotated, gives the illusion of motion. The slits prevent the images from blurring together, creating a succession of images that seem to be moving. The images seem to be alive; hence zoetropes are considered one of the earliest forms of animation. In fact, the name "zoetrope" comes from the Greek words for "life" and "turn" and could be taken to mean "wheel of life."

The modern cylindrical zoetrope was created in 1834 by British mathematician William George Horner. A patented, reusable version was then invented by an 18-year-old American student, William Ensign Lincoln, in 1865. The concept may have had much earlier beginnings, however. A bowl from Iran, dated at over 5,000 years old, featured a goat in various stages of motion. A Chinese inventor, Ding Huan, produced an early version of the zoetrope around 190 AD. He designed a lamp decorated with birds and other animals that rotated when the lamp was lit. The rotation was said to give the appearance of the animals moving naturally.

Questions

No.17　How might zoetropes have led to films?

No.18　What did early zoetropes depict?

ゾートロープ

　ゾートロープ（回転のぞき絵）とは，映画ができる前の動画装置の一形態であり，映画の前身だと考えられるかもしれない。ゾートロープは，垂直に切れ目が入った円筒と連続した静止絵を使ってできており，回転させると錯覚で動いているように見える。この切れ目は，絵が一緒になってぼやけてしまうのを防いでおり，絵を連続させることで動いているかのように見せている。絵が生き生きとして見えるので，ゆえにゾートロープは一番古い動画の一形態と考えられている。実際，「ゾートロープ」という名前は life（命）と turn（回転）を表すギリシャ語に由来し，wheel of life（命の輪）の意味だと理解することが可能だ。

　近代の円筒状のゾートロープは1834年に英国の数学者であるウィリアム・ジョージ・ホーナーによって作られた。その後，特許を受けた再利用可能なゾートロープを発明したのが18歳のアメリカ人学生であるウィリアム・エンサイン・リンカーンであり，1865年のことだった。しかしながら，その概念はずっと昔に存在していたかもしれない。5,000年以上前のイランに起源を持つ椀には，ヤギのさまざまな動きがよく描かれていた。中国人の発明家である丁緩は，初期の型のゾートロープを190年ごろに作った。彼が設計したランプにはトリやそのほかの動物が飾られており，ランプに火を灯すと回転した。この回転によって動物が自然に動いているように見えたと言われていた。

No. 17　解答　**2**

「ゾートロープはどのように映画につながった可能性があるか」

1 その円筒状の形が初期のカメラに影響した。　　**2** 静止絵を動いているように見せた。

3 動画を効果的にぼかした。　　　　　　　　　　**4** 最初のゾートロープはギリシャ人が作った。

解説　ゾートロープについては冒頭で the forerunner to films と述べている。その理由は It is made using a cylinder with vertical slits and a series of still images which, when rotated, gives the illusion of motion. とあり，ゾートロープは静止絵が動いているように見える装置だったことがわかる。**2**が正解。

No. 18　解答　**4**

「初期のゾートロープは何を描いていたか」

1 陶器や陶磁器をよく含んでいた。　　　　　　　**2** 数学的な概念と結びついていた。

3 発明家はランプやそのほかの円筒の物体を描いた。　**4** 初期の例はよく動物を描いていた。

解説　初期のゾートロープについては，イランの椀については featured a goat，中国のランプについては decorated with birds and other animals と説明がある。どちらも動物を描いているので**4**が正解。

(E)

Equality

　There can be a tendency to see equality as a modern construct. Recent history has seen advances in, for example, voting rights for women, the civil rights movement, and marriage equality. In fact, it is now established that early civilizations relied on equality and cooperation to survive. As humans became more advanced, this tendency towards equality increased. The development of tools, especially weapons, meant that it wasn't just the strongest who could dominate. This led to greater equality in early hunter-gatherer communities, even when it came to settling in one place.

　Equality in early societies can teach us much more than how to get along. Equal societies also tend to be more sustainable. People work together for the common good, rather than the strong subjugating the weak to demonstrate their superiority. Even what are generally seen as great civilizations may not be that great in hindsight. Evidence suggests that the success of the Roman Empire came with a loss of creativity and innovation, and perhaps even health. China, for example, was a more equal society. While Europe somewhat stagnated under colonization, China produced more ecological, technological and philosophical innovations including gunpowder and printing.

Questions
No.19 What has been the role of equality throughout human history?
No.20 What lessons can be learned from equality in early societies?

平等

　平等は近代に入ってから作られた概念だと見る傾向があるかもしれない。最近見られた前進には，例えば女性の投票権や公民権運動，同性結婚がある。実は，初期の文明社会は平等と協同に頼って生きていたことが今では立証されている。人間が進歩するにつれ，平等に対するこの傾向が強まったのだ。道具，特に武器の発達は，支配するのは最強の社会だけではないことを意味していた。そのおかげで，さらなる平等が初期の狩猟採集社会にもたらされたのである。それは１つの場所に定住した場合でも同じだった。

　初期社会の平等からわれわれが学べることは，仲良くやっていく方法だけでない。平等な社会はまた，高い持続性を持つ傾向があるのだ。人々は公共の利益のために一緒に働き，強者が弱者を従属させて優位性を見せつけたりはしない。一般にすばらしい文明だと見なされているものでさえ，後から振り返ってみれば，そんなたいそうなものではないかもしれない。ローマ帝国はその成功とともに創造性，革新，そしておそらくは健康さえも失ったという証拠がある。中国を例にすると，この国はもっと平等な社会だった。ヨーロッパが植民地化でいくぶん停滞していたころ，中国は生態学的，科学技術的，そして哲学的に新しいアイデアを生み出した。例えば火薬や印刷である。

No. 19　解答　**4**

「人間の歴史を通して平等の役割は何だったか」
1 先進社会がもたらした最近の傾向である。
2 平等は人間が洗練されていくにつれてあまり重要ではなくなった。
3 これまで最も強い社会の影響力を増してきた。
4 平等は初期の文明社会が起こったときから重要だと考えられてきた。
解説　パッセージは There can be a tendency to see equality as a modern construct. から始まっており，「しかしそうではない」という議論が続くと推測できる。その後で In fact, it is now established that early civilizations relied on equality and cooperation to survive. と述べているので，**4**が正解。

No. 20　解答　**3**

「初期の社会の平等からどのような教訓を学ぶことができるか」
1 公共の利益を促した植民地の方が健全だった。
2 どの文明が最も偉大だったかを決めるのは難しい。
3 平等が行きわたると社会も繁栄した。
4 高等な社会では，平等よりも革新に価値を置くべきである。
解説　初期の社会の平等については後半で述べられる。Equal societies also tend to be more sustainable. と，平等な社会ほど持続性が高いと述べている。さらに，創造性，革新，健康を失ったローマ帝国と，平等でさまざまな革新を遂げた中国の例を挙げており，**3**が正解だとわかる。

Part 3　🔊 043〜048

(F) *No. 21*　解答　**1**

This is FastEx calling. We located the package you were expecting last week. The label was not legible, so we delivered it to someone with a similar name on 5th Avenue. It was returned to the sender, who then shipped it a second time. When our driver stopped by 681, 7th Avenue, at 10 this morning, nobody was home, so he left a note. We don't deliver on weekends, so the earliest you could get it would be the 13th. If you need it before then, you could pick it up downtown at our 42nd Street Main Dispatch Office on Saturday from 9 a.m. to 5 p.m. Do not go to our local office in Highland Park as the package is not there.

状況：金曜日の夜遅く仕事を終えて帰宅すると，あなたは留守番電話で次のメッセージを聞く。あなたはどうしても12日までに小包が欲しい。

質問：あなたは明日何をすべきか。

FastExです。先週お客様がお受け取り予定だった小包の所在が確認できました。宛先ラベルが読めなかったため，5番街にお住まいのよく似たお名前の方に配達していました。小包は送り主に戻され，送り主から再度発送されました。当社のドライバーが今朝10時に7番街681番にお寄りしましたが，お留守でしたので，メモを残しました。当社は週末の配達を行っておりませんので，お届けは早くても13日になります。もしそれ以前に必要であれば，市内の42番通りにある当社の配送本部で，土曜日の午前9時から午後5時までお受け取りいただけます。小包はハイランドパーク支店にはありませんので，そちらには行かないでください。

1　42番通りの配送本部に行く。　　　　　　2　自宅で配送を待つ。

3　送り主から小包を受け取る。　　　　　　4　ハイランドパークにあるFastExの支店に電話する。

解説　状況から，小包は12日までに必要だが，the earliest you could get it would be the 13th と説明されている。続けて If you need it before then とあるので注意して聞くと，you could pick it up downtown at our 42nd Street Main Dispatch Office on Saturday from 9 a.m. to 5 p.m. という説明があるので，**1**が正解。

(G) No. 22 解答 **2**

Shoppers, we are slashing prices in our end-of-summer sale even further! Between now and 8 p.m., the cashier will give an additional 8.8 percent discount to members, or 4.4 percent for non-members. You can join for free today, but you won't get the full member's discount until the next time you visit our store. Today's special discount cannot be used in combination with our 6.6 percent senior citizen discounts. However, many items, including many discounted items, are also eligible for manufacturer's rebates of 15 percent off the purchase price if you apply within 30 days of purchase.

状況：あなたは買い物中に店内でアナウンスを聞く。あなたは店の会員であり，また高齢者である。

質問：トータルで最大の割引を利用するにはどうすればよいか。

お買い物中の皆さま，夏季最終セールの価格をさらに大幅値下げいたします！　今から午後8時まで，会員の方にはレジにてさらに8.8％の値引きを，会員以外の方には4.4％の値引きをいたします。本日無料で会員になることもできますが，正会員としての割引を受けられるのは，次回当店にお越しいただいてからとなります。本日の特別割引は，当店が行っている6.6％の高齢者割引との併用はできません。ですが，たくさんの割引品を含む多くの商品が，お買い上げから30日以内にお申し込みになれば，メーカーからお買い上げ価格の15％の割戻しを受けることもできます。

1　すべての買い物に対して割戻しを申請する。　　2　会員割引をしてもらい，割戻しを申請する。

3　高齢者割引と割戻しを組み合わせる。　　　　　4　最大割引のため午後8時以降に買い物する。

解説　割引には会員割引と高齢者割引があるが，Today's special discount cannot be used in combination with our 6.6 percent senior citizen discounts. という説明から，併用できないことがわかる。つまり割引率の高い会員割引を受ける方がよい。さらに，many items ... are also eligible for manufacturer's rebates of 15 percent off the purchase price とあるので，メーカーからの還元も受けることで割引は最大となる。**2**が正解。

(H) No. 23 解答 **3**

Your second molar on the upper right side is severely decayed. I recommend filling it instead of getting a root canal and crown or an implant. There are several choices for the filling material. An amalgam of silver and mercury is the cheapest, but some people worry about mercury in their body. A plastic composite is more expensive but has the same color as your tooth. A gold inlay is by far the strongest but also the most expensive, and some people don't find it attractive. But since the tooth is not so visible, I recommend the last if you have insurance.

状況：あなたは，歯科医師が治療の選択肢について説明するのを聞く。あなたは歯科保険に入っていない。

質問：彼のアドバイスに従うとしたら，あなたはどうすべきか。

右上の第二臼歯がひどい虫歯です。根管治療やかぶせ物，インプラントではなく詰め物をすることをお勧めします。詰め物の材質については，いくつか選択肢があります。銀と水銀の合金であるアマルガムが一番安価ですが，水銀が体内に入ることを心配する人もいます。プラスチック複合材はより高価ですが，歯と同じ色です。金のインレーは強度が断然高いですが，値段も一番高くて，見た目がよくないと感じる人もいます。ただし，この歯はそれほど目立たないので，保険にお入りでしたら，金のインレーをお勧めします。

1 悪くなった歯を抜く。　**2** 根管治療を受ける。　　**3** 詰め物をする。　　　**4** 金のかぶせ物をする。

解説　専門用語がたくさん出てくるが，I recommend filling it instead of getting a root canal and crown or an implant. が聞き取れれば正解を**3**に絞り込むことができる。cavity は「虫歯（の穴）」のこと。

(I) No. 24　解答　**3**

I'm sorry, but the road ahead is closed due to a wildfire in the vicinity. You're probably worried about your house and possessions, but we believe at this point that the firefighters will be able to keep the flames away from the structures on this hill. We can't be certain, however, especially if the wind changes. The fire crews are doing their best. For now, I need you to return down the hill. Here is the address for a temporary shelter or you may choose to stay with friends or family for the time being. The situation should become clear soon, so you'll want to listen to local news to keep up with events as they unfold.

状況：あなたが車で自宅の近くまで来ると，道路の前方に警官の姿が見える。彼はあなたの車を止め，何が起きているかを説明する。

質問：彼は，あなたにどうするように忠告しているか。

申し訳ありませんが，道路はこの先，付近の山火事のために閉鎖されています。自宅と家に置いてある物が心配だと思いますが，現状から考えて，消防隊によってこの高台にある建物への延焼を防ぐことができると思います。ただし，特に風向きが変わった場合など，どうなるか確信は持てません。消防隊は最善を尽くしています。取りあえず，坂の下へ戻っていただく必要があります。こちらが一時避難所の住所ですが，しばらくの間，友人や家族のところに滞在されても構いません。状況はじきに明らかになるはずですので，ローカルニュースを聞いて今後の事態の進展をチェックするようにしてください。

1 貴重な所有物のみ自宅から持ち出す。　　**2** 自宅で待つ間ニュースを聞く。

3 しばらくの間は自宅から離れる。　　　　**4** 建物を守ろうと努力している消防隊の手助けをする。

解説　警官は火事の状況を説明した後，For now, I need you to return down the hill. Here is the address for a temporary shelter or you may choose to stay with friends or family for the time being. と求めている。この内容を Stay away from your home と言い換えている**3**が正解。

(J) No. 25　解答　**3**

There are various promising investment options according to your plans, the amount of initial investment, and your age. I'm a big believer in real estate, either homes or apartment buildings. Unless you can put at least $60,000 down, your cash flow would be negative, which I don't recommend. Another real estate investment option, called Real Estate Investment Trusts, can be rewarding, but they don't usually pan out as well as stocks over the long run and they offer poor liquidity. Buying undervalued stocks is a time-tested winning strategy. Unless you have a lot of time for research and portfolio maintenance, though, buying individual stocks is tricky. That's why I recommend busy younger folks to go with an index fund. This gives you exposure to a wide variety of stocks to minimize risk. It also gives you liquidity if you need to divest your savings. Buying bonds that offer dividends can be great for retirees or those near retirement age.

状況：あなたは米国で投資セミナーに参加する。あなたは29歳で，退職後や将来いざというときに備えて投資したいと考えている。あなたは投資をやり繰りする時間があまりない。あなたは投資を始めるにあたって4万ドル用意している。あなたはフィナンシャル・プランナーから次のことを聞く。

質問：このフィナンシャル・プランナーよると，あなたは何をすべきか。

あなたのプラン，初期投資額，年齢ですと，有望な投資先がいろいろあります。私は不動産の価値を大いに信じています。家かアパート建物です。最低でも6万ドルは出さないとキャッシュフローがマイナスになるでしょうから，お勧めはしません。もう1つの不動産投資に，不動産投資信託と呼ばれるものがあります。やるだけの価値はあるでしょうが，長期的に見ると株式ほどの成果が上がらないことも珍しくありませんし，流動性も低いです。割安の株を買うことは，勝つための戦略として長年行われてきました。ただし，調査やポートフォリオの見直しに多くの時間をさくことができる場合を除き，個別株の購入は簡単ではありません。そのような理由で，私は多忙で若い方々にはインデックスファンドへの投資を勧めています。これは幅広い銘柄に関連することで，リスクを最小限に留めるものです。積み立てを売却する必要がある際の流動性もあります。配当金が支払われる債券の購入は，退職された方や退職間近の方にはとてもよいかもしれません。

1 個人用の家を買う。　　　　　　　　　　**2** 割安の株を買う。

3 インデックスファンドに投資する。　　　　**4** 配当金が支払われる債券に投資する。

解説　29歳のあなたは，将来への備えとして投資をしたいが，そのために使える時間はあまりなく，初期予算は4万ドルという状況。**1**と**2**はこうした条件に合わない。**4**は高齢者向きとある。残った**3**が正解。I recommend busy younger folks to go with an index fund. という説明もある。

Part 4 🔊 049〜050

★：Today, we have invited Gloria Mendez to talk about her work as a dietitian at a hospital. Welcome, Gloria.

☆：Thank you for inviting me.

★：Could you tell us what your normal working day is like?

☆：Sure. I supervise food preparers at the hospital where I work. Some hospitals outsource food preparation to a company, but at our hospital, we have our own kitchen facilities. I don't cook myself, but I have to make sure that all our food is safe to eat and that it tastes good. I spend a lot of my time checking our food's taste, making sure portions are the right size, and seeing that the presentation of the food is appealing. It's important that I also frequently check the kitchen to make sure that everything is clean.

★：Is that to avoid food poisoning?

☆：Yes, that's a big concern, as many of our patients have a weakened immune system. Some kinds of food we serve must be cooked at over 75 degrees centigrade to make sure that all germs are killed. We use a food thermometer to measure the temperature inside meats and other foods. Another important part of my job is ordering ingredients from suppliers. Before ordering, however, I must know how many patients we have and then estimate how many we will likely have in the next several weeks.

★：That sounds complicated.

☆：It is. My hospital is famous for helping patients with kidney diseases, and the number of kidney illnesses changes a lot according to the season. Many patients receive kidney dialysis two to three times a week, but during holiday seasons, families often leave dialysis patients at our hospital, so we must prepare more meals.

★：How do you decide what kinds of meals to prepare for patients?

☆：Doctors tell me about their patients, including such things as their medical conditions, results from blood tests, height, weight, that sort of thing. I've got to plan meals based on the information I receive, especially information about patients' medical conditions. Patients with heart disease, diabetes, kidney disease and high cholesterol all have different dietary needs. Several years ago, doctors used to tell us what kinds of food to prepare for their patients, but hospital dietitians make those decisions now. Our staff also works with critical-care patients. We have to manage their nutrition support, often through feeding tubes or IVs.

★：Do you ever visit patients?

☆：Oh, yes, often. Only dietitians get to meet patients directly, so it's important for me to talk to them and get feedback for the food preparation staff, which motivates them. I need to see how patients are eating and what they think of the food we prepare. Perhaps the thing that makes me happiest in my work is when I hear patients say, "The food here is really good. Thank you so much." One other thing I have to watch out for are patient needs that may not get communicated to me. For example, some patients need to have their food cut up in small pieces. I also give counseling and advice to patients about their diets so that they can get discharged more quickly and take better care of themselves after they are discharged.

★：This has been very interesting. Thank you for taking the time to be with us here today, Gloria.

☆：I've enjoyed being here.

Questions

No.26 What is one thing Gloria does to make sure the food is safe to eat?

No.27 What is one thing Gloria says about food preparation?

★：本日はグロリア・メンデスさんをお迎えしました。病院での栄養士の仕事についてお話ししていただこうと思います。ようこそ，グロリアさん。

☆：お招きいただきありがとうございます。

★：通常の勤務日がどのような感じなのか教えていただけますか。

☆：わかりました。勤務先の病院では調理担当スタッフを管理しています。病院によっては調理の準備を企業に外注しているところもありますが，当院は調理場が整っています。私自身は調理をするのではなく，すべての食べ物が安心して食べられ，味も良いことを確認しなければなりません。多くの時間を費やして食べ物の味をチェックし，分量が適当か確認し，見た目がおいしそうかどうかも確かめています。また，これも重要なことなのですが，調理場にあるものがすべて清潔に保たれているかどうかも頻繁にチェックします。

★：それはつまり，食中毒を避けるためですか。

☆：はい，それにはとても気を配っています。患者さまの多くは免疫力が低下しているからです。提供する食材によっては，摂氏75度以上で加熱調理し，確実に完全殺菌しなければなりません。食品用の温度計を使って，肉やそのほかの食べ物の内部温度を測っています。私の仕事でもう1つ重要なことは，材料を供給業者に発注することです。ただし，発注前には現在の患者数を把握しておかなければなりませんし，今後数週間の患者数の見通しも立てておく必要があります。

★：複雑そうですね。

☆：そうなんです。私の病院は腎臓に疾患をお持ちの患者さまの介助でよく知られており，腎臓病は季節によって多くなったり減ったりするんです。多くの患者さまは，腎臓の透析治療を週に2，3回受けていらっしゃいます。しかし，長期休暇の時期になると，透析の患者さまを入院させるご家族もよくいらっしゃるので，用意しなければならない食事が増えるのです。

★：患者さんにどんな食事を提供するのか，どうやって決めているのですか。

☆：医師が私に患者さまについて教えてくれます。病状や血液検査の結果，身長，体重，といったことです。献立は受け取った情報，とりわけ病状に関する情報を基に考えなければなりません。患者さまは心臓病なのか，糖尿病なのか，腎臓病なのか，コレステロール値が高いのかによって食事のニーズがそれぞれ異なります。数年前は，医師が私たちに患者さまにどんな種類の食べ物を用意するか指示していましたが，今では病院の栄養士が判断しています。当院のスタッフは重症の患者さまに対応することもあります。私たちは栄養面でのサポートを担うことが求められ，それは多くの場合，栄養チューブや静脈カテーテルを通して行われます。

★：患者さんを訪ねることもあるのですか。

☆：ええ，よくあります。栄養士しか直接患者さまに会えませんので，患者さまとお話しし，調理担当スタッフのためのフィードバックをいただくことは，私にとって重要なことなのです。こうしたフィードバックはスタッフのやる気につながります。患者さまがどのように食事をとり，私たちが用意した料理をどう思っているのかを確かめる必要があります。おそらく，私がこの仕事をしていて一番幸せを感じるのは，患者さまが「ここの料理は本当においしいね。どうもありがとう」とおっしゃるのを耳にするときです。もう1つ，私が注意しなければならないことは，患者さまのニーズには，私に伝わっていないものもあるかもしれない，ということです。例えば，食べ物を細かく切ってあげないといけない患者さまもいらっしゃいます。患者さまに食事に関するカウンセリングやアドバイスもします。そうすることで早期の退院が可能になりますし，退院後には自分自身の体調管理もしやすくなります。

★：とても興味深いお話でした。グロリアさん，今日は私たちのためにお時間を割いていただき，ありがとうございました。

☆：楽しかったです。

No. 26 解答 **3**

「食べ物が安全に食べられるか確認するためにグロリアがすることの1つは何か」

1 患者に出す前にスタッフに試食させる。

2 給仕の直前に医師に相談する。

3 食べ物が適切な温度で調理されていることを確かめる。

4 用意した食べ物を患者が食べるのを注意して見る。

解説　食べ物の安全確認については，Some kinds of food we serve must be cooked at over 75 degrees centigrade to make sure that all germs are killed. We use a food thermometer to measure the temperature inside meats and other foods. と話しているので，**3**が正解。

No. 27 解答 **1**

「食事の用意についてグロリアが述べていることの1つは何か」

1 医師が彼女に患者の病状に関する情報を与える。

2 彼女は個人的に個々の患者を訪ね，病状をチェックする。

3 医師が患者の病状に基づいてどんな食べ物を用意したらよいか指示する。

4 必要な情報はオンラインで見られる患者に関するレポートから得る。

解説　グロリアは献立作りに関して，I've got to plan meals based on the information I receive, especially information about patients' medical conditions. と説明している。**1**が正解。**3**は数年前までの話。

筆記試験＆リスニングテスト
解答と解説

問題編 p.54〜74

筆記

1

問題	*1*	*2*	*3*	*4*	*5*	*6*	*7*	*8*	*9*	*10*	*11*	*12*	*13*	*14*	*15*	*16*	*17*	*18*	*19*	*20*
解答	2	1	2	1	4	2	2	2	2	3	1	1	3	2	4	1	4	4	2	3

問題	*21*	*22*
解答	4	4

2

問題	*23*	*24*	*25*	*26*	*27*	*28*
解答	3	4	1	2	3	4

3

問題	*29*	*30*	*31*	*32*	*33*	*34*	*35*
解答	1	4	2	3	4	4	1

4　　**5**　　解説内にある解答例を参照してください。

リスニング

Part 1

問題	*1*	*2*	*3*	*4*	*5*	*6*	*7*	*8*	*9*	*10*
解答	1	3	4	1	1	1	1	2	1	1

Part 2

問題	*11*	*12*	*13*	*14*	*15*	*16*	*17*	*18*	*19*	*20*
解答	4	2	4	2	3	4	2	4	3	1

Part 3

問題	*21*	*22*	*23*	*24*	*25*
解答	3	3	4	3	1

Part 4

問題	*26*	*27*
解答	2	4

1

(1)　解答　**2**

「効果的な予防接種普及活動のおかげで, 小児まひは多くの国でほぼ根絶された病気の1つである」

解説　「効果的な予防接種普及活動のおかげで」とあるので, 小児まひはほぼ「根絶された」はず。**2**が正解。polio（= poliomyelitis）「小児まひ」。**1**「濃縮された」, **3**「差し控えられた」, **4**「強化された」。

(2)　解答　**1**

「タバコ業界は, 喫煙が肺がんを引き起こすという広く共有された認識を否認しようと頑張るのはあきらめた」

解説　the commonly accepted understanding「広く共有された認識」を目的語にとって文意が通るのは, **1**「〜を退ける, 否認する」。**2**「〜を強要する」, **3**「〜を格下げする」, **4**「〜を熟慮する, 直視する」。

(3)　解答　**2**

A「アルトゥルア社が破産するとたった今ジャックが耳にして, 彼はその件で1面に記事を書きたいと

言っています」

B「もし本当なら確かに報道する価値はあるのだが, 彼はその情報を 1 つの筋からしか得ていないのだ。記事が印刷される前に, われわれは**裏づけを取らなけ**ればならない」

解説 「彼はその情報を 1 つの筋からしか得ていない」のだから, 「裏づけ」が必要。**2**が正解。**1**「切望された」, **3**「若返らされた」, **4**「窒息させられた」。

(4) 解答 **1**

「テツオは記憶力がいい。彼は多くの事実や名前や日付を**覚えておく**ことができる」

解説 「記憶力がいい」のだから, 多くの事実を「保持できる, 覚えておく」ことができるはず。**1**が正解。**2**「〜を持ち上げる」, **3**「〜の多数を殺す」, **4**「〜を計画する」。

(5) 解答 **4**

「大手の自動車会社のうちの 1 社が, 昨年の販売実績不振のため生産を**削減した**」

解説 「販売実績不振」の結果として考えられるのは, 生産の「削減」。**4**「〜を切り詰めた, 削減した」が正解。**1**「〜(苦痛など)を軽くした」, **2**「〜の埋め合わせをした」, **3**「〜(人・感情など)をなだめた」。

(6) 解答 **2**

「その石油流出は, その沿岸地域がこれまで経験した最大の**環境災害**と考えられた」

解説 oil spill「石油流出」は environmental catastrophe「環境的な大災害」と言える。**2**が正解。**1**「(身体的な)障害」, **3**「不正行為」, **4**「結果」。

(7) 解答 **2**

「『平等の権利』を受け入れている社会においてすら**階層化**の傾向があることを, 社会科学者は今も明らかにすることができる」

解説 文中に even があることに注目。equal rights「平等の権利」と対照的な内容になるのは, **2**「階層化」。**1**「評決」, **3**「固執, 不屈」, **4**「決まり文句」。

(8) 解答 **2**

「契約書には, すべての発送品は期日通りに配達されねばならず, 遅れた場合は 1 日の遅延につき 100 ドルの罰金が発生すると**明記されていた**」

解説 契約書の役割を考えれば, **2**「〜を規定した」が正解だとわかる。**1**「〜を引き出した」, **3**「〜を叱責した」, **4**「〜を(神に)捧げた」。

(9) 解答 **3**

「麻薬は乱用されると人体に**有害な**影響を与え, 死につながることもある」

解説 leading to death から考えて**3**「有害な」が正解とわかる。narcotic drug は「麻薬」の意。**1**「統制的な」, **2**「説得力のある」, **4**「耳障りな」。

(10) 解答 **1**

「トイレから戻ったケンは, 机の上の誕生日プレゼントとカードを見て驚いた。彼が席を外している間に, 誰かが**こっそりと**置いていったのだ」

解説 机の上の誕生日プレゼントとカードを見て驚いた理由は, 誰かが「こっそり」置いていったからだと考えられる。**1**が正解。**2**「不注意に」, **3**「賢明に」, **4**「過去にさかのぼって」。

(11) 解答 **1**

「その国の憲法はこれまで 52 の**修正条項**が加えられてきたが, 憲法の妥当性が弱まったわけではない」

解説 constitution「憲法」に対してなされるものなので, **1**「修正条項」が加えられたと考えると文意が通る。**2**「受取人」, **3**「謎」, **4**「墓碑銘, 碑文」。

(12) 解答 **3**

「その 2 大政党間の合意は**目前に迫っている**ようだ。残されたいくつかの意見の相違を埋めるべく, 交渉担当者たちは夜遅くまで働いている」

解説 「残った意見の違いを解決すれば合意が成立する」という文脈なので, **3**「目前に迫った」が正解。**1**「不測の」, **2**「中世の」, **4**「あざけりの」。

(13) 解答 **2**

A「会議で何が議論されていても, ジムは必ず主要な論点をわかりやすく整理しますね」

B「そうだね。彼はいつも頭が切れるし**明敏だ**よ」

解説 sharp「頭が切れる」と and で並列されているので, **2**「明敏な, 頭脳明晰な」が正解。**1**「始まりの」, **3**「報復的な」, **4**「官能的な」。

(14) 解答 **4**

「仕事に出かける前, ジェームズはその日何か悪いことが起きる予感がした。それは結局本当のこととなった。なぜなら, 彼はほんの数時間後に軽度の自動車事故を起こしたのである」

解説 something bad would happen that day「その日何か悪いことが起こるだろう」ということを知らせるもので，後にそれが現実になったのだから，**4**「予感，虫の知らせ」が正解。**1**「診察，（専門家との）相談」，**2**「変化，変更」，**3**「報復，天罰」。

(15) 解答 1

「座りがちな生活スタイルが健康によくないというのは周知のことだ。日中はテレビやコンピュータから離れて運動することが大事である」

解説 どんな生活スタイルが健康によくないのかを考える。2文目には「運動することが大事」とあるので，**1**「座りがちな」生活スタイルが正解。**2**「精力的な，はつらつとした」，**3**「熱烈な」，**4**「質素な，切り詰めた」。

(16) 解答 4

「選挙での大敗の後，その上院議員は政界から引退することを決めた。その選挙で議員は完敗を喫したのだ」

解説 打ち負かされ，その結果政界を引退するというのだから，選挙は**4**「大敗」だったはず。**1**「熱弁」，**2**「躍進」，**3**「名残，残存者」。

(17) 解答 4

「市の警察署長が若いころ非行少年で何度か罪を犯したことがあると聞いて，市民たちはショックを受けた」

解説 「何度か罪を犯した」というのだから，**4**「非行少年［少女］」だったはず。**1**「熟考する人」，**2**「指数，割り当て」，**3**「協力者」。

(18) 解答 2

A「お邪魔だったかな。寄る前に電話すべきだったね」
B「気にしなくていいよ。別に何もしてなかったから」

解説 「あまり（　　）でなければいいけど。寄る前に電話すべきだったね」という流れから，Aの発言の1文目は相手への気遣いを示す発言になると考えられる。

2「押しつけがましい，目障りな」が正解。**1**「素っ気ない」，**3**「助けになる」，**4**「思いとどまらせる」。

(19) 解答 2

「2人のテニスチャンピオンは，誰が世界最高の選手かを決するべく，その国際杯の決勝戦で対決した」

解説 決勝戦ですることなので，**2**「対戦する」が正解。**1**「～を刺激した」，**3**「四方八方に散らばった」，**4**「煮こぼれた」。

(20) 解答 3

「長年にわたる研究の末，研究者たちはついに風邪の効果的な治療法に的を絞りつつあると確信している」

解説 **3**の zero in on ～ は「～に的を絞る，狙いを定める」という意味。長年にわたる研究の結果，ようやく治療法を見定めたということ。**1**「（価格など）を引き上げる」，**2**「～に磨きをかける，～をやり直す」，**4**「分け前を取る」。

(21) 解答 4

「事態は予想外の奇妙な展開を見せ，ブルースは結局妻と離婚し，結婚カウンセラーと結婚することになった」

解説 wound は動詞 wind の過去形。「最後に～することになる」という意味の wind up -ing を入れると文意が通る。twist は「予想外の展開」の意。**1**「～を引き上げた」，**2**「～を発見した」，**3**「～を与えた」。

(22) 解答 4

「ヘレンは送別会で大いに楽しんでいたが，スピーチの間はかなり言葉に詰まっていたようだった。私は彼女が泣き出すかと思った」

解説 泣き出しそうな様子を表す語句として適切なのは，**4**「（感極まって，声・言葉）を詰まらせた」。**1**「～をはぎ取った」，**2**「真面目に取り組んだ」，**3**「～を水で薄めた，（計画など）を骨抜きにした」。

Day
5

2

全訳

忙しさと創造性

　私たちはニュース，メッセージ，ソーシャルメディアのアップデートに攻められ，さらに至るところに存在するデジタル仲間からも攻められ，次第につのる忙しさの中で暮らしている。つまり私たちの頭はかつてよりずっと占領されているのだ。私たちは，ほんの25年前よりも最大5倍かそれ以上の情報を毎日消化していると見積もられており，私たちの関心のこの絶え間ない流出が，創造的能力に悪影響を及ぼすことが明ら

かになってきた。創造性はしばしば，スイッチを切って頭をぼんやりさせることで目覚める。だが情報の流れが私たちの脳を直線的思考モードでいることを要求するときには，それは難しい。それでは解決策は，表面的だとしても，絶えず考えているよりむしろずっと何も考えていないことなのだろうか。人生における多くの事柄と同じように，解決策は極端より中庸にある。

　過度の刺激に自分をさらすことで創造的になる能力が減らされるとはいえ，ある程度のリミットを設けることで，それを強化することができる。ニュージャージー州ライダー大学の心理学部による実験では，タスクに特定の制約を与えられた被験者たちはより創造的になり，それらの制約が解かれても創造的であり続けたことがわかった。このやや相容れないような研究結果は，一見したときほど矛盾しないのかもしれない。インターネットを常にチェックすることは私たちの多くにとって習性となっており，それゆえ習慣的で，常習性がある。私たちの創造性の井戸を活用することも，スマートフォンの制限を導入するような簡単なものかもしれない。

　忙しくすることと頭を自由に回転させることをうまく両立させるやり方のおかげで，世界で最も創造的な頭脳たちは，画期的な発明や理論を想像・発展させることができた。例えばアルバート・アインシュタインは，実験や考える時間から定期的な休憩を取り，リラックスしたり音楽を聞いたりしたし，ニコラ・テスラは散歩している最中に磁場を回転させることについての洞察を得た。そのほか，アップルの共同創設者スティーブ・ジョブズとスティーブ・ウォズニアックを含む多くの人が，創造のバッテリーを再充電するためにしばらく注意をそらすことのメリットを激賞している。長期間何もしないのは逆効果で，長時間連続して忙しいのも逆効果になり得るから，画面を離れるのは，ただ目を休めるよりもずっと効果的かもしれない。

(23)　解答　3

解説　段落の冒頭から，私たちが日々情報にさらされて暮らしていることを述べている。その内容を言い換えた**3**が正解。**1**「集中し続けられないこと」，**2**「この神経伝達物質に対する遮断」，**4**「ソーシャルメディアを絶えずアップデートする必要」。

(24)　解答　4

解説　文頭に譲歩・対照を示す While（…とはいえ）があるので，前半の内容を打ち消す内容**4**が入るのが自然。**1**「それは常習行為にはつながらない」，**2**「規

則の強制との衝突も伴う」，**3**「私たちはもはや適切な境界を設定することができない」。

(25)　解答　1

解説　創造力を育むことと，画期的な発明や理論を発展させるために良い方法について述べている段落。別の言葉で言い換えた**1**が正解。**2**「ソーシャルメディアで人と再び連絡を取るために」，**3**「そして長時間怠けることを受け入れる」，**4**「最も重要な仕事に集中するために」。

全訳
ハッシュタグ民主主義
　ソーシャルメディアが拡大し続ける猛烈なスピードは，友だちがわいせつで私的な詳細を過剰に公開するよりも波紋がはるかに大きく，民主主義はそれに追いつこうと奮闘している。今日，ティーンエイジャーから世界の首脳陣までが，大部分が検閲されていない見解を聞きたがっている人々に伝え，討論やディベートを行うことができるし，実際そうしている。ソーシャルメディアは自分を表現したい人々にはけ口を提供することで，メディアへのアクセスを民主化するのに大いに寄与したとも言えるが，その一方で政治的プロセスをかく乱し，それによって影響を与える役割を持つことも，ますます明らかになっている。

　今や米国の成人の60％以上がニュースのためにツイッターやフェイスブックのようなプラットフォームに頼り，政治家やそのほかの人々が彼らに発信する機会を得ていることもあり，ソーシャルメディアの影響は無視できない。しかし，今日，多数の報道機関が利用できるにもかかわらず，多くの人々は，自分自身が選んだ，多くの場合限定されたデジタルバブルの中でシェアされる記事に頼っている。これが，自由に見られるニュースの配信元の急激な成長率のおかげで，私たちの多くが自分自身を露骨に思想的なものに制限する結果となり，さらなる党派心と偏向した政治的意見の一因となるという，奇妙な矛盾へとつながった。この矛盾が民主主義そのものをむしばむことにつながると見る人もいる。

　誤情報キャンペーンがソーシャルメディア上で猛威をふるうことがあるが，ソーシャルメディアは大部分の伝統的な報道機関と異なり，同じ道徳的・法律的規準が守られていない。ツイッターやフェイスブックの類も，規模と伝達範囲からして事実上メディア企業になったのだから，ほかの放送事業者と同じ規則や罰則を順守するときが来たと多くが主張する。これらの情

報ルートでは深刻な問題が日常的に討論され，それが国民的議論に悪影響を与えることもあるが，ソーシャルメディアは民主主義を救う手助けとして使うこともできる。ソーシャルメディア・プラットフォームは，私たちが興味を持つかもしれない類似した項目の情報を強制的に詰め込もうと，アルゴリズムを使って視聴傾向を分析する。これがデジタルバブルをはじけさせる鍵となるかもしれない。こうしたアルゴリズムは，われわれを別の視点に触れさせることによって，議論と民主主義を強化するためのもっと前向きな用途で使われるべきだと多くが主張している。

(26) 解答 2

解説 空所は冒頭文の一部で，それ以降で述べられるソーシャルメディアと政治のかかわりを案じる一言が入る。2が正解。1「家族は当然心配している」，3「政治家たちは見て見ぬふりをしている」，4「効果は割合小さい」。

(27) 解答 3

解説 限定的な情報を視聴した結果どうなるか，という文脈なので，3が入る。1「政治思想へのより深い洞察」，2「社会問題への視野を広げる社会」，4「リベラル寄りの議題への支持の高まり」。

(28) 解答 4

解説 議論と民主主義を強化するためのアルゴリズムの前向きな用途を考える。4が正解。1「より好戦的に交流するよう私たちを奨励する」，2「ソーシャルメディア通信をアップグレードする」，3「民主主義に反対する人々を罰したり非難したりする」。

3

全訳

グローバリゼーションの歴史

　私たちのほとんどは，グローバリゼーションは人類の歴史の中でも比較的新しい概念だと思い込んでいる。つまり，世界規模の宅配便サービス，多国籍コーヒーチェーン店，インターネット，製造施設やコールセンターのオフショア化といったビジネストレンドによって特徴づけられる概念というわけである。実のところ，人類誕生の地であるアフリカを何万年も前に最初の人間が離れたときから，グローバリゼーションは私たちと共に存在し続けている。そのとき以来，移民，商人，宣教師，戦士などが自分たちの価値観，理念，習慣，商品などを世界の新たな地域に持ち込み，重大な変化を促してきたのである。グローバリゼーションを十分に理解するためには，単に経済，貿易，政治，宗教といった狭い文脈にとどまらず，最も広い文脈で考えるべきである。なぜなら，グローバリゼーションは，人類が織り成す広大な歴史に非常に多くのやり方で複雑に織り込まれてきたからである。

　『バウンド・トゥギャザー：貿易商・牧師・探検家・戦士がいかにグローバリゼーションを形成したか』の著者でエール大学グローバリゼーション研究センター員であるナヤン・チャンダは，グローバリゼーションは「何千年にもわたって名づけられることもなくひっそりと進行していたのであり，古代のはるかかなたの土地とわれわれを結んできたおびただしい糸の中を通り抜けているのである」と論じる。人間が移動し移住する限り，人間が交易をする限り，グローバリゼーションは常に私たちと共にあり続ける。この論点を強調するために，チャンダは自身のDNAを検査してもらい，全く当然のことだが，自分の大昔の血統がインドに，さらにその前にはアフリカにつながっていることを発見した。移住者の集団が地球上を動き回り続けていることを忘れてはならないとチャンダは言う。なぜなら，「世界のおよそ41の大国において，人口の2割を移民が占めている」のだ。

　チャンダの著書の主要な考えは，グローバリゼーションは人類の歴史の大部分を通じて徐々に展開したのであって，現在のグローバルな事業展開は過去に起源があるというものだが，多くの学者がこの考え方は単純過ぎると批判するかもしれない。しかし，グローバリゼーションという歴史的な進化の事象に関する彼の鋭い見識と，個人と社会と文化とを絡み合わせる彼の手法は，印象的であるとともに説得力がある。今日との類似を明らかにする際，近代の多文化企業はイングランド，ポルトガル，オランダなどで王家が出資した貿易会社を模したものだとチャンダは仮定する。それらの国々の広範な世界的影響は，はるか遠くメソポタミアの古代王国にまで起源をさかのぼることができる。さらに，近代的な交易の原動力である兌換通貨紙

幣やクレジットカードの発達は，財宝を母国に船で運んだ初期のスペイン人侵入者たちによるメキシコとペルーでの金銀採掘に起源をさかのぼることができるとチャンダは考える。

米国は近代グローバリゼーションの創始者だとしばしば見なされるが，ローマ帝国もモンゴル帝国も大英帝国も，全盛期には同様にグローバリゼーションの創始者であり推進者と見なされていた。グローバルパワーの交代は，将来も止まることはなさそうである。中国の成功は中国が支配するグローバリゼーション新時代の前兆だと考える人がいるため，西洋の強国は現在，大量の中国製品が世界中に投下されていることに恐怖心を抱いている。しかし，変化を阻止しようとする努力は無駄である。なぜならグローバリゼーションがもたらす急速な変化に追いつくのに現代人は苦労しているが，その変化を封じ込めることはできないからである。しかしながら，やはり過去から受け継いだ遺産である狭量な同族意識が邪魔をして，私たちは，世界的な気候変動，強力な流行病伝染，国際的な経済危機，人類規模の災害と闘うために必要な全地球レベルでの変化を実現できないでいる。私たちが同胞として生き残り，繁栄するつもりであれば，私たちは皆グローバリゼーションを違う角度から考察する必要がありそうだ。

(29) 解答 1

「グローバリゼーションの発展について何がわかるか」
1 人類が初めて遠い土地へと移住して以来，グローバリゼーションは何らかの形で私たちと共に存在している。
2 グローバリゼーションは人類の生活の中で長く役割を果たしてきたが，今日では著しく異なるものに発展した。
3 グローバリゼーション全体の発展を理解する試みは無益なので，特定の研究分野を通じて分析するのが最善である。
4 専門家たちは，グローバリゼーションはビジネスをする上で全く異なる道を開く現代の概念であるというほぼ一致した意見に達した。

解説 本論の重要ポイントである「グローバリゼーションは近年始まったものではない」という考えは第1段落で既に出ている。第2文の内容が1と一致する。2ではdramatically differentとあるが，本文はむしろ不変であることを強調しているので誤りとなる。3はparticular fieldsが第4文に反しているし，4はグローバリゼーションが最近の事象であることに意見が一致している，という点が誤り。

(30) 解答 4

「『バウンド・トゥギャザー：貿易商・牧師・探検家・戦士がいかにグローバリゼーションを形成したか』という作品について，筆者が暗に伝えていることは何か」
1 グローバリゼーションがどのように展開したかについて本の中で紹介された概念と，現代との比較はあまりにもシンプルである。
2 グローバリゼーションの歴史とそれが私たちの日常生活にどのように影響しているかについての，これまでで最高の本である。
3 グローバリゼーションの進化についてのチャンダの説明は，現代との彼の比較よりずっと説得力がある。
4 グローバリゼーションの過去の出来事のチャンダの理解と，複雑に絡み合った関係の解釈は見事である。

解説 著書について聞かれているが，この文章自体がその本に基づいてチャンダの考え方を紹介しているので，彼の考え方について問われていると考えてよい。第3段落第2文に見られるconvincingやimpressiveなどの褒め言葉がヒントになる。正解は4。2はdaily livesが本文で特に触れられていないので誤りとなる。

(31) 解答 2

「筆者はグローバリゼーションの進行について何を暗示しているか」
1 つまらない部族主義に傾く傾向を最もうまく制した国が，グローバリゼーションの主導者になりそうだ。
2 歴史的にグローバリゼーションの中心にいた国々はやがてその主要な役割を失う定めだ。
3 グローバリゼーションの進化は予測不可能なので，国々が自国の利益を必死で維持しようとするのは自然である。
4 世界中の商品を輸入するのに成功したため，中国はグローバリゼーションの新たな中心ではなくなる運命にある。

解説 最終段落で，グローバリゼーションを支配する国は時代とともに代わっており，その変化は避けられないと述べられている。2が正解。

全訳

音響環境学

私たちは聞く能力を失いつつあるのだろうか。私たちは音に囲まれている。都会の環境に関して言えば，音に「攻撃されている」と言う方がより適切かもしれない。しかし，大多数の人々は，周囲の音をほとんど意識することなく日々の生活を送っている。もしあなたが，音を聞いていないこのグループに自分は属さない

と思うならば，個人の聞き取り能力を評価する簡単な
テストを出してみよう。今日耳にした音を5つ挙げて
ほしい。数分間でリストを完成させることができなく
ても，決して自分だけではないと安心していい。

　意識して聞くという人間の能力の衰退，あるいは少
なくともこの現象を認識したことが1つの懸念となり，
カナダ人の音楽家であり，作曲家であり，情報工学の
元教授でもあったR・マレー・シェーファーは，1960
年代に音響環境学という学際的な分野を提案し展開さ
せ始めることとなった。シェーファーは，視覚機能が
過度にそして次第に強く社会を支配するようになって
おり，しばしば音への意識を損なうほどだと考えた。音
環境を音楽作品として聞き，社会の構成員がこの作品
の内容に責任を持つことを彼は提唱した。これは確か
に深遠な考え方であり，そのような意識に広範囲なレ
ベルで達成できる見込みはありそうもないのだが，
シェーファーはそれにもかかわらず，世界中の音への
意識を改善するために優れた貢献をした。

　シェーファーの重要な研究は，1970年代に彼が率
いた『世界サウンドスケープ・プロジェクト』という
名の野心的な活動に基づいていた。このプロジェクト
は，人間が住む音環境と人間の関係を調査し記録する
ことを目的としていた。プロジェクトの最初の試みは
カナダのバンクーバーのサウンドスケープ（音風景）
の実地調査で，音響レベルの測定，音の録音，そして
一連の音の特徴の記述という手法を用いた。このプロ
ジェクトに引き続き，ヨーロッパ各地のいくつかの小
さな町で同様の研究が行われた。さまざまなサウンド
スケープを分析して，シェーファーと彼の同僚は音源
を3つの大きなカテゴリーに分類した。根底にある調
性を表す背景音である「主音（キーノート）」，注意を
引く前景音である「音信号（サウンド・シグナル）」，そ
して岸に寄せる波，滝，野生動物，ベル，さまざまな
伝統的な活動が生み出す音など，特に顕著にほかと識
別される特徴である「音指標（サウンドマーク）」であ
る。この研究によって，ある特定の共同体の音は，自
然な音も人為的な音のどちらも，土地の建築物や慣習
や文化と同じように，その共同体の独自性を特徴づけ
表現し得るものであるという事実が明確にされた。

　しかし残念なことに，今も続く都市化の進展ととも
に多くの特異なサウンドスケープが消滅し，近代都市
の特徴であるほかと区別のつかない騒音の均質な攻撃
の下に埋もれてしまっている。さらに，自然界の音が，
われわれの都市環境を定義づける交通や建設などの不
快な音の特徴に次第に取って代わられるとともに，音
は次第に耳を傾けるものというよりは遮断しようとす

るものになりつつある。今日の社会において音への意
識が欠如しているのは，心に訴えかける音が欠乏して
おり，その結果私たちは精神の健康を守るために本当
に音を無視しなければならないからだと論じることも
可能だろう。しかしこの主張には欠点がいくつかある。
1つは，「悪い」音から自分自身を閉ざすことは，同時
に「良い」音を楽しむ可能性を制限するということで
ある。もっと重要かもしれないのは，意識レベルで周
囲の騒音をとにかく遮断しようと選ぶことは，ストレ
スをはじめとする精神の健康に対するマイナスの影響
といった，騒音の潜在意識における悪影響を見逃すこ
とになる，というものである。さらに，社会の構成員
全員がサウンドスケープを生み出した責任を持ってい
るというシェーファーの訴えを私たちは心に留めるべ
きであり，そして責任を持つ者として，生活環境の音
に注意を払い，好き嫌いを意識し，心地よい音を保存
し，不快な音を減らすか防ぐかする助けとなる適切な
行動を取るべきである。

　環境音への意識を高めるための1つの技法は，
シェーファーと彼の仲間が創始したいわゆる「サウン
ドウォーク（音の散歩）」である。さまざまな取り組み
方があるのだが，基本的な手法は，特定の場所をぶら
ぶら歩いて音の違いを区別しながらサウンドスケープ
に耳を傾け，同時に耳に入るそれぞれの音について批
判的評価を行い，それぞれの音の音環境全体への貢献
を判定することである。ほとんどの人にとって，耳に
入る1つ1つの音を注意深く聞くという集中力を要す
る作業は，通常は気づかないであろうおびただしい音
を必ずや明らかにするだろう。

　今日の音響環境学は，学者，都市計画者，社会学者，
エンジニア，建築家，サウンドアーティストなどが行っ
ている仕事を網羅する，幾分包括的な用語である。こ
の比較的新しい学問分野が及ぼす影響は広範囲にわた
る。騒音公害はずっとこの分野の特別な関心事であっ
たし，今もそうなのだが，これは極めて当然なことで
ある。交通量の増加と音を出す機械や技術の使用拡大
により，騒音レベルは上がり続けている。その一方で，
自然界の音は消滅の一途をたどっている。しかし，こ
のような過渡期にあっても，私たちの行動や健康に対
する音の影響は，ほとんど顧みられない話題のままで
ある。今こそこれまで以上に，音と，私たちの生活で
音が果たす役割をもっと深く理解することが必要であ
る。

(32) 解答 **3**

「文章によると，シェーファーが音響環境学という分野

を発展させる気になったのは…ためである」

1 音の環境の変化とそれがどのように人々に悪影響を与えるかについて関心があった

2 現代社会で消えつつある特異なサウンドスケープを記録したかった

3 人々が周囲の音に十分注意を払っていないと考えた

4 私たちが出会う視覚的様相と聴覚的様相は実際には切り離せないものだと主張した

解説　第2段落第1，2文にシェーファーがacoustic ecologyを提唱した背景が述べられている。第2文の，視覚的なものが支配的になり聴覚的なものへの意識が失われている，という記述が**3**のinsufficient attention to the sounds around themに相当する。

(33) 解答 4

「シェーファーは地域社会のすべての音は…と言う」

1 人々が気づいていなくても，視覚的様相と同じように市民の性格を形作る

2 共同体のサウンドスケープを作り上げ，それが「主音」という単位で測定できる

3 その特定の共同体の特性に合うように徐々に進化したので，ある意味自然だ

4 ほかの重要な文化的特徴と同じくらい，その共同体の独自性を反映する

解説　音と共同体の関係を述べているのは第3段落。シェーファーたちの結論は最終文にまとめられており，音と文化的特徴は共に共同体の独自性を反映している，という**4**の内容と一致する。

(34) 解答 4

「筆者は…と示唆する」

1 騒音公害は人々を永久的な難聴にしている

2 騒音公害を止めるためにできることはほとんどないと人々が考えるのは正しい

3 騒音公害を無視することで私たちのストレスレベルは下がるので，私たちの幸福にとって，それがほぼ間違いなく最善である

4 都市の騒音公害のおかげで，人々は環境のほとんどの音を無視したくなっている

解説　人間と音の関係を述べた選択肢が並ぶ。**1**では聴力のことを述べているが，本文では述べられていない。**2**は第4段落最終文の「行動を起こすべきだ」に反する上，第5段落では，サウンドウォークという具体的な手法も紹介されている。**3**は第4段落第5文と逆の内容になる。**4**は同段落第2文と一致する。

(35) 解答 1

「サウンドウォークとは…技法の一例である」

1 環境の中のさまざまな音を聞き，評価する能力を高める

2 音の物理的特徴と生活におけるその役割の理解を改善する

3 環境音の認識とそれぞれの音が私たちをどのように元気づけているかの認識を促進する

4 過去に聞いた音を想起できるように私たちの無意識を刺激する

解説　第5段落の第1文に「意識を高める」とあり，その後に，注意深く聞く，音に評価を与える，という手法が紹介されており，これが**1**と一致する。**2**は前半の「音の物理的特徴」が，**3**は後半の「元気づける」が誤り。**4**の最後にある「過去に聞いた音」に関する記述は本文にない。

4

問題文の訳

　アメリカ合衆国では10年ごとに，国の現在の人口を数えるために国勢調査が行われたあと，国政選挙の選挙区の形と規模が徹底的に見直され，新たに得られたデータと比較される。それから必要であれば，人口の変化を反映し，それぞれの国民にとって平等に代表が選出されることを確実にするために選挙区は変更される。しかしながら政治家の中には，「ゲリマンダリング」と呼ばれるテクニックを利用して，このプロセスに正直に取り組まない者もいる。これは選挙で不当に優位に立とうとして，選挙区の形と規模を変えてしまうものである。共和党も民主党もやましくもこの慣習をたびたび行ってきた。

　ゲリマンダリングはひどく非民主的で，200年以上の間存在してきた慣習である。特に，ゲリマンダリングは黒人などの少数派の人々がアメリカ政治において公正に代表してもらうことを困難にしてきた。例えば，人種差別主義の政治家は「クラッキング」と呼ばれるテクニックを使う可能性があるのだが，それは少数派の人々を複

数の選挙区に分断させるもので，彼らが支持政党から誰かを選出することをほぼ不可能にしてしまう。一方で，「パッキング」として知られるもう1つの方法では，少数派の有権者を1つの選挙区に集中させる。彼らがその1つの地域で代表を選出することは容易だが，他の選挙区で候補者を選出できる可能性は低い。

　人種に基づいたゲリマンダリングは，アメリカ合衆国では違法である一方，アメリカ合衆国最高裁判所は多くのケースでゲリマンダリングの利用を実質的に支持し，政党が選挙で優位に立つことを可能にしてきた。これはつまり，ある人物の人種とその人物が票を投じる政党の間には強い相関関係があるので，少数派の人々はいまだにその影響を受けているということである。この決定は，書き直された地図の方が国民をよりよく代表しており，特定のグループを差別するものではないと見せかけながら，政党が差別的な地図を守ることを可能にしてきた。

解答例	解答例の訳
Changes in the shapes and sizes of America's election districts are supposed to reflect changes in census data, but they are often based on gerrymandering, in which politicians try to gain political advantage by altering district shapes and sizes. This persisting issue is especially problematic for minorities, who are often split among districts so that they cannot vote as a block or are grouped together in one area so that their influence is decreased. Although race-based gerrymandering is prohibited, it can still be allowed in practice. Party affiliation is often correlated with race, so politicians are often able to discriminate through gerrymandering while claiming that they are not. (108語)	アメリカの選挙区の形と規模の変更は，国勢調査のデータの変化を反映していると考えられているが，ゲリマンダリングに基づいていることも多く，それによって政治家たちは，選挙区の形と規模を変えることによって政治的な優位性を得ようとしている。長年続いてきたこの問題は，特に少数派にとっては問題のあるもので，ひとまとまりになって投票できないように選挙区間で分断されることがしばしばあったり，あるいは影響力を減らすために1つの地域にまとめられてしまったりする。人種に基づくゲリマンダリングは禁止されているが，それでもなお実際には認められることもある。支持政党はしばしば人種と相関しているので，政治家は差別はしていないと主張しながらゲリマンダリングを利用して差別できることが多いのである。

解説　トピックは第1段落第3文 However, there are some politicians who do not approach this process honestly by utilizing a technique called "gerrymandering," which alters the shapes and sizes of voting districts in order to gain an unfair advantage in elections. から，「『ゲリマンダリング』と呼ばれるテクニックの問題」だとわかる。各段落の要旨は，第1段落：選挙区の見直しが行われるときに，政治家が自分たちに優位になるように選挙区の形や規模を変えようとする「ゲリマンダリング」という手法が横行している。第2段落：ゲリマンダリングのせいで，少数派の人々は自分たちの代表を政界に送り出すことが困難になる。第3段落：人種に基づくゲリマンダリングは違法だが，国勢調査の反映という名目でゲリマンダリングを利用することは実質的に認められるケースも多く，人種と投票先には強い相関があるので，結局のところ少数派の人々はゲリマンダリングの影響を受けるということになる。解答の際はこれらを問題文とは異なる表現に言い換えてまとめる。なお，第1段落の国勢調査の詳しい話については要約に含める必要はない。一方，第2段落の「クラッキング」や「パッキング」といった手法については，ゲリマンダリングを具体的に説明している同段落の重要な情報なので，要約に含めたい。解答例では，第1段落のゲリマンダリングが横行している現実について they are often based on gerrymandering と簡潔に説明している。第2段落の，クラッキングによって支持政党の候補者を選出できなくすることについては split among districts so that they cannot vote as a block と，またパッキングについては grouped together in one area so that their influence is decreased とわかりやすく言い換えている。第3段落の要旨については，politicians are often able to discriminate through gerrymandering と単刀直入に説明している。

問題の訳
TOPIC：高齢の親は自宅で面倒をみてもらうべきか。

解答例①

Many elderly people would rather live with their children than go into a care facility. However, this not only places great financial, physical, and mental burdens on their children, but can also be dangerous for the elderly people themselves.

Firstly, caring for one's elderly parents at home can be very expensive. This is not only because of the cost of things such as food and medicine, but also because a child or their spouse may have to leave their job in order to stay at home and care for a parent, thus reducing the income of the household.

Second, caring for an elderly person can also be exhausting physically and mentally. If a person suffers from dementia, for example, his or her behavior may be very unpredictable, and he or she may need round-the-clock care.

Lastly, living with adult children may be dangerous for elderly people, especially if their children are working and they are home alone. If they have a medical emergency, it may escape notice for a while. It would be safer for them to live somewhere where medical attention is available 24 hours a day.

While elderly people may wish to stay at home, given the financial, physical, and mental burden on the caregiver, not to mention the issue of safety, it is better for elderly people to be cared for in a facility. (227語)

解答例①の訳

多くの高齢者が介護施設に入るより，子供たちと一緒に暮らしたいと思っています。しかしながら，これによって大変な経済的，肉体的，精神的負担が子供にかかるだけでなく，高齢者自身が危険な目にあう可能性もあります。

まず，年老いた親を自宅で世話することは，非常にお金がかかります。これは食べ物や医薬品といった物の費用のせいだけでなく，子供やその配偶者が自宅で親の面倒を見るために仕事をやめざるを得ないかもしれず，そのせいで世帯収入が減ってしまうからです。

次に，高齢者の世話は肉体的にも精神的にも非常に疲れることです。例えば，痴ほう症の人は非常に予測不能な行動をする可能性があり，昼夜休みなく世話する必要があるかもしれません。

最後に，成人した子供と住むのは高齢者にとって危険かもしれません。特に子供たちが働いていて，高齢者が自宅にひとりでいる場合は危険な可能性があります。緊急医療が必要になっても，しばらく気づいてもらえないかもしれません。高齢者はどこか1日24時間医療を受けられる場所に住んだほうが安全でしょう。

高齢者は自宅にいたいと思うかもしれませんが，安全の問題は言うまでもなく，介護者にかかる経済的,肉体的，精神的負担も考慮すると，施設で面倒をみてもらった方がよいのです。

解説 序論では，トピックに対して反対の立場を表明し，費用の問題，心身にかかる負担の問題，そして高齢者自身にふりかかる危険を列挙している。第2段落から始まる本論はその詳しい説明で，第2段落では食費や医療費の問題に加え，介護離職が世帯収入に及ぼす影響についても触れている。第3段落は介護疲れの問題について述べている。第4段落では自宅でひとりになってしまう場合の危険性について丁寧に説明している。最終段落では，3つの理由に簡潔に触れることで全体をまとめている。

解答例②

Many people these days are very busy, and they find it hard to care for elderly parents at home. However, some people choose to do so for a number of reasons including finances, a sense of loyalty, and because it is better for the elderly people themselves.

First of all, decent care homes in Japan these days are extremely expensive. Even if people want to have their elderly relatives live in a care home, for most people the cost is prohibitive. It is far cheaper to have elderly people living at home.

Second, many people feel a deep sense of loyalty to their parents. Their parents raised them and paid for their education. They feel it would be ungrateful to send their father or mother off to a care home and prefer to take care of them themselves, even if it is hard.

And lastly, many elderly people do not like living in care homes. If they are able to live at home with their families, they may have a better quality of life and live longer, happier, and also healthier lives, which is also good for society.

If we consider the cost of care homes, our sense of duty to our parents, and the fact that most elderly people prefer to live at home, it makes sense for elderly people to live with their relatives. (226語)

解答例②の訳

最近では多くの人がとても忙しくしており，自宅で高齢の親の面倒をみるのはとても難しいと思っています。しかしながら，数々の理由から，そうすることを選ぶ人もいます。経済的な理由や家族を誠実に扱う気持ち，そしてそうすることが高齢者自身にとってよいことだからです。

まず，最近の日本の立派な介護施設は，極めて高額です。高齢の家族に介護施設に住んでもらいたいと思っていても，大半の人々にとってその費用は法外です。高齢者を自宅に住まわせている方が，ずっと安く済みます。

第2に，多くの人には親を心から誠実に思う気持ちがあります。親は彼らを育て，教育の費用を払ってくれました。彼らは父や母を介護施設に入れるのは恩知らずな行為と感じ，たとえ大変でも自分で面倒をみたいと思っています。

そして最後に，多くの高齢者は介護施設で暮らすことを好みません。自宅で家族と一緒に暮らせるのなら，生活の質としてはその方がよいかもしれず，もっと長生きができ，幸せで，さらに健康的な生活を送れるかもしれません。それは社会にとってもよいことです。

介護施設の費用，親に対する責任感，そしてほとんどの高齢者が自宅で暮らしたいと思っている事実を考えれば，高齢者が家族と暮らすのは理にかなっています。

解説 序論では，トピックに対して賛成の立場を表明し，その理由として経済的な問題，家族を思う気持ちの問題，そして高齢者自身の希望の問題に触れている。本論では，まず第2段落で経済的な問題を扱っており，高額な施設に入れるよりも自宅で面倒をみた方が安く済むと述べている。第3段落は家族を誠実に扱いたいという人々の気持ちの問題に触れており，親を施設に入れるのは恩知らずだと彼らは思うのだと述べている。第4段落は高齢者自身の気持ちに焦点を定めており，親が望む通りに自宅で暮らすことでよりよい生活を送れると述べている。最終段落では，3つの理由を別の言葉で繰り返すことで全体をまとめている。

Day
5

69

Listening Test

Part 1 🔊 051～061

No. 1 [解答] **1**

★：Hello, Sally.

☆：Hi, John. How was your first week at our office?

★：It was great. Thanks for asking. Are you coming to the office party tomorrow night?

☆：I haven't decided for sure, but probably. It's a good chance to talk to colleagues outside the office, and the catering's awesome.

★：Yes, I'm looking forward to it. Do you think I should wear something formal?

☆：No, I don't think so. Our parties are very casual. You can wear something like a polo shirt and jeans.

★：Good. That was one thing I wasn't sure about.

Question：What do we learn from this conversation?

★：やあ，サリー。

☆：あら，ジョン。私たちのオフィスでの最初の1週間はどうだった？

★：とてもよかったよ。聞いてくれてありがとう。明日の夜の会社のパーティーには来るかい？

☆：まだはっきりとは決めてないけど，たぶん行くわ。職場の外で同僚と話す良い機会だし，ケータリングがすごいのよ。

★：そうか，楽しみだ。何かフォーマルなものを着ていくべきかな。

☆：いいえ，それはないわ。うちのパーティーはとてもカジュアルなの。ポロシャツとジーンズみたいなものを着てもいいのよ。

★：よかった。それだけ確信が持てなかったんだ。

質問：この会話から何がわかるか。

1 ジョンはこの会社のパーティーに不慣れである。　**2** ジョンは会社のパーティーに出席したくない。
3 ジョンは職場に友達が少ない。　**4** ジョンは同僚と仲良くなれればよいと思っている。

[解説] 女性の最初の発言 How was your first week at our office? より，男性がこの職場で働き始めたばかりということがわかる。その後も女性がパーティーの雰囲気について男性に教えてあげており，男性はドレスコードに確信が持てないでいたことが分かる。**1**が正解。

No. 2 [解答] **3**

☆：Hey, Jacob. Are you going to the party tonight at Tim's?

●：Maybe, Rachel. It's supposed to start around 6:30, but I have to work till 8:00 or so. If it's still going on at 9:00, I might drop in. I'll give Tim a call to find out first.

☆：Oh, don't worry about that. Things will just get going from 9:00. Tim's last party didn't slow down until 2:00 a.m. There might not be much food left, but there should be plenty of drinks and company.

●：Well, in that case, I'll just buy some snacks and bring them around 9:00. Please let Tim know.

☆：Great. See you later.

Question：What will Jacob probably do before going to the party?

☆：ねえ，ジェイコブ。今夜ティムの家でやるパーティーには行く？

●：たぶんね，レイチェル。パーティーは6時半ごろ開始のはずだけど，8時かそこらまで仕事なんだ。9時になってもまだやっていたら，顔を出すかもしれない。まずティムに電話して確かめるよ。

☆：ああ，それなら心配しないで。9時ならやっと動き始めるところよ。この前のティムのパーティーは午前2時まで盛り上がりっ放しだったの。食べ物はあまり残っていないかもしれないけど，飲み物と仲間はたくさん残っているはずよ。

●：そうか，そういうことなら，ちょっとした食べ物を買って9時ごろ持っていくよ。ティムに知らせておいて。

☆：よかった。また後でね。

質問：パーティーに行く前にジェイコブはおそらく何をするか。

1 ティムに電話する。　　**2** レイチェルに会う。　　**3** 食べ物を買う。　　**4** 職場を早めに出る。

解説　今夜のティムのパーティーについて話している。ジェイコブは仕事で遅くなるのでパーティーに間に合わないことを心配していたが，ティムのパーティーは遅くまで盛り上がることを知り，I'll just buy some snacks and bring them と言った。**3**が正解。

No. 3　解答　**4**

☆：Hi, Steve. Well, back to another week of teaching English. How's your class at JCO Technologies going? Is the business-English textbook I recommended working out?

★：No, the students are too advanced, so I decided not to use it. It's a small class and most of the students have lived overseas, so I needed something more challenging.

☆：Oh, so what are you using, then?

★：I found some useful business case studies used in American MBA programs that are perfect. We first study the vocabulary and content. Then I break them up into groups to discuss solutions.

☆：Sounds interesting.

★：It is. They can practice critical thinking and put all their knowledge to work.

Question：What curriculum did the man choose for his English class?

☆：こんにちは，スティーブ。英語指導の新しい1週間が始まりましたね。JCO テクノロジーズでの授業はどうですか。私がお勧めしたビジネス英語の教科書は役に立っていますか。

★：いや，生徒たちの英語力はとても高くて，それは使わないことにしたんです。少人数の授業ですし，大半の生徒は海外に住んでいた経験があります。だからもっとやりがいがあって難しいものが必要だったのです。

☆：まあ，では何を使っているのですか。

★：アメリカのMBAプログラムで使われているビジネス・ケーススタディーでとても役に立つものを見つけて，これが申し分ないんです。まず語彙と内容の学習をします。それから生徒たちをグループ分けして解決策を話し合うんです。

☆：面白そうですね。

★：はい。クリティカル・シンキングの練習もできますし，すべての知識を仕事に役立てられるのです。

質問：男性は英語の授業のためにどのようなカリキュラムを選んだか。

1 アメリカのMBAのために勉強している生徒のために書かれた教科書。
2 英語学習者のためのビジネス英語の教科書。
3 生徒たちが自分で行ったケーススタディー。
4 ビジネスの研究をしている大学院生のためのケーススタディーの素材。

解説　男性は最初 business-English textbook を使ってみたのだが，受け持っている生徒には簡単すぎると感じたため，I found some useful business case studies used in American MBA programs that are perfect. と言っている。**4**が正解。それは教科書ではないので，**1**は誤り。

No. 4　解答　**1**

☆：I'm so angry at Derrick that I don't know what to do. Remember my idea about automating certain parts of the assembly line?

★：Oh, yeah. You've been talking about that idea for several months. So what happened? Did your boss turn it down?

☆：デリックには本当に頭にきてしまって，どうしたらいいのかわからないわ。組み立てラインの一部を自動化するという私のアイデアを覚えている？

★：ああ，うん。ここ数カ月，君が話しているあのアイデアだね。それで，どうしたんだい？　君

☆：No, he loved it, and he's putting the new plan in action. But Derrick claimed at Friday's meeting that it was his idea and Maggie, our supervisor, is giving him credit for it.

★：That's terrible. Why didn't you put Derrick in his place at the meeting?

☆：And make a public scene? No, but I'll tell Maggie how I was stabbed in the back when I meet her in private tomorrow morning.

Question：What will the woman do tomorrow morning?

の上司がそれを認めてくれないのかい？

☆：いいえ，彼はとても気に入ってくれて，実行しようとしているの。でも，デリックが金曜日の会議でそれは自分のアイデアだと言い張って，監督者のマギーは，彼の功績だと思っているのよ。

★：それはひどいね。どうして会議でデリックのでたらめを正さなかったの？

☆：それで人前で大騒ぎするの？ いいえ，でもマギーには私がどのように裏切られたか伝えるつもりよ。明日の朝，個人的に会うときにね。

質問：女性は明日の朝何をするか。

1 監督者にデリックの偽りの主張について知らせる。
2 組み立てラインを効率化するための彼女のアイデアを提示する。
3 自動化装置の問題を解消する手伝いをする。
4 デリックの間違った主張に関して彼と対峙する。

解説　女性は最後の発言で翌朝の予定について I'll tell Maggie how I was stabbed in the back when I meet her in private tomorrow morning. と述べている。be stabbed in the back は「裏切られる」という意味。ここではデリックが手柄を横取りしたことを指している。**1**が正解。

No. 5　解答　**1**

●：You know the new job as Marketing Director I took at Sendax? I was assured that 80 percent of my time would be spent meeting clients with only a smidgen of administration work.

☆：I hope you're not going to tell me you're overwhelmed with admin stuff.

●：It's actually worse than that. I have to make cold calls pretty much all day, the exact kind of sales I just can't stand. Of course, I get hung up on most of the time.

☆：Wow. Talk about deception. I hope you can speak to someone who can help you reshape your work into something closer to what was initially described.

Question：What is the man's problem?

●：僕がセンダックスで就いた，新しいマーケティング・マネージャーの仕事があるだろう？ 時間の8割はクライアントとの打ち合わせに使って，管理業務は少ししかないと言われていたんだ。

☆：その管理業務でまいっているなんて言わないでよね。

●：実際にはもっと悪いんだよ。一日中かなりの勧誘電話をかけないといけないんだ。正に僕が大嫌いなタイプの営業だよ。もちろん，たいていは電話を切られるんだ。

☆：まあ。だまされたもいいとこよね。もともと言われていた仕事になるべく戻せるよう助けてくれそうな人に相談できるといいわね。

質問：男性の問題は何か。

1 責務が約束通りではない。
2 管理業務にほぼ一日費やしている。
3 管理職としてふさわしい肩書が欲しい。
4 顧客と一緒に仕事をするのが極めて難しい。

解説　男性は2番目の発言で I have to make cold calls pretty much all day, the exact kind of sales I just can't stand. と言い，これを受けて女性が I hope you can speak to someone who can help you reshape your work into something closer to what was initially described. と言っている。つまり，当初説明を受けていた業務内容と違っていることが問題だとわかるので，**1**が正解。

No. 6　解答　1

★: You know, my account has doubled in size the last few years, but our staff size hasn't kept pace. Everyone's overworked and overwhelmed. Two people have quit recently, and there are plans to fill only one of the positions.

☆: Seriously? But the company's hired over twenty new employees this year. So why do you think it is that you're not getting the additional help you need?

★: Good question. The vice-president of sales and our manager don't seem to get along, so I think it has something to do with office politics.

☆: Very unprofessional. By not giving clients the care they deserve, we're shooting ourselves in the foot.

Question: What does the man imply?

★：ねえ，僕の取引は規模にしてここ数年で倍になったのに，スタッフの規模が伴っていないんだ。みんな働きすぎでまいっているよ。最近2人辞職したのに，たった1人しか補充しない計画なんだよ。

☆：本当に？　でも会社が今年採用した新入社員は20人を超えたわよね。なのに，どうして必要な支援を追加で受けられないのかしら。

★：いい質問だね。営業副本部長とうちの部長のそりが合わないみたいなんだ。だから僕は社内政治に関係していると思っているよ。

☆：とてもプロらしくないわね。顧客にふさわしい対応をしないと，私たちは墓穴を掘ることになるわ。

質問：男性は何を示唆しているか。

1 営業副本部長は不公平である。　　2 女性の取引は重要だと見なされていない。
3 採用は非公式に凍結されている。　　4 会社の全スタッフが働きすぎである。

解説 男性が言っていることは，仕事が増えているのに人手が足りていないこと，人手不足をカバーできない要因は営業副本部長と部長のそりが合わないことに原因があると見られること，である。後半の内容に合う**1**が正解。

No. 7　解答　1

☆: Phillip has been in middle school now for two months, right? How's he getting along in his new school?

●: Not so good, actually. He's used to going to a small private school, so he feels overwhelmed being in a huge middle school.

☆: Too bad. My daughter's having adjustment problems too, so we're getting some family counseling. Have you thought about what you're going to do?

●: Charlene and I met Phillip's teacher to discuss options. We've decided to give it another few months and if it doesn't work out by then, move him back to a smaller school.

Question: What have Phillip's parents decided to do?

☆：フィリップは中学校に通い始めてもう2カ月よね。新しい学校ではうまくやっているのかしら。

●：そうでもないみたいなんだ，実際はね。もともと小さな私立学校に通っていたから，大規模な中学校に圧倒されているんだ。

☆：それはあんまりね。うちの娘も適応の問題を抱えていて，家族でカウンセリングを受けることにしているの。あなたはどうしようか考えたことある？

●：シャーリーンと一緒にフィリップの先生に会って，選択肢について話し合ったんだ。もう数カ月は様子を見て，それまでにうまく事態が進まないようなら，もっと小規模な学校に彼を戻すことにしたんだ。

質問：フィリップの両親はどうすることにしたか。

1 最終判断を下すまで時間をかける。　　2 フィリップをもっと小さな学校にやる。
3 家族でカウンセリングを受ける。　　4 フィリップの先生にアドバイスをもらう。

解説 質問にある Phillip's parents とは，男性とシャーリーンのこと。男性は最後に We've decided to give it another few months and if it doesn't work out by then, move him back to a smaller school. と言っている。しばらくは様子見なので，**1**が正解。

No. 8 解答 2

☆：My train was delayed again, so it took over two and a half hours to get to the university. The train was so crowded that I couldn't even concentrate on my reading.

●：That's crazy. If I were you, I'd think about finding a place that is more accessible to the university. It would make life so much easier.

☆：I know, but I live with my parents, so it's free rent. I'm saving up for a trip to Europe.

●：Yes, but think about it. If you lived within 30 minutes, you'd have several more hours each day to do other things, including working part-time if you really need the money.

Question：What does the man suggest the woman do?

☆：電車がまた遅れたの。だから大学に着くのに2時間半もかかったのよ。電車はとても混雑していて，読書に集中することすらできなかったわ。

●：正気の沙汰じゃないね。僕だったら，大学にもっと通いやすい所に住む場所を見つけようと考えるだろうね。その方が生活しやすくなるよ。

☆：わかっているけど，私は両親と住んでいるから，家賃はかからないの。ヨーロッパ旅行の費用を貯めているのよ。

●：ああ，でも検討してみてごらんよ。30分圏内に住めば毎日数時間浮いて，ほかのことができるよ。どうしてもお金が必要ならアルバイトをする時間も持てる。

質問：男性は女性に何をするように提案しているか。

1 自宅にもっと近い大学を見つける。　　**2** もっと便利な場所に引っ越す。
3 読書にもっと集中する。　　**4** 引き続き両親と住む。

解説　男性は最初の発言で If I were you, I'd think about finding a place that is more accessible to the university. と言い，最後の発言でも think about it と重ねて言っている。**2**が正解。

No. 9 解答 1

★：Thank you for calling Biotech Medical. How may I help you?

☆：I'm calling to inquire about the job vacancy you posted last week for an administrative assistant position in your company. Could you please tell me the deadline for applications?

★：Yes, of course. Applications will be accepted until 5:00 p.m. on Friday the 24th. That's October, of course.

☆：OK, thank you. And could you also tell me when you plan to begin interviewing applicants for the position?

★：Well, we don't have specific dates set, but interviews will probably start one week after the application deadline. We intend to make our final decision by the end of November.

☆：I see. I'll send my application this week, but I'll be out of town for two weeks, and I'm concerned that I'll miss the chance for an interview.

★：In that case, maybe you should make a note of the dates you'll be away on your application. If you seem like a strong candidate, I'm sure someone could arrange a mutually convenient time to

★：バイオテック・メディカル社にお電話いただきありがとうございます。どのようなご用件でしょうか。

☆：先週掲示された，御社の課長補佐の空席の件についてお尋ねしたくて電話いたしました。応募の締め切り日を教えていただけますか。

★：はい，もちろんです。応募は24日金曜日の午後5時まで受け付け予定です。もちろん，10月の。

☆：わかりました，ありがとうございます。それから，そのポジションへの応募者の面接はいつから開始するつもりかも教えていただけますか。

★：そうですね，具体的な日取りは決まっていませんが，おそらく面接は応募締め切りの1週間後に始まります。11月末までに最終決定を行うつもりでいます。

☆：わかりました。今週中に応募書類をお送りしますが，2週間留守にするので，面接の機会を逃すのではないかと心配なんです。

★：それでしたら，留守にされる日程を応募書類に書いておくといいかもしれません。有力な選考対象者になるようであれば，お互いが会うのに都合のいい時間をきっと誰かが設定できるでしょう。

meet.

☆：Yes, I'll do that. But do you think it might be possible to have an interview early next week? I'm very interested in this job.

★：Well, if you give me your name and number, I'll pass on your request to the person in charge of hiring, and she can get back to you about that.

☆：Oh, thank you. That would be great.

Question：What does the man agree to do?

☆：はい，そうします。ただ，来週の前半に面接を行っていただくことは可能でしょうか。この仕事にとても興味があるんです。

★：では，お名前と電話番号をいただければ，採用担当者にご要望を伝えます。彼女からこの件について折り返しご連絡しますよ。

☆：ああ，ありがとうございます。そうしていただけると大変助かります。

質問：男性は何をすることに同意しているか。

1 女性の要望を伝える。

2 女性の応募を検討する。

3 重要な情報を伝えるため電話を折り返す。

4 来週の面接を設定する。

解説 男性が同意したのは，女性の面接関連の要望を担当者に伝える（pass on）ことである。このpass onをconveyと言い換えた **1** が正解。男性は直接採用業務に携わっているわけではないので，ほかの選択肢は誤り。

No. 10 解答 1

●：Mr. and Mrs. Martin, I'm afraid we're fully booked. There are no seats available on the 11:00 a.m. flight.

★：No seats available? There must be some mistake. I confirmed our reservation yesterday!

●：I'm terribly sorry, but we've obviously overbooked the flight, and I apologize for that. There is another flight leaving at 1:00 p.m., and I know that one has seats available.

☆：But we can't wait until 1:00 p.m. We have a wedding to attend. Isn't there any other option?

●：I understand. Well, there is actually one seat available in business class.

☆：In that case, why don't you go first, honey? I don't mind joining you at the reception.

★：No, I think we should go together. We should probably change airlines.

●：Well, I'll see if one of the other passengers would be willing to change to the later flight.

☆：And what if no one is willing to give up their seat?

●：There is plenty of time until boarding, and we offer excellent compensation. We usually have a few people who accept our offer, so let me announce that now.

★：Alright, please do. We will check other airlines just in case, though.

Question：What does the airline staff imply to the couple?

●：マーティンさま，あいにく満席となっております。午前11時の便には空席がございません。

★：席がないって？ 絶対に何かの間違いです。昨日予約を確認したんですよ！

●：大変申し訳ありませんが，この便についてはオーバーブッキングをしてしまったようで，お詫びいたします。ほかに午後1時発の便がありまして，そちらには空席がございます。

☆：でも私たちは午後1時まで待てないわ。結婚式に参列しなければならないの。ほかに選択肢はありませんか。

●：わかりました。実は，ビジネスクラスが1席空いております。

☆：それなら，あなたは先に行ったらどう？ 私は披露宴であなたと合流しても構わないわよ。

★：いや，一緒に行くべきだと思う。たぶん航空会社を変えた方がいいだろう。

●：ええと，ほかのお客さまの中で1人，後の便に変更してくれる方がいらっしゃるか確認いたします。

☆：それで誰も席を譲りたい人がいなければどうするのですか。

●：搭乗までたっぷり時間はありますし，当社はとても待遇のよい補償をお出ししています。いつもは応じてくださる方が数名いらっしゃるので，今アナウンスをさせてください。

★：わかりました，そうしてください。念のため私たちはほかの航空会社も確認してみますが。

質問：航空会社のスタッフは夫婦に対して何を示唆しているか。

1 彼らは午前11時の便の席を得るだろう。

2 彼らはおそらく午後1時の便に乗らなければならないだろう。

3 彼らは遅延に対する補償をたっぷり受けられるだろう。

4 彼らはほかの航空会社の席を得られるだろう。

解説 オーバーブッキングされてしまった夫婦の選択肢を考える。会話の前半では男性だけ先に行く話が出ているが、男性はそれを却下している。後半でスタッフが伝えているのは、補償を受ける代わりに席を譲ってくれる人がきっといるだろうということ。正解は**1**。

Part 2 🔊062〜067

(A)

Classifying the World's Languages

For several centuries, a number of linguists attempted to classify the world's languages. Before the twentieth century, the most common approach was to find language families which were believed to have developed over time in the same way that biological species develop through evolution. However, any attempt to find only one classification system for all the world's languages will certainly fail because many languages are very similar to each other in some ways but totally different in others. Languages that share similar vocabulary —for example, Chinese and Japanese—are not at all alike in grammar or sound. In fact, Chinese is in many ways closer to English than it is to Japanese. On the other hand, Japanese is much closer in word order to Turkish than Turkish is to the languages of countries that have had the most contact with it throughout history.

Even if one person, using a massive computer, could enter the data of the approximately 6,000 world languages existing today, the results would be contradictory, depending on the grammar, the sound system, the vocabulary, or other criteria used by linguists to describe human languages. All we can do when classifying human languages throughout the world is to carefully limit the ways in which we place different languages into categories of similarity or difference. One kind of classification might be based on word order; another might be based on historical similarities and vocabulary; yet another might be based on how words are formed in different languages. Yet each categorization is valid within its own context.

Questions

No.11 How did linguists attempt to classify languages in centuries past?

No.12 What is the biggest problem with the classification of the world's languages?

世界の言語の分類

　数世紀にわたり、多くの言語学者が世界の言語を分類しようと試みてきた。20世紀以前の最も一般的な手法は、生物学的な種が進化によって発達するのと同じように、長年にわたって発達したと信じられている語族を発見することであった。しかし、世界のすべての言語を分類するただ1つの体系を見つけようとする試みは、どんなものでも間違いなく失敗することになる。なぜなら、多くの言語は、ある点では互いに非常に似通っていながら、別の点では全く異なるものだからである。似ている語彙を共有する言語、例えば中国語と日本語は、文法や音韻の面では全く似ていない。実際、中国語は多くの点で日本語よりも英語に近い。一方、日本語は語順の点ではトルコ語に近く、その度合いは、トルコ語と、トルコ語が歴史を通じて最も多く接触してきた国々の言語との類似の度合いを大きく上回る。

　たとえ誰かが大型コンピュータを使って、今日存在するおよそ6,000の世界の言語のデータを入力できたとしても、文法や音韻体系や語彙によって、あるいは言語学者が人間の言語を記述するために用いるそのほかの基準

によって，分析結果は相いれないものとなるだろう。世界中の人間の言語を分類する際にわれわれにできるのは，さまざまな言語を類似や相違といった分類に入れる方法を注意深く限定することだけである。ある種の分類は語順に基づくかもしれず，別の分類は歴史的な類似と語彙に基づくものかもしれず，また別の分類は異なる言語における語形成のあり方に基づくかもしれない。だが，いずれの分類も，それ自身の文脈の中では有効なのである。

No. 11　解答　**4**

「過去数世紀にわたり，言語学者はどのように言語を分類しようとしたか」

1 似た単語やフレーズを持つ語族がある場所を突き止めた。

2 主に文法的な違いから語族を区別した。

3 主に地理的な近さから語族の説明をした。

4 言語を，発展した経緯を共有する語族にグループ分けした。

解説　言語の分類の仕方については，the most common approach was to find language families which were believed to have developed over time in the same way that biological species develop through evolution という説明がある。発展の歴史に言及している **4** が正解。

No. 12　解答　**2**

「世界の言語の分類に関する最大の問題は何か」

1 大量のデータを分析しなければならないこと。

2 異なる分類体系が異なる結果を生むこと。

3 世界の言語を分類することに対する関心がほとんどないこと。

4 世界には言語があまりにも多く存在していること。

解説　前半部分で any attempt to find only one classification system for all the world's languages will certainly fail because many languages are very similar to each other in some ways but totally different in others と述べており，それを後半部分でさらに the results would be contradictory, depending on the grammar, the sound system, the vocabulary ... と説明している。この部分に合う **2** が正解。

(B)

For Goodness' Sake

Traditionally, big business has focused on the formula that greed is good. However, University of Michigan Professor Kim Cameron says that virtuous companies can also be financial winners.

Cameron defines this so-called organizational virtue in terms of human impact, moral goodness, and social betterment. He argues that corporations which focus on such areas are likely to outperform their more cutthroat competitors. A study of the airline industry, for example, showed that companies which considered both the financial and human impact of business decisions performed better than those that focused solely on profits. When corporations employ organizational virtue, says Cameron, there is a positive effect on the corporate culture. Employees become more cooperative and feel much greater loyalty to their organization.

Nevertheless, organizational virtue is not without its naysayers. In ruthless business environments, some argue that every virtuous act comes at a price, whether it is higher employee costs or reduced income. Many business leaders argue that it may be unethical for publicly traded companies to consider the human impact of decisions as it is the shareholders—to whom corporate management is answerable—that ultimately pay the price.

Questions

No.13　What does Kim Cameron say about the way corporations operate?

No.14　What do many business leaders say about organizational virtue?

善意に基づいて

伝統的に大企業は，貪欲は善なりという公式に焦点を当ててきた。ところが，ミシガン大学のキム・キャメロン教授は，高い道徳的理念を掲げる企業はまた経済的勝者ともなり得ると語る。

キャメロンは，このいわゆる企業の道徳的理念を，人に与える影響，道徳に照らした善，社会の改善の観点から定義づけている。彼は，そのような分野に焦点を合わせる企業の方が，より冷酷な競合他社に勝る業績を上げる可能性が大きいと主張する。例えば，航空業界に関するある調査では，企業が財政・人の両面への影響を考慮して決定を行っている場合の方が，単に収益だけを重視する企業よりも業績が良いという結果が出ている。企業が組織として道徳的理念を掲げる場合，企業文化に良い影響が現れ，従業員がより協力的になり，さらに以前より自らの属する組織に対してはるかに大きな忠誠心を感じるようになるとキャメロンは語っている。

とは言え，組織の道徳的理念に対しては反対者もいる。過酷な経営環境下では，あらゆる道徳的理念に基づく行動が，人件費の増加であれ，収益の減少であれ，何らかの代償が伴うと反論する人たちもいる。多くの産業界のリーダーたちは，最終的にその代償を払うことになるのは株主であり，企業経営は株主に対して責任を負うものなのだから，株式公開企業が，その決定が人間に及ぼす影響を考慮すること自体，企業倫理に反するかもしれないと主張する。

No. 13 解答 **4**

「企業が活動するあり方について，キム・キャメロンはどのように述べているか」
1 競合他社を打ち負かすためにもっと非情である必要がある。
2 航空業界の過ちから学ぶべきである。
3 徳について助言する立場にない。
4 道徳的に行動することで利益を増やすことができる。
解説 キム・キャメロンの主張の要点は，virtuous companies can also be financial winners ということ。financial winners を boost profits と言い換えている **4** が正解。

No. 14 解答 **2**

「組織の道徳的理念に関して，多くの産業界のリーダーたちはどのように述べているか」
1 無慈悲なビジネス界では欠かせないものである。
2 株主のニーズの方が優先順位が高い。
3 それを取り入れる前に今一度よく調べる必要がある。
4 不要な従業員を排除するために使うことができる。
解説 organizational virtue については最後の方に Many business leaders argue that it may be unethical ... to consider the human impact of decisions とあり，その理由を it is the shareholders—to whom corporate management is answerable—that ultimately pay the price と述べている。つまり，道徳的理念よりも優先されるのは，最終的な責任を持つ株主だと言っているので，**2** が正解。

(C)

The Taj Mahal

The Taj Mahal is one of the most recognizable buildings in the world and stands on the right bank of the Yamuna River in Agra, India. It was commissioned and built by Mughal emperor Shah Jahan in memory of his third wife, Mumtaz Mahal, who tragically died during childbirth. The construction of the Taj Mahal began in 1632 and took around 16 years to complete. Over 20,000 people and 1,000 elephants were used during construction, with materials coming from countries including China and Sri Lanka. The mausoleum is not only beautiful but also perfectly symmetrical.

The Taj Mahal is a very popular tourist destination, attracting between two and four million visitors each year. In 1983, it became a UNESCO World Heritage Site, and in 2007, it was chosen as one of the

New Seven Wonders of the World. Its popularity, however, could be affecting its conservation. Pollution from both surrounding areas and further afield is causing some of its pure white marble to turn yellow, and loss of groundwater could be affecting its wooden foundations. To counter these effects, the government set up a series of buffer zones in order to protect this architectural gem for future generations.

Questions

No.15 Which of the following is true about the Taj Mahal?

No.16 How could its fame be affecting the Taj Mahal?

タージ・マハル

　タージ・マハルは世界で最もよく認識されている建物であり，インドのアグラを流れるヤムナー川の右岸に立っている。その建設を進めたのはムガル帝国の皇帝シャー・ジャハーンであり，出産時に悲劇的に亡くなった3番目の妻，ムムターズ・マハルを追悼して建立した。タージ・マハルの建設工事は1632年に始まり，完成まで約16年かかった。2万超の人々と1,000頭を超えるゾウが建設に従事し，資材は中国やスリランカを含む諸外国から集められた。大霊廟は美しいだけでなく，完璧な左右対称を描いている。

　タージ・マハルは旅行者に非常に人気の場所であり，毎年2,000万から4,000万人の訪問者を引きつけている。1983年にはユネスコの世界遺産になり，2007年には新世界の七不思議の1つに選ばれた。しかし，その人気ぶりがその保存にも影響を及ぼしかねない状況となっている。周辺地域の汚染のみならず，遠く離れた場所の汚染も，純白の大理石が黄色に変色する原因になっており，地下水の枯渇が木製の土台に影響を与えているかもしれない。こうした影響に対処するため，政府は一連の緩衝地帯を設け，この珠玉の建築物を将来の世代のために守ろうとしている。

No. 15　解答　**3**

「タージ・マハルについて正しいものは次のうちどれか」

1 世界最古の大霊廟である。　　　　　　　　　**2** 皇帝が子供の誕生を記念して建てた。

3 どちら側も他方が鏡に映った像をしている。　　**4** ゾウを使った資材の運搬に16年以上かかった。

解説　英文全体がタージ・マハルの説明になっているので，特定の箇所だけを根拠に答えを出すのは難しい。The mausoleum is not only beautiful but also perfectly symmetrical. を a mirror image of the other「他方が鏡に映った像，左右対称になった像」と説明している**3**が正解。

No. 16　解答　**4**

「タージ・マハルの名声はタージ・マハルにどんな影響を及ぼしかねない状況か」

1 訪問者が飲用にする水がない。　　　　　　　**2** 何百万人という訪問者がその保全に協力している。

3 政府がその修復のための基金を設立した。　　　**4** 環境的な悪状況に悩まされている。

解説　タージ・マハルの popularity「人気」が及ぼしかねない影響については，Pollution from both surrounding areas and further afield is causing some of its pure white marble to turn yellow, and loss of groundwater could be affecting its wooden foundations. と説明している。Pollution from both surrounding areas and further afield を adverse environmental conditions と言い換えている**4**が正解。

(D)

Lido

　The United Kingdom isn't exactly known for its tropical weather, yet outdoor swimming is surprisingly popular. It's for this reason that lidos are something of a British tradition. A lido is an outdoor swimming pool with surrounding facilities such as a café and areas for sunbathing. The 1930s were considered the golden age of lidos, when outdoor swimming surged in popularity, with 169 lidos

リド

　イギリスはその熱帯的な天候で有名なわけではないのだが，屋外スイミングが驚くほど人気がある。そのため，リドはイギリスの伝統のようになっている。リドは屋外型のスイミングプールで，周囲にはカフェや日光浴のための場所がある。1930年代はリドの黄金時代と考えられており，屋外スイミングの人気が急上昇した当時，レクリエーションのために英国中に169のリドが建設された。多くのリドは，ビーチや海，屋外スイミングを楽しめるように海岸近くに建てられた。リドという言葉は実のところ，海岸を意味するイタリア語である。

　国外旅行が安くなり一般大衆が利用しやすくなるにつれ，リドの人気は下がった。その結果，多くのリドは閉鎖されたが，近年は人気が再び上昇しており，多くが再オープンした。夏の気温が上がっていることが，再び関心が高まっている要因だと言う人もいる。イギリス人はかつてほど裕福でなくなり，そのせいで人々が倹約しているので，外国での休暇の人気がなくなったと言う人もいる。さらに，屋内スイミングプールで連想される塩素が屋外スイミングプールにはないので人気が高まっていると言う人もいる。理由が何であれ，イギリスではリドが浸透している。

No. 17　解答　**2**

「なぜリドはイギリス特有の現象になっているのか」

1 1930年代により多くの人々が沿岸部を訪れた。

2 イギリスの天気は特に屋外スイミングには適していない。

3 イタリア人の名前がついた場所はとても人気がある。

4 イギリス人はカフェで日光浴をするのが好きである。

解説　冒頭で The United Kingdom isn't exactly known for its tropical weather, yet outdoor swimming is surprisingly popular. と言っているので，**2**が正解。isn't exactly が選択肢では is not particularly に言い換えられている。

No. 18　解答　**4**

「リドに何が起きているか」

1 外国旅行が以前よりも安くなったので，最近閉鎖してしまった。

2 金持ちは化学物質が好きではないので，閉鎖してしまった。

3 気温の上昇に伴って諸外国でもオープンし始めている。

4 さまざまな理由で今一度人気になりつつある。

解説　質問は現在完了形で尋ねられていることから，過去ではなく，最近のリドの動向が問われているとわかる。後半に recent years have seen their popularity rise once again and many have reopened とあり，その理由がさまざま紹介されているので，**4**が正解。

(E)

Ballpoint Pens

Fountain pens write beautifully, but they are also quite messy to use. We have László Bíró to thank for the largely mess-free ballpoint pen. While working as a journalist, he noticed that the ink used to print newspapers dried quickly and didn't smudge. Intrigued, he tried to use the same ink in a fountain pen but found that it was too thick to flow into the tip and simply blocked the pen. However, he remained intent on using the ink to write with and set about developing what would later become the ballpoint pen.

Working with his brother, Bíró developed a pen tip which consisted of a ball that could move freely in a socket. As it rolled, the ball would pick up ink and deposit it onto the paper, hence the name ballpoint pen. The first ballpoint pens were presented at the Budapest International Fair in 1931. The initial versions were made of metal, but cheaper disposable plastic versions were developed soon after. This affordability, coupled with the ease of use, made ballpoint pens hugely popular around the world. Nowadays, ballpoint pens can be found everywhere, and many people still refer to them as "Biro's."

Questions

No.19 What inspired Bíró's idea for the ballpoint pen?

No.20 What is true about modern ballpoint pens?

ボールペン

万年筆は美しく書けるが，使い方がかなりやっかいだったりもする。ほとんどやっかいなことがないボールペンがあるのはラースロー・ビーローのおかげである。彼はジャーナリストとして働いているときに，新聞を印刷するのに使用されているインクがすぐに乾き，にじまないことに気づいた。興味を持った彼は，同じインクを万年筆に使おうとしたが，どろっとしすぎていてペン先まで流れず，単にペン先を詰まらせてしまうことに気づいた。しかしながら，筆記用にそのインクを用いるという彼の熱心さは変わらず，後のボールペンとなるものの開発に取りかかった。

兄弟で一緒に作業をしながら，ビーローはソケット内で自由に動くことができるボールからなるペン先を開発した。それは回転すると，インクを集めて紙の上に押し出した。だからボールペンという名前なのである。最初のボールペンは，1931年のブタペスト国際フェアでお披露目された。最初のバージョンは金属製だったが，すぐに安くて処分可能なプラスチック製のバージョンが開発された。この値段的な手軽さが，使いやすさと相まって，ボールペンを世界中で大人気製品にした。今ではボールペンはどこにでもあり，多くの人々がいまだに「ビーロー」と呼ぶ。

No. 19 解答 3

「何からビーローはボールペンの着想を得たか」

1 彼の万年筆がインクで詰まってしまうことへの不満。　　**2** 新聞社で働いているときに執筆した記事。

3 新聞の印刷に使われていたインクの特性。　　**4** 以前に行った速乾性のあるインクを使った実験。

解説　ボールペン開発のきっかけについては，While working as a journalist, he noticed that the ink used to print newspapers dried quickly and didn't smudge. とある。速乾性のあるインクを何とか使いたいという思いが，set about developing what would later become the ballpoint pen へとつながっていったので，**3** が正解。

No. 20 解答 1

「現代のボールペンについて正しいことは何か」

1 それを呼ぶとき発明者の名前を使う人もまだいる。　　**2** 使い捨てタイプのものしかない。

3 最初のバージョンと見分けがつかない。　　**4** もはや金属を使っていない。

解説　最後の many people still refer to them as "Biro's" から **1** が正解。金属製からプラスチック製に改良された話はあるが，現在金属製のボールペンがないとは言っていないので，**4** は誤り。

(F) *No. 21* 解答 3

All students participating in next Monday's field trip to Painted Stone State Park need to turn in a permission slip with the parent's authorization by Friday. You can find permission slips on the Cloverfield Elementary School website. We will provide lunch. We cannot accommodate special meal requests nor provide a list of foods served in advance, so if your child has any issues with certain foods, parents are requested to prepare a bag lunch for their children to bring with them. The weather is expected to be hot, so children should dress appropriately, including wearing hats or caps. Remember that you can purchase a special school cap at the office for $5. If you think your child may find the field trip physically or emotionally challenging, please call the school. A teacher will be on hand that day at the school to take care of students not participating in this event.

状況：あなたの幼い子供が遠足に行くことになっていて，すでに許可書を提出している。あなたの子供は，卵とピーナッツに対してアレルギーがある。あなたは放課後，学校に電話し，次の録音された音声を聞く。

質問：学校はあなたに何をするよう求めているか。

今度の月曜日に予定されている，ペインテッド・ストーン州立公園への遠足に参加する生徒は全員，金曜日までに保護者が承諾したことを示す許可書を提出する必要があります。許可書はクローバーフィールド小学校のウエブサイトにあります。ランチは学校で用意します。特別食の要望にはお応えできません。また，事前に食べ物のリストをお渡しすることもできません。お子さんが特定の食べ物に問題を抱えている場合は，保護者がお弁当を用意し，お子さんに持たせるようお願いいたします。天候は暑くなる見込みですので，帽子をかぶるなど，適切な服装での参加をお願いします。特別な生徒用の帽子を事務室にて5ドルで購入できますので，お忘れなく。お子さんにとって遠足が肉体的あるいは精神的に困難かもしれないと思われる場合は，学校にお電話ください。当日は教師が1人学校に残り，この行事に参加しない生徒たちの世話をします。

1 娘のアレルギーについて学校の事務室に電話する。　　**2** 食事に関するオンラインの要望書に記入する。

3 娘のために昼食を用意する。　　　　　　　　　　　　**4** 特別食を購入する。

解説　状況からあなたの子供に食物アレルギーがあることがわかる。その場合の対応としては，parents are requested to prepare a bag lunch for their children to bring with them と指示されているので，**3**が正解。

(G) *No. 22* 解答 3

Following this presentation, we'll have several breakout sessions. For those going to any of the EU countries or Great Britain, please meet in room 1404. For those who are interested in study programs in the United States but have not yet made any firm plans, please meet in 1601. There are several tables set up with brochures, and there are teachers and students who have completed overseas study programs. For those who plan to study in America sometime this year but who have not yet applied for a student visa, there are a few changes to the application process that you should be aware of. Please meet in 1604 to discuss the process as well as obtain useful information about completing your documents. Those planning to go to New Zealand or Australia this year, or who have interest in going there for study in the future, should attend the session in room 1412.

状況：あなたは今年9月に米国に行き，カリフォルニアの大学で勉強するつもりだが，まだビザの申請をしていない。あなたは留学を計画しているほかの生徒たち全員と説明会に出席し，学生課の課長から次のことを聞く。

質問：あなたは何をするべきか。

この説明会の後，いくつかに分かれて分科会を行います。EU各国ならびにイギリスに行く方は，1404号室に集まってください。米国での勉強プログラムに興味があるけれども，まだ計画を確定できていない方は，1601号

室に集まってください。パンフレットとともにいくつかテーブルを用意しています。先生や留学プログラムを修了した生徒もいます。今年のうちにアメリカ留学を計画していて，まだ学生ビザを申し込んでいない方は，知っておかなければならない申請手続きの変更があります。1604号室に来てください。手続きについて話すだけでなく，書類の記入に関する役立つ情報も得られます。今年ニュージーランドかオーストラリアに行く計画を立てている方，あるいは将来そこで勉強することに興味がある方は，1412号室で行われる会に参加してください。

1 テーブルが用意されている1601号室に行く。　　**2** 1404号室でアドバイスをもらう。
3 1604号室で援助を受ける。　　**4** 1412号室で行われる分科会に参加する。

解説　状況から今年アメリカに留学するが，まだビザの申請をしていないことがわかる。つまり those who plan to study in America sometime this year but who have not yet applied for a student visa のための会に参加することになる。Please meet in 1604 と言っているので**3**が正解。

(H) No. 23　解答　4

Your doctoral committee will serve as mentors and evaluators and help you through the steps towards obtaining your doctoral degree. You should now choose members of your committee. Here's the list of approved faculty members to direct dissertations. You'll see that Dr. Carlson is not on the list since she isn't in our department. To gain approval to have her on your committee, you must consult with the Director of Graduate Studies, Robin Wright. As soon as you get an answer from her, fill out the Doctoral Committee Form and have all members you've chosen for your committee sign it. Submit the form to the Graduate School office on the fourth floor of Southerland Hall by December 15th. Your committee will help you schedule your comprehensive exam, which is necessary for gaining admission to candidacy. You'll need to fill out the Admission to Doctoral Candidacy form and follow all instructions provided on the form and accompanying paperwork.

状況：あなたは米国の大学の博士課程で学んでいる。学部の指導教官に会い，次のように言われる。あなたは博士論文審査委員会にシーラ・カールソン博士に加わってもらいたいと思っている。
質問：あなたが最初にすべきことは何か。

博士論文の審査委員会は，助言をし，評価をくれる場であり，あなたが博士号取得に向けて前進するのに役立ちます。もう自分の審査委員会のメンバーを選んでおいた方がよいでしょう。こちらが委員として博士論文の指導をすることが認められている教職員のリストです。カールソン博士の名前がリストにないことに気づくと思いますが，それは彼女の学部が違うためです。彼女をあなたの審査委員会に迎えることを認めてもらうには，大学院研究科長のロビン・ライトに相談しなければなりません。彼女から返答をもらったらすぐに博士論文審査委員会申請書に記入し，委員会に選んだ全委員の署名をもらってください。申請書はサウザーランド・ホールの4階にある大学院研究科事務局に12月15日までに提出すること。委員会は総合試験の予定を組む手伝いをしてくれます。博士候補となる許可を得るのに必要な試験です。博士候補許可の申請書に記入し，申請書ならびに付随する書類に記されているすべての指示に従う必要があります。

1 総合試験の予定を組む。　　**2** 認可された教職員のリストを要求する。
3 博士論文審査委員会の申請書に記入する。　　**4** ロビン・ライトとの約束を取り付ける。

解説　今すべきことは You should now choose members of your committee. から委員を選ぶことだが，その際，状況にあるシーラ・カールソン博士を呼ぶには，To gain approval to have her on your committee, you must consult with the Director of Graduate Studies, Robin Wright. という説明がある。**4**が正解。

(I) No. 24　解答　3

A member of volunteer programs will be waiting for you in the arrival lobby of the International Airport in Phnom Penh. Technology volunteers will then be taken to our program's apartment complex in Phnom Penh to deposit your belongings. There, you'll receive a briefing at our office on your first or second day, depending on your time of arrival. Conservation volunteers will spend their first night in Phnom Penh at a guesthouse, where you'll receive your bus tickets. You'll catch a public minivan at the main bus station, Poy Japon, the following day. A member of the conservation team will pick you up at the bus stop on Poy Japon beach and take you to the pier, where you'll take a speedboat to Koh Sdach Island. Medical volunteers will first be taken to one of the four hospitals to meet staff and then will be taken to a dormitory attached to the hospital.

状況：あなたはフォワード・イン・カンボジアと呼ばれるプログラムのボランティアで，出発前のオリエンテーションに参加している。あなたはカンボジアの環境保護グループとともに働くことになっている。プログラムの事務局長から次のことを聞く。

質問：プノンペンに着いたらまずどこに行くか。

ボランティア・プログラムのメンバーの1人がプノンペンの国際空港の到着ロビーであなたを待っています。それから科学技術ボランティアの人たちは，プノンペンにあるプログラム用アパートに連れて行ってもらい，荷物を降ろします。そこにある事務所で事前説明を行いますが，到着時刻によって初日か2日目に開催します。環境保護ボランティアは，最初の晩はプノンペンのゲストハウスに宿泊し，そこでバスのチケットを受け取ります。翌日，ポイジャポンという一番大きいバス乗り場で公共のミニバンに乗ります。環境保護チームのメンバーの1人がポイジャポンビーチに面したバス停まであなたを迎えに行き，桟橋まで送ります。そこからスピードボートに乗り，コスダック島に行きます。医療ボランティアはまず，4つある病院のいずれか1つに行ってスタッフに会い，それから病院付属の寮に向かいます。

1 健康診断を受けに病院に行く。　**2** 自分の荷物を置きにアパートに行く。
3 1泊するゲストハウスに行く。　**4** ミニバンに乗るためにバス乗り場に行く。

解説　ボランティアが3タイプに分かれているので整理して聞く必要がある。状況からあなたは環境保護ボランティアに加わることがわかる。その最初の行動については，Conservation volunteers will spend their first night in Phnom Penh at a guesthouse, where you'll receive your bus tickets. と説明がある。**3**が正解。

(J) No. 25　解答　**1**

Attention, passengers. If this is your final destination, you must go through immigration, baggage claim, and customs. U.S. citizens and Green Card holders should follow the green lines. All other immigrants should follow the red lines, unless instructed otherwise by an official. Please follow the blue signs to your next flight if you are a transit passenger. If any person has a fever or does not feel well, you must report to the quarantine counter for an interview. Also, travelers who recently visited countries and regions shown on the sign, which are affected by epidemics, must see a representative and complete a questionnaire.

状況：あなたは客室乗務員によるアナウンスを聞く。あなたは別の便に乗り換える予定である。

質問：あなたは何をすべきか。

ご搭乗の皆さまにご案内いたします。当地が最終目的地のお客さまは，入国手続きを済ませ，手荷物を受け取り，税関へとお進みください。米国籍の方，ならびにグリーンカード（永住ビザ）を保有している方は，緑の線に沿ってお進みください。そのほかの入国される方は，係官から別の指示がない限り，赤い線に沿ってお進みください。お乗り継ぎのお客さまは，青い標識に従って乗り継ぎ便までいらしてください。熱がある方，またはご気分のよくない方は，検疫カウンターにお寄りください。お話を伺います。また，標識に表示されている国や地域を最近訪問なさった方は，伝染病が流行している地域ですので，担当者にお申し出いただき，アンケートに記入していただくことになっております。

1 青い標識に従う。　　**2** 赤い線に沿って進む。　　**3** 担当者に会う。　　**4** 入国手続きをする。

解説　状況からあなたは別の便に乗り換える必要がある。アナウンスでは，Please follow the blue signs to your next flight if you are a transit passenger. と指示されているので，**1**が正解。

☆：Today we have with us a very distinguished travel writer and lecturer, Mr. Kenneth Stevenson. Welcome to the program.

★：I'm glad to have the chance to talk with you and your audience.

☆：To start with, could you give us a little background information about your career as a world traveler and writer?

★：Well, since I was very small, I've wanted to see new places and experience different cultures. I think I first became attracted to travel from looking at copies of *National Geographic*, which my parents had subscribed to for years.

☆：And the writing?

★：Well, it just came naturally, and it was a perfect way to support my travels. I always liked to read travel magazines and travel books, even before I had ever left my home country.

☆：Could you give us some idea of one of those early books you read that really impressed you?

★：Sure, one book I always remember is a book titled *The Royal Road to Romance*, written by Richard Halliburton. It's a classic of travel writing.

☆：You've just finished a book about hiking through Central Asia. Could you comment on that trip and on writing the book?

★：Yes, well, one of my hobbies is reading historical novels and straight history. I'd read some fascinating books on Mongolia several months before the trip, and that persuaded me to go. It was a wonderful experience, and the Mongolian people were so friendly and... and generous. It's a vast country with an ancient, proud culture.

☆：Well, it certainly looks to be a wonderful, wonderful book. My best wishes for its success.

★：Thank you. I might mention that several major television networks are interested in filming a documentary on the trip, which would be a very interesting and new experience for me.

☆：Well, I hope that works out well. I'm sure all of us would enjoy seeing the result. Before we wrap up our interview, could you please tell us about the next region you're interested in visiting?

★：Well, I might stay close to home next time, and do some writing about the people living in the flood plains along the Mississippi River. I've always been fascinated by why these people continue to live along rivers that will invariably flood every few years or so. Also, as a boy I loved the writings of Mark Twain, which were set on the Mississippi.

☆：Well, Mr. Stevenson, I want to thank you very much for your comments and look forward to talking with you again after your next few projects are completed.

Questions

No.26 What is one reason Kenneth decided to travel through Central Asia?

No.27 What is one reason Kenneth wants to write about people living along the Mississippi River?

☆：本日は，大変著名な旅行作家で講演者でもいらっしゃる，ケネス・スティーブンソンさんにおいでいただいています。番組にようこそ。

★：あなたと観客の皆さんとお話しする機会をいただき，うれしく思います。

☆：まず，世界を旅行する作家としてのあなたの経歴について，少し予備知識をいただけますか。

★：はい，私は小さいころから，新しい場所を見たい，違う文化を体験したいと思っていました。最初に旅に興味を持ったのは，両親が長年購読していた『ナショナル・ジオグラフィック』誌を見たからだと思います。

☆：執筆に関しては？

★：そうですね，自然に書くようになっていましたし，私の旅を支える手段として申し分なかったのです。私は

ずっと旅に関する雑誌や本を読むのが好きでした。まだ外国に出たことのないうちからそうでした。

☆：若いころに読んで印象に残った本について教えていただけますか。

★：はい，いつも思い出すのは，『ロイヤル・ロード・トゥ・ロマンス』というタイトルの，リチャード・ハリバートンが書いた本です。旅行記の古典です。

☆：スティーブンソンさんは，中央アジアを巡った徒歩旅行に関する本を書き上げられたばかりでしたね。その旅と旅行記の執筆に関して，何かお話しくださいますか。

★：はい。私の趣味の1つは，歴史小説や歴史の本そのものを読むことです。この旅行に出る数カ月前にモンゴルに関するとても魅力的な本を何冊か読んでいて，旅に出る気になりました。素晴らしい経験になりましたし，モンゴルの人々はとても親切で心が広かったです。モンゴルは昔からの誇り高い文化を持つ，広大な国ですよ。

☆：実に素晴らしい本のようですね。ご成功をお祈りしています。

★：ありがとうございます。これもお話しさせていただきたいのですが，大きなテレビネットワークがいくつか，旅のドキュメンタリーを撮ることに興味を示してくれています。私にとって大変興味深い新しい経験になりそうです。

☆：うまくいくといいですね。きっとみんながその結果を楽しく見ると思います。インタビューを終える前に，次に訪問したいと思っている地域について教えてください。

★：そうですね，次は身近な所に目を向けて，ミシシッピ川の洪水地帯に住む人々について書こうかと思います。数年ごとに決まって洪水が起きる川の流域になぜ人々が住み続けるのか，ずっと興味がありました。それに少年のころは，マーク・トウェインの作品が大好きだったのです。ミシシッピ川が舞台になっていますよね。

☆：スティーブンソンさん，お話しいただきまして大変ありがとうございました。次のいくつかのプロジェクトが終わったころに，またお話しするのを楽しみにしています。

No. 26 解答 **2**

「ケネスが中央アジア旅行をしようと決めた理由の1つは何か」

1 子供のときに『ナショナル・ジオグラフィック』誌で中央アジアについて読んだ。

2 旅の計画をする以前に，モンゴルに関する興味深い本をいくつか読んだことがあった。

3 中央アジアの人々は友好的で寛容だと聞いたことがあった。

4 いくつかのテレビネットワークのために旅のドキュメンタリー映画を撮りたかった。

解説　きっかけについてスティーブンソン氏は I'd read some fascinating books on Mongolia several months before the trip, and that persuaded me to go. と説明している。**2**が正解。**3**は旅行した結果わかったこと。

No. 27 解答 **4**

「ケネスがミシシッピ川沿いに暮らす人々について書きたいと思っている理由の1つは何か」

1 『ロイヤル・ロード・トゥ・ロマンス』というミシシッピ川での冒険記を読んだことがあった。

2 世界旅行で疲れ果てており，しばらくは自宅に近い所にいたいと思っている。

3 子供のころから，マーク・トウェインのような作家になり，ミシシッピ川沿いに住む人々について書きたいと思っていた。

4 決まって氾濫する川沿いに人々が住む理由に魅了されている。

解説　スティーブンソン氏は理由を2つ挙げている。1つは，I've always been fascinated by why these people continue to live along rivers that will invariably flood every few years or so. であり，もう1つは Also, as a boy I loved the writings of Mark Twain, which were set on the Mississippi. なので，1つ目の理由に合致する**4**が正解。少年のときにマーク・トウェインの作品には魅了されたが，彼のような作家になりたいと思っていたという説明はないので，**3**は誤り。

筆記試験＆リスニングテスト
解答と解説

問題編 p.76～96

筆記

1

問題	1	2	3	4	5	6	7	8	9	10	11	12	13	14	15	16	17	18	19	20
解答	1	4	3	1	2	4	1	3	4	3	2	3	2	2	3	4	2	1	4	4

問題	21	22
解答	1	1

2

問題	23	24	25	26	27	28
解答	2	4	1	2	3	4

3

問題	29	30	31	32	33	34	35
解答	3	4	3	3	3	1	3

4　　**5**　　解説内にある解答例を参照してください。

リスニング

Part 1

問題	1	2	3	4	5	6	7	8	9	10
解答	1	3	1	1	1	4	3	2	3	2

Part 2

問題	11	12	13	14	15	16	17	18	19	20
解答	1	1	2	1	3	4	4	2	3	4

Part 3

問題	21	22	23	24	25
解答	2	1	2	3	2

Part 4

問題	26	27
解答	4	1

Day
6

1

(1) 解答 **1**

「タンニンとして知られる赤ワインに含まれる物質は、高脂肪食物による有害な作用を抑えると考えられているので、少量の赤ワインは体に良いと考える栄養士もいる」

解説　good for you「体に良い」のだから、有害な作用を「抑える」と考えられる。**1**が正解。**2**「～を無効にする」、**3**「（人）をそそのかす、扇動して～させる」、**4**「～を収縮させる、引っ込める」。

(2) 解答 **4**

「教授はクラスの学生たちに非常に腹を立て、彼らを叱責し怒鳴った。教授の説教は10分以上続いた」

解説　教授は腹を立てて大声を張り上げていたのだから、その「長い非難演説」は長く続いたはず。**4**が正解。**1**「標本」、**2**「激潮水域、激流」、**3**「後援」。

(3) 解答 **3**

「アパート近くの高速道路から聞こえる絶え間ない車の騒音に男性の神経はすり減ってしまい、彼は引っ越

すことにした」

解説 引っ越さざるを得ないほどだったのだから，神経は**3**「すり減って」いたはず。one's nerves are frayed で「神経がすり減る」という意味。**1**「やり損なった」，**2**「外皮で覆われた」，**4**「邪魔された」。

(4) 　解答　**1**

「その大富豪は亡くなるとき，彼の現代美術のコレクションを国立美術館に遺贈した。『このような寄贈を受け，非常に喜ばしく思います』と美術館の広報担当者は述べた」

解説 大富豪が亡くなったのを機に美術館は贈り物を受け取ったのだから，**1**「～を遺贈した」が正解。**2**「～をひどく嫌った」，**3**「（海外からの逃亡犯）を引き渡した」，**4**「～を告発した」。

(5) 　解答　**2**

「その家は広々として美しかったが，庭はろくに手入れされておらず，そのため地所全体の外観を損ねていた」

解説 庭は「ろくに手入れされていなかった」のだから，「外観を損ねた」と考えられる。detract from ～ で「～を損なう」という意味。**1**「（病気など）を悪化させた」，**3**「～を略奪した」，**4**「～を照らした」。

(6) 　解答　**4**

「その市の至る所に遍在するコーヒーショップは，この飲み物の人気が上昇している証しだ」

解説 「コーヒー人気で街の至る所にあるコーヒーショップ」を形容する語として適切なのは，**4**「遍在している」。**1**「（子供が）ませた」，**2**「率直な」，**3**「荒れ果てた」。

(7) 　解答　**1**

「交渉が手詰まりになった後，解決策を調停して成立させるための第三者に加わってもらうことで双方は同意した」

解説 行き詰まった結果，bring in a third party「第三者に加わってもらう」理由は，解決策を**1**「調停して成立させる」ため。**2**「～を征服する」，**3**「～を立証する」，**4**「～を自由にする，解放する」。

(8) 　解答　**3**

「医者たちはジャックの病気が治ったものと信じていたが，その年のうちに病気は突然再発した」

解説 「病気が治ったものと信じていた」と対照的な内容になるので，**3**「再発」が正解。**1**「反論」，**2**「残

骸，がれき」，**4**「（太陽や月の）食」。

(9) 　解答　**4**

「そのフットボール選手は肩の手術後，故障した選手のための施設で，トレーニングに戻れるようになるまで回復するための時間を与えられた」

解説 「故障した選手のための施設」の目的を考えれば，**4**「健康を回復する」が正解だとわかる。**1**「打つ，衝突する」，**2**「剽窃する」，**3**「さまよう」。

(10) 　解答　**3**

「豪雨のため，1週間以上誰もその山村にたどり着けなかった。生活必需品が不足し，村人たちは非常に困っていた」

解説 誰も村に近づけない状況なので，村人は生活必需品が**3**「不足」したはず。**1**「供給過剰」，**2**「魅力，（魚釣りの）ルアー」，**4**「豪雨，大洪水」。

(11) 　解答　**2**

「多くの国では，ウェイターの収入全体に給料の占める割合は半分未満である。普通ウェイターは給料よりチップの稼ぎの方が多い」

解説 目的語に less than half of their total income「収入全体の半分未満」をとって文意が通るのは，**2**「～を構成する，占める」。**1**「～のふりをする」，**3**「～を製造する，でっち上げる」，**4**「～を駆り立てる」。

(12) 　解答　**3**

A「いなくなることについてのアリスの謎めいたコメントはどんな意味があったのだろう」

B「よくわからないけれど，辞めるつもりだとほのめかしていたんだと思うよ」

解説 comment を修飾する語として適切なのは**3**「謎めいた」。**1**「潜在的な」，**2**「均質的な」，**4**「無気力な」。

(13) 　解答　**2**

「城の周りの景色はわびしいもので，葉のない木々や黒っぽいごつごつした岩があるだけだった。地元の人間は城に寄りつかなかった」

解説 「葉のない木々や黒っぽいごつごつした岩があるだけ」なのだから，景観は**2**「わびしい，荒涼とした」と考えられる。**1**「支払い能力のある」，**3**「温和な」，**4**「非常に裕福な，ぜいたくな」。

(14) 解答 **2**

「捜査はまだ初期段階であり誰も告訴されたわけではないのだから，マスコミが取りざたしている見解は単なる憶測でしかない，と警察署長は強調した」

解説 「捜査はまだ初期段階」なのだから，メディアの見解は **2**「憶測」にすぎないはず。**1**「刻み目，くぼみ」，**3**「仲裁，調停」，**4**「完成，達成」。

(15) 解答 **3**

「その患者は，手術中に失った血液を補うため輸血を受けた」

解説 「手術中に失った血液を補う」ためにすることは，**3**「輸血」。**1**「伝達，伝染」，**2**「浸軟，浸漬」，**4**「移住」。

(16) 解答 **4**

「著者が通例1人でいるのを好む非常に内向的な人として知られていることを考えれば，彼が熱心にスピーチしたがったことにファンは驚喜した」

解説 who usually prefers to be alone「通例1人でいるのを好む」のは **4**「内向的な」人。**1**「楽観的な」，**2**「厳格な」，**3**「実現可能な，便利な」。

(17) 解答 **2**

「ケリーは，設計士が彼女のオフィスにしたことを目にして不快なショックを受けた。というのも，美的に喜ばしいと思える新しいものが何ひとつなかったのだ」

解説 unpleasantly shocked「不快なショックを受けた」のだから，**2**「美的に」喜ばしいもの何ひとつ加えられていなかった，と考えると文意が通る。**1**「不安定に」，**3**「手当たり次第に」，**4**「大胆に」。

(18) 解答 **1**

「科学者たちは最新の実験結果を論理的に説明できなかったので，その結果は例外と見なされた」

解説 論理的に説明がつかない実験結果をどう見なしたか考える。**1**「例外，変則」が正解。**2**「覚醒，喚

起」，**3**「寄付」，**4**「大建築物，組織」。

(19) 解答 **4**

A「どうしてロイドは最近ジャロドとつるんでいないのかな。前は2人は一番の仲良しだったよね」
B「ロイドは彼と仲違いしたんだよ。どちらも同じ女の子とデートして，結局うまくいかなかったのさ」

解説 ロイドとジャロドは同じ女の子とデートしたというのだから，**4**「仲違いした」と考えるのが自然。**1**「辞退した」，**2**「～を殴り倒した」，**3**「約束を破った」。

(20) 解答 **4**

「スティーブが中古車に対して受けた提示額は期待ほど高くなかったので，彼はもっと良い提示があるまで粘ることにした」

解説 金額が予想ほど高くなかったのだから，**4**「粘る」ことにしたと考えられる。hold out for ～で「～を要求して粘る［譲らない］」という意味。**1**「完全に失敗する」，**2**「～を繰り越す」，**3**「～を取り外す」。

(21) 解答 **1**

「報告書は40ページ以上あり，会議の前にじっくり検討する時間はなかった。私はページをめくってざっと目を通すのがやっとだった」

解説 「報告書をじっくり検討する時間はなかった」のだから，**1**「～のページをぱらぱらめくる」のがやっとだったと考えられる。**2**「そばをやっとのことで通る」，**3**「活動や興味を広げる」，**4**「～を応援する」。

(22) 解答 **1**

「その報道記者は，担当したインタビューを録音することに加えて，話を聞く際ちょっとメモを取るのが好きだった」

解説 記者がすることで，目的語に notes がきている。**1**「（メモ）を書き留める」が正解。**2**「～をののしる」，**3**「～について思い悩む」，**4**「～の状態に陥る」。

2

全訳

言語が死ぬとき

　世界にはおよそ6,500の言語が現存している。20世紀だけで約400語が消滅したことを知らなければ，桁

外れの数に思えるだろう。現在，世界の人口の約半数は上位10の言語を話し，さほど広く話されていない言語は危機的状況に瀕しており，専門家の推定では現存する言語の50％が今世紀末までに消滅しかねない。ユ

ネスコは消滅危機言語地図の中で危機に瀕する言語を追跡調査しているが，目下のところかなり存続が危ぶまれている言語は576記載されており，さらに1,000以上が危険にさらされているか，その恐れがあると見なされている。

　こうした言語が失われることは，単に地域方言が使われなくなるだけではなく，もっと大きな意味がある。危機に瀕しているのは，無名と思われている言語の喪失だけではなく，関連した文化，感情，習慣の喪失でもある。それらはしばしば口頭伝承で伝えられ，必ずしも翻訳できるというわけではないからだ。消滅が目前に迫っている独特で不思議な言語の1つの例がsfyriaで，言葉を全く使わない。その代わりに，その言葉を「話す」人々は口笛を吹くのだ。sfyriaはギリシャの山岳地帯に限られ，2,000年以上話されており，話し手は4キロ以上という驚くような距離で意思を伝達することができる。主に注意深く守られた秘密として世代から世代へと受け継がれてきたが，今ではほんの一握りの人々が話すだけとなり，若い世代はアテネでのより大きな経済的チャンスを求めて田舎を離れるため，もう1つの経済的犠牲となることが確実視されている。

　驚くべきことに，sfyriaは口笛を使う唯一の言語ではなく，ヨーロッパやアフリカ全土にもほかに存在し，本格的な保護制度の関心を引いているものもある。カナリア諸島で口笛を使って話されているスペイン語，シルボ・ゴメーロは2009年にユネスコの人類の口承及び無形遺産の傑作に宣言され，以来幾分よみがえっているのを目撃されている。政府はまた国定カリキュラムの一部としたり，観光キャンペーンに使ったり，祭りや儀式の目玉にすることで，言語を保護しようとしている。

(23)　解答　2

解説　存続が危ぶまれている言語数を示した後なので，**2**が適切。**1**「毎日新しい言語が密かに生まれているのだが」，**3**「そしてほかの多くは飛躍的に回復している」，**4**「有益な言語発展と考えられている」。

(24)　解答　4

解説　伝承言語を受け継ぐべき若い世代が田舎を離れる理由について述べた部分なので**4**が正解。**1**「結局言語不足で阻止された」，**2**「そして文化的秘密をあまねく広げた」，**3**「教育と言語の困難さのため」。

(25)　解答　1

解説　口笛言語の保護に関して述べられているので，**1**が正解。**2**「新しい音調の言語の開発の原因となった」，**3**「記憶から消えて行くのを許されている」，**4**「今や衝撃的な新しい形を取っている」。

全訳
素足と最小主義ランニング

　2009年，クリストファー・マクドゥーガルの本『走るために生まれた』は，ランニングというスポーツに広範囲かつ大規模な予期せぬ変化を引き起こした。訓練のコツや有名ランナー，注目を集めるレースなどを扱うランニングについての多くの本と異なり，『走るために生まれた』にはそうしたことはほとんど書かれていない。北部メキシコのタラウマラ族の，古タイヤやそのほかのくずから作られた薄っぺらいサンダルで長距離を走る人々と著者の出会いを記録し，さらに人類の歴史を通じてのランニングの社会人類学的側面に関する研究を記録した本だ。人間はなぜどうやって走るのかについての，この微妙に異なる見解は，それ以降，近代的なランニングシューズについての社会通念を覆し，企業を揺るがす激変と，素足と最小主義ランニングへのにわかな関心の高まりを引き起こした。

　多くの人が，ランニングのより自然なやり方への単なる回帰ではなく，おそらく長距離ランナーとしての生得権の開拓とさえ考えたことに付随して起こったのは，次第に長距離を目指すランナー数の急激な増加だった。50キロから200キロ，さらにそれ以上の距離のウルトラマラソンへの参加が急激に増え，かつては勇敢で向こう見ずとも言える人々によって競われてきた小規模のイベントを主流にした。タラウマラ族の偉業に張り合おうとするランナーがどんどん増えるにつれ，最小主義者の履物の新しい需要に追いつくために靴メーカーは苦戦した。確かに著しくはあったが，最小主義の急激な増加は比較的短命であった。

　2015年ごろには逆方向に人気の振れ子が振れ始め，当初素足と最小主義ランニングに魅了された人々は，従来の近代的ランニングシューズの緩衝や保護が恋しくなった。メーカーは最小主義から最大主義へと重点を移し，固有受容感覚を増すための非常に薄い靴底を，雲に浮かんでいるかのような心地がするようにデザインされたふかふかの柔らかい靴底へと変えた。しかし，最小主義ランニング，素足ランニング，ウルトラランニングを流儀として採用した多くの人々にとっては，スポットライトが移ったことは，いつかそれが戻ってくるかどうかにかかわらず，ほとんど影響がない。

(26) 解答 2

解説 空所直後の why and how we run から，**2**が正解。**1**「文明があまり進んでいない地域社会やグループの知恵」，**3**「オリンピック種目に関する慣習や規則」，**4**「集団で走る傾向の高まり」。

(27) 解答 3

解説 空所直後の文に長距離マラソンの参加者が急激に増えたとあるところから，**3**が正解。**1**「それらの目立った減少」，**2**「隔世遺伝のコミュニティーの再生」，**4**「昨今の勇敢な人物のまね」。

(28) 解答 4

解説 文の後半に人々は従来のランニングシューズが恋しくなった，とある。最小主義の人気が衰えたという意味の**4**が自然。**1**「まもなく人類学の流行がやって来て」，**2**「著者はメキシコを離れ旅をして」，**3**「最大主義を慕わせたものすべてが変わって」。

3

全訳

文化的気候変動

　気候変動の科学的根拠は，その真相をいまだに否定したいと願う人々におかまいなく，今やほとんど明白である。われわれは悲しいことに，異常気象，干ばつ，海抜上昇，大量絶滅などたくさんの未来に向きあうことになるということを耳にするのに慣れてきている。こうしたシナリオは非常に現実的な問題を提示しているにもかかわらず，それらを世間に示した人々は，気候変動が文化的レベルでどれほど根本的に影響を及ぼし得るかについてはしばしば見逃しており，そのせいで，常に反対を唱える人々を説得する大きな心理的な道具を手に入れ損なっているのだろう。ほかの悪いニュースと同様，われわれは欲求不満で首を横に振ったり，不確かな未来にやきもきしたりするかもしれないが，日々の生活をこなすことができる。多くの人々にとっては影響は直近ではなく，差し迫った不安を引き起こすほど切実ではないからだ。それらはいわばすぐ近くにはないので，今は締め出しておけるのだ。しかしほかのところでは，人々はそれほど無頓着でいるわけにはいかない。

　世界のいくつかの場所では，サーフィン，水泳，セーリングや単なるビーチでの日光浴といった海を中心に展開するアクティビティーは，その地域の経済的持続可能性の中心であるばかりか，地域社会を結びつけている文化の中心でもある。山岳地方では，登山，ハイキング，そしてスキーやスノーボードといったウィンタースポーツが同じ機能を果たしており，地域の文化と生活様式の基準となっている。海やビーチや山々，そのほかの地理的特色が気候変動のせいで脅威にさらされると，それに頼っている文化と地域も同様に脅威にさらされてしまう。これは伝統的な建築方法や地元の技能の喪失，食物資源の死滅，集団移動による地域社会の離散，文化的な絆の破壊を意味する。このような気候変動の深刻で非常に現実的な影響は，影響を受ける人々にとっては大きな問題であるが，行政機関の研究やプログラムではめったに検討されない。

　こうした感情的影響は芸術に利用され，人々が日常生活に関連づけられるようなやり方で気候変動の危険性を伝えることに成功している。数え切れないほどの書籍，映画，演劇や詩が未来の反ユートピア的眺望を描き，多くがはっきりとあるいは漠然と，人為的気候変動をほのめかす。芸術は一般大衆にとっては科学出版物よりもずっとわかりやすいので，より多くの人々に感銘を与える力を持つ。パオロ・バチガルピによる『ねじまき少女』，ハミッシュ・マクドナルドによる『有限性』，ダニエル・クランプによる『ここから』といった作品は，すべて気候変動を主題としている。どの作品も，状況が劇的に変わらない場合，未来を明るく描いてはいない。

　全作品が言及しているのは，破壊された地域社会，社会基盤の崩壊，食料と飲料水の不足，地域社会全体を破壊する異常気象，電気やガスなどわれわれが当たり前と思っている快適さの喪失といった，毎日人々が直面する現実の影響だ。この，より差し迫った具体的な見通しは，将来の気候変動に取り組むこと，そしてわれわれの環境とそれが支える文化を守ることの両方にとって，鍵となり得る。

(29) 解答 3

「気候変動を取り扱った報道が増えた結果として何が記事中で言及されているか」

1 人為的な気候変動の証拠はさほど圧倒的ではないので，世界の人々は心配しなくてよい。

2 気候変動は地球に影響を与えているように思えるが，科学者は明らかな因果関係を示すことができず今なおいら立っている。

3 地球への気候変動の物理的影響はどんどん知らされているが，文明全体への影響については忘れがちである。

4 海抜が上がり，移住が増えるにつれ，われわれは水を閉めだし，不十分な建築を防ぐために家を強化する必要がある。

解説　第1段落第3文の「こうしたシナリオは非常に現実的な問題を提示しているにもかかわらず，それらを世間に示した人々は，気候変動が文化的レベルでどれほど根本的に影響を及ぼし得るかについてはしばしば見逃しており」という部分の内容に，**3**が一致する。

(30)　解答　4

「地域社会は気候変動のどのような脅威にさらされているか」

1 気候変動の影響が増すにつれ，政府は財政的支援を小さな地域社会から地域全体の維持へと変えることを余儀なくされる。

2 地域社会は気候変動と戦うために，定着した生活様式を次第に犠牲にすることを求められている。

3 より多くの人々がスキーよりサーフィンに行くようになるので，地域社会の観光業は悪影響を受けることになるだろう。

4 地理的要因のまわりに築かれた地域社会は，気候変動のせいで自分たちの生活そのものが消えるのを見ることになるだろう。

解説　第2段落の中盤に，「海やビーチや山々，そのほかの地理的特色が気候変動のせいで脅威にさらされると，それに頼っている文化と地域も同様に脅威にさらされてしまう」とある。その後にも様々な影響が述べられており，これに一致する**4**が正解。

(31)　解答　3

「懐疑的な大衆に気候変動の危険性を警告することにおいて，科学者よりも芸術はどのように成功できているか」

1 反ユートピア的文学は地域社会の崩壊と資源不足について人々が楽観的になるのを概して助けている。

2 科学者たちは気候変動についての詩や歌を書き，インターネットで効果的に配信することができる。

3 芸術は気候変動を個人向けに変えるので，大衆はそれが実際的な面で自分たちの生活にどのように影響を及ぼすかをより正確に感じることができる。

4 科学文献は多くの読者にとって感情的すぎるため，芸術は破滅と快適さの喪失から一時の逃避を提供する。

解説　第3段落第3文の「芸術は一般大衆にとっては科学出版物よりもずっとわかりやすいので，より多くの人々に感銘を与える力を持つ」と，最終段落冒頭の文の内容に一致する**3**が正解。**1**の反ユートピア的文学の役割は誤り。科学者は気候変動について詩や歌を書いていないので**2**も誤り。科学文献が感情的という話題はないので**4**も不適である。

全訳
侵入種の影響

　科学者たちは長い間，侵入種によって生態系に昨今起こっている変化について懸念を抱いてきた。ハーバード大学の著名な生物学者エドワード・O・ウィルソンは，種の絶滅に対する影響という点においては，外来種の侵入は生息地の破壊に次いで深刻なものだと論じた。1958年の先駆的研究『動植物による侵略の生態学』で侵入外来種の科学的調査に着手した英国の生態学者チャールズ・エルトンは，「われわれは間違いを犯してはならない。われわれは世界の動植物相の歴史上最も大きな混乱状況の1つを目の当たりにしているのだ」と書いた。エルトンらの研究者によるチームは，基本的パターンを明らかにしたり，「特定の種は侵入によりうまく適応しているのか」，「ハワイ諸島のような特定の環境はなぜ侵入を受けやすいのか」，「アメリカのトウブハイイロリスがイギリス諸島での大繁殖に成功したのはなぜか」といった疑問に答えたりすることで，外来種の影響をより理解しようと考えた。研究者たちは，これらの疑問や別の疑問に答えるため，大量の事例研究を収集した。

　生物学的多様性，つまりある生態系における種の多様性や個体数と，その生態系全体の健全性には関連があるとエルトンは論じた。多様性がより大きな生態系では，生態系の完全な状態を維持するために役立つ「生命の抵抗力」がより大きい。彼の医学モデルでは，十分な多様性を持ち侵入されていない生態系は健全で，一方外来種に侵入された生態系は病んでいると考えられた。エルトンは自らが観察した進行中の移行を説明するのに役立つよう，別のモデルを導入した。就職口すなわちニッチ（市場でのすき間，生態系での地位）の数に限りがあるという点で，生態系は市場と類似していると彼は論じた。多数の志願者が1つの就職口に応募するのと同じように，在来種であれ外来種であれ，すべての種はニッチのために競争しなければならない

というのである。

　ニッチというこの考えによって，エルトンと後に続く生態学者は，ハワイのような小さくてより隔離された生態系がより侵入を受けやすい理由を説明しやすくした。その生物多様性は，より大きな生態系，特に大陸の生態系ほど複雑ではなく，維持する種も少ない。そのため，侵入種のためのニッチがより多く存在した。また，より小さな生態系の在来種はより大きな生態系よりも競争が少なく，それゆえ，たくましさと抵抗力で劣っていた。「比較的単純な動植物共同体のバランスは，より多様な動植物共同体よりも簡単に乱され，従って侵入にさらされやすい」とエルトンは書いている。

　エルトンの初期の研究以来半世紀にわたる調査によって，侵入種は，従来種に病気を広めたり，自らの生き残りに有利になるよう環境を変えたり，ほかの種を食べたりするなどのさまざまな方法で，生態系を変化させることができ，また実際に変化させていることが確認されている。しかし，収集された事例によって，エルトンが予想だにしなかっただろうパターンが明らかになっている。それは，外来種が在来種を追い払うことはめったにないということである。エルトンが特に興味を持っていたトウブハイイロリスの事例を見てみると，トウブハイイロリスの数の増加は，イギリス人が愛するユーラシア産のキタリスの個体数の減少と一致していた。現在イギリスにいるこのキタリスの数は3万に満たない。侵入種が在来種の生息域を荒らし，在来種の減少の直接の原因となったことはほとんどの観察者にとって明らかと思えた。

　しかし，外来種がいかに在来種を追い払うかを例証する一般的なモデルとなったこの事例は，実際は当初信じられていたものよりももっと複雑である。事実，キタリスの減少の原因はトウブハイイロリスだけではないという証拠がある。キタリスの減少は，強敵と考えられるトウブハイイロリスが到着するはるか以前に始まっていたのである。19世紀には，イギリス諸島の一部の地域ではキタリスは既に姿を消しており，再移入させられなければならなかった。とはいえ，全トウブハイイロリスの3分の2がキタリスの感染しやすいウィルス性皮膚病の保菌者であり，このことがキタリスの減少を早めたのも確かである。

　侵入外来種の大半は，競争して相手に勝つというよりも，有害な影響を与えることなく，自らが選んだ生態系に単に適応する。なぜなら，どんな生態系を取ってみても，そのほとんどはより大きな多様性を身の内に取り込むことができるのであり，エルトンやウィルソンが思い描いた厳格に構成されたシステムとは程遠

いものなのである。「侵入が明らかにしてきたのは，利用されていない資源がたくさんあるということです」とカリフォルニア大学デイビス校の海洋生物学者テッド・グロショルツは言う。「生態系は多くの新種を吸収できるのです」。外来の動植物相が行き交う交差路である南フロリダは，300種の新たな侵入種植物の宿主となってきた一方，サンフランシスコ湾では，少なくとも250種の在来種ではない種をこれまで研究者たちは数えている。船をはじめとする輸送手段が遠い国々から意図せずにさまざまな形態の生物を持ち込んできたことから，海洋の生態系は侵入種に対して特に開かれていることが過去数世紀を通して明らかになってきた。それでも，外来の甲殻類，海綿動物，寄生虫，貝類，および海の病気がサンフランシスコ湾に入ってきたにもかかわらず，侵入種によって絶滅させられたと明らかにされた海洋の在来種は1つとしてないのである。

　これらの事実から得られる結論は，地上と海洋の生態系における侵入は，1つの新種が別の種を駆逐するといった，勝つか負けるか，差し引きゼロの勝敗争いという単純なものではないということである。以前は生態系の被害や崩壊が懸念されたにもかかわらず，侵入された生態系がより豊かな多様性を提供することを，研究者たちは発見している。

(32)　解答　3

「侵入種についてのエドワード・O・ウィルソンの説はチャールズ・エルトンの説とどのように比較されているか」

1 長年の研究で，どちらも侵入種は最初に思われたよりも無害だという結論に達した。

2 ウィルソンは侵入種は小さな問題だと考えたのに対し，エルトンは侵入種の破壊力を非常に恐れた。

3 どちらも生態系が侵入種に攻撃されており，その結果が深刻なものになり得ると考えていた点で似ていた。

4 どちらも侵入種の影響について数多くの質問をしようとしたが，満足のいく答えは得られなかった。

解説　ウィルソンの考えは第1段で説明されており，侵入種の危険性を訴えている。その後はエルトンの考えの紹介がしばらく続くが，彼も侵入種は危険と見している。**3**が正解。

(33)　解答　3

「ニッチについてエルトンは何を暗示したか」

1 ニッチは基本的に特定の生態系における在来種の数

を表し，非在来種が侵入したときには減少する。

2 多様な種がニッチのために常に競争しているので，侵入種の導入は最終結果に総合的な悪影響をもたらす。

3 ニッチが少ない生態系は多様性が大きく，それゆえニッチが多い生態系よりも強かった。

4 小さい生態系は大きな生態系よりもニッチが少ないので，大きな生態系の方が外来種に対して弱くなる。

解説 ニッチについては，第2段落後半と第3段落で説明されている。第3段落第3文Therefore, they（= certain smaller, more isolated ecosystems）had more niches available ... の内容を裏返すと**3**になる。

(34)　**解答** **1**

「イギリスのキタリスの個体数の減少の事例は…という考えを裏づけている」

1 在来種の消滅は必ずしも侵入種の直接の結果ではない

2 侵入種が持ちこんだ病気は，ほかのどの原因よりも多くの絶滅を引き起こす

3 在来種の導入は，大部分の研究者が予測するよりも劇的な結果を伴う

4 お互いに似通っている2つの種は，結局は同じ生態系で共存できない

解説 キタリスの減少についての説明は第4段落後半から始まる。第5段落第2文の内容が**1**と合致する。**2**は，病気がキタリスの減少を sped up「加速させた」とあるが，最も大きな原因とはされていない。**3**は，在来種のリスが再導入された後のことに関する記述はない。**4**は，2種のリスに数の増減はあっても共存が不可能だとは書かれていない。

(35)　**解答** **3**

「侵入種に関する筆者の結論は何か」

1 有史以来，種は生態系に侵入し続けており，このような侵入は進化の過程の自然な一部である。

2 ほとんどの場合，侵入種は第二の故郷に十分に適応して長く生き残ることができない。

3 生態系はかつて思われたよりも適応性があり，外来種の導入からもしばしば恩恵を受ける。

4 生態系の複雑さのせいで，研究者たちは侵入種の在来種への影響を完全に理解することができないだろう。

解説 筆者の結論については最後の2つの段落に書かれている。南フロリダやサンフランシスコ湾の例が，生態系のオープンな柔軟性を表している。また最終段落で「侵入された生態系はより多様性が増す」と言っている点からも，筆者が楽観的な結論を出していることが読み取れる。正解は**3**。

4

問題文の訳

　旅行が環境に及ぼしうる影響を旅行者はますます意識するようになっており，多くの旅行者がエコツーリズムに目を向けつつある。エコツーリズムはしばしば，世界を探検するより持続可能な方法であると言われる。この産業はとても人気が高まっており，今では世界で1,700億ドル以上の価値があると見積もられている。理屈の上では，エコツーリズムは，旅行者が環境に与える負の影響を最小限にしながら，自然の景観，野生生物，そして地域の文化を保護することを重視するものである。これにもかかわらず，批判的な人たちはエコツーリズムに関して，特にこれまでケニアとタンザニアのマサイ族のような先住民族に与えてきた負の影響について，頻繁に懸念を表明している。

　アフリカの驚くべき野生生物，文化，そして眺めのよい景色を披露している数々の旅行者向け公園が，伝統的にマサイ族の人々のものである土地に設立され，エコツーリズムをこれらの国の相当な収入源にするのに役立ってきた。しかしながら，公園は主に西側諸国の企業によって運営されていたので，マサイ族自体が利益の配当にあずかることはめったになかった。さらにエコツーリズムは，マサイ族の人々にとって土地と資源の喪失という結果にも行き着いた。マサイ族の人々は，自分たちの先祖伝来の領地に保護地域を設立されたため，強制退去させられてきた。これらの地域は彼らが放牧地や神聖な場所に行くことを制限してきたが，そのような場所は彼らの暮らしにとっても文化的アイデンティティにとっても必要不可欠である。

　エコツーリズムはマサイ族にとって歴史的に決して理想的ではなかった一方，マサイ族のコミュニティをかか

わらせ，権限を与えることを目的とした，持続可能なエコツーリズム構想もたくさんある。例えば，カンピ・ヤ・カンジやマーラ・ナボイショ・コンサーバンシーは，参加型の包括的なアプローチをうまく採用し，マサイ族が意思決定や管理運営のプロセスにかかわってきた。さらにそうした構想では，マサイ族がエコツーリズム活動から，雇用機会や収入の創出，インフラ開発といった公正で公平な利益を確実に受け取るようにもしてきた。

解答例	解答例の訳
While ecotourism is becoming a notable industry economically and is said to lessen the environmental impact of travel, it may also have disastrous consequences, especially for indigenous peoples. For instance, people like Africa's Maasai have generally not profited from the tourist facilities on their territory. Additionally, they have been forced to move away and also have suffered culturally due to ecotourism. Fortunately, though, some efforts have been made to help the Maasai by involving them in the ecotourism industry and by making sure that they receive economic benefits from it. (90語)	エコツーリズムが経済的に注目すべき産業になりつつあり，旅行が環境に及ぼす影響を減らすと言われている一方で，それは特に先住民族にとっては悲惨な結果をもたらすこともあるかもしれない。例えば，アフリカのマサイ族のような人々は，自分たちの領地にある旅行者向けの施設からたいてい利益を得てこなかった。さらに彼らは，エコツーリズムのせいで立ち去ることを強制されたり，文化的に苦しんだりもしてきた。ただし幸運なことに，マサイ族をエコツーリズム産業にかかわらせたり，それから経済的な利益を確実に受け取るようにしたりすることで，彼らを助ける努力もなされてきた。

解説　トピックは第1段落最終文 Despite this, critics frequently express concerns about ecotourism, particularly the negative effects that it has had on indigenous peoples, such as the Maasai of Kenya and Tanzania. より「エコツーリズムが先住民族に及ぼす負の影響」だとわかる。各段落の要旨は，第1段落：人気が高まり市場規模も大きくなっているエコツーリズムだが，先住民族に及ぼす負の影響も懸念されている。第2段落：マサイ族の土地に旅行者向けの公園を整備しておきながら，先住民族は経済的なメリットを享受できておらず，むしろ暮らしや文化的アイデンティティのために必要な場所がある自分たちの領地を追われてきた。第3段落：成功した構想では，マサイ族が意思決定と管理運営にかかわり，利益を得ていた。解答の際はこれらを問題文とは異なる表現に言い換えてまとめる。なお，第1段落の1,700億ドルというエコツーリズム市場の大きさや，第2段落の「アフリカの驚くべき野生生物，文化，そして眺めのよい景色を披露している」という旅行者向け公園の説明，第3段落の「カンピ・ヤ・カンジ」や「マーラ・ナボイショ・コンサーバンシー」といった名称については要約に含めなくてよい。解答例では，第1段落の，エコツーリズムの人気が高まって市場規模も大きくなっていることについて，ecotourism is becoming a notable industry economically と簡潔に述べ，負の影響についてはit may also have disastrous consequences とまとめている。notable は important，disastrous は very bad の意味で使える。第2段落の，マサイ族が経済的メリットを享受してこなかったことについてはnot profited from the tourist facilities on their territory とすっきりとまとめている。第3段落の成功した構想についても，some efforts have been made to help the Maasai by involving them in the ecotourism industry and by making sure that they receive economic benefits from it と，簡潔ながらも十分に説明できている。

Day
6

5

問題の訳
TOPIC：賛成か反対か：自由貿易は望ましい

解答例①

There are several reasons why free trade is undesirable. These include the threat to domestic producers, the neglect of environmental protection laws, and the fact that it can lead to a weakening of cultural diversity.

Labor and manufacturing costs differ from country to country. Where free trade is allowed and imported goods from low-wage countries are allowed to flow in, many domestic businesses are unable to compete. They go out of business and lay off their workers. This is a high price to pay for cheaper goods.

Free trade also can be bad for the environment. Under free trade regulations, it is relatively easy for manufacturers, in the pursuit of higher profits, to move their businesses to countries that have less strict environmental protection laws. Governments in such countries are powerless to complain about problems such as the pollution of the local environment because they fear that companies will move their facilities elsewhere.

And lastly, there is a possibility that free trade may have a negative impact on cultural diversity. This is because certain countries have more economic power and thus a bigger impact on global markets. As the cultures of these stronger countries spread across the world, local cultures disappear.

Free trade can be good for large corporations and can lead to the availability of cheaper consumer goods. However, due to negative impacts on domestic businesses, the environment, and local cultures, it is hard to see it as desirable. (240語)

解答例①の訳

自由貿易が望ましくない理由がいくつかあります。国内の生産者にとって脅威になることや，環境保護法の軽視は，文化的多様性の衰退につながりかねないという事実が理由に数えられます。

人件費と製造コストは，国によって違います。自由貿易を認め，低賃金国からの輸入品の流入を許可している場所では，多くの国内企業は太刀打ちできません。会社は倒産し，従業員は解雇されます。これでは安い製品の代償が高くつくことになります。

自由貿易は，環境のためにもよくない可能性があります。自由貿易のルールの下では，メーカーは比較的簡単に，より高い利益を追求して，環境保護法があまり厳しくない国に事業を移すことができます。そのような国の政府には，地域の環境汚染などの問題について不満を伝える力がありません。企業がどこかよそに設備を移してしまうことを恐れているからです。

最後に，自由貿易は文化的多様性に悪影響を与える可能性があります。一部の国にはほかの国より強大な経済力があり，その結果，世界市場に対する影響力も大きくなります。そのような強国の文化が世界中に広まると，地域の文化が消失します。

自由貿易は大企業のためにはなると言えますし，その結果，安い消費財を手に入れることができます。しかしながら，国内企業，環境，そして地域文化への悪影響のせいで，好ましいとは考えにくいのです。

解説　序論では，トピックに対して反対の立場を表明し，その理由として国内の生産者にとって脅威になること，環境保護法の軽視，文化的多様性の衰退を挙げている。本論では，それぞれの理由を順に詳しく説明しており，第2段落では自由貿易によって国内企業が太刀打ちできなくなる可能性を指摘し，その代償は高いと断言すること

で，自分の考えに対する自信をのぞかせている。第3段落では環境保護法は国によって厳しさが違うことを指摘し，それが環境汚染につながる理由をわかりやすく説明している。また，環境が汚染されても強気に出られない地元政府の悲哀に触れることで，読み手の興味を強く引いている。第4段落では自由貿易によって文化的多様性がどのように失われるかを説明しており，因果関係を明確に説明することで主張をいっそうわかりやすいものにしている。最後の段落では理由を改めてまとめ，主張を繰り返すことで結論としている。

解答例②

There has been a lot of debate about free trade recently, with some in favor and others violently opposed to it. It is my opinion that free trade is desirable for reasons related to economic growth, greater consumer choice, and world peace.

The first advantage of free trade is that it promotes economic growth by allowing nations to specialize and trade in the products they are best at producing. As all countries have different natural resources, it makes sense that a country should be able to export the product or service they are best at providing, and then purchase the other products they require at competitive prices.

Another positive aspect of free trade is that it allows for greater consumer choice. This is especially beneficial to the poorer members of society who, thanks to free trade, are able to buy essential items such as imported food and clothing at competitive prices.

It is also the case that free trade can lead to a more peaceful and stable world as it allows countries to gain resources through trade rather than conquest as in the past. Free trade between nations also reduces the chance of war because countries are unlikely to go to war with their important trading partners.

In conclusion, free trade is desirable because it encourages economic growth, provides inexpensive goods for the poor, and lowers the risk of war. (230語)

解答例②の訳

　最近では自由貿易に関する議論が活発で，賛成意見もあれば，激しい反対意見もあります。私の意見では，自由貿易は好ましいものであり，その理由は経済成長，消費者の選択肢の拡大，そして世界平和に関係しています。

　自由貿易の第一の利点は，経済成長を促すことです。自由貿易のおかげで，国家は製造を最も得意とする製品に特化して取引することが可能になるからです。すべての国に異なる天然資源があるため，国は提供することを最も得意としている製品やサービスを輸出し，そのほかの必要な製品を安く購入することは道理にかなっていると言えます。

　自由貿易のもう1つの良い点は，消費者の選択肢を拡大させることです。この利点を特に享受できるのは社会を構成する貧しい人々であり，自由貿易のおかげで，輸入食品や衣料品といったとても重要な商品を安く買うことができます。

　さらにこれも事実なのですが，自由貿易はより平和で安定した世界につながる可能性があります。自由貿易のおかげで各国は，過去にあったような征服という手段ではなく，交易という手段で資源を獲得できるからです。国家間の自由貿易により，戦争が起こる可能性も低くなります。重要な貿易相手国に対し，戦争を始める可能性はあまりありません。

　結論として，自由貿易は好ましく，その理由は経済成長を促すこと，貧しい人々に安価な製品を提供すること，そして戦争のリスクを低減させることです。

解説 　序論では，賛否両論があると言ってから賛成の立場を表明しており，自分の主張は客観的に考えた結果導き出されたものだということを伝えている。その理由として挙げているのが「経済成長」，「消費者の選択肢の拡大」，「世界平和」であり，一見すると自由貿易とは関係なさそうな「世界平和」を理由として挙げることで，読み手の興味を強く引いている。本論ではそれぞれの理由を順番に説明している。第2段落では得意な分野に特化して製造・輸出することで経済成長が期待できるとし，同時に安価な製品を輸入できる点も挙げている。第3段落では，特に貧しい人の立場から選択肢が増えるメリットを説明している。注目の第4段落では，歴史的な視点

に立って資源の獲得が戦争につながってきたことに触れ，自由貿易では戦争が回避される理由を丁寧に説明している。最後の段落では理由と主張を簡単にまとめて結論としている。

Listening Test

Part 1 🔊 076〜086

No. 1　解答　**1**

○：Hello, thank you for calling National Airlines. How may I help you?

★：I'd like to know if you have a seat available in business class on today's 2:00 p.m. flight to Mexico City.

○：There shouldn't be a problem, sir, but give me a moment to check. Could you tell me your name and customer number, please?

★：Certainly. The name is Eric Hamilton, and the number is 3456782. By the way, I'll be paying for the ticket with my National Airlines credit card.

○：Sounds good. Yes, there is a seat available, Mr. Hamilton. I'll reserve the seat for you, and the details will be sent to your e-mail address in a minute.

★：Thanks.

Question：What do we learn about the man?

○：はい，ナショナル航空にお電話いただきありがとうございます。ご用件は何でしょうか。

★：今日午後2時のメキシコシティ行きの便のビジネスクラスに空席が1つあるかどうか知りたいのですが。

○：大丈夫だと思いますが，確認のため少々お時間をいただきます。お名前とお客さま番号を教えていただけますか。

★：わかりました。名前はエリック・ハミルトンで，番号は3456782です。ところで，チケットの代金はナショナル航空のクレジットカードで支払います。

○：結構です。はい，ハミルトンさま。お席はございます。席のご予約をさせていただきます。詳細はすぐにお客さまのEメールに送信されます。

★：ありがとう。

質問：男性について何がわかるか。

1 彼はこの航空会社の常連である。　　　　　　**2** 彼は仕事での出張を計画している。

3 彼はすでにメキシコの住所を取得している。　**4** 彼は空港で支払いをしたい。

解説　男性が電話で航空チケットを予約している。男性はNational Airlinesのお客さま番号を答えており，この会社のクレジットカードも保有している。正解は**1**。

No. 2　解答　**3**

★：Excuse me, but is this Doctor Thomas' office?

☆：Yes, it is. How may I help you?

★：I'd like to see her as soon as I can for a checkup.

☆：OK. This week is a little tight, but when could you come in?

★：Any time on Tuesday morning would be fine, but on any other day I'd have to come after 5 p.m.

☆：We can squeeze you in at 10:30 on Tuesday. Would that work?

★：That's super. I appreciate it.

★：すみません。こちらはトマス先生の医院ですか。

☆：はい，そうです。どうかなさいましたか。

★：検査のためにできるだけ早く先生にお会いしたいのですが。

☆：わかりました。今週はやや予約が詰まっているのですが，いつでしたらお越しになれますか。

★：火曜の午前でしたら何時でも大丈夫ですが，それ以外の日は午後5時以降になります。

☆：火曜の10時半に何とか予約を入れられます。それで構いませんか。

Question：Why did the man call the doctor's office?

★：非常に助かります。ありがとうございます。

質問：この男性は何のために医院に電話したのか。

1 彼の予約を変更するため。   **2** 彼の予約をキャンセルするため。

3 新しく予約を取るため。   **4** 彼の予約時間を確かめるため。

解説 医院の事務と患者の会話。I'd like to see her（= Doctor Thomas）as soon as I can より男性は予約を取りたがっているので，**1**と**3**に絞られる。特に事前に予約をしていた話題はないので，**3**が正解。

No. 3 解答 **1**

○：I've been through everything in your closet. You simply have too much stuff, so I've picked out these things to get rid of.

★：Oh no, not that jacket! I just bought it last summer.

○：And you've gone through the fall and winter without wearing it once. Let's give it to your nephew. He needs a good jacket.

★：And why are you throwing out my favorite sweater?

○：Are you kidding? Look at the holes. And these worn out shirts have got to go.

★：Well, I guess they're rather dated.

○：You still have a lot left over, and your newer things look so much better on you.

Question：What does the woman say about the man's wardrobe?

○：あなたのクローゼットにあるものをすべて見たわ。端的に言って物が多すぎね。だから処分しようと思ってこれらを選んでおいたの。

★：そんな，そのジャケットはやめて！ 昨年の夏に買ったばかりなんだ。

○：そして秋も冬も1回もそれを着ないですごしてきたじゃない。あなたの甥にあげましょう。彼には良いジャケットが必要よ。

★：そしてどうして僕のお気に入りのセーターを捨ててしまうんだ？

○：冗談でしょ？ 穴が開いているでしょう。それからこれらのぼろぼろのシャツも処分しないとだめね。

★：まあ，それらはちょっと時代遅れかな。

○：でもまだたくさん残っているし，新しいものの方があなたにはよく似合っているわ。

質問：女性は男性が持っている服について何と言っているか。

1 使っていない物は手放すべきだ。   **2** 男性は新しいスタイルの服を買う必要がある。

3 クローゼットを季節に応じて整理する必要がある。   **4** 残っている服の大半はとてもみすぼらしい。

解説 女性は最初の発言で You simply have too much stuff, so I've picked out these things to get rid of. と言い，その後の発言でも同様のことを言っている。**1**が正解。

No. 4 解答 **1**

★：Weren't you supposed to go to the dentist this morning?

☆：Oh, no! I completely forgot about it. That's the second time I've missed an important appointment this week.

★：You've got to write things down in your schedule book.

☆：I do. I write down all my appointments in my smartphone calendar app, but then I forget to check my calendar.

★：Then you've got to make it a habit to check your

★：今朝は歯医者に行くはずだったんじゃないの？

☆：ああ，なんてこと！ 完全に忘れていたわ。重要な予定を忘れたのは，今週2回目よ。

★：スケジュール帳に書いておかないとだめだよ。

☆：書いているわ。予定はすべてスマートフォンのカレンダーアプリに記録しているのよ。でもその後カレンダーをチェックし忘れてしまうの。

★：だったら毎日同じ時間にカレンダーをチェックすることを習慣にしないと。そうしないといつまでも忘れ続けることになるよ。

☆：あなたの言う通りね。朝起きたらまずチェック

calendar at the same time every day. Otherwise, you'll keep missing things.

☆: You're right. I'll make it a rule to check it when I first get up in the morning.

Question: What did the woman resolve to do?

することにするわ。

質問：女性は何をすることにしたか。

1 毎朝まずスマートフォンのカレンダーを見返す。　**2** 歯科医に電話して予約を忘れたことを謝る。

3 スマートフォン用に新しいアプリを手に入れる。　**4** すべての予定をカレンダーに書き留める。

解説　女性の問題は，スマートフォンのアプリで予定を書いても忘れてしまうこと。男性に Then you've got to make it a habit to check your calendar at the same time every day. と言われ，I'll make it a rule to check it when I first get up in the morning. と答えているので，**1** が正解。

No. 5　解答　**1**

★: Did you pick up the dry cleaning on your way home?

○: Yes, here it is. It looks like they didn't get the stain out on your pants.

★: That's not good. They charged me extra to take out the stain and assured me they could do it.

○: Well, look at it for yourself. You're not going to want to wear them again, so I'd chuck them if I were you.

★: No, not before I take them back to the cleaners. If they couldn't remove it like they said they could, then they at least need to reimburse me for the extra charge.

Question: Why is the man upset?

★: 帰りにクリーニングを取ってきてくれた？

○: ええ，どうぞ。ズボンのシミは取れていないみたいね。

★: それはよろしくないな。そのシミを取るのに追加料金がかかったし，シミは取れるとはっきり言われたのに。

○: まあ，自分の目で確かめて。もうそのズボンを履くつもりになれないと思うから，私なら捨てるわ。

★: だめだよ，クリーニング店に戻すまではね。彼らが言った通りに除去することができなかったのなら，少なくとも追加料金は返してもらわないと。

質問：男性はなぜ動揺しているか。

1 クリーニング店が約束通りの仕事をしなかった。　**2** クリーニング店員がズボンを捨てるように提案した。

3 新しいシミがズボンにあった。　**4** クリーニング店は法外に高い。

解説　シミが残っていると聞いた男性は They charged me extra to take out the stain and assured me they could do it. と言い，最後の発言では If they couldn't remove it like they said they could, then they at least need to reimburse me for the extra charge. と言っている。クリーニング店が約束通りにシミを取らなかったことが問題なので，**1** が正解。

No. 6　解答　**4**

☆: Atsuko and I are going to an event this Saturday called "New Age of Health." Would you like to go? Some famous speakers will be there.

★: No, I've got my regular Saturday tennis game.

☆: Yes, but you can give up one day to come to this event. You're interested in holistic healing, right?

★: I think tennis would be better for my health than wading through some crowded event.

☆: But won't you at least look at this website and see

☆: アツコと私は今度の土曜日に「新時代の健康」というイベントに行くの。あなたも来る？　有名人が何人か話すのよ。

★: いいや，土曜日はテニスの定期試合があるんだ。

☆: そうね，でもこのイベントに出るために1日くらいあきらめてもいいんじゃない。ホリスティックヒーリングには興味があるでしょう？

★: 混み合ったイベントに何とか参加するよりも，テニスの方が僕の健康にはいいと思うよ。

what it's about? Besides, Atsuko's husband Doug is coming along.

★：Really? I haven't seen him in ages. In that case, I'll consider it.

☆：Great. He'd be delighted to see you.

Question：Why is the man thinking about going to the event?

☆：でも，少なくともこのウェブサイトは見て，どんなイベントか確かめるべきよ。それに，アツコのご主人のダグも来るのよ。

★：本当かい？　彼には随分会っていないな。だったら検討してみるよ。

☆：よかった。彼もあなたに会えば喜ぶわ。

質問：男性はなぜイベントに行くことを考えているのか。

1 テニスでのけがを治したいと思っているから。

2 ホリスティックヒーリングに関することに興味があるから。

3 有名な講演者の話を聞きたいから。

4 そこで知り合いに会えるから。

解説　男性はイベントに乗り気でなかったが，女性に Atsuko's husband Doug is coming along と言われ，Really? I haven't seen him in ages. In that case, I'll consider it. と答えている。Doug に会えるならイベントに参加してみてもよいと考えているので，**4**が正解。

No. 7　解答　**3**

☆：Hey, Jessie, I didn't expect you to come in to work today. I thought you'd still be at the conference.

★：You know the hurricane that's going to hit Atlanta? We were told we wouldn't be able to depart Atlanta during the storm, which could last days, so I came back early.

☆：That's too bad.

★：Well, I was lucky to change my ticket, since many other passengers wanted to do the same thing.

☆：So how was the conference?

★：Not so great. There was one speaker I was really hoping to see, but he cancelled due to illness. And I missed the presentation I wanted to see yesterday because of my flight change.

Question：Why did the man leave the conference early?

☆：まあ，ジェシー。今日は仕事に来ると思っていなかったわ。まだ協議会に出ているものだと思っていたけど。

★：ハリケーンがアトランタに上陸しそうなのは知っているだろう？　ハリケーンが来たらアトランタから離れられなくなるって言われたんだ。数日はハリケーンの荒れた天気が続くだろうから，早く帰ってきたんだ。

☆：それは残念ね。

★：まあ，幸運にもチケットの変更ができたしね。同じことをしようとした乗客がほかにもたくさんいたから。

☆：それで協議会はどうだったの？

★：あまりよくはなかったね。どうしても会いたいと思っていた講演者が1人いたんだけれど，病気でキャンセルになったんだ。飛行機を変更したせいで，昨日は見たかったプレゼンテーションを見逃すしね。

質問：男性はどうして早く協議会を去ったのか。

1 協議会で気分が悪くなったから。　　**2** 欲しいチケットが取れなかったから。

3 遅れて戻るのを避けたいと思ったから。　**4** 会議はつまらないと思ったから。

解説　男性は最初の発言で We were told we wouldn't be able to depart Atlanta during the storm, which could last days, so I came back early. と説明している。came back early を avoid a delayed return と言い換えている**3**が正解。

Day **6**

No. 8　解答 2

★：Hello, Professor Lim. How are you?

○：I'm fine, Joe. May I ask where you're off to?

★：To the post office to pick up a package from my parents.

○：Oh, I'm headed there, too, to post a few letters. Shall we walk together?

★：I can drop those off for you, if you'd like.

○：That would be very helpful, actually. I've got a faculty meeting in 15 minutes, and that would ensure I won't be late. Thanks a lot, Joe.

★：No problem.

Question：What will Joe do for Professor Lim?

★：こんにちは，リム教授。ご機嫌いかがですか。

○：元気ですよ，ジョー。どこへ行くところなの？

★：両親からの小包を受け取りに郵便局に行くんです。

○：あら，私も手紙を何通か出しに行くところなのよ。一緒に歩きましょうか。

★：よろしければ，代わりに出してきますけど。

○：実を言うと，そうしてもらえると助かるわ。15分後に教授会があるのだけど，それであれば遅刻せずに済むわ。どうもありがとう，ジョー。

★：いいですよ。

質問：リム教授のために，ジョーは何をするか。

1 彼女が遅れることを何人かに伝える。　　**2** 彼女の手紙を何通か出す。

3 彼女の小包を受け取る。　　**4** 彼女に郵便局がどこにあるか教える。

解説　キャンパスでの教授と学生の会話と思われる。聞き取れないと困るのは，I can drop those off for you というジョーの申し出。drop off は「（郵便物など）を出す，投函する」という意味で，正解の **2** はこれを Mail で置き換えている。

No. 9　解答 3

★：How do you feel things are going at the Call Center?

☆：I think OK, but I've only been Center Manager for three months, so I still have a lot of things to learn.

★：For your information, we've conducted a customer survey and there appears to be one major issue of concern, which I'd like to address this morning.

☆：Really? What is it?

★：Four customers reported they weren't given the information they required from Call Center agents to solve problems related to privacy concerns and security issues.

☆：Oh, no! I wish I'd known that earlier.

★：Well, that's partly our fault in Operations. We need to get information to you faster so you can make adjustments. I'll work on that on our end.

☆：Perhaps our agents need more training.

★：Well, they can't be expected to know everything. The major problem I see relates to referral of certain types of complicated calls to specialists.

☆：I see. I'll need more details to pass on to my staff.

★：And that's exactly what I've prepared for you,

★：コールセンターの業務はどのように進んでいると感じていますか。

☆：問題はないと思うのですが，まだセンター・マネージャーになって3カ月ですから，覚えなければならないことがたくさんあります。

★：ご参考までにお伝えしておくと，顧客調査を行ったところ，気がかりな大きな問題が1つあるようで，今朝はその問題を扱いたいと思っているのです。

☆：本当ですか。何ですか。

★：4人のお客さまから，プライバシーやセキュリティーに関連した問題の解決に必要な情報をコールセンターの係員に要求したところ，情報をもらえなかったというお知らせがあったのです。

☆：まあ，なんてこと！　もっと早く知っていれば。

★：まあ，その責任の一部は私たちのオペレーション部にあります。あなたへ情報をもっと迅速に伝える必要がありますね。そうすればあなたも対応できるでしょう。私の方で対処するようにします。

☆：たぶん係員はもっと研修が必要です。

★：そうですね，すべてを知っているものと期待することはできませんね。私が思う大きな問題は，

including a list of names and issues each specialist can deal with. This should make your staff's work easier and better equip them to satisfy customer needs.

Question: What does the man suggest?

あるタイプの複雑な電話を専門スタッフに回すことに関連しています。

☆：わかりました。スタッフに伝えるためさらに詳細が必要になると思います。

★：まさにその準備をしておきました。各専門スタッフの名前とそれぞれが扱える問題のリストもあります。これであなたのスタッフも働きやすくなって，お客さまのニーズを満たすための準備がさらに整うはずです。

質問：男性は何を提案しているか。

1 さらに複雑な質問を扱えるよう係員を研修する。
2 定期的に顧客満足度調査を実施する。
3 特定の電話を専門の係員に回す。
4 オペレーション部ともっと定期的に意思疎通をはかる。

解説 男性の提案として，We need to get information to you faster so you can make adjustments. や The major problem I see relates to referral of certain types of complicated calls to specialists. と言っている。状況がつかみづらいかもしれないが，最後の that's exactly what I've prepared for you, including a list of names and issues each specialist can deal with から，要は複雑な問題に関する問い合わせは専門のスタッフに対応させるということ。**3**が正解。

No. 10 解答 **2**

☆：George, why isn't the report finished? The client is furious.

★：I'm sorry. I thought I could finish it last night, but then I realized one section had to be redone. I'm working on it right now.

☆：Right now is too late! The client had told us it was urgent, and it was supposed to be delivered this morning.

○：Kim, it's not completely his fault. I also had George working on the new proposal. I should have let him focus on finishing the report first.

★：No. I'm responsible for the delay. I should have told both of you first thing this morning that the report wasn't finished and that I was having problems getting it done.

☆：I want to be informed before a deadline if there's a problem with a project, not after the deadline has passed.

★：I know. I'm sorry.

○：I'll call the client to apologize and tell them we'll send it to them as soon as possible. When will that be ready, George?

★：I'll have it done in less than three hours.

☆：ジョージ，なぜレポートができていないの？ クライアントがかんかんよ。

★：すみません。昨日の夜に完成できると思っていたんですが，セクションを1つ書き直さなければならないことに気づいたんです。今取りかかっています。

☆：今では遅すぎるわ！ クライアントは大至急とおっしゃられていて，今朝には納品するはずだったのよ。

○：キム，彼だけの責任ではないのよ。私もジョージに新しい提案の作業をしてもらっていたの。まずはレポートを完成させることに集中してもらうべきだったわ。

★：いいえ。遅れたのは私の責任です。今朝一番に，レポートが完成していないことと，まとめるのに苦労していることをお2人にお伝えすべきでした。

☆：プロジェクトに問題があるときは，締め切りがすぎてからではなく，その前に知らせてもらいたいわ。

★：そうですね，すみません。

○：私はクライアントに電話でおわびをして，できるだけ早くお送りすると伝えるわ。いつ出来上

☆：OK. And remember to keep me up to date on your progress. I don't want any more surprises like this in the future.

★：There won't be any. I promise.

Question：What does George's boss ask him to do in the future?

がるの，ジョージ？

★：3時間以内に仕上げます。

☆：わかったわ。それから，進行状況をその都度私に知らせるのを忘れないでね。今後はこんな不意打ちはしてほしくないわ。

★：もうありません。約束します。

質問：ジョージの上司は今後何をするよう頼んだか。

1 直接クライアントに謝罪する。　　　　**2** 彼女に逐次報告をする。

3 効率的にマルチタスクをこなすよう努める。　　**4** 進捗レポートを更新する。

解説　気の毒にもジョージが怒られてしまっているのは，仕事が終わっていないことと，何よりその報告が遅れたことが原因である。remember to keep me up to date on your progress と言われているので，これを言い換えている**2**が正解。

Part 2 🔊087～092

(A)

Amazing Chalk

Everyone knows what chalk is; that white substance used to write on blackboards in classrooms all over the world. We have various hues of chalk today: yellow, green, red, and other colors of the rainbow, but none of those are the original color of chalk. Many people know that chalk provides the beautiful white glow of the famous "cliffs of Dover," and the white stone faces of similar geological formations in Austin, Texas and the South of France.

Yet, few non-scientists know that chalk is actually the remains of extremely small sea animals that lived in the ocean over 65 million years ago. At one time, the chalk that teachers use to write on their blackboards came from living things, and later, it was a kind of soupy substance that formed what scientists now call the "Chalk Sea." The small animals that made up chalk lived near the surface of oceans and seas. After dying, their shells and skeletons floated downward and settled on the ocean floors, forming thick layers that eventually hardened. The tiny shells composing chalk are known to be the smallest fossils yet discovered, requiring powerful microscopes to observe them. The next time you see a teacher write something on a blackboard, you are watching a person smear 65-million-year-old fossils across the board.

Questions

No.11　What is Dover famous for?

No.12　How was chalk formed?

驚くべきチョーク

チョークが何なのかは誰でも知っている。世界中で教室の黒板に字を書くのに使うあの白い物質である。黄，緑，赤，ほかに虹に含まれる色など，今日のチョークにはさまざまな色合いがある。しかし，そのどれもチョーク本来の色ではない。有名な「ドーバーの崖」に美しい白い輝きを与え，テキサス州オースティンやフランスの南部にある同様の地質的岩層に白い石の表面を与えているのがチョークであることを，多くの人が知っている。

しかし，チョークが実際には6,500万年以上前に海に生息していた極めて微小な海洋動物の死骸だということを知る人は，科学者以外ではほとんどいない。教師が板書に使うチョークは，かつて生物から生じたのであり，そして後に，科学者が現在「チョーク（白亜）の海」と呼ぶものを形成した一種のスープ状物質になったのである。

チョークの元となった微小動物は，大洋や海の海面近くで生きていた。死後，その殻と骨格は下方へと浮遊して海底に定着し，厚い層を形成して最後には硬化した。チョークを構成する微細な貝は，これまで発見された中で最小の化石として知られており，観察するには高倍率の顕微鏡が必要である。この次教師が板書しているのを見たら，それは，黒板に 6,500 万年前の化石をこすりつけている人を見ていることになる。

No. 11　解答　1

「ドーバーは何で有名か」

1　その有名なチョークの崖。
2　近くにあるチョークの海。
3　チョークが作られている工場。
4　さまざまな色のチョーク。

解説　chalk は日本語でも「チョーク」と呼ぶが，素材の chalk は「白亜」と呼ばれる石灰岩のこと。Many people know that chalk provides the beautiful white glow of the famous "cliffs of Dover," から 1 が正解。

No. 12　解答　1

「チョークはどのように形成されたのか」

1　微生物の残骸が海底に沈んだ。
2　化石が強い海流で分解された。
3　小さな生き物が岸壁に堆積物を残した。
4　軟体動物が持つ貝殻が海面へと漂い，固まって岩になった。

解説　chalk is actually the remains of extremely small sea animals that lived in the ocean over 65 million years ago から，チョークは微生物の残骸であることがわかる。さらに After dying, their shells and skeletons floated downward and settled on the ocean floors, forming thick layers that eventually hardened. から，残骸が海底にたまり，固まったことがわかるので，1 が正解。

(B)

Monument to the Sun

There is an ancient and mysterious monument that sits on a hilltop about 250 miles north of Lima, Peru. For many years, explorers, researchers, and tourists visited the lonely structure, but none were able to figure out why it was built, and what purpose it once served. The ruins are comprised of three concentric stone walls that surround a fortress and thirteen towers. Researchers believe the structures were built by a pre-Incan civilization of farmers, traders, and llama herdsmen, collectively called the Chavin. Some guessed that the monument was used for religious ceremonies, others thought it was for military defense, and still others surmised it was a gathering place for the elite.

The debate continued until archeologist Ivan Ghezzi of the Catholic University of Peru finally cracked the riddle. He realized that the ruins formed the oldest solar observatory in all of the Americas. From a temple within the inner circle, the Chavin could observe the sun rise between the stone towers, which were precisely spaced to calibrate the days, weeks, and seasons according to the position of the sun. It would have been useful as a calendar for the agricultural community, but it was probably even more important to the civilization's rulers, who were able to gain valuable information from the monument: the ability to predict the movement of the sun. With the knowledge gained from these massive stone calendars, this chosen elite could convince the common people that they controlled the movement of the sun, thus solidifying their own authority.

Questions

No.13　What did Ivan Ghezzi believe was the main purpose of the Chavin monument?

No.14　How was the information gathered by the Chavin in the monument used?

太陽の遺跡

　ペルーのリマから北へ約250マイル行った丘の頂に，古代の謎めいた遺跡が立っている。長年，探検家や研究者や観光客がこのぽつりと立っている建造物を訪れたが，なぜこれが建てられたのか，かつてどんな目的に使われていたのかを解明することは誰にもできなかった。遺跡は，1つの要塞と13の塔を同心円状に囲む3重の石壁から成っている。この建造物を建てたのは，集合的にチャビンと呼ばれる，農夫と商人とラマ飼いから成る前インカ文明だと研究者は考えている。ある者はこの遺跡は宗教儀式に使われたと推測し，ある者は軍事防衛用だったと考え，またある者はエリート層の集会場だったと推測した。

　ペルー・カトリック大学の考古学者イヴァン・ゲッチがついに謎を解き明かすまで，議論は続いた。この遺跡が南北アメリカ全体で最古の太陽天文台を形作っていることに，彼は気づいたのである。内側の円の中の寺院から，チャビンは石塔の間から昇る太陽を観測することができた。石塔は，太陽の位置に従って日と週と季節の長さを定めるために，正確な間隔で配置されていた。それは農業共同体の暦として有用だったのだろうが，おそらくこの文明の統治者たちにとってもっと重要だった。彼らはその遺跡から貴重な情報，つまり太陽の動きを予測する能力を手に入れることができた。この選ばれたエリート層は，この巨大な石の暦から得られる知識を手に，自分たちが太陽の動きを支配していると一般民衆に信じ込ませることができ，そうすることで自らの権威を確固たるものにしたのである。

No. 13　解答　**2**

「イヴァン・ゲッチは，チャビンの遺跡の主たる目的は何だと考えたか」

1 主に軍事防衛用であった。　　　　　　　**2** 正確な太陽暦としての役目を果たした。

3 重要な宗教的儀式に利用された。　　　　**4** チャビンのエリートが集まる場所だった。

解説　イヴァン・ゲッチの見立てでは，チャビンは the oldest solar observatory であり，could observe the sunrise between the stone towers, which were precisely spaced to calibrate the days, weeks, and seasons according to the position of the sun であったとある。a precise solar calendar と一言でまとめている**2**が正解。Some guessed that the monument was used for religious ceremonies, others thought it was for military defense, and still others surmised it was a gathering place for the elite. につられて**1**，**3**，**4**を選ばないように注意。

No. 14　解答　**1**

「チャビンが遺跡で集めた情報は，どのように利用されたか」

1 首領たちによって政治的な道具として使われた。　　**2** 文明の軍事強化のために使われた。

3 農家の重要性を強固にした。　　　　　　　　　　　**4** 一般の人々を教育するのに利用された。

解説　最後に this chosen elite，つまり the civilization's rulers であるエリートが，この太陽暦を使ってしたことがまとめられている。convince the common people that they controlled the movement of the sun, thus solidifying their own authority とあるので，これを a political tool と表している**1**が正解。

(C)

Jailed for Reading?

　Books have the power to change ideas and lives, in positive and negative ways. Some books are banned in some countries while being celebrated in others. It is very rare, however, to hear of people being arrested for reading. Yet this is what happened to fifteen political and human rights activists in Angola. They were arrested in 2015 for organizing a public discussion of two books about peaceful challenge to authoritarian regimes. The activists were involved in campaigns for numerous social justice issues and tried to make the government answer their concerns. The government, in turn, accused them of plotting a coup.

　The events put Angola in the international spotlight for all the wrong reasons. Although it is one of

Africa's fastest growing economies, the wealth generated by its abundant natural resources is rarely distributed to the general population. In fact, over 70 percent of the population live on less than $2 a day, while the ruling elite live in luxury. Support for the book-reading activists came from all corners of the globe, with groups like Amnesty International calling for their release. Despite the outcry, however, the decision to publicly discuss ideas written in books led to the group being jailed for rebelling against the government.

Questions

No.15 What led to the arrests in Angola?

No.16 What does the speaker highlight about Angola?

読んだために投獄？

　本は良い方向にも悪い方向にも，考えや生活を変える力を持っている。ある国では禁止される本が，ほかの国で称賛されることもある。しかし，人々が読んだだけで逮捕されるのを聞くことは，非常に珍しい。だが，これはアンゴラで15人の政治及び人権活動家に起こったことだ。2015年，彼らは独裁政権に対する平和的な異議申し立てに関する2冊の本の公開討論を組織したために逮捕されたのだ。活動家たちは数多くの社会正義問題運動にかかわり，政府に自分たちの懸念について答えさせようとした。その結果政府は，クーデターを起こそうとした罪で彼らを告発した。

　その出来事のおかげでアンゴラは悪い理由で世界の注目を集めることになった。アンゴラはアフリカで最も急速に発展している経済圏の1つにもかかわらず，豊富な自然資源から生まれる富はめったに一般住民に配分されることはない。実際，支配層エリートがぜいたくに暮らしている一方，国民の70％以上が1日2ドル以下で生活している。アムネスティ・インターナショナルのような団体が彼らの釈放を要求するなど，読書活動家への支援は世界中から集まった。しかし，激しい抗議にもかかわらず，本に書かれていた思想を公開で討論しようとした決断のせいで，グループは政府に対する反逆の罪で投獄されることになった。

No. 15　解答　**3**

「アンゴラにおける逮捕につながったのは何か」

1 活動家たちはクーデターを企てた。

2 何冊かの本について否定的な書評があった。

3 活動家たちは政府に異議を申し立てるために本を使った。

4 出版記念パーティーが手に負えなくなった。

解説　第1段落中盤に They were arrested in 2015 for organizing a public discussion of two books about peaceful challenge to authoritarian regimes. とある。これを言い換えた**3**が正解。

No. 16　解答　**4**

「話者はアンゴラについて何を強調しているか」

1 国内の反逆者の数。　　　　　　　　**2** 地元の経済の珍しい成功。

3 禁止された本を読むことの危険性。　　**4** 国民の間の富の格差。

解説　第2段落の前半からアンゴラの経済について述べている。自然資源は豊富だが，一般の人々には行き渡らないと説明した後で，In fact, over 70 percent of the population live on less than $2 a day, while the ruling elite live in luxury. と具体的な数字を挙げている。したがって，**4**を強調していると考えられる。

(D)

Gaslighting

　The term gaslighting is used by psychologists to describe how a person covers their own lies by deflecting, distracting and blaming others. The name comes from the 1944 movie *Gaslight* starring

Ingrid Bergman. In the movie, a husband tries to convince his wife, played by Bergman, that she is going insane in order to cover up a murder he committed. He is ultimately unsuccessful, but in real life, many others have used similar techniques to cause considerable harm to partners and spouses. Psychologists say that the effects of gaslighting can be deeply traumatic, with recovery being difficult and time-consuming.

Although it is most common within relationships between couples, psychologist Stan Tatkin warns that in today's political climate, society as a whole could be at risk. He suggests that we are in committed relationships with our leaders which depend on a basis of trust. A gaslighter manipulates this trust by blaming others, distracting our attention from things he or she is trying to hide, or simply lying about something. On a national or international level, this can be particularly dangerous as it undermines both trust in government and in democracy itself. Unsurprisingly, therefore, it is often used by dictators.

Questions

No.17　In psychology, what does gaslighting mean?

No.18　How can gaslighting work at a national or international level?

ガスライティング

　ガスライティングは，人がどのように他人の気をそらし，混乱させ，また他人を責めることで自分の嘘を覆い隠すのかを説明するために，心理学者によって用いられている用語である。その名前は1944年の映画，イングリッド・バーグマン主演の『ガス燈』が由来である。この映画では，ある夫がバーグマン演じる妻を説得して，彼女が正気ではなくなりつつあると信じ込ませ，自分が犯した殺人を隠そうとする。彼は最後には成功しないのだが，実生活では多くの人々が似たようなテクニックを使ってパートナーや配偶者をかなり傷つけてきた。心理学者が言うには，ガスライティングのせいで深い心の傷を負うこともあり，その回復は困難で時間がかかる。

　恋愛関係の中では非常によくあることだが，心理学者のスタン・タトキンは，今日の政治情勢では社会全体が危機的になりかねないと警告する。その主張によれば，われわれは信頼を礎にする献身的な関係をリーダーと築いている。ガスライティングをする人は，他人を非難することでこの信頼を巧みに操作し，リーダーが隠そうとしていることからわれわれの注意をそらしたり，単に嘘をついたりする。国あるいは国際的なレベルでは，これは特に危険なことになりかねない。政府ばかりか民主主義そのものへの信頼も根底から崩壊してしまうからだ。それゆえ，それが独裁者がよく用いる手段だとしても，驚くようなことではない。

No. 17 　解答　**4**

「心理学ではガスライティングはどのような意味か」

1 有名な映画の筋書き。

2 誰かを狂わそうという成功することのない試み。

3 困難で時間を要する診断。

4 ごまかしを隠すためのさまざまなテクニックの使用。

解説　心理学におけるガスライティングの意味は，to describe how a person covers their own lies by deflecting, distracting and blaming others という説明がある。**4**が正解。『ガス燈（*Gaslight*）』という映画の登場人物がこのテクニックを使っていることから，その名がきている。

No. 18 　解答　**2**

「国あるいは国際的なレベルでガスライティングはどう作用する可能性があるか」

1 リーダーが外国政府と関係を築くときに利用する。

2 政府に対する人々の信頼に影響を与えかねない。

3 リーダーがリスクの高い政策を採用するのに役立つ。

4 そのおかげで独裁者は自身を社会から疎外させることができる。

解説　国あるいは国際的なレベルでは，this can be particularly dangerous as it undermines both trust in government and in democracy itself と警鐘が鳴らされている。これをシンプルに言い換えた**2**が正解。

(E)

Running

For virtually as long as humans have been walking upright, we have also been running. Perhaps our early ability to run allowed us to escape immediate threats. It is endurance running, however, that truly sets us apart from other running animals. Early humans were thought to run long distances in order to tire their prey and make them easier to catch. This endurance ability made up for a relative lack of physical power. Evidence suggests that running led to evolutionary changes in humans like many sweat glands, larger joints in the legs, and more muscle around the hips.

Nowadays, running is a very popular recreational activity and a multibillion-dollar industry. Competitive running grew from early religious celebrations to the huge number of events and races we have today. Athletes compete in races that range from a few seconds to multiple days. Courses range from specially-created tracks to mountains and deserts. Those who are successful can expect to earn a great amount of money from sponsorship and prize money, and many become celebrities. It's a far cry from early competitions when runners who failed to win could be jailed, publicly flogged or even executed.

Questions

No.19 In what way did running help early humans?
No.20 How has the sport of running changed?

走る

実質的に人間が立って歩いているのと同じ期間, われわれは走ってきた。おそらく, もともと走る能力があったおかげで人は目の前の脅威から逃げられたのだろう。しかし, ほかの走る動物とわれわれを本当に区別しているのは, 持久走である。昔の人間は獲物を疲れさせて捕まえやすくするために長距離を走ったと考えられている。この持久力が, 相対的に不足している身体的な強靭さを補っていたのだ。走ることが人間の進化上の変化につながったことを示す証拠もある。変化の例は, 汗腺が多いこと, 脚部の関節が大きいこと, 腰回りの筋肉が多いことなどである。

今日では, 走ることはとても人気のレクリエーション活動であり, 数十億ドル規模の産業である。競って走ることは昔の宗教的なお祝いから, 今日開催されている無数のイベントやレースへと成長した。アスリートは数秒から数日間に及ぶものまであるレースで競う。コースは特別に用意されたトラックから, 山, 砂漠までさまざまだ。成功した者はスポンサーや賞金で大金を稼ぐことが期待でき, 多くが有名人になる。勝てなかったランナーが投獄されたり, 人前でむちで打たれたり, 処刑されたりすることすらあった昔の競走とはまるで違う。

No. 19 解答 **3**

「走ることはどのように昔の人間を助けたか」

1 高いレベルで競うことができた。　　　　　　**2** より大きな獲物を圧倒する能力を発達させた。
3 さらに首尾よく狩りができた。　　　　　　　**4** 立って歩くことができた。

解説　昔の人間にとっての走る利点については, Perhaps our early ability to run allowed us to escape immediate threats. や Early humans were thought to run long distances in order to tire their prey and make them easier to catch. という説明がある。後者に一致する**3**が正解。

No. 20 解答 **4**

「走るスポーツはどのように変化したか」

1 ほとんど変化していない。
2 現代のアスリートは以前よりも長く自分たちのキャリアを続けられる。
3 競って走ることは宗教的になった。
4 多様化し, もうかるようになった。

走ることの変化は，Competitive running grew from early religious celebrations to the huge number of events and races we have today. の後で詳しく説明されている。まとめると，現在では時間やコースが多様になり，成功すれば大金を稼ぐことができ，有名にもなれるということなので，**4**が正解。

Part 3 🔊 093~098

(F) No. 21 解答 2

Currently, many experts say we're in a real estate bubble, so it might be best to wait a few years to see how the economy pans out. Many commercial real estate investors have over-extended themselves on loans and are stretched thin. During a recession, banks will foreclose on many of these over-leveraged properties and you'll be able to pick them up at steep discounts. There are several shopping malls available at a discount right now, but we're going through what's called a retail apocalypse. Fifteen percent of shopping malls are expected to fold within the next decade. A better, low-risk option if you need to invest in something soon would be a so-called lifestyle center, a new shopping center concept with a beautiful main street and architectural details like cobblestone sidewalks, fountains, and attractive landscaping. They're located on smaller properties than traditional malls but offer upscale brand stores along with fancy restaurants and fun entertainment options.

状況：あなたは日本の投資グループを代表し，米国の投資銀行の経営者と，不動産について協議する。あなたには6カ月以内に投資しなければならない資金がある。投資銀行の経営者はあなたに次のアドバイスをする。
質問：アドバイスによると，あなたにとって最適な投資先は何か。

最近では多くの専門家が不動産バブルだと言います。ですから，数年は経済の成り行きを見守っているのが最善の策かもしれません。商業用不動産に投資している方の多くは，自分の返済能力を上回るローンを組み，余力がありません。景気後退の局面では，銀行が借り入れ過多の物件の多くに対して担保権を実行しますので，こうした物件を非常に割安に手に入れることができます。直近では割安なショッピング・モールがいくつかありますが，われわれはリテール・アポカリプス（小売業の崩壊）と呼ばれるものを経験しているところです。今後10年間でショッピング・モールの15％は閉店すると見込まれています。もっと良い低リスクの選択肢が，もし何かにすぐ投資する必要がある場合ですが，いわゆるライフスタイル・センターでしょう。これは新しいコンセプトのショッピング・モールで，美しいメインストリートがあり，玉石を敷き詰めた歩道や噴水，魅力的な景観といった建築の細部まで考えられています。ライフスタイル・センターがある場所は，従来のショッピング・モールほど大きな土地ではないのですが，高級ブランド店が入っていて，豪華なレストランや楽しいエンターテイメント施設も備えています。

1 チェーン展開しているレストラン。   **2** ライフスタイル・センター。
3 従来のショッピング・モール。   **4** 新しいタイプのエンターテイメント施設。

解説 この投資銀行経営者は最終的に，A better, low-risk option if you need to invest in something soon would be a so-called lifestyle center と言い，ライフスタイル・センターを勧めている。**2**が正解。**3**に対しては悲観的。**1**と**4**については触れていない。

(G) No. 22 解答 1

These courts are owned and maintained by the city, so prices are very reasonable—$10 per hour for indoor courts and only $2 an hour for outdoor courts. As you know, a storm is approaching, and it's expected to rain all day on Saturday. Most of the indoor courts are already reserved, but we have one court that's available from 3 p.m., if you'd like. Sunday is booked up until 2 p.m., but after that, we have both indoor and outdoor courts available. But nobody knows if the weather will be okay by then. What I can do, if you'd like, is to reserve one indoor and one outdoor court, and you can cancel one of them at least 24 hours in advance, so there won't be a penalty. We'll probably have a better idea of what Sunday's weather will be by Saturday.

状況：あなたは今週末にテニスコートを予約し，友人と一緒に利用したいと思っている。あなたは午前10時から午後4時までの2時間プレイできる。お金はなるべく使いたくない。予約係が次のように言う。

質問：予約係によると，あなたはどの予約を入れるべきか。

こちらのテニスコートは市が所有・管理していますので，値段はとてもリーズナブルです。室内コートが1時間10ドル，屋外コートは1時間たったの2ドルです。ご存じのとおり，嵐が近づいていますので，土曜日は1日中雨の見込みです。室内コートはすでにほぼ予約で埋まっているのですが，よろしければ午後3時から利用可能なコートが1面あります。日曜日は午後2時まで予約がいっぱいなのですが，その後は室内コート，屋外コートともに利用可能です。ただし，そのころまでに天候がどうなっているかは知るよしもありませんね。よろしければ，室内コート1面と屋外コート1面の予約をお取りしましょうか。24時間前にどちらかキャンセルすれば，違約金は発生しません。おそらく土曜日には，日曜日の天気がどうなるかもっとはっきりわかるでしょう。

1 日曜日の午後2時に2面。　　　　　　　　　**2** 土曜日の午後2時に屋外コートを1面。
3 土曜日に1面，日曜日にもう1面。　　　　　**4** 土曜日まで予約を入れない。

解説　予約係の提案内容に注意して聞く。状況より，なるべく値段の安い屋外コートを使用するべきなので，屋内コートしか空きがない土曜は選択肢から外れる。日曜の状況は予約係によると both indoor and outdoor courts available で，reserve one indoor and one outdoor court, and you can cancel one of them at least 24 hours in advance と提案されている。one indoor and one outdoor court を Two courts と言い換えた **1** が正解。

(H) No. 23　解答　2

This is Bob Finch from Testing. We've run several tests on the software product that was coded by InTech Company and have run into some major issues. These are not just bugs. The product simply fails to meet the specs we agreed on during the requirements stage, so it needs to be almost completely recoded. I don't know how this could have happened, as we were very clear about specifications. If we have a contract with them guaranteeing compliance to the requirements, don't make payment. The work was so shoddy that we'll want to consider hiring a different coding company, in which case we'll need to consult our company legal team immediately. If we don't have a binding contract, we'll just have to send it back to InTech and watch them like a hawk until they do the coding correctly. Either case will mean some serious delays in getting product to market. Get in touch with me after you've decided what to do.

Day 6

状況：あなたは，自身が働いている会社でソフトウエア開発を任されている検査チームから携帯電話にメッセージを受け取る。あなたはプログラミング会社と返金保証つきの契約をしている。

質問：メッセージによると，あなたはまず何をするべきか。

検査のボブ・フィンチです。InTech 社がプログラムを作成したソフトウエアの検査を数回行いましたが，いくつか大きな問題があることがわかりました。単なるバグではありません。要件を決める段階で合意したスペックを全然満たしていないので，ほぼすべてプログラムを作成し直す必要があります。スペックについてわれわれはとても明確にしていたのに，どうしてこうなったのかわかりません。要件を守ることが契約で保証されているのでしたら，支払いはしないでください。あまりにも雑な仕事なので，別のプログラミング会社の採用を検討したいと思います。その場合は社の法務チームに直ちに相談しなければならないでしょう。法的な拘束力のない契約の場合は，ソフトウエアをInTech社に戻し，彼らが正しくプログラムを作成するまで厳しく見ておくしかありませんね。いずれにしろ，製品の上市はひどく遅れることになるでしょう。対応を決めたら，私に連絡してください。

111

1 新しいプログラミング会社を探す。　　2 法律の専門家に相談する。
3 InTech 社に電話をしてさらに情報をもらう。　4 InTech 社と支払い金額の値引き交渉をする。

解説　If we have a contract with them guaranteeing compliance to the requirements の後を注意して聞く。we'll want to consider hiring a different coding company に続けて in which case we'll need to consult our company legal team immediately と言っていることから，正解は **2**。our company legal team を legal experts と言い換えている。

(I) *No. 24*　**解答** 3

You asked if extra storage capacity for our mainframe is necessary, and I have to say emphatically that it is. The additional hardware I need is expensive, I know, but the cost is typical for mainframes. You can't compare the costs to PC hardware. Mainframe equipment costs more by a factor of 10, sometimes even 100. I know what you're thinking—just replace our mainframe with workstations, but you can't. Even the best workstations will bog down with the calculations that mainframes process. As a research company, we simply can't give up that power. A few years down the road, workstations will probably do the trick, but not yet.

状況： あなたは調査会社の購買責任者である。技術スペシャリストがあなたにアドバイスをする。
質問： 技術スペシャリストによると，短期的にあなたはどうすべきか。
わが社のメインフレーム・コンピュータに記憶容量の追加が必要かというお尋ねでしたが，その通りと声を大にして申し上げなければなりません。私が必要とする追加のハードウェアは確かに高価ですが，メインフレーム・コンピュータなら当たり前の価格です。パソコンのハードウェアとは価格は比較になりません。メインフレーム・コンピュータ用機器は，その10倍，時に100倍もします。メインフレーム・コンピュータをワークステーションで代用すれば済むとお考えでしょうが，そうはいかないのです。最高性能のワークステーションでさえ，メインフレーム・コンピュータが処理する計算では，遅々として進まなくなるでしょう。調査会社としてわが社は絶対にその力を手放せません。数年先には，たぶんワークステーションで用が足りるようになるでしょうが，今はまだ無理です。
1 より強力なメインフレーム・コンピュータを購入する。
2 強力なワークステーションに乗り換える。
3 彼女が必要としているハードウェアを購入する。
4 一番お買い得なものを探す。

解説　あなたがすべきことが問われているが，話者である「技術スペシャリストによると」ということなので，彼女の言い分をつかむ。冒頭の You asked if extra storage capacity for our mainframe is necessary, and I have to say emphatically that it is. The additional hardware I need is expensive ... の部分から **3** が正解。それ以降は彼女がそう考える理由の説明になっている。

(J) *No. 25*　**解答** 2

The plenary session will begin in 30 minutes in the Grand Conference Room in Building One, so we need to move along. Those giving a poster presentation are asked to go to Conference Room B in Building Three now to choose a space and put up your posters. Those participating in one of the forum presentations should go to the room next door, Room 2003, where you'll split into topic groups. Those participating in the round-table exchange are asked to stay here to meet other panelists to decide how you'd like to carry out the discussion. And those giving short presentations are asked to go to your assigned presentation rooms now and make sure you have the appropriate audio-visual equipment and that it functions properly with your computers, cables, and USB devices. If you have any questions or problems, please see conference staff at the check-in table in the lobby of Crystal Hall.

状況：あなたは会議でポスター発表を行う予定で，本会議が始まる前にほかのプレゼンターとともに打ち合わせに出ている。会議運営者から次のことを聞く。

質問：あなたはこれから何をするよう求められているか。

本会議は30分後に1号棟にあるグランド・コンファレンス・ルームで始まりますので，移動する必要があります。ポスター発表を行う方はこれから3号棟のコンファレンス・ルーム B に行き，場所を選んでポスターを掲示してください。発表討論会のいずれかに参加される方は，隣の2003号室に行ってください。そこでトピックによるグループ分けをします。円卓会議に参加される方は，こちらに残っていただき，ほかのパネリストと顔合わせをして，討論の進め方を決定してください。ショート・プレゼンテーションを行う方は，割り当てられたプレゼンテーション・ルームにこれから向かい，AV 機器が正しくそろっていて，あなたのコンピュータやケーブル，USB 機器とともに正常に機能することを確認してください。質問や問題がある方は，クリスタル・ホールのロビーの受付テーブルに会議のスタッフがいますので，ご相談ください。

1 隣の部屋に行く。　　　　　　　　　　**2** 3号棟にある割り当てられた部屋に行く。
3 使用予定の全 AV 機器のチェックを行う。　**4** クリスタル・ホールのロビーで受付を済ませる。

解説　さまざまなプレゼンテーション，会議が開催されるが，あなたが参加するのは「ポスター発表」なので，Those giving a poster presentation ... から特に注意して聞くと，go to Conference Room B in Building Three という説明があるので**2**が正解。Conference Room B を選択肢では your assigned room と言い換えている。those giving short presentations are ... につられて**3**を選ばないように注意。

Part 4　🔊 099〜100

☆：Today, our special guest at Tech News is Bernard Silverman, Director of Jump Start, Japan. Thank you for taking time from your busy schedule to be with us today, Bernard.

★：You're welcome.

☆：Can you describe to our listeners what your company does, exactly?

★：Jump Start is an incubator, accelerator, venture capital firm, and corporate innovation platform all wrapped into one.

☆：Can you explain that in simpler English for our less technically-inclined listeners?

★：Sure. Just like an incubator helps newborn babies at risk, we help fledgling technology-based startups get the support they need to survive and grow. And as an accelerator, we help startups make the connections and receive the training and funding they need to grow more quickly. Startups need and benefit from legal support, access to advice and consultants from experts in their field, marketing support and training, investor access, and a whole bunch of other things. And as a venture capital firm, we've invested in over 120 startups, including such hugely successful startups as DropIn and OnSite.

☆：And what do you do exactly as a corporate innovation platform?

★：We have nearly 250 large corporations worldwide that are investors and partners with Jump Start who are looking for specific kinds of innovation for their own products and markets. This is not just an extra benefit for corporations. The competitiveness in industries has greatly accelerated over the last few decades, and corporations that fail to introduce their share of technological breakthroughs to maintain competitiveness are the ones who face obsolescence. That's why corporations require access to startups that can provide them with cutting-edge technologies. We offer fifty accelerator programs globally, which provide in-depth training workshops and ongoing support for startups, and each of these programs is sponsored by several of our corporate partners. We are industry-specific, offering an innovation platform in such fields as IoT, or the "internet of things," fintech, technology for the financial services sector, and mobility, which is advanced technology for the automotive industry.

☆：What specifically brought you to Japan?

★：There are many Japanese corporations with a keen interest in the startup community, both in Japan and abroad. Before I opened our Tokyo branch last year, we already had 35 Japanese corporate partners at our headquarters in Silicon Valley, so it made sense to have an office here to better serve them. But there is another reason for opening shop here. Currently, the startup ecosystem in Japan is underdeveloped. There are too few startups in general, and most of those are focused only on the domestic market rather than the global. Japanese universities are not producing enough entrepreneurs, and startups do not receive much in the way of government support or private investment from corporate partners or investors. Jump Start is here to do what our company name implies—jump start the startup ecosystem and build it up to a scale that you would expect from one of the world's leading economies.

☆：How do your company's global connections play a role in this?

★：Well, they play a role in different ways. First, through our twenty-eight offices around the world, we can introduce our Japanese corporate partners to new startup technology that is a good fit for the Japanese market. And in a similar way, we assist Japanese startups to reach overseas markets.

☆：That wraps up our program. Thank you, Bernard, for being our guest speaker today.

★：My pleasure.

Questions

No.26 What is one thing Bernard says about Jump Start's accelerator programs?

No.27 What is one thing Bernard says about the startup platform in Japan?

☆：今日のテック・ニュースのスペシャルゲストは，バーナード・シルバーマンさんです。日本のジャンプ・スタート社で取締役をしていらっしゃいます。バーナードさん，本日はお忙しいスケジュールの中，お時間を割いていただきありがとうございます。

★：どういたしまして。

☆：リスナー向けに，バーナードさんの会社が何をしていらっしゃるのか，正確なところをご説明いただけますか。

★：ジャンプ・スタート社は，インキュベーター，アクセラレーター，ベンチャーキャピタル，そしてコーポレート・イノベーション・プラットフォームとしてのすべての役割を1社で担っています。

☆：もっと簡単な英語で，技術的なことにあまり関心がないリスナーでもわかるように説明していただけますか。

★：わかりました。インキュベーター（保育器）が危険な状態にある新生児を助けるのと同様に，技術力を土台にして創業したばかりの企業を助け，事業の存続・拡大に必要な支援を受けられるようにしています。アクセラレーターとしては，創業した会社が他とつながりを持ち，早い成長を実現するのに必要な研修と資金を受ける手伝いをしています。新しい会社が必要としていることには，法務上のサポート，同じ分野の専門家からアドバイスをもらい相談を受け付けてもらうこと，マーケティングの支援と研修，投資家との接点，そのほかとても多くのことがあり，こうしたことから利益も得られるのです。ベンチャーキャピタルとしては，120社を超える新興企業に投資してきました。その中には，ドロップインやオンサイトといった大成功を収めている企業もあります。

☆：そしてコーポレート・イノベーション・プラットフォームとしてですが，実際のところどのようなことをするのでしょうか。

★：全世界で250社近くの大企業が，投資会社やパートナー企業としてジャンプ・スタート社とともにあり，自社製品や市場のために具体的なイノベーションを求めています。これは企業にとって単にメリットが増えるという話ではありません。産業界の競争は過去数十年で大いに加速しています。必要な技術的打破が実現できず競争力を保てない企業は，廃退に直面するのです。だからこそ企業は，最先端技術を提供できる新興企

業との接点を必要としています。当社は50のアクセラレーター・プログラムを世界的に提供しており，徹底した研修を行って，新興企業を継続的に支えています。各プログラムを後援しているのは，数社のパートナー企業です。当社は業界に特化してイノベーション・プラットフォームを提供しており，例として IoT，つまりインターネットオブシングスや，金融サービスセクターで利用されるフィンテック・テクノロジー，自動車産業の先進技術であるモビリティーなどの分野があります。

☆：具体的にどういった理由で日本に来たのですか。

★：日本の国内外を問わず，新興企業のコミュニティーに強い関心を持っている日本企業はたくさんあります。昨年，東京支社を開設しましたが，それまでにシリコンバレーの本社には，日本の企業パートナーがすでに35社ありました。だからもっと彼らの役に立つためにここに事務所を構えることは理にかなっていたのです。しかし，ここで事業を始める理由はもう1つあります。現在，日本では新興企業のエコシステムがまだ形成途上です。一般的に見て新興企業の数があまりにも少なく，その大半がグローバルな市場ではなく国内市場にしか目を向けていません。日本の大学は起業家を十分に輩出しておらず，政府による支援という点，あるいはパートナー企業や投資家からの民間投資という点では，あまり多くのものを得ていません。ジャンプ・スタート社がこの国ですることは，当社の社名が示唆しています。つまり，新興企業のエコシステムをジャンプ・スタート（活性化）し，世界有数の経済大国として期待される規模になるまで，それを築きあげていくのです。

☆：その点において，御社の世界的なつながりはどのような役割を果たすのですか。

★：そうですね，さまざまな方法で役割を果たします。まず，当社が世界に有する28の拠点を通じて，日本のパートナー企業には，日本市場に合った新興技術を紹介することができます。同様に，日本の新興企業が海外市場に進出する支援もします。

☆：これで番組は終わりになります。バーナードさん，本日はゲストスピーカーとしてお越しいただきありがとうございました。

★：どういたしまして。

No. 26 解答 4

「バーナードがジャンプ・スタート社のアクセラレーター・プログラムについて述べていることの1つは何か」

1 ジャンプ・スタート社の法人投資家のために企業の技術開発を加速させる。

2 企業や新興企業を教育して，事業拡大に役立つ新技術を教える。

3 企業を起業家に紹介し，新興企業の新しい技術を利用できるようにする。

4 新興の起業家に研修と支援を提供し，彼らの事業の成長を助ける。

解説　アクセラレーター・プログラムについては，We offer fifty accelerator programs globally, which provide in-depth training workshops and ongoing support for startups と説明している。**4**が正解。

No. 27 解答 1

「バーナードが日本の新興事業について述べていることの1つは何か」

1 日本は単に起業家や新興企業の数が少なすぎる。

2 日本企業は外国企業と比較すると新興企業への関心が低い。

3 日本の大企業は新興企業と直接競合し，抑え込んでしまう。

4 海外の新興企業のほうが積極果敢で，日本の新興企業を圧倒する。

解説　日本の新興企業についてバーナードはThere are too few startups in general, and most of those are focused only on the domestic market rather than the global. と説明しているので，**1**が正解。なお，この対話での ecosystem は「生態系」の意味から派生したビジネス用語で，業界における企業同士のネットワークや協業によって収益をあげるシステムのこと。

筆記試験＆リスニングテスト
解答と解説

問題編 p.98〜118

筆記

1

問題	1	2	3	4	5	6	7	8	9	10	11	12	13	14	15	16	17	18	19	20
解答	2	3	2	3	4	2	2	1	1	3	1	2	1	3	1	1	4	4	3	4

問題	21	22
解答	4	2

2

問題	23	24	25	26	27	28
解答	3	4	2	1	1	1

3

問題	29	30	31	32	33	34	35
解答	2	3	3	3	2	4	2

4 **5** 解説内にある解答例を参照してください。

リスニング

Part 1

問題	1	2	3	4	5	6	7	8	9	10
解答	4	4	2	2	1	2	4	3	1	1

Part 2

問題	11	12	13	14	15	16	17	18	19	20
解答	1	1	4	2	3	2	3	1	2	4

Part 3

問題	21	22	23	24	25
解答	4	2	3	2	2

Part 4

問題	26	27
解答	1	3

1

(1) 解答 **2**

「普通『有機園芸』は，土の肥沃度を高めるのに役立つよう，生物分解性廃棄物と葉から成る堆肥を利用する」

解説 園芸に必要なのは，**2**「堆肥」。**1**「抗生物質」，**3**「取るに足りないこと」，**4**「かす，くず」。

(2) 解答 **3**

「政府は農業経営者に対し割当量を設定することで，コメの生産量を削減した」

解説 政府はコメの生産量を調整しているので，**3**「割

り当て（量）」が設定されたと考えられる。**1**「注釈」，**2**「球，天体，範囲」，**4**「茎」。

(3) 解答 **2**

「この大学を退学処分となったいかなる学生も復学を申請してよい。学部長が最終決定を行う」

解説 「退学処分となったいかなる学生」も許可されることは，**2**「復帰，復学」を申請すること。**1**「弁償，報酬」，**3**「高潔，誠実」，**4**「至福」。

116

(4) 解答 **3**

「重度の卒中が原因の脳の損傷による影響が緩和されるよう，その医者は薬を処方した」

解説 「重度の卒中が原因」とあるので，**3**「脳の，大脳の」損傷があると考えられる。**1**「共同社会の，共有の」，**2**「同じ性質の」，**4**「本物の」。

(5) 解答 **4**

「その2国の大統領は，両国が共有する国境沿いに平和維持軍を配置する内容が盛り込まれた和平案を退けた」

解説 peacekeeping forces「平和維持軍」は**4**「配置，配備」するもの。**1**「否認，否定」，**2**「態度，品行」，**3**「中傷，誹謗(ひぼう)」。

(6) 解答 **2**

「自転車のこれらのギアは，時間の経過による摩耗を防ぐため，オイルやグリースで定期的に油を差すべきだ」

解説 「オイルやグリース」を使ってされることなので，**2**「油を差されて，滑らかにされて」が正解。**1**「助長されて」，**3**「補強されて」，**4**「無効にされて」。

(7) 解答 **2**

「その政治漫画家は，影響力のある人々の顔立ちを誇張して滑稽に見せる風刺漫画で有名である」

解説 政治漫画家がすることは，影響力のある人々の**2**「風刺漫画，戯画」を描くこと。**1**「ことわざ」，**3**「愛国者」，**4**「郊外」。

(8) 解答 **1**

「新薬の効能と安全性を検査するため，研究対象の3分の1にはその薬が，別の3分の1には偽薬が与えられ，残りの3分の1には何も与えられなかった」

解説 新薬の検査で，「3分の1には新薬，3分の1には何も渡さなかった」とあるので，残りの3分の1には**1**「偽薬，プラシーボ」が渡されたと考えるのが自然。プラシーボは，薬効はなく臨床試験の対照剤として使用される。**2**「つねること」，**3**「(船舶・列車などの) 積荷目録」，**4**「突風」。

(9) 解答 **1**

「その会社の最新の製品の安全性を問題にしたテレビ報道の後，その会社には電話が殺到した」

解説 テレビ報道で製品の安全性が問われたのだから，電話が**1**「殺到した」はず。be inundated with ～ で「～が殺到する」の意味。**2**「ふびんに思った」，**3**「包

まれた」，**4**「飾られた」。

(10) 解答 **3**

A「この嵐で多くの被害が出たよ。水浸しの中心街の映像を見たかい」

B「もちろん見たわ。ほとんど完全に水没した車もあったの。かろうじてその屋根が見えるくらいだったわ」

解説 町の中心地では洪水が発生しているのだから，車はほとんど**3**「水没した」はず。**1**「ぎょっとした」，**2**「引き伸ばされた」，**4**「力を弱められた」。

(11) 解答 **1**

A「新しいプロジェクトチームにジャックはいらないと君が言っていると，ジャックは聞いたらしい。彼は少し怒っているよ」

B「彼が聞いた話は誤解されているわ。私はぜひ彼をプロジェクトチームに入れたいんだけど，彼は既にやるべき仕事を十分すぎるほど抱えているのよ」

解説 Bは「ジャックはいらない」と言ったと思われているが，実際には「ぜひ欲しい」と思っている。つまり，「ジャックはいらない」という彼女の発言は「誤解されている」とわかる。**1**「誤解された」が正解。**2**「懐疑的な」，**3**「はっきりと確定できない」，**4**「非現実的な，実体のない」。

(12) 解答 **2**

「冬休みの前日で生徒たちは気もそぞろだったので，先生は彼らに楽しい活動をさせてやることにした」

解説 on the day before their winter vacation「冬休みの前日」から生徒たちの心理状態を考えれば，**2**「(心・注意が) 散漫な」が正解だとわかる。**1**「ばかにされた」，**3**「外観を損なった」，**4**「手の込んだ」。

(13) 解答 **1**

「メアリーは自分の最初の小説が最高の文学賞を受賞したと聞き有頂天だった。彼女は祝賀パーティーを開くことにした」

解説 文学賞を受賞し，自ら祝賀パーティーまで開くことにしたのだから，その様子は**1**「有頂天」と言える。**2**「落胆した」，**3**「怒った」，**4**「自発的な」。

(14) 解答 **3**

「刑事たちは容疑者を一人一人尋問して強盗事件の真相を聞き出そうとしたが，彼らの話は矛盾していて，捜査員はいっそう混乱するばかりだった」

解説 刑事の仕事は真相を**3**「引き出す」こと。

contradictoryは「矛盾した」の意味。**1**「～を即興で作る」，**2**「～を奇襲する」，**4**「～を空中に浮かせる」。

(15) 解答 **1**

「ケンの母親は，鮮やかな色でほかにないデザインの，特徴のある服を着るのを好む」

解説 「鮮やかな色でほかにないデザイン」の服は**1**「特徴のある」服である。**2**「疑われる」，**3**「冷淡な，無感覚な」，**4**「手ごわい，恐るべき」。

(16) 解答 **1**

「ビルは自動車の組立ラインで働くのを心待ちにしていたが，数カ月してその仕事が退屈になり，新しい仕事を見つけたくなった」

解説 新しい仕事を見つけたくなったのだから，今の仕事は**1**「つまらない」と思っていると考えられる。**2**「ずるい」，**3**「輝く，明快な」，**4**「天の，神聖な」。

(17) 解答 **4**

「もし黙ったままで人としゃべらずにいるなら，無関心でよそよそしいと思われるだろう」

解説 黙っていて人と話さない人は，無関心で**4**「よそよそしい」人だと言える。**1**「荒れ狂った」，**2**「みだらな」，**3**「理不尽な」。

(18) 解答 **4**

「その社員は職務をおざなりに行った。実際，彼女の仕事は非常にずさんでサービスも粗悪だったので，顧客からよく苦情がきた」

解説 2文目からこの社員のずさんな仕事ぶりがわかるので，**4**「おざなりに，いい加減に」が正解。**1**「便宜上」，**2**「博学で」，**3**「遺伝的に」。

(19) 解答 **3**

「チャールズは夜ほとんど起きて小論文を書いていた

ので，授業中に居眠りするのをこらえ切れなかった」

解説 ほぼ徹夜だったというのだから，授業中に**3**「居眠りをする」のをこらえられなかったと考えられる。**1**「（人が）死ぬ」，**2**「興奮する，夢中になる」，**4**「～を箱に詰める」。

(20) 解答 **4**

「誤配線がおそらくその火事の原因だったが，徹底的な調査が済むまでは放火の可能性を除外しないと火災調査員は言った」

解説 「徹底的な調査が済むまで」とあるので，別の可能性を**4**「除外」しないのだと考えられる。arson は「放火」。**1**「（会話・交際）を始める，（曲）を演奏し始める」，**2**「～を保釈する」，**3**「～を考え抜く，案出する」。

(21) 解答 **4**

「多くのボランティアがハリケーンの後，熱心に協力し片付けの手伝いをしたので，町は当局の当初の予想よりずっと早く復旧した」

解説 「ハリケーンの後に…して清掃を手伝った」という流れにふさわしいのは，**4**「協力する」。**1**「認める，白状する」，**2**「くんくんかぎ回る」，**3**「～を削除する，切り離す」。

(22) 解答 **2**

「パーティーは8時に始まる予定で，たくさん人が来る。いいものを食べたいなら8時半までにジルの家に着いた方がいい」

解説 パーティーの時間が話題になっている。ジルの家に「到着する，姿を見せる」という意味になる**2**が正解。**1**「殴りかかる」，**3**「～を見捨てる，放棄する」，**4**「～を副産物として生み出す」。

2

全訳

ニコラウス・コペルニクスの影響

　15世紀後半，惑星論は論争を起こす問題であり，「天文学」と「占星術」という用語はほとんど同義で，どちらもより大きな「星の科学」の下位区分だった。現代の用語では占星術を，主に占星図と毎年恒例の予言

に関連して疑似科学のようなものだと考える人もいるだろうが，当時は明確な区別はされていなかった。後から見ると簡易で誤りがあるように見えるかもしれないが，当時，天をより微細に理解するために数学的技術は広く使われており，惑星の状態や動きを説明するための理論的手段や運動表を作り出していた。

この歴史的背景は，ニコラウス・コペルニクスの発見と理論が非常に画期的だった理由の一部を成す。当時，天体の一般的に認められた理解は，宇宙の中心に動かない地球を置き，ほかの惑星や星がその周りを回っているというもので，その順序も激しい論争の的となっていた。コペルニクスは，動かない太陽を中心に据え，地球を含むほかの惑星が決められた順序と軌道上にあるという宇宙の地動説を展開した。コペルニクスは自分の発見を1543年，革新的な本『天球の回転について』で発表し，それがガリレオ，ニュートン，ケプラーのような人々によるほかの偉大な発見の道を開いた。

コペルニクスは宗教が非常に重要でカトリック教会が相当な権力をふるっていた時代に生きており，それゆえ彼の著書のうわさがバチカンの興味を引いたとき，励ましと懸念の両方の原因となった。教会は天文学を含む科学の主要な出資者ではあったが，時には新しい科学理論を提起したものを迫害することもあった。この背景で，コペルニクスが最初，特に宗教界からの軽蔑と批判を恐れ，『天球の回転について』の出版に反対していたこと，そして本をローマ教皇パウルス3世に捧げるきっかけとなった理由の説明がつく。彼の本は，生存中はさほど論議を呼ぶことはなかったものの，本で提起した理論の弁護は16世紀におけるガリレオの悪名高い裁判につながった。

(23) 解答 **3**

解説 現代では占星術がどう見られているか，という文脈。占星図と予言から連想されるのは**3**。1「主として学究的世界の領域」，2「綿密な思想や過程を完全に欠いている」，4「単なるつまらない見せかけ」。

(24) 解答 **4**

解説 宇宙の地動説の説明がされているので，**4**が正解。1「宇宙論の用語では事実上無関係」，2「不定の星や物質の周りを回転している」，3「天体の順序の妥当性を得るために争っている」。

(25) 解答 **2**

解説 宗教界からの批判を恐れていたという文脈の中なので**2**が適切。1「自分の理論の死後の出版を求める」，3「出版権に桁はずれな料金を要求する」，4「経済学と外交関係の分野に焦点を絞る」。

全訳

アブラヤシ農園

ヤシ油は世界の植物油市場の33％を占め，料理からバイオ燃料の生成まであらゆるものに使われている。しかし，国際自然保護連合（IUCN）による最近の研究は，アブラヤシ農業が環境にとって破滅的だということを示している。インドネシアやマレーシアのような国々では，アブラヤシ農園が原生林を侵略しており，壊れやすい生態系を徹底的に破壊している。アブラヤシ農園の拡大は，オランウータン，ギボン，トラを含む190種以上の絶滅危惧種を脅かしているのだ。さらに悪いことに，ヤシ油の需要が高まるにつれてさらなる開発が進むと，全絶滅危惧哺乳類の半分以上と全絶滅危惧鳥類のおよそ3分の2の環境が脅かされることになる。

「持続可能」というお墨付きのヤシ油は，人跡未踏の熱帯雨林の破壊の防止という点ではほんのわずかましなだけである。持続可能性の認定は，アブラヤシ農園が森林破壊を引き起こしているのではないと消費者に請け合うために作られたものだ。全ヤシ油の約20％を保証する，持続可能なパーム油のための円卓会議（RSPO）の広報担当者は，保証システムは大いに良い影響をもたらしてきたと主張する。不完全ではあるが，システムは森林破壊に対する戦いにおいて重要な役割を果たしてきた。しかし，グリーンピースUKのリチャード・ジョージは，それは全く正しくないと断言する。彼の広告監視機関は「オランウータンの生息環境を破壊したのを含め，RSPOのメンバーがアブラヤシのために森林破壊を行う現場を何度も押さえた」ということだ。

あいにく，問題に対する簡単な解決策はない。1つの大きな問題は新しいアブラヤシ農園の状況だ。これまでに耕作された農園の複雑な所有権問題を処理するより，原生林を切り倒す方が簡単な場合がよくある。加えて，しばしば農園は作物収穫量が低い荒廃地に追いやられている。さらなる環境被害を止める試みとして，EUは2030年までにバイオ燃料におけるヤシ油の使用を禁止する法律を通した。ただし，ヤシ油を完全に禁止すれば，おそらく大豆やトウモロコシ，菜種などほかのタイプの油の生産増加につながるだろう。そうした油料作物はアブラヤシ農園が占める土地の9倍もの耕地を使うので，そうなるとアルゼンチンやブラジルといった，世界のほかの地域の野生生物の生態系の大量破壊を引き起こす。言い換えれば，ヤシ油の禁止は，おそらく問題をほかの生態系に移動し，より広範囲の破壊と生物多様性の喪失をもたらすことになるの

だ。

(26) 解答 **1**

解説 アブラヤシ農園が生態系を破壊しているという文脈なので，**1**が適切。**2**「古い農園に替わっており」，**3**「さまざまな絶滅危惧種の生息地となっており」，**4**「最新の農業技術を導入しており」。

(27) 解答 **1**

解説 保証システムを作った団体の広報担当者の主張

なので，**1**が適切。**2**「あまり期待できなさそうだ」，**3**「ほかの国々に拡大するべきだ」，**4**「改良する必要がある」。

(28) 解答 **1**

解説 続く文は農園の所有権問題，荒廃地の問題などに触れているので，これらをまとめる**1**が正解となる。**2**「熱帯の生態系の壊れやすさ」，**3**「アブラヤシ収穫の複雑さ」，**4**「ヤシ油の競争上の優位性」。

3

全訳

科学を助けるハンターたち

　捕鯨は何世紀にもわたってアラスカ土着の文化の一部だったが，1977年，国際捕鯨委員会（IWC）はホッキョククジラ捕鯨定数をゼロとすることによってそれを危うくした。IWCは，クジラの数が危険なほど少ないと結論づけた。なぜなら，クジラは氷を怖がると考え，開放水面で泳いでいるのが見えるクジラだけを数えたからである。アラスカ先住民の捕鯨リーダーたちは抗議して，自らグループを作り，クジラは氷を恐れないこと，そして先に見積もられたよりも数はずっと多いことを証明しようとした。別の科学者グループが彼らの主張を支持し，禁止令は解除され，生計のために捕鯨を行っている地域社会にとって救済になったばかりか，ハンターと科学者の新たな提携の始まりともなった。

　こうした関係のおかげで，ハンス・テウィッセンのような科学者たちは，これまではできなかったやり方でクジラに近づき，かつては不可能だった実験を行うことが可能になった。クジラは保護種なので，テウィッセンと科学者たちは普通遠くから観察するしかなく，新鮮な死体で実験をする機会はほとんどなかった。少し恐ろしいように思えるが，捕鯨リーダーたちの季節ごとの漁を追うことで，彼はクジラの行動と生態を理解する上でいくつもの大発見をすることができた。それにはホッキョククジラが嗅覚を有するという発見も含まれる。これについても，クジラが嗅覚を有するという示唆はハンターたちからもたらされた。焚き火をしているとクジラは岸から離れて泳ぐので，焚火の匂いがわかるのだと彼らは信じるようになったのだ。クジラに匂いがわかるという示唆は，最初は退けられた。

水の中で暮らす動物には空中の匂いを嗅げることなど無用だからだ。しかし，テウィッセンは新しいホッキョククジラの頭を入手して，脳を調べた後，意外にもそれは本当だと証明した。

　ハンターたちが科学的に知られていなかったクジラの骨格に関する情報を含め，知識だけでなく捕獲したクジラまで進んで共有したことは，科学者たちの研究を大いに助けた。こうした協力はしかし，必ずしも進んで提供されたわけではなく，信頼を築くまでにはそれを育む長い時間が必要だった。最初，多くのハンターが1977年のIWC割り当てにまだ動揺しており，自分たちが与えた知識は政府に漁禁止のために利用されるのではないかと心配していた。見返りとして科学者たちは，自分たちが漁についていきたいのは純粋に科学のためで，政治や，多くが野蛮な行為だと信じていたことを暴露したいという動機のためではないとわかってもらえるよう努力しなくてはならなかった。捕鯨反対の風潮は世界中で高まり続け，地域の生息環境を脅かす環境問題と相まって，アラスカにおける捕鯨の伝統に終止符を打ちかねない。この件については，科学者たちの記録が，将来の世代のためにクジラに関する地元の知識を保存するのに役立つだろう。

(29) 解答 **2**

「IWCのクジラの頭数の見積もりはアラスカ先住民のハンターたちのデータに比べてどうだったか」

1 IWCの調査結果は，クジラは寒さが嫌いだと指摘したアラスカ先住民が正しかったことを裏づけた。

2 この件におけるハンターたちの知識は，IWCが達した当初の結論より優れていることが判明した。

3 ハンターたちとIWCの間の問題を解決するために，

科学者たちはデータを説明することを申し出た。

4 何世紀にもわたる漁が行われてきたにもかかわらず，クジラの数は安定していることをIWCは発見した。

解説　クジラの頭数に関する記述は第1段落にある。IWCは氷の下にクジラがいないと考え，海面から観察できる頭数だけを数えたが，アラスカのハンターたちはクジラは氷を恐れないので，IWCの見積もりよりずっと数は多いと主張したとある。従って，この内容に合う**2**が正解。

(30) 解答 3

「科学者とハンターの研究は，クジラの理解にどのような効果を及ぼしたか」

1 研究のおかげで科学者は焚き火のための新鮮な肉を得て，ぞっとするような漁について学ぶことができた。

2 科学者たちは，遠くから観察したおかげで，クジラについて広く信じられているいくつかの考えを退けることができた。

3 科学者たちは，かつてはできなかったクジラへの近接からだけでなく，現地の専門知識からも恩恵を受けた。

4 社会学的観点からは貴重だが，研究は新たな科学的知識は生まなかった。

解説　科学者とハンターの研究については第2段落に説明されている。第3文に，クジラの行動と生態を理解する上でいくつもの大発見をすることができたとある。直接脳を調べたこと，ハンターの知識がもたらした情報も手助けをしたという内容に一致するのは**3**。

(31) 解答 3

「アラスカ先住民のハンターと科学者の関係は，時間とともにどのように発展したか」

1 最初は友好的だったが，双方にプログラム全体をだめにしそうになるほどのますますの不信がある。

2 ハンターと科学者のどちらも，捕鯨産業について広がりを見せる懸念を政治化しようと働いた。

3 最初の懸念にもかかわらず，関係は効果的で，アラスカ先住民のハンターが伝統を守るのにも役立つかもしれない。

4 最初は有益だったが，漁と侵略的な科学実験が今や環境を脅かしている。

解説　最終段落では，ハンターと科学者の関係の推移が説明されている。ハンターたちは，最初は政治的に利用されるかと心配していたが，最終的に信頼関係が築かれたこと，さらに最終文には，将来の世代のため

にクジラに関する知識を保存するのに科学者の記録が役立つだろうとある。この内容を網羅した**3**が正解。

全訳

AI軍隊の増大

　殺人ロボットの概念はたいてい『ターミネーター』や『ロボコップ』のようなSF映画のイメージを思い出させるが，自律型殺傷兵器は開発されているだけではなく，現在使われている。韓国政府のためにサムソンが開発した定位置監視銃は，監視して，報道によると自主的に発砲することができるが，それができるのはこの銃だけではない。英国は人間が操縦する戦闘機の代わりになるドローンを開発中である。空対空，また空対地兵器を運び，大陸間で作動するだけではなく，完全な自律性も組み込まれる。ロシアとアメリカを含むほかの国々は，戦車，軍艦，潜水艦，人型ロボットを含む自律型兵器を開発中だ。

　特に米国政府の下で開発されている2つのシステムについては，人間を完全に無防備にしかねないと学者たちは警告している。アメリカ国防高等研究計画局（DARPA）は操作者との連絡から独立して，ターゲットを追跡し殺傷することができるドローンを作ろうとしている。カリフォルニア大学バークリーのコンピュータ科学教授スチュアート・ラッセルのような学者たちは，このような研究はジュネーブ協定を破りかねず，人類が道徳基準を持たない機械の管理下に置かれるという終末論的シナリオにつながりかねないと主張している。テクノロジーが進歩を続ける速度は，うわべは自覚を持った高度に武装した機械が，数十年と言わず数年のうちに戦闘に配備されるだろうことを意味している。それが不安の度合いを非常に高めているのだ。

　人工知能（AI）とロボット工学企業の創設者やシリコンバレーの重役たちを含む，ロボット技術とAIの最先端にいる人々でさえ，自律型兵器のさらなる発展と使用を禁止するよう国連を促し続けている。こうした兵器を禁止しろという要求の裏にある理由は，殺人ロボットのための現在の兵器開発競争を止め，これ以上先に行くことを防ぐためだ。26カ国100人以上の専門家が署名した国連への手紙は，このような兵器開発競争は火薬と核兵器の開発と使用に続く「戦争の第3革命」を引き起こしかねないと主張している。この兵器開発競争は，過去に見られたものとは全く異なるものになるだろう。なぜなら自律型殺傷兵器は，ほとんど想像できないほどの規模の武力紛争を可能にするからだ。

Day
7

もう1つの大きな懸念は，人間的な要素の，ひいては道徳的要素の除去である。単にターゲットを探して破壊するようプログラムされた機械は，そのターゲットが何であるかに関係なく，そうすることができる。これは，何の罪もない人々がテロリストや独裁者の目標とされるという恐ろしい可能性を提起する。自律型殺傷兵器システムを，化学兵器やそのほかの兵器とともに，国連の特定通常兵器使用禁止制限条約（CCW）の下，禁止兵器のリストに加えるべきだという要求を促したのは道徳的要素である。さらに，すべてのコンピュータ制御機械と同様，機能不全とハッキングという副次的なリスクもある。これらとそのほかの理由で，さらなる産業化した戦争よりもむしろ平和のためのAIを追求すべきだという声が次第に高まっているのだ。

「人工知能の名づけ親」という名で呼ばれる男性，ジェフリー・ヒントン教授でさえ，これが人々を全体としてのAIに敵対させるべきではないとしながらも，自立型兵器の配備には反対している。彼は兵器化されたAIシステムに反対するばかりか，民間人に対する監視をますます強めるために政府によってAIが使用されることや，彼の研究がセキュリティー・サービスによって乱用されることを恐れてもいる。こうした懸念を抱えながらではあるが，ヒントンはAIの有効利用については楽観的な姿勢を崩さない。最初の妻をがんで失くし，2人目の妻も同じ病いに屈するのを目撃したヒントンは，AIを利用すればコストが大きく減り人間のミスがほぼゼロになるのだから，医学ははるかに有能になると信じている。

道徳性は，戦闘におけるAIの使用に関連する唯一の人間的要素ではなく，それこそが軍が戦場でこのようなシステムを使いたがっている理由なのかもしれない。知能ロボットは疲れることがなく，作動しながら学ぶことができ，費用効率が非常に高く，おそらくミスを犯しにくい。戦争がどれほど隊員と，影響を受ける社会を疲弊させるかを考えると，潜在的結果が壊滅的だとしても，軍が軍事目的でAIを利用したがるのも無理もない。工場で反復作業を行う機械は厳しく監視でき，必要ならプラグを抜いて電気を切ることもできるのに対して，極秘に何千マイルも離れた所で自律して稼働する知的戦闘機械はずっと操作が難しい。自律型機械によって罪のない命が失われ残虐行為が行われるリスクはつまり，これ以上の開発を注意深く監視する必要があるということを意味する。戦争の未来はSFの領域に向かっているのかもしれない。科学者，軍事戦略家，政治家やそのほかの指導者たちが革命に対処する

準備ができているかどうか，現時点では不明である。

(32) 解答 3

「世界の自律型兵器システムの現在の状態について正しいのはどれか」

1 自律型兵器システムの開発は，非常に速い速度で進んでおり，兵器はすでに操作者に逆らっている。

2 道徳心がない機械は，国際的な操作が認められ，定位置に制限されないことを要求している。

3 軍は，人間から独立して稼働するだけではなく，人間に取って代われる兵器システムを開発中だ。

4 自律型兵器システムは厳しい法的制約の下でのみ，戦車や潜水艦とともに戦闘に配備される運命にある。

解説 第1段落最終文に，「ロシアとアメリカを含むほかの国々は，戦車，軍艦，潜水艦，人型ロボットを含む自律型兵器を開発中だ」とある。この内容を言い換えた**3**が正解。

(33) 解答 2

「自律型兵器の使用について，ますます多くの技術専門家や指導者たちはどう感じているか」

1 AI技術の専門家は自律型兵器の禁止は新たな兵器開発競争につながると考えている。

2 AIシステムの開発を導いた人々でさえ，それが武力衝突に使われることについて懸念している。

3 AI兵器の開発に関わった多くの人々は，国連がAI兵器の配備を妨げるべきではないと感じている。

4 そうした指導者たちは武力衝突を革命的に変化させる手助けをしており，配備へのバリアが引き上げられるのを見たがっている。

解説 technology specialists and leaders と同義の表現は第3段落の冒頭にある those at the forefront of robotics technology and artificial intelligence (AI) である。従って，この段落に彼らの考え，感じていることが述べられている。正解は**2**。

(34) 解答 4

「一部の人々はなぜ，AIシステムの禁止に関する道徳議論は，安全に関する議論と同じように重要だと考えているか」

1 そうした兵器を自律型にすることは，型破りな方法と戦略を使ってターゲットを破壊することにつながる。

2 関連するテクノロジーはハッキングやテロリズムと戦うことに役立てるべきだ。

3 自律型兵器は現在単純すぎて，政府が平時の国民を

監視するのにあまり役立たない可能性がある。

4 その技術は罪のない国民を数え切れないほどの有害なやり方で標的にしかねない。

解説　第4段落第3文に「何の罪もない人々がテロリストや独裁者の目標とされるという恐ろしい可能性を提起する」とある。この内容に合った**4**が正解。

(35)　解答　**2**

「人間とAIシステムを差別化するどのような要素が，戦闘で自律型兵器を使う前に徹底的に検討される必要があるか」

1 AI兵器システムのコストが，兵士やそのほかの軍事人員に置きかえるメリットをはるかに超える。

2 自律型兵器は肉体的限界は感じにくいが，戦争犯罪を防ぐ行動規範に欠ける。

3 AIシステムは武力衝突の潜在的結果の概念がなく，自分たちのミスを正すことができない。

4 ロボット兵器システムは，軍指導者と政治家よりずっと武力衝突の将来の備えがある。

解説　最終段落の第2文に「疲れることがなく，作動しながら学び，費用効率が高く，ミスを犯しにくい」という知能ロボットのメリットが説明されている。しかし最後の3文では，AIには「自律型機械によって罪のない命が失われ残虐行為が行われるリスク」があると述べられている。この内容に合った**2**が正解。

4

問題文の訳

　近年，世界中で熱波や自然災害が増えていることが示す通り，地球温暖化は極めて深刻になりつつあり，現在の削減努力は功を奏していないのかもしれない。結果的に人類にとっての一番の希望は，「地球工学」として知られる考えを探求することかもしれないと示唆している研究者の数が増加している。これは，世界規模で地球温暖化の影響に対抗するために先進技術を利用することを指している。それにより，より持続可能で低炭素の未来へと移行する貴重な時間稼ぎになるだろうと考えている科学者は多い。

　可能性がある地球工学の手法の1つは太陽放射管理であり，それには少量の太陽エネルギーを反射させて宇宙に戻すことが含まれる。これはエアロゾルと呼ばれる微小の粒子を大気の上層部に注入して人工の雲を作り出したり，巨大なスペースミラーを利用したりすることにより達成できるだろう。これらの雲，あるいは鏡が，火山灰がこれまで地球を冷やしてきたのとまさに同様に，太陽光が地球を暖めるのを防ぐだろう。もう1つの方法は二酸化炭素の除去であり，炭素を本物の葉より効率的に吸収するプラスチック製の葉を持つ人工樹木といった装置が利用される。吸収された炭素はその後，地中やその他の長期貯蔵施設に保管されるだろう。

　地球工学は期待が持てる一方で，深刻な懸念も引き起こしている。例えば，生態系や天候に意図しない結果を生じさせるかもしれない。ありうることの1つとして，地球表面の反射率を変えると降雨パターンに影響が出て，局地的に気候を乱してしまうかもしれない。さらに，「応急措置」として地球工学に頼ると，温暖化ガスの放出を減らす緊急性に潜在的な影響を与えかねない。これは，より環境にやさしいエネルギーシステムをもたらすための努力の妨げになりうる。したがって，持続可能な行動と再生可能なエネルギー源を通じて温暖化ガスを減らす努力を引き続き優先させつつ，慎重に，そしてその潜在的な影響力を深く理解しながら地球工学に取り組んでいくことが極めて重要である。

解答例

　The environmental crisis is becoming so serious that some researchers are suggesting the use of geoengineering, which is the use of advanced technology to disrupt global warming, until other solutions can be found. Two examples of these geoengineering techniques are solar radiation management, in

解答例の訳

　環境危機はとても深刻になりつつあるので，一部の研究者は，別の解決法が見つけられるまで地球工学の利用を提案している。それは地球温暖化が進まないようにするために先進技術を利用するものである。こうした地球工学のテクニックの2つの例として，太陽放射管理という地球に届く太陽光の量を減らすことと，人工樹木のような装置を利用した二酸化炭素の除去が

which the amount of sunlight reaching the Earth would be reduced, and carbon dioxide removal through devices like artificial trees. However, there are worries that geoengineering could result in damaging changes in climate patterns or that it may distract society from creating a greener energy system. Therefore, geoengineering proposals should be thoroughly studied as we keep our main focus on using sustainable methods and renewable energy. (110語)

ある。しかしながら，地球工学は結果的に気候パターンの有害な変化につながりかねないという懸念や，より環境にやさしいエネルギーシステムの創造から社会の注意をそらしてしまうかもしれないという懸念がある。したがって，持続可能な方法と再生可能なエネルギーを利用することに最も集中し続けながら，地球工学の提案は徹底的に検討されるべきである。

解説 トピックは第1段落第1文の global warming is becoming extremely serious, and current efforts to reduce it may not be effective と，第2文 As a result, a growing number of researchers are suggesting that humanity's best hope may be to explore a concept known as "geoengineering." より，地球温暖化を解決する手段としての「地球工学」だとわかる。なお，この英文は「地球工学」について，地球温暖化対策の観点から詳しく述べたもので，全体を通して具体的な話が続く。そのため，これまでのDayのように各段落の要旨をまとめるのは簡単ではないかもしれない。端的に言うと，第1段落は「地球工学」の提示，第2段落は「地球工学」でできること，第3段落は「地球工学」の弊害についてである。それを踏まえた各段落の要旨は，第1段落：地球工学を使うことで，地球温暖化の影響に対抗し，環境にやさしい将来に移行するまでの時間稼ぎができる可能性がある。第2段落：地球工学を利用した方法の例として，人工の雲を作ったり，スペースミラーを利用したりして太陽光を反射させる太陽放射管理と，人工樹木を利用してより効率的に二酸化炭素を吸収する二酸化炭素の除去がある。第3段落：地球工学の利用は生態系や天候に思わぬ影響を与える可能性があるので，その利用は慎重にすべきであり，温暖化ガスを減らす努力を優先的に進めていかなければならない。解答の際はこれらを問題文とは異なる表現に言い換えてまとめる。解答例では，第1段落の地球温暖化の影響を軽減することを disrupt global warming と表現している。第2段落の具体的な手法については，Two examples are solar radiation management and carbon dioxide removal. という構造の文を使い，solar radiation management と carbon dioxide removal それぞれについて非制限用法の関係詞などを使って説明を加えることできれいにまとめている。第3段落の，温暖化ガスを減らす努力を優先的に進めていかなければならないことについては，keep one's main focus on ～ という表現を使い，we keep our main focus on using sustainable methods and renewable energy と自分の言葉で説明している。

5

問題の訳
TOPIC：賛成か反対か：動物を使った実験は直ちに禁止すべきだ

解答例①

　Every year billions of sentient animals, including dogs, monkeys, rabbits, and rats, are tortured and killed in experiments to provide evidence that new products are safe for humans. However, animal testing is immoral, unreliable, and unnecessary.

解答例①の訳

　毎年，イヌやサル，ウサギ，ネズミなど，何十億もの感覚を持つ動物が，ひどい苦痛を与えられ，殺されています。人間が新製品を使っても安全であることを証明する実験のためにです。しかし，動物を使った実験は道徳に反し，当てにならず，不必要なのです。

　動物を使った実験に反対する上でまず言っておきた

The first argument against animal testing is that it is immoral. Animals are sentient beings with central nervous systems. They feel fear and pain just like humans do and suffer greatly when confined to cages and experimented on. Even if animal testing was effective, it would still be morally indefensible to use animals in this way.

Animal testing is also extremely unreliable. The bodies of animals are not exactly the same as our own. The results of animal experiments can be very misleading, as drugs that may be beneficial to humans can cause illness in animals, and vice versa. In fact, 90 percent of medicines that pass animal testing go on to fail human trials. This is a massive waste of life, time, and resources.

And finally, animal testing is simply unnecessary. These days, there are many methods of testing drugs that are superior to animal testing. These include computer models and experimenting on cell cultures.

In conclusion, animal testing is an outdated system that is both morally indefensible and unreliable. As it is also unnecessary, it would be better for both humans and animals to abolish animal testing as soon as possible and replace it with modern technology instead. (236語)

いことは，道徳に反するということです。動物は中枢神経系を備えた，感覚を有する生き物です。人間同様，恐怖や痛みを感じます。そして，かごに閉じ込められ，実験対象とされると，大いに苦しむのです。たとえ動物を使った実験が効果的だとしても，このような方法で動物を使うことは道徳的に擁護のしようがないでしょう。

動物を使った実験は，極めて当てにならないものでもあります。動物の体は私たちのものと全く同じわけではありません。動物実験の結果は誤解を招く可能性があります。ある薬は，人間には効果があるかもしれなくても，動物に投与すると病気になることがあり，その逆もまた然りなのです。実際，動物を使った試験で合格した医薬品の90％は，人間で試すと不合格となります。これは命，時間，資源の大変な無駄使いです。

そして最後に，動物を使った実験はただ単に不必要です。最近の医薬品検査の方法には，動物を使った実験に勝るものがたくさんあります。例えばコンピュータモデルを使った方法や，細胞を培養して行う実験などです。

結論としては，動物を使った実験は時代遅れで，道徳的に弁護の余地がなく，当てにもならないシステムです。さらに不必要であり，動物を使った実験は即刻廃止し，代わりに最近の技術を導入した方が，人間のためにも動物のためにもなるでしょう。

解説　序論では，賛成の立場を表明した上で「道徳に反する」，「当てにならない」，「不必要」と断じ，本論でどうしてそう考えるのかを詳しく説明している。第2段落では「道徳に反する」と考える理由を説明しており，動物にも感覚があることを根拠にしている。第1文の The first argument against 〜 is that ... は表現として覚えておくとよい。第3段落では「当てにならない」と考える理由を説明しており，具体的な数字を出して説明することで主張に説得力を持たせている。第4段落では「不必要」と考える理由を説明しており，具体的な代替手段を紹介している。最後の段落では理由と主張を改めてまとめている。この解答は動物を使った実験のことをとてもよく勉強している人の解答であり，実際にはここまで具体的に論じることは難しいだろう。あまりなじみのないトピックについては，具体例はある程度推測しても構わないので，自分の立場と理由は必ず明確にしておこう。

解答例②

Most companies are required by law to test their new medicines on animals. Therefore, an immediate ban on animal testing is unrealistic. Instead, we should make efforts to reduce the number of experiments by choosing cruelty-free products, taking care of our health, and encouraging alternative testing methods.

解答例②の訳

大半の企業では，法律によって動物を使って新薬の実験を行うことが義務づけられています。従って，直ちに動物を使った試験を禁止することは現実的ではありません。代わりに，私たちは動物実験件数を減らすためにあらゆる努力をするべきです。そのために残酷な手段を用いていない製品を選び，健康に気を使い，別の実験方法を推し進めていくのです。

Animal testing is mainly done for new household products and cosmetics. However, in most cases there are cruelty-free versions already available. We can reduce animal testing greatly by using our consumer power to buy these products instead. We can also choose not to buy new versions of existing medicines, as every new medicine is required by law to be tested on animals.

Another way we can reduce animal testing is by taking better care of our health. At present, many people suffer from lifestyle-related diseases, and a lot of animal research is on drugs for these diseases. If we make efforts to eat more healthily and exercise more, we could reduce our dependence on drugs and animal experiments.

And finally, we can encourage the use of alternative testing methods. In the case of Europe, cosmetic tests on animals were discontinued after non-animal methods were shown to be safe. If we continue to invest in new technologies, animal testing for medicines will also become redundant.

A ban on animal testing is not possible at present. As such, we should focus on reducing the number of animal experiments and also encourage alternative testing methods. (239語)

動物を使った実験は主に，新しい家庭用品や化粧品のために行われています。しかし，たいていの場合，残酷な手段を用いていない製品がすでに入手可能なのです。私たちはこうした製品を代わりに購入するという消費者パワーを使うことで，動物を使った実験を大幅に減らすことができます。また，既存の薬の新製品を買わないことを選ぶこともできます。新しい薬はすべて法律によって動物を使った実験が求められているからです。

動物を使った実験を減らすもう1つの方法は，自分たちの健康にもっと気を使うことです。現在，多くの人々がライフスタイルに関係する病気を患っており，多くの動物を使った研究はこうした病気の薬に関するものです。もっと健康的な食事をとり，運動を増やす努力をすれば，薬や動物実験にあまり頼らずに済むでしょう。

そして最後に，別の実験方法の利用を推し進めていくことができます。ヨーロッパの場合，動物を使った化粧品の実験は，動物を使わない方法でも安全であることが判明すると，中止になりました。新しい技術への投資を続ければ，動物を使った医薬品の実験も不要となるでしょう。

動物を使った実験の禁止は，現在は可能ではありません。それならば，私たちは動物実験の件数を減らすことに注力するべきであり，さらに代わりとなる実験方法も奨励していくべきなのです。

解説 序論では，「動物実験を直ちに禁止する」という考え自体は「現実的ではない」として否定している（反対の立場）。その後，「禁止をする代わりに消費者ができることがある」という話の展開にすることで，その手段を自分の立場を支持する理由としている。このように，単純に理由を3つ考えるのが難しい場合，少し視点を変えて理由づけすることも1つの方法である。解答例で述べられている3つのポイントは，「動物実験に頼らない製品を選ぶ」「健康に気を使い，動物実験が関係している薬に頼るのをやめる」「別の実験方法を推し進める」である。結論においても，動物実験の禁止よりもまずはその数を減らすべきだと述べて締めくくっている。このように，序論と結論は内容がほぼイコールになるようにすることで，書き手の一貫した考えが伝わる。

Listening Test

Part 1 🔊 101~111

No. 1 解答 **4**

★：Thank you, ma'am. Your change is $4.75, out of $70.

☆：Are you sure that's right? I thought it cost just a little over $60, so I should be getting more than $5 back.

★：You must be from out of state.

☆：Yes, I'm from Wyoming.

★：Ah, well, we pay over 8 percent sales tax here in California, not like you lucky people in Wyoming.

☆：Oh, yes, that's right. Sorry. I completely forgot about that.

Question：Why did the woman make a mistake?

★：ありがとうございます。70ドルお預かりしましたので，お釣りは4ドル75セントです。

☆：本当にそれで合っている？　60ドルちょっとだと思ったのだけど。だからお釣りは5ドル以上あるはずよ。

★：あなたは州外からいらっしゃいましたね。

☆：ええ，ワイオミングから来たわ。

★：ああ，あのですね，ここカリフォルニアでは8％以上の売上税を払うんですよ，幸運なワイオミングの皆さんとは違いましてね。

☆：あら，ええ，そうだったわね。ごめんなさい。そのことをすっかり忘れていたわ。

質問：女性はなぜ間違えたのか。

1 彼女は値引きをしてもらえると思った。　　**2** 彼女は売上税が上がったのを忘れていた。
3 彼女は商品の値段を正しく覚えていなかった。　　**4** 彼女は州による税金の違いを考えていなかった。

解説　女性はワイオミング州とカリフォルニア州で売上税率が異なることを忘れていたが，店員に指摘をされて，州による税率の違い（state tax differences）に気付いたのである。**4**が正解。

No. 2 解答 **4**

★：Hello, long-distance operator.

○：Hello. I'd like to place a long-distance collect call.

★：All right. Who is calling, please?

○：Olivia Jackson. And I'm making a call to Indianapolis, Indiana.

★：OK. And the number, please?

○：The number is 317-522-6098.

★：Just a minute while I check if the party you want to reach is available.

Question：Who is Olivia Jackson?

★：もしもし，長距離通話オペレーターです。

○：もしもし。長距離のコレクトコールをかけたいのですが。

★：かしこまりました。お名前をおうかがいできますか。

○：オリビア・ジャクソンです。インディアナ州インディアナポリスへの通話です。

★：わかりました。電話番号をどうぞ。

○：番号は317-522-6098です。

★：あなたがおかけになりたい相手の方がいらっしゃるか確認しますので，少々お待ちください。

質問：オリビア・ジャクソンとは誰か。

1 長距離通話オペレーター。　　**2** 女性が電話をかけている相手。
3 インディアナポリスにいる女性の顧客。　　**4** この電話をかけている人物。

解説　女性が話したい相手はインディアナにおり，そのために長距離オペレーターに電話をかけた際の会話である。ただし男性の Who is calling, please? が聞き取れれば，**4**が正解とわかる。Who is [Who's] calling? は電話口で「どちらさまですか」という意味。

No. 3 解答 **2**

★：I'm so mad at Carrie for telling the manager I'm not doing my job. Nobody works harder than I do.

○：I don't think Carrie would really say something like that. You know that William likes to play his team against each other.

★：You might be right about that. But why does he think disharmony and chaos are good for the department?

○：He feels that he has more power when the team is afraid to confide in each other.

★：Well, I don't like it. Let me check with Carrie, and if she didn't make those remarks, I'm going to give William a piece of my mind.

Question：According to the woman, what is the source of the problem?

★：僕が仕事をしていないとマネージャーに言ったことで，僕はキャリーにすごく怒っているよ。誰も僕ほど仕事をしていないのに。

○：キャリーが本当にそんなことを言うとは思わないわ。ウィリアムがチームのみんなを競争させたがるのは知っているでしょう。

★：君の言う通りかもしれない。でもどうして彼は不和と混乱が部署のためになると思うんだろう。

○：チームがお互いに信頼することを恐れているときの方が，彼はより権力を感じるのよ。

★：そうか，僕はそれはよくないと思う。キャリーに確認してくるよ。そしてもし彼女があの発言をしていなかったら，ウィリアムに遠慮なく言ってやる。

質問：女性によると，問題の源は何か。

1 キャリーは同僚に批判的すぎる。　　**2** マネージャーが意図的に信頼を壊している。
3 チームメンバーの何人かは信頼できない。　　**4** ウィリアムは特定のチームメンバーを選り好みする。

解説　男性は最初キャリーに対して怒っている。すると女性は，マネージャーであるウィリアムが（キャリーについて男性に嘘をつくことで）チームの競争心をあおっているのだと推測する。**2**が正解。

No. 4 解答 **2**

☆：Shall we watch another episode of *Hell's Rangers*? I want to know what happens next.

★：You know I can only watch it in small doses. There's too much blood and gore for me to binge-watch.

☆：But you know it's not real. And you said you like the acting and stories.

★：True, but I need to watch something less dark and morbid most of the time, especially when we're eating or right before bed.

☆：But you watch true-life crime programs, and some of those crimes are very intense.

★：Yes, but they're not nearly as graphic.

Question：What does the man say about *Hell's Rangers*?

☆：『ヘルズ・レンジャーズ』のエピソードをもう1つ見ましょうか。次に何が起きるのか知りたいの。

★：僕がちょっとずつしか見られないのは知っているだろう。あまりに流血が多いから一気には見られないよ。

☆：でも現実のことではないのよ。それに演技やストーリーは好きだって言っていたじゃない。

★：そうだけど，大半の時間は，それほど暗くなくて病的でないものを見る必要があるよ。特に食事中や就寝前にはね。

☆：でもあなたは実際に起きた犯罪の番組を見るじゃない。その中にはかなり強烈な犯罪もあるわよ。

★：ああ，でもそれほど生々しくはないよ。

質問：男性は『ヘルズ・レンジャーズ』について何と言っているか。

1 彼はその番組を見ることに耐えられない。　　**2** 彼は一度に数話しか見ない。
3 彼はそのストーリーは好きだが演技は好きでない。　　**4** 彼はそれを実際に起きた暴力事件よりも楽しんでいる。

解説　男性は最初の発言で You know I can only watch it in small doses. と言っている。in small doses を a few episodes at a time と言い換えている**2**が正解。

128

No. 5　解答　1

★：I'd like to retire in the British Virgin Islands. Remember how nice it was when we stopped there on our Caribbean cruise?

○：It was spectacular, but I wouldn't want to live there.

★：Why not? We could invite our family and friends, so we wouldn't get lonely. Besides, you mentioned the idea of retiring abroad.

○：Yes, but it's too remote and has a tiny population.

★：The U.S. is only a few hours away. Imagine going to an uncrowded beach every day.

○：We'd both get bored of that in no time. I need a city within reach for shopping and entertainment.

Question：What does the woman think of the man's retirement idea?

★：定年後はイギリス領バージン諸島に住みたいな。カリブ海クルーズで立ち寄ったときにどんなにすばらしかったか思い出してごらん。

○：すばらしかったわよね。でも私はそこには住みたくないわ。

★：なぜだい？　家族や友人を招くことができるから，寂しくはならないよ。それに外国で定年後をすごすアイデアは君が口にしていたじゃないか。

○：ええ，でも都会から離れすぎているし，人口もわずかなのよ。

★：米国からたった数時間だよ。毎日人があまりいないビーチに行くのを想像してごらん。

○：私たちは2人ともたちまちそれに飽きてしまうわ。私には買い物や娯楽がすぐに楽しめる街が必要なのよ。

質問：女性は男性の定年後のアイデアについてどう思っているか。

1 都市部に住む方がいいと思っている。　　2 外国で定年後をすごしたいと思っていない。
3 ビーチの近くで暮らす方がよい。　　4 もっと米国の近くに住みたい。

解説　男性のアイデアは I'd like to retire in the British Virgin Islands. というもの。これに対して女性は I wouldn't want to live there や it's too remote and has a tiny population と言い，最後には I need a city within reach for shopping and entertainment. と都会に住みたいとはっきり言っている。**1**が正解。

No. 6　解答　2

☆：It's great that we got our visas the same morning we applied for them.

★：Yes, considering the embassy website said they'd send back our passports five days after we turn in our application at the embassy. This was a lot faster than expected.

☆：Their site also said the embassy would be open at 9 a.m., but they didn't open until 10.

★：So we ended up waiting in the hot sun for 40 minutes. Ugh. And that's after walking 20 minutes from the train station and getting lost along the way.

☆：I wish they'd update their application explanation to avoid confusion.

Question：What are they complaining about?

☆：申し込んだその朝のうちにビザが取れたなんて，すばらしいわね。

★：そうだな，大使館のウェブサイトに，大使館に申請書を提出してから5日後にパスポートを返送すると書いてあることを考えるとね。思っていたよりずっと早い。

☆：ウェブサイトには大使館は9時に開くとも書いてあったけど，10時まで開かなかったわね。

★：だから暑い太陽の下で40分も待つはめになったんだよね。やれやれ。しかも駅から20分も歩いて，途中で迷った後だったしね。

☆：混乱を避けるために，大使館が申請に関する説明を更新してくれたらいいのに。

質問：彼らは何について不満を述べているか。

1 ビザの取得に予想よりも時間がかかった。
2 大使館のオンラインの情報は不正確だった。
3 パスポートを大使館に置いてこなければならなかった。

4 ビザの申請は必要以上に複雑だった。

解説　女性の最後の発言 I wish they'd update their application explanation to avoid confusion. から**2**が正解。ほかの発言からも，ビザの取得に必要な日数や大使館の開く時間がウェブサイトと異なっていたことがわかる。

No. 7　解答　4

☆：Excuse me, Professor Jenson, but could you tell me my grade for the semester?

★：Of course. Have a seat. Let's see ... oh, here we are. You got a B.

☆：Really? I was hoping for an A. What could I have done better? Was my final report the problem?

★：No, you got an A on the report. You received a B on the midterm and an A on the final test. However, you really didn't speak up in class much, and active participation was an important part of the grade. That really affected your grade.

☆：I see.

★：You'll have another chance during the fall semester.

Question：What brought the student's grade down the most?

☆：すみませんが，ジェンソン教授，今学期の私の成績を教えていただけませんか。

★：もちろんですよ。座って。どれどれ…ああ，これだ。君の成績はBです。

☆：本当ですか？　Aを取りたいと思っていたのですが。どうすればよかったのでしょうか。私の最終レポートが問題でしたか。

★：いいえ，レポートの成績はAですよ。中間試験はBで，期末試験はAでした。でも，授業であまり発言しませんでしたね。積極的な授業参加も成績の重要な部分でしたから。それがあなたの成績にとても影響したのです。

☆：わかりました。

★：秋学期にまたチャンスがありますよ。

質問：学生の成績を低下させた最大の原因は何か。

1 最終レポート。　　　　　　　　　　　**2** 中間試験。

3 期末試験。　　　　　　　　　　　　　**4** 授業への参加が十分でなかったこと。

解説　教授は2番目の発言の However 以下で，you really didn't speak up in class much, and active participation was an important part of the grade. That really affected your grade. と述べている。**4**が正解。

No. 8　解答　3

☆：I've always wanted to own my own restaurant. I'm thinking about quitting my job and looking for a restaurant for sale.

★：You're a great cook, and I'm even willing to invest our savings in a business. But frankly speaking, the restaurant business is risky. You've got to approach it the right way.

☆：You don't think I can succeed, do you?

★：It's not that. It would be far better to have experience in the business before you venture out on your own.

☆：All right, then. Let me see what jobs are available in the restaurant field, but I don't want to get stuck working in someone else's restaurant for too long.

Question：What does the woman agree to do?

☆：ずっと自分のレストランを持ちたいと思っていたの。仕事をやめて売りに出ているレストランを探そうかと思っているのよ。

★：君は料理がとても上手だからね。それに僕らの貯蓄を何かビジネスに投資したいと思っているよ。でも率直に言って，飲食業はリスクが大きいよね。うまく着手しないと。

☆：私は成功できないと思っているでしょう。

★：そういうことではないんだ。自分で事業に乗り出す前に，事業の経験を得た方がずっといいと思うんだ。

☆：だったら，わかったわ。レストランの分野でどんな仕事ができるか調べてみるわ。でも他人のレストランにとどまって長いこと働くのはごめんだわ。

質問：女性は何をすることに同意したか。

1 自分のレストランを開くこと。　　**2** ほかの資金源からお金を得ること。
3 専門的知識を得るために仕事をすること。　　**4** 現在の仕事を続けること。

解説 男性に It would be far better to have experience in the business before you venture out on your own. と経験を積むように言われた女性は, All right, then. Let me see what jobs are available in the restaurant field と答えている。have experience in the business を gain expertise と言い換えている**3**が正解。

No. 9　**解答**　**1**

★：I'm really impressed with Maximum Property Management. We've had almost no problems with renters, rent collection, or maintenance.	★：マキシマム・プロパティ・マネジメントは本当に素晴らしいね。賃借人，賃料の回収，メンテナンス，どれもほぼ何の問題もなかったよ。
○：Yes, I've been working closely with them and have observed their day-to-day operations, including how they thoroughly screen applicants. That's why problems and turnover have decreased.	○：ええ。私は彼らとずっと近くで働いてきて，日々のオペレーションをよく見てきたわ。彼らがどれだけ徹底して申込者をスクリーニングしているかとかね。だから問題の発生やテナントの空きが減少したのよ。
★：Would you recommend them for all of our properties?	★：すべての資産に彼らを推薦するかい？
○：For sure. Standard Management has been a disaster, so we've been planning on dropping them anyway. Maximum's pushing us to let them handle all our properties. As a come-on, they've offered a significant reduction in management fees if we go with them. There would certainly be benefits to consolidating.	○：絶対に。スタンダード・マネジメントはひどかったから，私たちはいずれにしろ彼らをボツにするつもりだったわね。マキシマムは私たちのすべての資産を任せてほしいと促してきているわ。売り文句としては，彼らに決めれば管理料を大幅に値下げすると言ってきたの。まとめれば確かに利益はあるわね。
★：Well, let's contact them and draw up a formal agreement with all these details spelled out. Make sure our attorney's there.	★：そうだね，彼らに連絡して，詳細をすべて説明した正式な合意文書を作ろう。必ず弁護士も同伴させるように。
Question：What do these people decide to do?	**質問**：この人たちは何をすることに決めているか。

1 新しい取り決めに関してマキシマムと連絡を取る。
2 期待を下回っているプロパティ・マネージャーにもっと多くのことを要求する。
3 スタンダード・マネジメントに連絡して彼らの決定について知らせる。
4 どちらの管理会社にもより良い仕事ぶりを求める。

解説 資産の管理会社の選定について男性と女性が話している。女性は一貫して Maximum Property Management を評価していて，男性も最後には Well, let's contact them and draw up a formal agreement with all these details spelled out. と言っている。**1**が正解。

No. 10　**解答**　**1**

☆：Hi, Christina. Do you know why we've called you in for a talk today?	☆：こんにちは，クリスティーナ。今日われわれが何の話であなたを呼んだかわかる？
○：Does it have anything to do with the interview I gave to Computer Life Magazine?	○：コンピュータ・ライフ・マガジン誌でのインタビューに関することでしょうか。
★：Exactly. You can imagine that some of your answers didn't show our company in the best light. Even more problematic, you announced the date of our new smartphone's release, which	★：その通りだよ。君が答えた内容には，当社のことを好意的に伝えていないものがあったことはわかるね。さらにもっと問題なのは，当社の新型スマートフォンの発売日を言ってしまったこ

hasn't yet been formally announced.

○：I understand completely. The interviewer asked me to lunch and told me that any comments would be off the record. I assumed it was safe to be open at that time.

☆：I can tell you from my experience in the Marketing Department that nothing's ever off the record.

○：I want to apologize about that. I realize I've made a huge mistake, and I promise to be more careful in the future. That is, if I still have a future with the company.

★：You won't be let go, if that's your concern. However, consider this an unofficial warning. If this happens again, we'll give you a written warning that goes into your personnel file.

☆：And before you give any more interviews, please check with someone in Marketing first so we can at least get our stories straight.

Question：What mistake did Christina make?

とだ。まだ正式発表していないのにね。

○：おっしゃることはすべて理解しています。記者が私をランチに誘って，一切のコメントはオフレコだと言っていたのです。オープンでいるのは問題ないとそのときは思ったのですが。

☆：マーケティング部での私自身の経験から言わせてもらうと，オフレコなんてものはないのよ。

○：その点はおわびしたいと思います。大失敗をしてしまったと認識していますし，今後はもっと注意するようにします。つまり，まだ会社にいていいのでしたら。

★：君がやめさせられることはないよ，もしその心配をしているならね。ただし，これは非公式の警告だと考えておきなさい。同じことがまた起きたら，個人記録として残るような文書化した警告を出すことになるよ。

☆：それから今度インタビューを受けることがあれば，その前にマーケティング部の誰かとチェックしてちょうだい。そうすれば少なくとも口裏を合わせることはできるわ。

質問：クリスティーナはどんな間違いをしたか。

1 機密情報をマスコミに教えること。
2 不正確な情報を彼女の上司に与えること。
3 マーケティング部の社員がいないところでマスコミと会うこと。
4 与えられた警告を無視すること。

解説 　クリスティーナのミスは，男性の最初の発言ですべて集約されている。雑誌のインタビューについて，You can imagine that some of your answers didn't show our company in the best light. Even more problematic, you announced the date of our new smartphone's release, which hasn't yet been formally announced. と述べているので，**1**が正解。

(A)

The Power of Sound

Sounds, including music, can alter emotions and behavior. Julian Treasure, a former drummer for punk bands in the 1970s and 80s, knows the power of sound well. Today, Treasure is the head of Sound Agency, a consultancy that helps businesses profit from tailoring sounds to please customers. Treasure sees himself as an audio interior designer, who removes unpleasant sounds and music and replaces them with more appealing sounds. Sometimes, the sounds are used to boost a business' identity or capture the essence of a particular brand.

Companies sometimes make mistakes when they try to choose the right sounds for themselves. A chain of British toy shops chose to play children's nursery songs in its stores to set the mood for children and toys. However, Treasure informed them that their target buyers were not children, but adults, so the music should really be pleasing to adult ears. The children's songs were likely irritating to adults after a short time. The stores started playing relaxing classical music, and sales jumped 10 percent.

For most shops, classical compositions or gentle ambient noises help shoppers relax and slow down. Customers who are able to slow down are more likely to browse longer and find a product to purchase, which is good for business. As competition in shops, restaurants and hotels increases, more and more businesses are likely to consider the total sensory experience they provide to their customers, including sounds.

Questions

No.11 How does consultant Julian Treasure basically perceive himself?

No.12 How did Treasure help the chain of British toy shops?

音の力

音楽を含めて，音は感情や行動を変える力を持つ。1970年代と80年代にパンクバンドでドラマーをしていたジュリアン・トレジャーは，音の持つ力をよく知っている。現在トレジャーはサウンドエージェンシーというコンサルタント会社の代表を務め，客を楽しませる音作りの注文に応じることで，企業の収益増に貢献している。トレジャーは自身のことを音のインテリアデザイナーと考えている。不快な音と音楽を除去し，より魅力的な音に置き換えるわけである。音は，時に企業の個性を強化したり，特定のブランドの核心を捉えたりするのに用いられることもある。

適切な音を自分で選ぼうとすると，企業は時として間違いを犯す。あるイギリスの玩具チェーン店は，子供とおもちゃにふさわしいムード作りのため，店内に童謡を流すことにした。だがトレジャーは，そのチェーン店がターゲットとする客は子供ではなく大人であり，音楽は実際に大人の耳に快適なものにすべきだと彼らに教えた。その童謡は，短い時間聞いただけで大人をいらいらさせそうなものだったのである。そのチェーン店が心地よいクラシック音楽を流し始めたところ，売り上げは10%伸びた。

ほとんどの店で，クラシックの作品や静かなアンビエントサウンド（環境音）は，買い物客がリラックスしてのんびりするのに効果がある。のんびりすることのできる客は商品を見て歩く時間も長くなり，買いたいものが見つかる可能性も高くなる。これは商売上ありがたいことである。商店やレストランやホテルの競争が激しさを増す中で，音を含め，客に提供するトータルな知覚体験を考慮する企業がますます増えそうである。

No. 11 解答 **1**

「コンサルタントのジュリアン・トレジャーは，基本的に自分自身のことをどのように見ているか」

1 音のインテリアデザイナー。

2 音楽の愛好家であり，クリエイター。

3 ほかの企業人を理解している企業人。

4 企業の個性の考案者。

解説　前半に Treasure sees himself as an audio interior designer という部分がある。これを an interior designer of sounds と言い換えた **1** が正解。

No. 12　解答　1

「イギリスの玩具チェーン店を，トレジャーはどのように支援したのか」
1 本当の客に集中させることで。
2 魅力的な子供の歌を流すよう説得することで。
3 店のブランドイメージに合った音を選ぶことで。
4 買い物客をのんびりさせるために玩具にやさしい音楽を演奏させることで。

解説　中ほどの Treasure informed them that their target buyers were not children, but adults が鍵。この target buyers を true customers と言い換えた **1** が正解。

(B)

Leif Erikson

Christopher Columbus is widely credited with "discovering" North America, but he was not the first European to land there. Columbus arrived in 1492, financed by the Spanish monarchy, but Leif Erikson landed in Canada nearly 500 years before him. Erikson was born in Iceland around 970 AD and followed in his father's footsteps as an explorer, eventually taking over colonies his father established in Greenland. He did not settle permanently in North America, but his expeditions became legendary. Despite not having the financial backing Columbus later enjoyed, he was able to successfully explore Europe and North America.

If stories are to be believed, however, Erikson wasn't the first European to see North America. An Icelandic merchant may have spotted the land after being blown off course during an expedition to Greenland. The stories about Erikson and his contemporaries, including their extraordinary feats, are recorded in the Icelandic Sagas. Two stories in particular, the Vinland Sagas, feature the expeditions of Erik the Red and Leif Erikson. Although the sagas are judged to be more or less historically accurate, the oral tradition of Icelandic storytelling means they cannot be completely verified.

Questions
No.13　What happened to Leif Erikson?
No.14　How true are the Icelandic Sagas?

レイフ・エリクソン

　クリストファー・コロンバスは北アメリカを「発見」したと広く信じられているが，彼はそこに上陸した最初のヨーロッパ人ではなかった。コロンバスはスペイン王室から資金提供を受け，1492年に到着したが，レイフ・エリクソンは彼より500年近く前にカナダに上陸した。エリクソンは西暦970年ごろアイスランドで生まれ，探検家の父親の歩んだ道をたどり，やがて父親がグリーンランドに築いた植民地を受け継いだ。彼は北アメリカに永住はしなかったが，その探検旅行は伝説的だった。コロンバスが後に享受した資金援助がなかったにもかかわらず，彼は無事にヨーロッパと北アメリカの探検を達成したのだ。

　しかしながら，話が本当だとすると，エリクソンは北アメリカを目にした初めてのヨーロッパ人ではなかった。アイスランドの商人がグリーンランドへの遠征の途中，強風で進路からそれて陸を見つけたかもしれない。エリクソンと彼と同時代の人々についての物語は，その途方もない功績も含め，アイスランド・サガ（歴史物語）に記されている。特に2つの物語から成るヴィンランド・サガはエリック・ザ・レッド（赤毛のエイリーク）とレイフ・エリクソンの探検旅行を特筆している。サガはだいたい歴史的に間違いないと判断されてはいるが，アイスランドの口承文学の言い伝えは，それらは完全には確かめられないということを示している。

No. 13 解答 4

「レイフ・エリクソンに何が起こったか」

1 スペイン王室の資金提供を受けた遠征に参加した。
2 グリーンランドに上陸することを許されなかった。
3 カナダでクリストファー・コロンバスと長年競い合ってすごした。
4 父が植民した土地をその後相続した。

解説　前半の eventually taking over colonies his father established in Greenland にヒントがある。これを inherit と言い換えた **4** が正解。

No. 14 解答 2

「アイスランド・サガはどの程度真実か」

1 言語学者によってのみ証明できる。
2 概して事実だと受け止められている。
3 真実と考えるにはあまりに突飛だと見なされている。
4 アイスランドでは全く的外れだと思われている。

解説　アイスランド・サガについては後半に Although the sagas are judged to be more or less historically accurate とあるので，おおむね真実であると見なされていることがわかる。正解は **2**。

(C)

Fastest Known Times

Ultra-endurance running has seen a rise in popularity in recent years, especially ultra-marathons. Some athletes, however, are taking things to a whole new level, pushing the levels of human endurance and ability. These runners are pursuing fastest known times, or "FKTs" as they are known. The idea is simple in theory but much harder in practice. Runners choose a route and then attempt to run it in the fastest time. Many runners are choosing to compete for fastest known times rather than in organized events, and sports manufacturers are taking notice.

Advancements in technology like GPS and digital cameras mean that FKTs can now be accurately recorded, monitored and verified. This has resulted in more interest and a change in the way the events are watched. Rather than simply recording them, filmmakers have produced documentaries which follow not just the record attempts but also the stories behind them. And these stories are resonating with a lot of people. In an era where professional athletics are tainted with drug scandals and many are wary of world records, these ultra-runners are attracting more and more sponsors. For some, pursuing FKTs is now a full-time job.

Questions

No.15　How have athletes responded to the popularity of FKTs?
No.16　What is one thing the speaker says about FKTs?

最速として知られるタイム

　限界を超えた持久走は，近年人気度が上がってきており，特にウルトラマラソンはその1つである。しかしながら，何人かのアスリートたちは自分たちの力を全く新しい段階にまで上げ，人間の限界や力量のレベルを押し上げようとしている。このランナーたちは，最速として知られるタイムを追求している。これは「FKT」として知られている。この発想は理論的にはシンプルだが，実際はそれ以上に非常に大変なことである。ランナーたちはルートを選択し，それを最速で走ろうとする。多くのランナーたちは組織的なイベントよりも最速として知られるタイムを競うことを選んでおり，スポーツメーカーはそれに目を留めている。

　GPSやデジタルカメラなどの技術の進歩は，今 FKT を正確に記録し，監視し，実証できることを意味している。これが結果的にさらなる興味につながっており，イベントを見る目の変化に繋がった。映像作家たちは単に

それらを記録するだけでなく，ドキュメンタリー番組を制作してきた。記録への挑戦にとどまらず，その背景にあるストーリーを追うドキュメンタリーだ。そしてこれらのストーリーは多くの人々の共感を得ている。プロスポーツ選手が薬物スキャンダルで腐敗し，多くの人が世界記録を注意深く見ている時代に，この限界を超えたランナーたちは，より多くのスポンサーを魅了している。中には，FKTの追求が現在ではフルタイムの仕事となっている者もいる。

No. 15　解答　**3**

「アスリートたちはFKTの人気にどんな反応をしているか」

1 一部のランナーたちはFKTが十分やりがいがあると思っていない。

2 組織的なレースよりもシンプルだと見なされている。

3 ランナーの一部にはほかのイベントよりもFKTを優先している者もいる。

4 彼らはスポーツ用品メーカーにもっとFKTに投資をするよう要求している。

解説　FKTに対するアスリートの姿勢については，Many runners are choosing to compete for fastest known times rather than in organized events という説明がある。これを prioritize them over other events と説明している**3**が正解。

No. 16　解答　**2**

「FKTに関して話者が言っていることは何か」

1 新技術の進歩につながってきた。

2 スポーツイベントの見方を変えた。

3 記録への挑戦について人々を懐疑的にした。

4 スポンサーに共感されるスポーツイベントが少なくなっている。

解説　全体が FKT の説明になっているが，This has resulted in more interest and a change in the way the events are watched. という説明に一致する**2**が正解。

(D)

Writer's Block

Writer's block is a condition where a writer cannot produce any new work, which can last for years. There can be many causes, such as depression, negative feedback or illness. For some, the condition can end their careers. The ways writers deal with it also vary. Some, like Maya Angelou and Neil Gaiman, recommend writing through the block. That means they will write anything, just to keep writing, until inspiration returns. Others, like Hilary Mantel, suggest doing anything but writing: walking, baking, meditating, anything other than worrying that the words won't come.

It's not only writers that can be affected, of course. Artists, designers, musicians and others can be affected by creative dry spells. This is known as creative block, and a whole industry has been built around it. Creatives seeking to rekindle their inspiration can turn to psychologists, self-help books, group therapy and much more to overcome their problem. Unfortunately, this could lead to further problems. Some creative types have complained of being duped by unscrupulous people trying to cash in on real problems. Rather than finding themselves cured, they have reported their condition getting worse and, in some cases, end up bankrupt.

Questions

No.17　How do writers deal with writer's block?

No.18　What has the problem of creative block led to?

作家のスランプ

作家のスランプは新しい作品を生み出せなくなる状態で，何年も続くことがある。落ち込み，否定的な反応，病

気など多くの原因が考えられる。作家によっては，その状態がキャリアを終わらせることになる。作家がそれに対処する方法も多様である。マヤ・アンジェロウやニール・ゲイマンといった作家たちは，書いてスランプを突破することを勧める。つまり彼らは，ひらめきが戻るまで，ただ書き続けるために何でも書くのだ。ヒラリー・マンテルのように，書くこと以外何でもしろと勧める作家もいる。ウォーキング，お菓子作り，瞑想など，言葉が浮かばないと悩むこと以外の何でもだ。

　もちろん，スランプに襲われる可能性があるのは作家だけではない。アーティスト，デザイナー，ミュージシャンなどの人たちも創造力が枯渇してしまう呪縛に影響されることがある。これはクリエイティブブロックとして知られ，それを取り巻く1つの業界ができているほどだ。ひらめきを呼び戻そうと求めるクリエイターたちは，問題を克服するために心理学者，自己啓発本，グループセラピー，そしてさらに多くのものに頼る。あいにく，これがさらなる問題を招くことになる。一部のクリエイターは，現実の問題を利用しようとする，たちの悪い人々にだまされたと不満を言う。彼らは治るどころか，さらに状態が悪くなったと報告しており，場合によっては破産してしまうのだ。

No. 17　解答　3

「作家はスランプにどのように対処するか」
1 彼らは否定的な反応や気が滅入るニュースを避ける。
2 ほとんどの作家はキャリアを終わらせることを決意する。
3 作家によって異なる方法を採用する。
4 作家たちはひらめきから意識をそらす。
　解説　作家のスランプへの対処法について述べているのが，The ways writers deal with it also vary. という部分。これを言い換えた**3**が正解となる。

No. 18　解答　1

「クリエイティブブロックの問題はどのようなことにつながるか」
1 経済難を引き起こすこともある。
2 多くのクリエイターは自分たちの業界について不満を言う。
3 自助グループは問題に取り組むのに失敗した。
4 今や治せない病気として認められている。
　解説　クリエイターたちが陥ってしまうさらなる問題についてはUnfortunately以降で述べられており，最後のend up bankruptを言い換えた**1**が正解。Unfortunately という言葉の後はマイナスの事実が述べられ，質問に関連する内容となることが多い。

(E)

Day 7

Vegetarianism

　Vegetarianism is the choice to avoid eating meat and fish. The reasons for adopting a vegetarian diet vary from person to person, including ethical and religious concerns. Others claim they follow a vegetarian diet for health reasons, and these claims can hold some truth. A vegetarian diet may help to reduce the risk of obesity, heart disease and some cancers, but the diet needs to be balanced. Risks with an unbalanced vegetarian diet include vitamin deficiencies and low bone density. In particular, vegan diets can be low in calcium and vitamin B if foods like tofu and leafy greens aren't consumed.

　Although vegetarian diets are sometimes considered to be a modern phenomenon, this is far from the case. The term "vegetarian" was coined in Manchester, UK in the middle of the 19th century, but the history of vegetarianism stretches back much further. Some believe the earliest record of vegetarianism is from the Indus Valley Civilization as early as the 7th century BC, and reliable evidence for vegetarianism comes from Greece in the 6th century BC. Vegetarianism has also been practiced throughout Indian

Questions
No.19 How might a vegetarian diet affect health?
No.20 When did people first become vegetarian?

菜食主義

　菜食主義は肉や魚を食べるのを避けるという選択である。菜食主義を採用する理由には倫理的，宗教的問題など，人によって異なる。健康上の理由で菜食を守ると主張する人もいて，その主張にも一理ある。菜食は肥満，心臓病，一部のがんなどのリスクを減らせるかもしれないが，食生活はバランスが取れたものでなくてはならない。アンバランスな菜食のリスクには，ビタミン不足や骨密度低下が含まれる。特に完全菜食は，豆腐や葉物野菜などの食物を摂取しないと，カルシウムやビタミンＢが不足しがちになる。

　時に菜食は現代的な現象だと考えられることがあるが，事実とは大違いだ。「菜食主義者」という言葉は19世紀半ばにイギリスのマンチェスターで作られたが，菜食主義の歴史は，はるか昔にさかのぼる。菜食主義の最初の記録は早くも紀元前7世紀のインダス文明から，さらに紀元前6世紀にはギリシャから菜食主義の確かな証拠が出ていると考える人もいる。菜食主義はまた，動物に対する非暴力という文化の態度の一部として，インドの歴史を通じて実践されてきた。

No. 19　解答　**2**

「菜食は健康にどのように影響するか」

1 バランスを保ち骨を強くする助けとなる。　　　**2** バランスの取れた菜食は健康を改善できる。
3 菜食はがんのリスクを上げると考えられている。　　**4** 完全菜食は採用してはいけない。

解説　前半の A vegetarian diet may help to reduce the risk of obesity, heart disease and some cancers, but the diet needs to be balanced. とその次の「バランスの取れていない菜食のリスク」に関する説明にヒントがある。この内容に **2** が一致する。

No. 20　解答　**4**

「人々が初めて菜食主義者になったのはいつか」

1 19世紀後半。
2 インド人が古代にギリシャに紹介した。
3 最初の菜食主義者はマンチェスターに住んでいた。
4 菜食主義は紀元前7世紀にさかのぼるかもしれない。

解説　後半に Some believe the earliest record of vegetarianism is from the Indus Valley Civilization as early as the 7th century BC と説明されている。従って，この内容に一致する **4** が正解。

(F) No. 21 解答 4

OK, marathoners and supporters, we've arrived at Ridgely Stadium. Marathoners should first show their registration form at the check-in table located near the stadium entrance. You'll be given your number, a map of the marathon route, and information about water, toilets, and medical booths at different locations on the course. You'll also be assigned a starting zone on the track. There's water available at tables located at each zone, and restrooms throughout the stadium are clearly marked. You should not consume water or energy drinks within 45 minutes before the marathon begins. We recommend you visit a restroom before you go to your zone. Be at your assigned zone 20 minutes before the race commences. You should not leave the zone thereafter. Starting zones will be crowded, so be sure to do your stretches or any other warm-up routine beforehand in the designated warm-up areas.

状況：あなたは海外でマラソンをすることになっており，あなたが乗っているチャーターバスが，マラソンが始まる競技場に到着する。あなたはバスで次のアナウンスを聞く。

質問：話者は，マラソンが始まる前の最後の20分間で何をするよう勧めているか。

さて，マラソン参加者とサポーターの皆さん，バスはリッジリー・スタジアムに到着しました。ランナーの皆さんはまず，スタジアムの入口近くにある受付テーブルで登録用紙を提示してください。ナンバーとマラソンコースの地図が渡され，コース上の何箇所かに設置されている給水地点，トイレ，救護所に関する情報をもらいます。トラック内のスタート・ゾーンも指定されます。水は各ゾーンのテーブルの上にあります。トイレはスタジアムのあちこちにあり，標識ではっきりと示されています。水やエナジードリンクは，マラソンが始まる45分前になったら飲まない方がよいでしょう。スタート・ゾーンに向かう前にトイレに行っておくことをお勧めします。レースが始まる20分前には決められたスタート・ゾーンに必ずいるようにしてください。その後はスタート・ゾーンを離れないでください。スタート・ゾーンは混み合いますので，あらかじめ指定されたウォームアップエリアで，ストレッチやそのほかのふだんしているウォームアップをしておいてください。

1 最後のストレッチをしたり，ふだんしているウォームアップをしたりする。
2 水を最後に1口飲む。
3 最後にもう1度トイレに行く。
4 スタート・ゾーン内にいる。

解説　問われているのは出発までの20分間にすること。Be at your assigned zone 20 minutes before the race commences. You should not leave the zone thereafter. から**4**が正解。**1**はスタート・ゾーンに行く前にすべきこと。**2**はスタートの45分前までにすべきこと。**3**は，20分前にはスタート・ゾーンにいないといけないので，それまでに済ませておく必要がある。

(G) No. 22 解答 2

Our Auction and Book Fair will be held on Saturday, October 16th. We appreciate the response from many of you who have agreed to help, with 64 volunteers signed up so far. We request that parents of first through third graders be here the week before the Fair to sort through books and auction items and prepare them for sale. Parents of fourth through sixth graders are asked to canvass local stores, including bookstores, to request books and other product donations for the auction. We have a list of stores here to divvy up. Parents of seventh and eighth graders are requested to be on hand to sell books and carry out the auction on October 16th. We also have a group of volunteers preparing cakes, cookies, and other baked items for auction. For the guys here, we certainly don't discriminate against men when it comes to making baked goods.

状況：あなたの子供は，米国の小学校に通う2年生である。あなたは学校でPTAの会議に参加する。あなたは毎年学校で行われているオークション＆ブック・フェアを手伝うと自ら申し出た。PTA会長から次のことを聞く。
質問：あなたは何をするよう求められているか。

オークション＆ブック・フェアが10月16日の土曜日に開催されます。多くの皆さんから手伝いを引き受けるとのお返事をいただき，誠に感謝しております。これまでに64名のボランティアの申し込みがありました。お願いしたいことは，1年生から3年生までの親御さんは，フェアの前の週にこちらにお集まりいただき，本とオークションに出す品に目を通し，販売の準備をしてください。4年生から6年生の親御さんは，書店など地元のお店を訪問し，本やそのほかの品を寄付していただけないか，お願いして回ってください。ここに店のリストがあるので，分担してください。7年生と8年生の親御さんは，本の販売とオークションの実施のため，10月16日に会場にいるようにしてください。さらに別のボランティアグループが，ケーキやクッキーをはじめとする焼き菓子類をオークション用に準備してくれます。こちらにいらっしゃる男性の皆さん，焼き菓子作りに関しては，もちろん男性を差別待遇することはありませんよ。

1 寄付を募るために地元の店を訪ねる。　　2 フェアの前に販売する品を用意する。
3 オークション用に焼き菓子を用意する。　4 寄付された品を10月16日に売る。

解説 子供の学年によってフェアでの役割が異なるので整理して聞く。2年生の保護者に関しては，We request that parents of first through third graders be here the week before the Fair to sort through books and auction items and prepare them for sale. と説明している。sort through books and auction items and prepare them for sale を Organize sale items と言い換えている**2**が正解。

(H) No. 23　解答 **3**

We do have rooms available for tonight, but I'm afraid we cannot offer you the same pricing you got online. I can tell you some other ways to save, though. If you show me a company card or other verification that you work for a company, we can offer you a corporate discount of 15 percent. Or if you're 55 years or older, we can offer you a 10 percent senior's rate. However, to get the rock-bottom rate, you must book the same way you did for your current reservation. You can go to our business center and use one of our computers for that purpose, if you'd like.

状況：あなたは58歳の会社役員で，休暇中である。4つ星ホテルに滞在中で，一晩延泊することにした。可能な限り安い料金で泊まりたいと思っている。
質問：フロント係はあなたにどうするように勧めているか。

今夜は確かに空室がございますが，残念ながらオンラインでご予約いただいたものと同じ料金ではご提供できません。ですが，ほかに節約する方法をいくつかお教えします。社員証もしくは会社員であると確認できるものを何かご提示いただければ，15％のコーポレート割引をいたします。あるいは，お客さまが55歳以上であれば，10％のシニア割引をいたします。しかし最安値をお望みであれば，このたびご予約いただいたのと同じ方法で予約してください。よろしければ，予約のために当ホテルのビジネスセンターに行き，パソコンをお使いください。

1 シニア割引を受ける。　　　　　　　　2 コーポレート割引をお願いする。
3 オンラインで部屋を予約する。　　　　4 ホテルで直接部屋を予約する。

解説 rock-bottom rate は「最低価格」という意味。そのために必要なことは book the same way you did for your current reservation という説明がある。もともと男性はインターネット経由で予約していたので，the same way とはネット予約のこと。**3**が正解。

(I) No. 24　解答　2

This is Tim Ericson. We've got a big problem again this morning. Janet isn't feeling well as usual and is taking the day off. Tomoko called to say she's too tired to come in. She wants to save her voice for the conference she's presenting at tomorrow. That leaves only me to teach all math and science classes today. I'll have to combine several classes to cover them. This has been an ongoing nightmare. I know you're probably tired of my complaints, but this isn't good for the students, either. We need an emergency meeting first thing Monday morning and have all teachers on hand to confront them with these issues. If that's not possible, then please at least send them an email saying that absences cannot be permitted without evidence of illness or emergency. We can hold the meeting the following Monday. If no one's willing to change, then we need to start recruiting other teachers right away.

状況：あなたは大学の人事部で働いており，付属高校で数学と理科を担当している教務主任から携帯電話にメッセージが届く。あなたは高校の教師を監督する立場にある。あなたは，直近の月曜日は出張の予定である。
質問：あなたはまず何をするべきか。

ティム・エリクソンです。今朝，また大問題がありました。ジャネットが例によって体調が優れず，休みを取っています。トモコは，疲れがひどすぎて出勤できないと電話してきました。明日彼女が登壇する協議会のために，声を保護しておきたいと思っているのです。その結果，今日は私1人で数学と理科を全クラス受け持たなくてはなりません。それをやるにはいくつかのクラスをまとめないといけないでしょう。こんな悪夢がずっと続いているのです。あなたがおそらく私の愚痴にうんざりしていることはわかっているのですが，こんなことでは生徒のためにもなりません。月曜日の朝一番で緊急会議を開き，今いる先生方全員に出席してもらいこうした問題に向き合ってもらう必要があります。それができないのなら，せめて彼らにメールを送って，病気や緊急事態を証明するものがない場合，休みは認められないと伝えてください。その次の月曜日に会議を開いてもいいです。もし誰も改めてくれないなら，直ちにほかの教師を採用しないといけません。

1 問題解決のために教師陣を集める。　　　　**2** 教師にメールを送る。
3 ティムをサポートするために学校に出向く。　**4** 新しい教師を探し始める。

解説　このメッセージがいつ届いたかは不明だが，ティムが最初に提案しているのは「（週が明けた）月曜一番での緊急会議」である。しかし，直近の月曜日はあなたは出張なので**1**は誤り。ティムはIf that's not possible ... と代替案を出しており，ここで述べられる「教師陣へのメール」が**2**の内容と一致する。

(J) No. 25　解答　2

You have three options for driver's license renewal. Most people choose to renew online, which is an option for anyone except those convicted of a moving violation or felony or those who have had a change of address since they last renewed four years ago. You can renew by mail if you send in your application to us at least 60 days before your current license expires. Finally, you can come into any DMV office to apply for renewal. Be sure to pick up a driver's license application form DL40 as you come through the door. The form needs to be an original, not a downloaded copy or other copy. We recommend you make an appointment reservation online beforehand, which will speed up the process once you arrive at the DMV.

状況：あなたは運転免許証の更新を予定しているため陸運局に電話をかける。あなたは最も簡単で早い更新方法を求めている。免許証は45日後に失効する。あなたは昨年転居した。あなたは次のアドバイスを聞く。
質問：あなたは何をするべきか。

運転免許証の更新には3通りあります。ほとんどの人はオンラインで更新します。誰でも利用できる方法ですが，交通違反や重罪で起訴された人，前回の4年前の更新時から住所が変わっている人は利用できません。郵便での更新も可能です。その場合，遅くとも現在の免許証が失効する60日前までにこちらに申請書を送ってください。最後の選択肢として，どこでもいいのでDMVのオフィスにお越しいただいて，更新の手続きをすることもでき

ます。入るときに運転免許証申請書DL40を忘れずに取ってきてください。書類は原本でなければならず，ダウンロードしたものやそのほかの複製した書類は使えません。事前に訪問の予約をオンラインで取ることをお勧めします。その方がDMVに着いてからの手続きが迅速に行われます。

1 オンラインで申請書をダウンロードする。　　**2** オンラインでDMVに行く予約を取る。

3 オンラインで免許証を更新する。　　**4** 郵便で免許証を更新する。

解説　オンラインでの更新は誰でもできるが，その例外に those who have had a change of address since they last renewed four years ago があり，あなたも該当する。郵便での更新は send in your application to us at least 60 days before your current license expires という条件があり，45日しか期間がないあなたは利用できない。残された方法はDMVに出向くこと。その際，予約を入れておくことが勧められているので，**2**が正解。**1**のダウンロードした申請書は直接出向く場合，利用できない。

Part 4 🔊 124～125

○：Today, we welcome Matt Benton, who will tell us what it's like to work as a real estate agent. Welcome, Matt.

★：Thanks for inviting me.

○：How did you first become interested in real estate?

★：I've always been interested in personal finances and came to realize that a home is usually a person's biggest investment. I liked the idea of helping people choose their home and making the investment work for them. I also am self-motivated and wanted to have a job where I was my own boss. Real estate was the best choice for me.

○：Does being your own boss give you more freedom?

★：Well, since I work an average of 60 hours a week, I don't have a lot of free time. On the other hand, I love what I do and meet a lot of great people.

○：What is your typical day like?

★：One of the things I like about my job is that there is no typical day. Things change constantly. I do everything from lead generation to marketing to house closings. A real estate agent has a lot of administrative duties and paperwork to handle. Fortunately, I have an assistant who handles most of the admin stuff for me and helps me in a whole bunch of other ways, like keeping track of scheduling issues. This allows me to leverage my time more effectively and to be more productive.

○：What do you find to be the most effective way to generate leads?

★：I send out fliers, run ads, and do open houses, which exposes me to a lot of people and brings in new clients. But by far the most effective way to generate leads is by focusing on the people I already know, such as family, friends, neighbors, classmates, and social contacts. I ask them to introduce people they know to me, and this is the way I get most of my leads. Most people will buy a house at some point in their life, so in that sense, every person I meet is a potential client. That's why I spend a lot of time meeting and speaking with a lot of people and then keeping in touch with my growing network.

○：What is the most challenging part of your job?

★：Keeping a steady flow of income into our business. When the economy is doing well, I get more business than I can handle and refer clients to other agents. But real estate is a cyclical business, just as the economy goes through cycles of recession and expansion. There are many fewer buyers during the down times, and agents compete to get those. Many agents have to give up and change their job during particularly long recessions. My company has a safeguard against the down times. I manage over 100 rental properties for clients, and I receive a rental commission each month. This is consistent income, and it's sufficient to help me through slower times. Moreover, since I offer a rental management service, I can more easily attract investors who want to buy rental properties. One of the good things about having investors as clients is that they usually buy several properties, so they are return customers, so to speak.

○: This has been very interesting, Matt. Thank you for sharing your knowledge with us.

★: You're most welcome.

Questions

No.26 What is one reason Matt was attracted to the real estate business?

No.27 What is one thing Matt does to protect himself from recessions?

○：今日はマット・ベントンさんをお迎えし，不動産業者の仕事がどういうものかお話ししていただきます。マットさん，ようこそ。

★：お招きいただき，ありがとうございます。

○：そもそも不動産に興味を持ったきっかけは何だったのですか。

★：パーソナル・ファイナンスにはずっと興味があり，家はたいていの場合，個人の一番大きな投資だと気付くようになったのです。人が家を選ぶ手伝いをして，投資が彼らにとってうまくいくようにするという考えが気に入りました。さらに，私は自発的な性格なので，自分で判断して動ける仕事をしたかったのです。不動産業界は私にとってぴったりの選択でした。

○：自分の好きなように働くということは，自由が多いということですか。

★：そうですね，週に平均60時間は働きますから，自由な時間はあまりありません。一方で，自分の仕事は大好きで，素晴らしい人に大勢会っています。

○：典型的な1日はどのようなものですか。

★：私が自分の仕事で気に入っている点の1つは，典型的な1日などないということです。物事が常に変化します。私は見込み客の獲得から，マーケティング，家の売買契約の完了に至るまで，すべて行っています。不動産業者はたくさんの管理業務や事務仕事を処理しています。幸いなことに，私の場合はアシスタントが管理に関することをほとんどやってくれていて，そのほかの多くの点でも私を助けてくれています。例えば最新のスケジュールを把握しておくことなどですね。そのおかげで時間をもっと有効に使えますし，生産性も上がります。

○：見込み客を獲得する最も効果的な方法は何だとお考えですか。

★：私はチラシを送り，広告を打ち，物件を公開します。そうすることで多くのお客さまに自分を知っていただき，新しいお客さまが舞い込んでくるのです。しかし一番効果的な見込み客の獲得方法は，すでに知っている人に焦点を絞ることです。家族や友人，ご近所さん，クラスメートや社会的なつて，などです。知り合いを紹介してくれるようにお願いして，そうやって私は大半の見込み客を得ています。ほとんどの人は，人生のどこかのタイミングで家を買います。その意味では，私にとってはお会いする方は全員，潜在的なお客さまです。そういうわけで，時間をたくさんかけて大勢の人々と会って話し，拡大するネットワークの中で連絡を取り合っているのです。

○：仕事で最も困難でやりがいがあるのは，どんなことですか。

★：事業収入を安定して得ることです。経済が好調なときは手に余るほどの仕事が来ますから，顧客をほかの不動産業者に紹介します。しかし不動産業は周期的な動きのある商売です。経済が後退と拡大を周期的に経験するのと同じです。景気が悪い時期は不動産の買い手がぐっと減りますので，業者は買い手の獲得競争をします。多くの不動産業者は，特に景気低迷が長期化すると，仕事をやめて別の仕事をしなければなりません。私の会社では景気後退の時期に備えて防衛策を講じています。100件を超す賃貸物件をお客さまに代わって管理していて，毎月，賃貸手数料を得ているのです。この収入は途切れないので，景気が低迷しているときの十分な助けになります。さらに，うちでは賃貸管理サービスを提供していますから，賃貸物件を購入したいと考えている投資家の皆さまをより簡単に引きつけることができます。投資家を顧客として抱える良い点

の1つは，彼らはたいてい数件の物件を購入しますので，いわばリピーターなのです。

○：とても興味深かったです，マットさん。いろいろ教えていただき，ありがとうございました。

★：どういたしまして。

No. 26　解答　**1**

「マットが不動産ビジネスに魅力を感じた1つの理由は何か」

1 経済学と，人の投資を手伝うことに興味があった。

2 建築が人々がより良い生活を送る上でどのように役立っているのかに興味があった。

3 友人が不動産業者をしていて，事業について話してくれた。

4 両親が不動産事業を営んでおり，いずれは跡を継いでもらいたいと思っていた。

解説　聞き手に How did you first become interested in real estate? と聞かれたマットは，I've always been interested in personal finances and came to realize that a home is usually a person's biggest investment. I liked the idea of helping people choose their home and making the investment work for them. と答えている。**1** が正解。personal finance「パーソナル・ファイナンス」とは個人的なお金のやりくりのこと。

No. 27　解答　**3**

「マットが景気後退から自身を守るためにすることの1つは何か」

1 不動産業者の広いネットワークを維持し，そこから見込み客を獲得する。

2 景気が後退している時期だけ販売の見込みがある客を紹介してくれるよう知り合いに頼む。

3 家の販売以外に，別の種類の不動産ビジネスを続けている。

4 景気のよい年にお金を貯めて，厳しい時期のビジネスの支えにしている。

解説　景気が悪いときの防衛策について，I manage over 100 rental properties for clients, and I receive a rental commission each month. This is consistent income, and it's sufficient to help me through slower times. と述べている。景気が悪いときにも別の収入源があるのである。**3** が正解。**1** と **2** は普段のビジネスでもやっていること。

7日間完成

文部科学省後援

英検®1級
予想問題ドリル

[6訂版]

解答と解説

Obunsha